AF478257

RALF PETERS UNTIL TODAY

**Der Katalog wurde maßgeblich gefördert durch /
This catalogue was co-funded by**

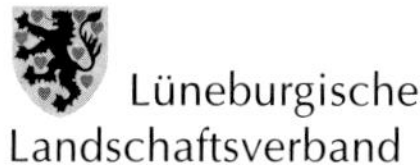 Lüneburgischer
Landschaftsverband

Lüneburgischer Landschaftsverband
Tel. +49 (0)581 827262
www.lueneburgischer-landschaftsverband.de

**Ausstellung / Exhibition
2010/11**
Fotomuseum im
Münchner Stadtmuseum
Sankt-Jakobs-Platz 1
D-80331 München
Tel. +49 (0)89 23322370
www.stadtmuseum-online.de

RALF PETERS UNTIL TODAY **Hrsg. / Ed.** Bernhard Knaus

Texte von / Texts by
Klaus Honnef, Heinz Kattner, Renate Puvogel & Raimar Stange

Galerien, die Ralf Peters vertreten /
Galleries representing Ralf Peters

Bernhard Knaus Fine Art
Niddastr. 84
D-60329 Frankfurt am Main
Tel. +49 (0)69 24450768
knaus@bernhardknaus.de
www.bernhardknaus.de

Base Gallery
Koura Daiichi Bldg. 1F,
1-1-6 Nihombashi
Kayabacho Chuo-ku
J-Tokyo 103-0025
Tel. +81 3 56236655
info@basegallery.com
www.basegallery.com

Galleria Torbandena
Via Tor Bandena 1/b
I-34121 Trieste
Tel. +39 040 630201
info@torbandena.com
www.torbandena.com

Diana Lowenstein Fine Arts
2043 North Miami Avenue
USA-Miami FL 33127
Tel. +1 305 5761804
info@dlfinearts.com
www.dlfinearts.com

Zonca & Zonca
Contemporary Art
Via Ciovasso 4
I-20121 Milano
Tel. +39 02 72003377
info@zoncaezonca.com
www.zoncaezonca.com

Nusser & Baumgart
Steinheilstr. 18
D-80333 München
Tel.+49 (0)89 221875
info@nusserbaumgart.com
www.nusserbaumgart.com

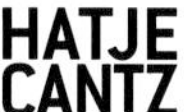

INHALT / CONTENTS

DIE NEUE SICHTBARKEIT DER FOTOGRAFIE ZU ZWEI WERKGRUPPEN VON RALF PETERS / PHOTOGRAPHY'S NEW VISIBILITY ON TWO GROUPS OF WORKS BY RALF PETERS Klaus Honnef

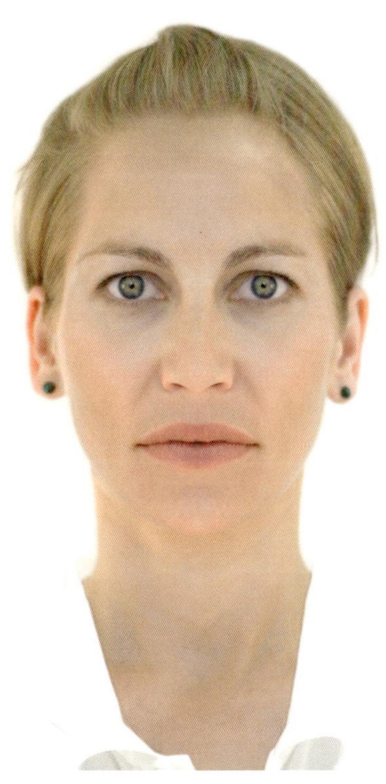

DIFFERENT PERSONS
ANETTE 76 × 52 cm / 29.92 × 20.47 in. 2006

Sie könnten Geschwister sein. Sind es aber nicht. Nicht einmal entfernt verwandt und mutmaßlich auch nicht verschwägert. Die Ähnlichkeit der zwölf Frauen ist dennoch verblüffend. Oberflächlich betrachtet, könnte jede auch dieselbe in freilich unterschiedlicher Maske sein. *Different Persons* nennt Ralf Peters die Reihe ihrer Bildnisse deshalb. Mit ernstem Gesicht ohne Ausdruck und offenen Augen blicken sie in die Kamera (S. 127–138). Wer einen Anflug von Lächeln auf den vollen, wohlgeformten Lippen sieht, erliegt wohl einer Autosuggestion. Andererseits – wäre es nicht möglich, dass gerade die Folge einer intensiven Anschauung das Wahrnehmen eines angedeuteten Lächelns ist?

Denn nur durch intensive Anschauung kristallisieren sich die Unterschiede in den frontal aufgenommenen Gesichtern aus. Und je länger der Blick auf den Gesichtern ruht, desto unverwechselbarer werden sie. Der erste flüchtige Eindruck provoziert lediglich ein Vorurteil; etwa jenes, dass Frauen eines bestimmten Alters aus der Mittelschicht gleich aussähen, weil sie einem identischen Schönheitsideal folgten. »Sie haben keine Gesichter mehr«, stöhnte die große Porträtfotografin Liselotte Strelow am Ende ihrer Laufbahn.

Kommerzielle Medien, Mode, Werbung, Kosmetikindustrie und plastische Chirurgie gäben das Modell vor, heißt es in kulturkritischen Einwürfen. Optische Unterschiede würden im Interesse eines standardisierten Ideals nivelliert. Mit Trugbildern erweckten sie den Eindruck, das wirksame Antidot gegen Enttäuschung, Alter und Tod zu sein, reflektierten aber allein sich selbst. Sie dienten vor allem als Schmiermittel eines ökonomischen Systems, das auf Versprechen basiere, welche zu brechen seine Funktion sei. Wer genauer hinsieht, vermag derlei Einsichten aus den typisierten Bildnissen durchaus zu gewinnen. Zumal Ralf Peters, der Autor der Aufnahmen, eine ganze Reihe von Voraussetzungen geschaffen hat, um sie zu befördern.

Zweifellos suchte er seine Modelle nach einem verbreiteten Vorstellungsbild aus. Wahrscheinlich hat er sich an den Gesichtern orientiert, die in populären Filmen, Fernsehspots, Magazinen und Reklamen für Mode- und Kosmetikartikel erscheinen, um das Bild

They might be sisters. Only they aren't. They aren't even distantly related, and we may assume they aren't related by marriage. Nevertheless, the similarity between the twelve women is astonishing. At a cursory glance, each one could be the same woman, just differently made up. Yet Ralf Peters calls this series of portraits *Different Persons*. They gaze at the camera seriously, expressionlessly, and open-eyed (pp. 127–138). Anyone finding a hint of a smile on their full, well-formed lips would undoubtedly be deluding themselves. On the other hand, couldn't it be that perceiving the trace of a smile is precisely what comes from looking intently at these images? For it is only by looking intently that the differences between these frontal portraits emerge. And the longer one gazes at the faces, the more distinct they become. The first cursory impression really only confirms certain preconceptions; like the one that middle-class women of a certain age look the same because they aspire to an identical ideal of beauty. At the end of her career, the great portrait photographer Liselotte Strelow bemoaned the fact that "they don't have faces any more."

According to many cultural critics, it is a type of look promoted by the commercial media, advertising, and the fashion, cosmetics, and plastic surgery industries. Visual differences, they claim, are being homogenized in the interests of a standardized ideal. These industries produce images aimed at deluding people into thinking they offer an effective antidote to disappointment, old age, and death; in reality, though, they only hold up a mirror to themselves. They serve first and foremost to oil the wheels of an economic system that functions by breaking the promises it makes. Anyone looking more closely may well derive insights of this kind from these typified portraits, especially because, in constructing these pictures, Peters has used a number of devices to encourage such insights.

He evidently used a widely held ideal of physical beauty as the basis for selecting his models. It seems most likely that he based his criteria on faces that appear in popular films, television commercials, fashion magazines, and clothes and cosmetics advertisements, using these to construct his image of a "dream

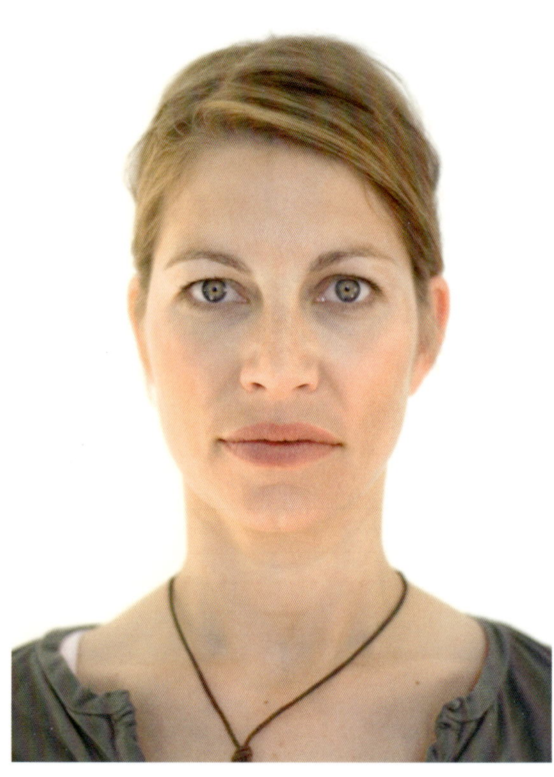

DIFFERENT PERSONS **TINA**
76 × 52 cm / 29.92 × 20.47 in.
2006

der »Traumfrau« zu entwerfen. Die Augenbrauen gezupft, die Haut makellos, die Augen klar, riesig groß kraft Blitzlicht, geschwungene Lippen, nicht zu dünn und nicht zu breit, helle Haare in sämtlichen Schattierungen des Blond, schmale, gleichförmige Nase, wohlgerundetes Kinn, ovale Kopfform – davon träumen ... ja wer? Die Männer. Aber offenbar auch die Frauen. Es besteht der begründete Verdacht, dass viele von ihnen diesem makellosen Bild nacheifern.

Trotz gemeinsamer Merkmale, die ohne Frage einem typologischen Schema entsprechen, entgehen nur dem zerstreuten Blick die Signale des Individuellen. Die Differenzen verraten sich in der Nuance. Die Farbe und Stellung der Augen, das Fallen der Haare, der Schmuck oder der Verzicht darauf, die Oberbekleidung. Zwar ist Ralf Peters in einschlägigen Modelagenturen fündig geworden. Die eine oder andere junge Frau hat er auch auf der Straße angesprochen, um sie für ein Shooting zu gewinnen. Aber nach genauer Inspektion fällt es schwer, die fotografierten Gesichter auf ein optisches Klischee zu verkürzen. Zwar weichen ihre Abbilder von den früheren Idealbildern des Weiblichen in der Kunst deutlich ab – aber welches Glamourmagazin würde die *Mona Lisa*, die Schöne mit dem geheimnisvollen Lächeln, je aufs Cover heben: zu rund das Gesicht, zu grob die Nase.

Angesichts des Problems der immanenten Subjektivität seiner Modelle bleibt die Haltung des Fotografen nichtsdestoweniger ambivalent. Mit dem Titel der Werkgruppe, *Different Persons,* und durch die Praxis, jedes einzelne Bild mit dem Vornamen des fotografierten Modells zu versehen, betont Peters die faktische Differenz der Frauen, die sich ablichten ließen. Gleichwohl lässt sich nicht leugnen, dass er bei Auswahl und Aufnahme ein eng konturiertes Segment im Spektrum des Bildnisgenres angesteuert hat.

Manches eher unscheinbare Detail deutet auf seinen gezielten Eingriff hin; etwa die fast einheitlichen Frisuren; straff nach hinten aus der Stirn gekämmt – unbeschadet der Frisur, die sie wirklich tragen. In jedem Fall beruht die strikt frontale Ausrichtung der Modelle, ihre markante Platzierung vor hellem Fond in der Bildmitte sowie die Kalibrierung der Quadrage, die ihren Schnitt unterhalb des Halsansatzes führt, auf

woman." It is a woman with plucked eyebrows, perfect skin, clear eyes, made to look very large by the illumination of flash, curved lips, neither too thin nor too thick, light-colored hair in various shades of blonde, a narrow, regular nose, a well-rounded chin, and an oval face—who actually dreams of this ideal? No doubt men do. But evidently women do as well. It is reasonable to suppose that many of them strive to emulate this image of perfection.

Despite these common features that clearly conform to a schematic type, only the most distracted viewer could overlook the tell-tale signs of the individual person. The differences betray themselves in nuances. The color and position of the eyes, the way the hair falls, the jewelry or lack thereof, the outer clothing. While Peters found most of the young women at the kind of modeling agencies you'd have expected him to use, he also approached a couple of them on the street and persuaded them to pose for a photo shoot. On closer inspection, though, it becomes difficult to reduce the faces in the photographs to visual clichés. Indeed, the images distinctly diverge from ideal images of femininity from the past. For which glamour magazine today would have on its cover the *Mona Lisa*, the beautiful woman with the enigmatic smile? Her face is too round, her nose too large.

The photographer's attitude to the problem of his models' immanent subjectivity is no less ambivalent. By entitling the group of works *Different Persons,* and by giving each individual picture its subject's first name, Peters emphasizes the actual differences between the women who appear in the photographs. Nevertheless, it cannot be denied that his approach to selecting and taking photographs is based on a very narrow definition of what portraiture is.

Many of the less conspicuous details point towards what he is really aiming at; they include the uniform arrangement of the hair, combed back tightly from the forehead in a way that ignores the kind of hair-do they actually have. In each case, the rigorous frontal positioning of the model, her prominent central placement against a light background, and the calibration of the quadrants so that they intersect just below the top of the neck, is the result of careful aesthetic decisions made by the photographer. At

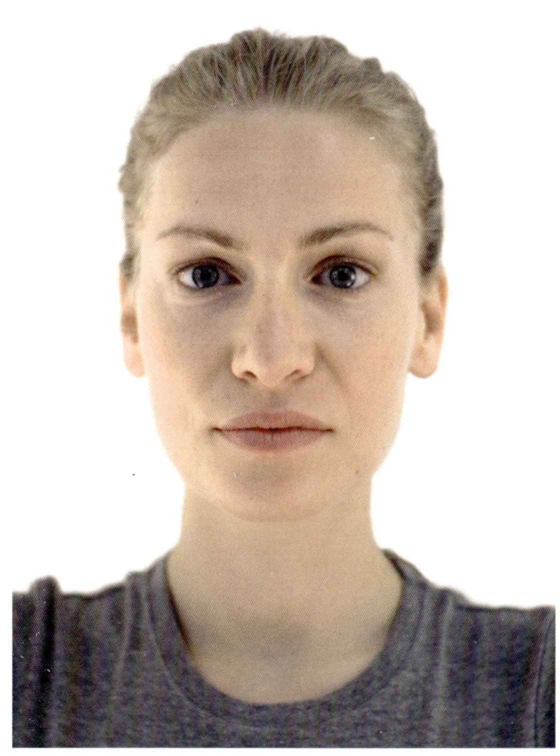

pointierten ästhetischen Entscheidungen des Autors. Zugleich sind es paradoxerweise aber die anschaulichen Ergebnisse dieser Entscheidungen, die den typologischen Charakter gegen den individuellen Anspruch in Geltung halten.

Indem Ralf Peters das eine betont, ohne das andere zu vernachlässigen, schärft er das Gespür für die prozessuale Seite des Sehens. Die ist den Menschen so selbstverständlich, dass sie unbewusst verläuft. Im Zuge der Wahrnehmung seiner Bilder, genauer, in dem, was Roland Barthes »studium« nennt, differenziert sich der Blick durch Reflexion vom zerstreuten Sehen und wird zur Rezeption. Offenbar löst der changierende Charakter der Bildnisse zwischen Modell- und Individualporträt, vom Fotografen durch die scheinbar unentschiedene Einstellung stimuliert, jene Reaktion aus, die das Selbstverständliche der Selbstverständlichkeit entkleidet, das Vertraute sozusagen fremd erscheinen lässt und so in ein »sehendes Sehen« (Max Imdahl) überführt.

Insofern könnte es sein, dass der eigentliche »Gegenstand« dieser Bildnisse nicht eine besondere Form des Abbildes ist, sondern das komplexe Phänomen der optischen Wahrnehmung, die während des Vorgangs bewusster Wahrnehmung selber zum Gegenstand wird. Aus diesem Grund ist auch nicht ein möglicher Wiedererkennungseffekt das Bestreben seiner ästhetischen Strategie, keine wie auch immer geartete Porträtähnlichkeit, sondern die offenkundige Ambivalenz des Bildnisses auszuloten, das eher eine Projektionsfläche der Betrachter ist als ein Ebenbild der fotografierten Modelle.

Einen solchen Eindruck bestätigen die Bildzyklen, die Ralf Peters durch vermeintliche Fenster mit Blick auf die Außenwelt realisiert hat. Besonders, wenn man sie mit den Bildnissen der zwölf »unterschiedlichen« Frauen in Beziehung setzt. Sofort wird klar, dass sie in Korrespondenz wirken. Mit anderen Worten: Die eine Werkgruppe ergänzt die andere. Im gegenseitigen Wechselverhältnis erweitern sie das Feld des potenziell Sichtbaren. Noch aufschlussreicher wird der Vergleich dank des Umstandes, dass es sich bei einigen der Fensterbilder, wie den in *Seoul* versammelten, um digital bearbeitete Fotografien handelt; oder wie bei den drei »Originalaufnahmen« der Werkgruppe

the same time, though, it is—paradoxically enough—the visual outcomes of these decisions that maintain the schematic character of these faces against their claims to individuality.

By emphasizing one of these elements without neglecting the other, Peters makes us more aware that looking is a process—one that occurs so naturally in human beings that it is largely unconscious. In the act of looking at his pictures, or more precisely, in the act of what Roland Barthes calls "studium," our gaze becomes reflective, distinguishing it from distracted forms of seeing and enabling it to become receptive to the work. Clearly the way in which the images are able to switch between being portraits of models and portraits of individuals, a deliberate effect of the photographer's apparently indecisive approach, enables us as viewers to strip the natural of its naturalness, and see the familiar as something strange, as it were, transforming it into what Max Imdahl calls a "seeing seeing."

In this respect, it could be that the real "subject" of these portraits is not only a particular kind of photograph but the complex phenomenon of visual perception, which becomes itself an object of perception in the process of conscious seeing. For this reason, Peters's aesthetic strategy isn't one of possible recognition; he isn't aiming at a portrait-likeness, however you might want to define it, but at exploring the possibilities of the manifest ambiguity of portraits, which are more a screen onto which the viewer projects than a true likeness of the photographed model.

This impression is confirmed by the series of images that Peters has made, which offer a view out of an imaginary window onto the world outside. This is especially the case if you compare it with the portraits of the twelve "different" women. For it immediately becomes clear that they are related. To put it another way: the one group of works complements the other. The way they interrelate broadens the field of what might potentially become visible. The comparison becomes still more revealing in view of the fact that some of the photographs taken from windows, such as those in the series *Seoul,* have been digitally altered, while the three "original photographs" from the series *Indoor* (pp. 101–103) show "almost empty"

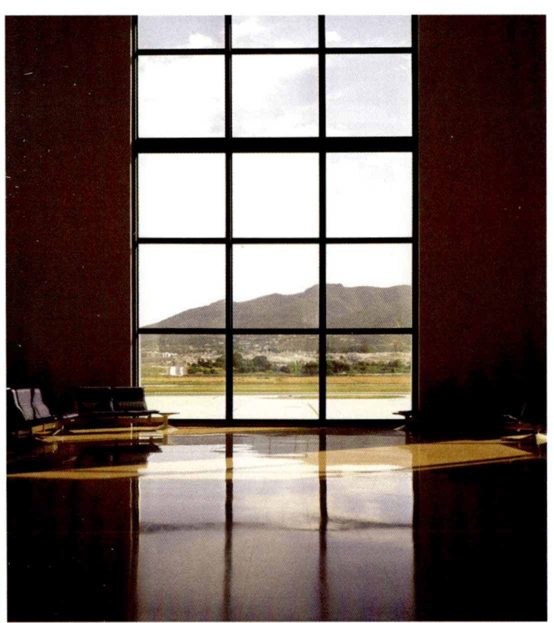

INDOOR **#1** 120 × 110 cm /
47.24 × 43.31 in. 2001/02

Indoor (S. 101–103) um »die fast leeren« Bilder, »die am Computer frei geträumt worden« sind (Peters). Was erblicken die Betrachter? Einen Widerschein des Realen oder eine bloße Computersimulation? Auch diese Frage lässt sich nicht so einfach beantworten. *Seoul* bildet eine Gruppe von drei gleichformatigen nahezu quadratischen (90 × 84 cm) Bildern von identischer Struktur (S. 158, 159). Oben und unten sind die Bilder mit einem Binnenrahmen versehen, rechts und links angeschnitten, wobei der Schnittrand durch zwei unweit davon aufstrebende Vertikalen in der Binnenfläche noch einmal verfestigt wird. Die Bilder entwerfen eine Art Fenster im Fenster. In der oberen Hälfte durchschneidet eine schmale Horizontale die gesamte Bildfläche. Dahinter entfächert sich ein gitterförmiges Gefüge. In der mittleren Partie ist es deutlicher sichtbar als in der unteren. Das Gitter setzt sich jenseits der Binnenrahmen andersfarbig fort. Es ist bald vollständig, bald nur zum Teil, bald transparent übertüncht, als hätte jemand mit weißer Farbe darüber gestrichen. Pure Illusion. Kein Maler hat Hand angelegt. Selbst das feine Relief der Binnenrahmen und die jedes Bild abschließende Konsole mit Reliefwirkung sowie der Balken auf der Konsole im zentralen Bild des Triptychons sind das Werk einer elaborierten Rechenoperation. Ob bewusst oder unbewusst, Peters zitiert das aus sich leuchtende »Glanzlicht« der Malerei, das sich laut Ernst Gombrich dem Apelles, dem überragenden Maler der Antike, verdankt. Ist es in diesem Zusammenhang wirklich bloßer Zufall, dass kein originales Gemälde von ihm überliefert ist? Dabei sind es bei Peters ausschließlich diese glänzenden Relieflinien, die den Charakter des Fensterbildes schaffen und so etwas wie eine räumliche Dimension wenigstens suggerieren.

Widerschein des Realen oder Computersimulation? Weder noch, sowohl als auch, gleichermaßen. Zu sehen ist lediglich, was zu sehen ist, präziser, was sich vermöge genauen Anschauens entfaltet, ganz im Sinne von Frank Stellas »What you see is what you see«. Doch anders als Stella geht es Ralf Peters nicht um die Herstellung eines selbstreferenziellen Bildobjektes, vielmehr um die Herstellung von Sichtbarkeit. Nichts ist weniger selbstverständlich als das.

images that according to Peters "were dreamt up on the computer." What are we looking at? Is it a reflection of reality or a mere computer simulation? Even this question can't be answered easily. *Seoul* is made up of a group of three, almost square pictures (90 × 84 cm) with an identical format and structure (pp. 158, 159). Each has an internal frame running along the top and the bottom, which is cut away along the left- and right-hand sides. The cut edges are strengthened by two adjacent rising verticals in the interior part of the picture. The pictures show a kind of window within a window. In their upper half, a narrow horizontal line cuts across the entire surface of the picture. Behind it, a grille-like structure fans out. It is more clearly visible in the middle than in the lower part. Beyond this inner frame, the grille continues in a different color. In some places it is fully intact, in others only partly, and in others it is painted over in a translucent white, as if someone had whitewashed it. It is all pure illusion. No painter has put his hand to it. Even the delicate rendering of the internal frame and the rendered brackets at the edge of each picture, as well as the beams on the brackets in the central picture of the triptych, have been produced by an elaborate computer operation. Whether consciously or unconsciously, Peters is quoting here the shining "luster" of painting, which Ernst Gombrich believes originated with Apelles, the outstanding painter of Antiquity. Given this, is it really pure coincidence that no original painting of his has survived? For in Peters's work it is only these lustrous outlines of forms rendered in light and shade that establish the character of the window-picture and at least suggest three-dimensionality.

Is this a reflection of reality or a computer simulation? It is equally neither and both. All that can be seen is what is to be seen, or more precisely, what may emerge on closer inspection, very much in the sense of Frank Stella's "what you see is what you see." Unlike Stella, though, Peters is not interested in producing a self-referential visual object, but rather in producing visibility itself. There is nothing more natural than this. Diane Arbus once noted in her diary that people don't see things because they're visible; rather the other way round, they are visible because

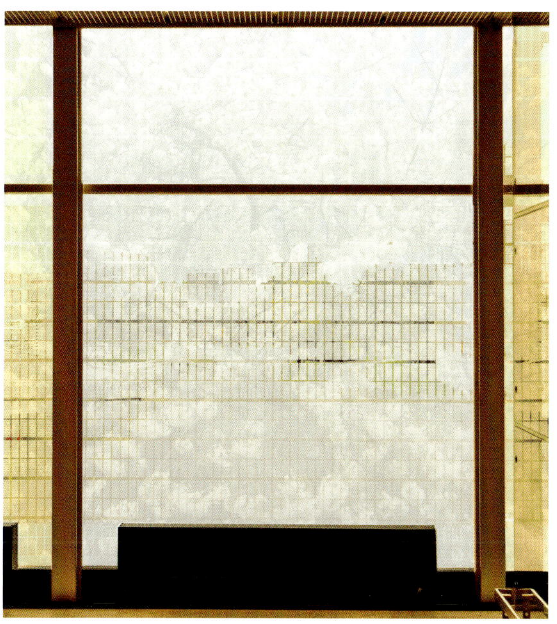

SEOUL **# 2** 90 × 82.6 cm / 35.43 × 32.52 in. 2009

Denn: »Die Dinge werden nicht gesehen, weil sie sichtbar sind, sondern umgekehrt, sie sind sichtbar, weil sie gesehen werden«, notierte Diane Arbus in ihrem Tagebuch. Die große Fotografin fasste in der kurzen Sentenz zusammen, was die Kunst, seit sie sich in der westlichen Welt aus dem Banne der Religion löste, gewissermaßen im Auge gehabt hat: Die Dinge sichtbar zu machen. Die sichtbare Welt ist letzten Endes das Produkt von Bildern.

Inzwischen decken die visuellen Massenmedien mit abgeschliffenen und zu Klischees verkommenen Bildern wieder zu, was die Kunst in die Sphäre der Sichtbarkeit navigiert hat. Die avancierte Kunst reagiert auf die optische Vermüllung, indem sie die Bedingungen der Bilder einer anschaulichen Reflexion unterwirft. Konkret: Die Sichtbarkeit ist ihr Motiv und nicht mehr die Darstellung eines bestimmten Motivs. Anstelle eines in Wirklichkeit tatsächlich abwesenden Motivs, eines auf »Realität« verweisenden Zeichens, werden demzufolge in Peters' »fotografischen« Bildern vor allem die Möglichkeiten, Sichtbarkeit zu erzeugen, sichtbar. So wenig die Augen der *Different Persons* den Betrachtern erlauben, in ihre Seele zu blicken, so wenig gerät vor den Fenstern des Triptychons *Seoul* die südkoreanische Metropole ins Blickfeld. Stattdessen erblickt man potenzielle Bilder von Menschen und Dingen, deren Referenz auf die Welt außerhalb der Bilder äußerst fragil und unsicher ist. Allenfalls Spuren der Realität haben sich erhalten. In der Konsequenz verschiebt Ralf Peters den Fokus in seinen perfekt anmutenden Bildern von der Zeichenhaftigkeit des »Fotografischen« zur Veranschaulichung der genuinen Sprache der Bilder. Der Gegensatz von analoger und digitaler Fotografie hebt sich unabhängig von ihrer jeweiligen technischen Grundlage auf. Das Ergebnis ist eine scheinbare Tautologie: Jedes Bild des Künstlers vermittelt vor allem anderen zunächst seine Bildlichkeit; konkret: Es ist ein Bild. Darin manifestiert sich nicht zuletzt auch die kritische Komponente von Peters' Werk.

people see them. In this short sentence, the great photographer summarized what western art has had its eye on, so to speak, since breaking free of the spell of religion: to make things visible. In the final analysis, the visible world is the product of images.

In the meantime, the visual mass media have been using polished and clichéd images to cover over again what art had mapped out in the realm of the visible. Critical art has reacted to this trashing of the visual by reflecting clearly on the conditions of visual representation. More specifically, its subject is now visibility itself, and no longer the representation of a particular subject. Instead of a subject that isn't there at all but is merely a symbol referring to "reality," what Peters's "photographic" pictures show are the possibilities for producing visibility. Just as the eyes of the subjects of *Different Persons* scarcely allow the viewer to gaze into their souls, so the window in the triptych *Seoul* offers no more than a glimpse of the South Korean capital. Instead, what one catches sight of are potential images of people and things, whose relation to the world beyond images is extremely fragile and uncertain. At the most, they are able to preserve traces of reality.

As a result, Peters shifts the focus of his apparently perfect pictures from photography's natural tendency to produce symbols to an illustration of the actual language of images. The opposition between analog and digital photography resolves itself independently of their respective technical wherewithal. The result is an apparent tautology: each of the artist's pictures conveys first and foremost its own nature as an image; in other words, that it is an image. And it is this that forms the critical aspect of Peters's work.

TANKSTELLEN / PETROL STATIONS 1998

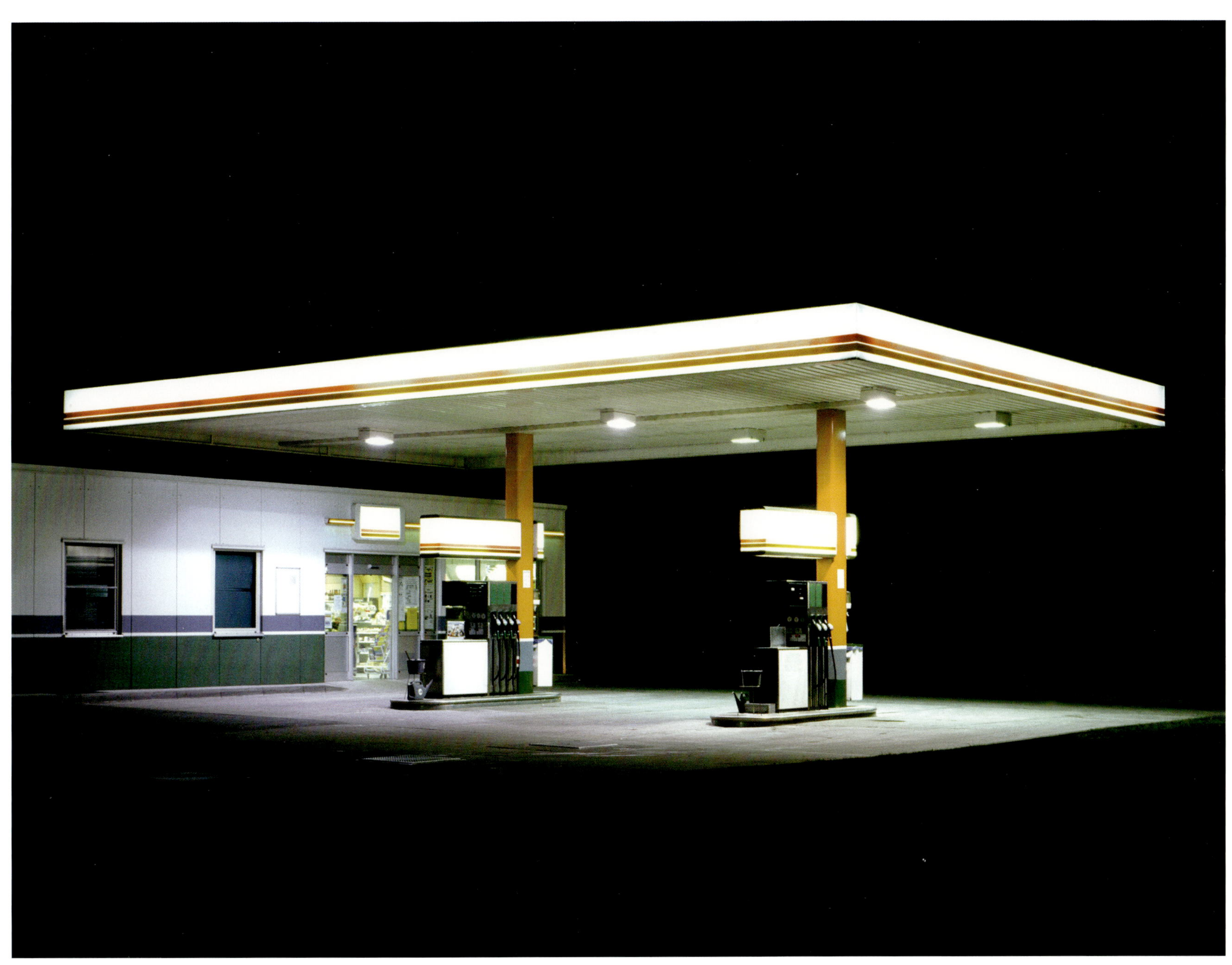

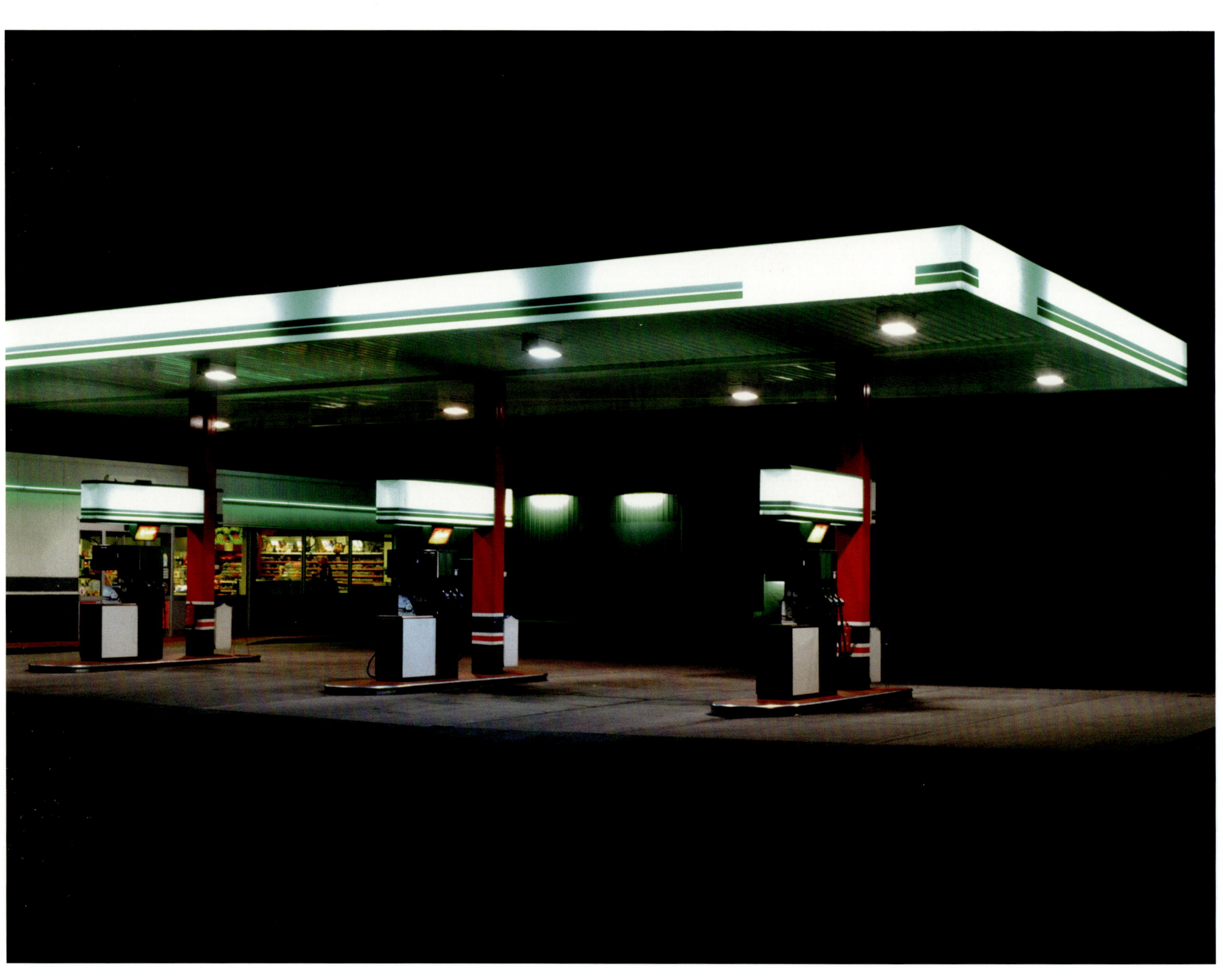

 GRÜN/WEISS / GREEN/WHITE 60 × 80 cm / 23.62 × 31.5 in.

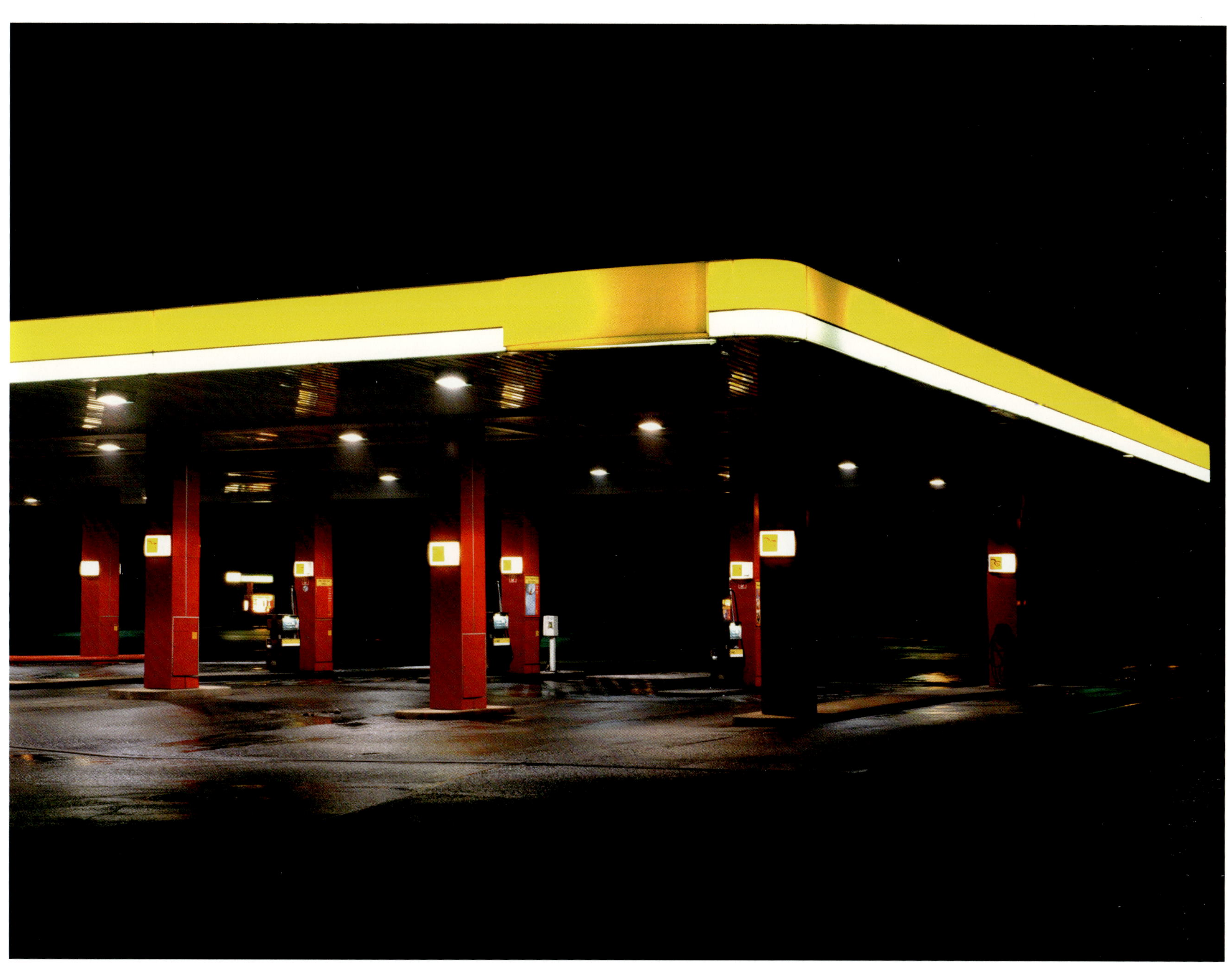

ROT/WEISS/GELB / RED/WHITE/YELLOW 60 × 80 cm / 23.62 × 31.5 in.

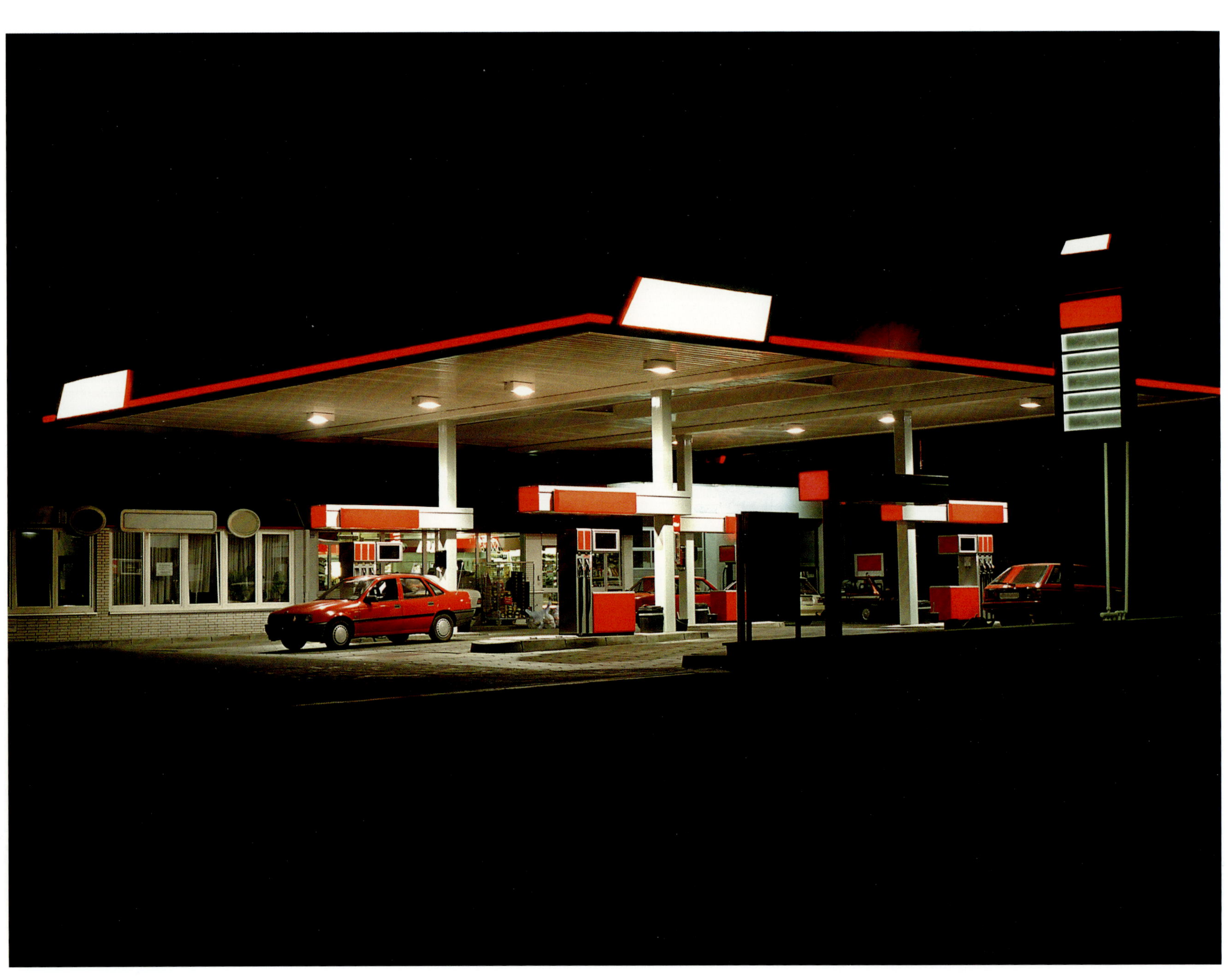

16 **ROT/SCHWARZ / RED/BLACK** 60 × 80 cm / 23.62 × 31.5 in.

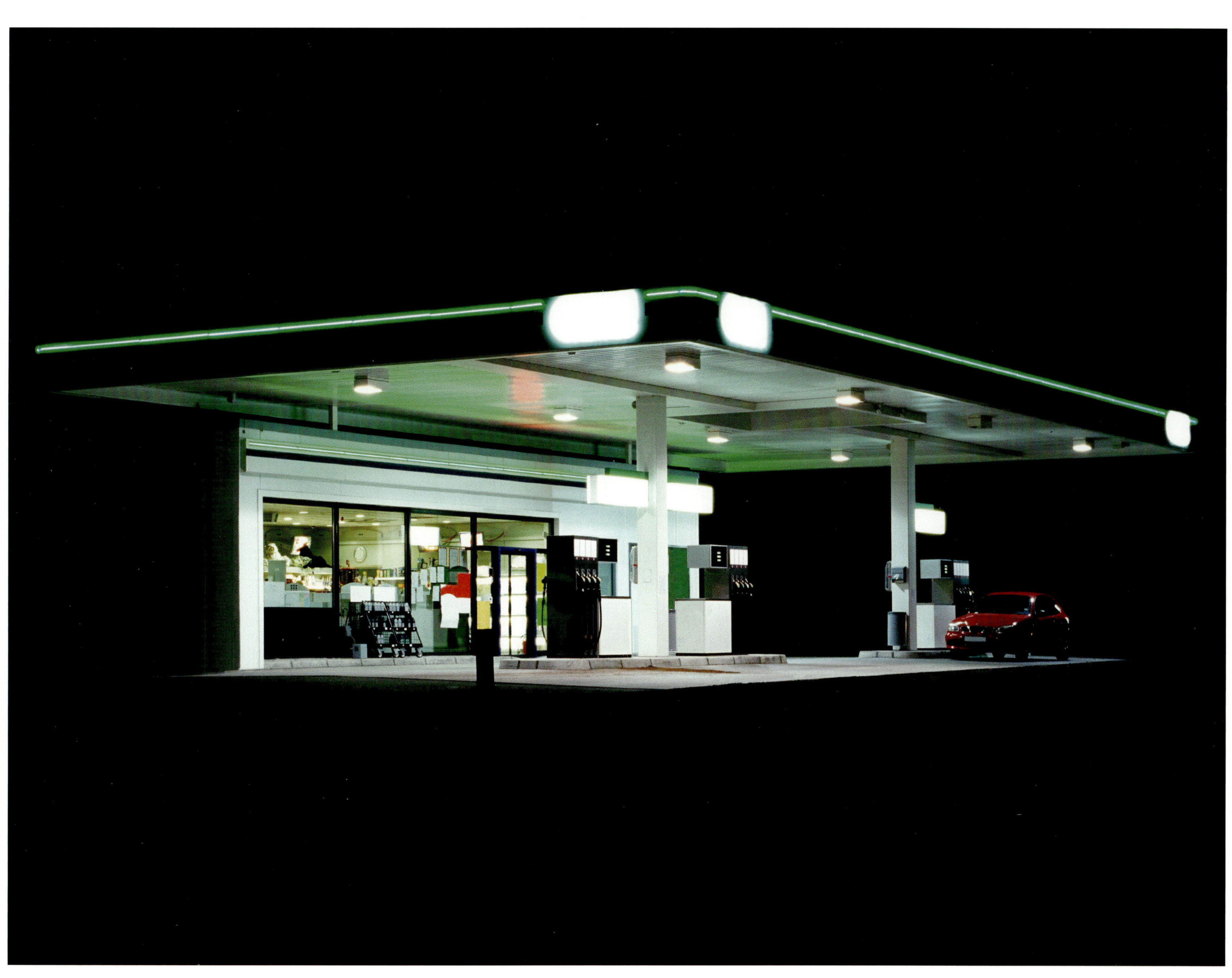

GRÜN/SCHWARZ / GREEN/BLACK 60 × 80 cm / 23.62 × 31.5 in.

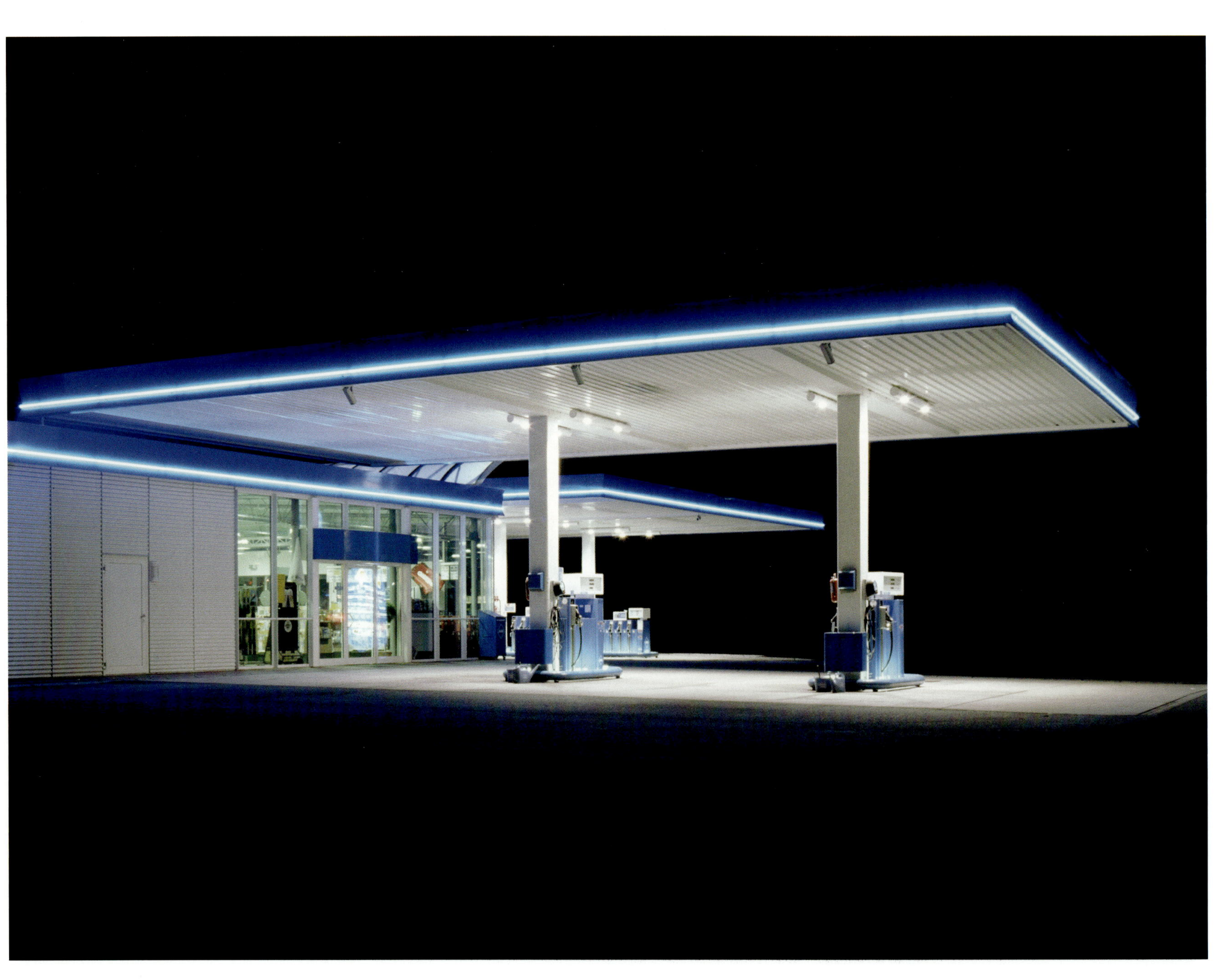

 WEISS/BLAU / WHITE/BLUE 60 × 80 cm / 23.62 × 31.5 in.

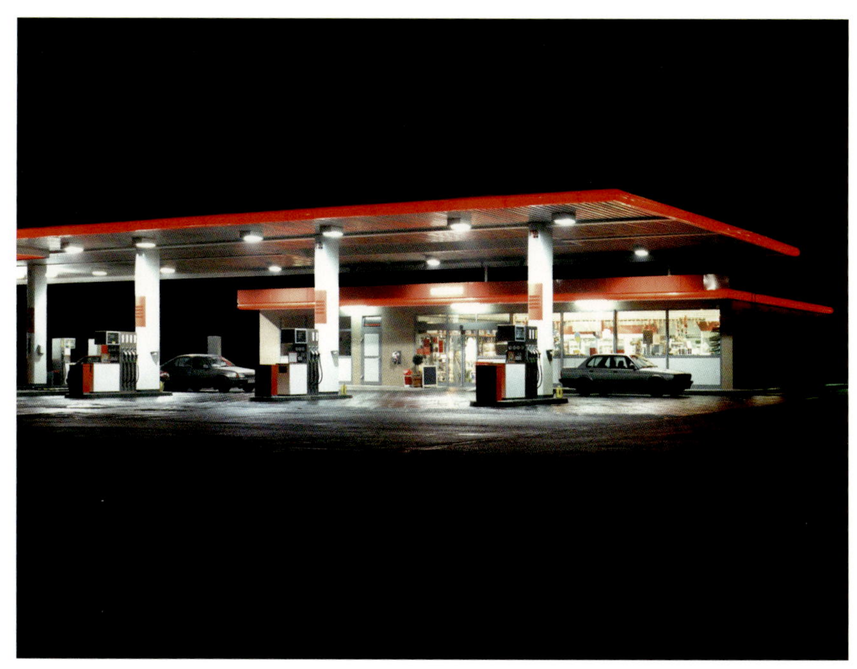 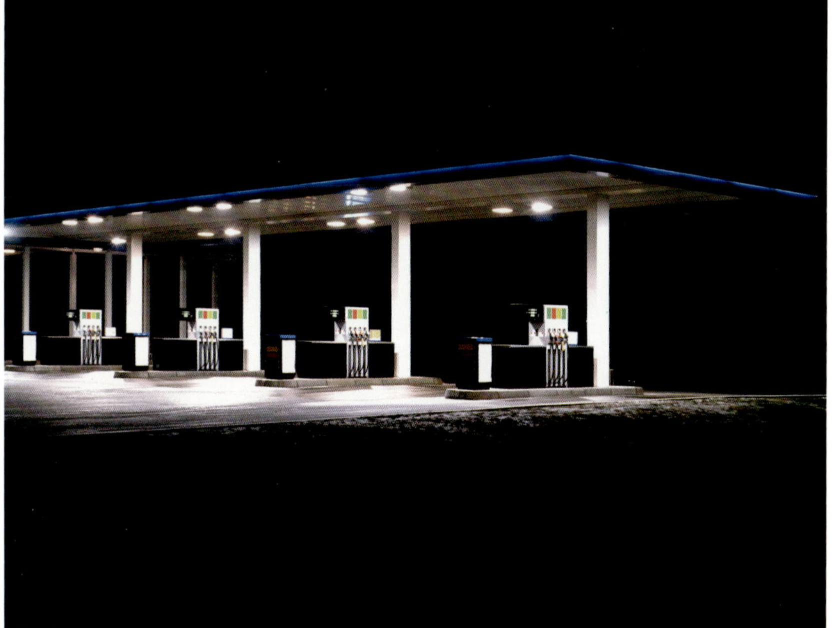

ROT/WEISS/ROT / RED/WHITE/RED   BLAU/WEISS / BLUE/WHITE   60 × 80 cm / 23.62 × 31.5 in.

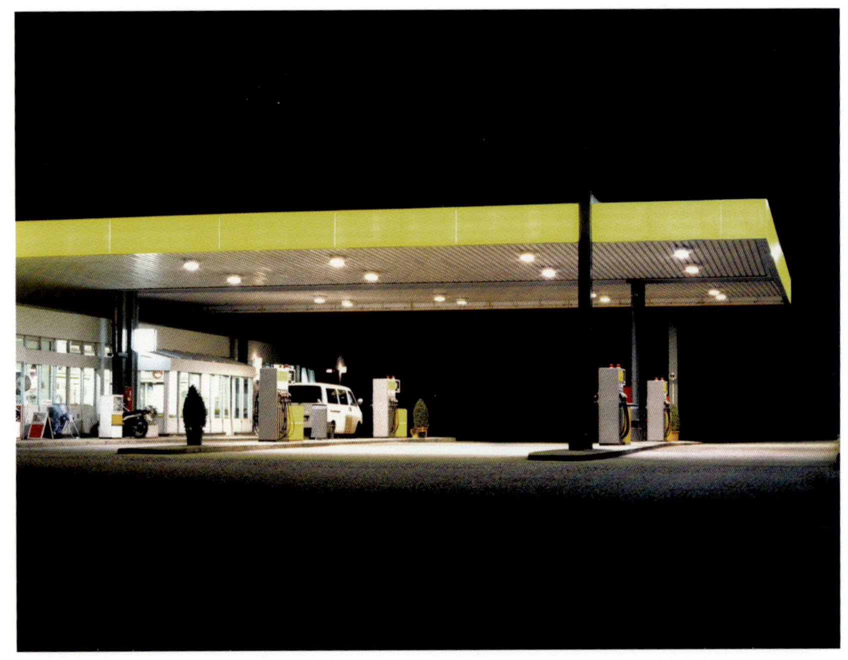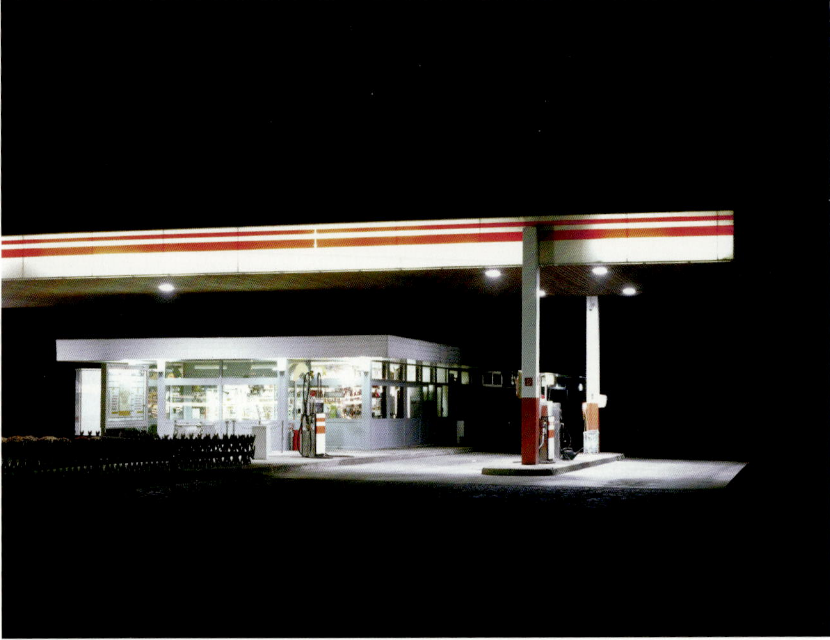

  GELB/SCHWARZ / YELLOW/BLACK   ROT/GELB / RED/YELLOW   60 × 80 cm / 23.62 × 31.5 in.

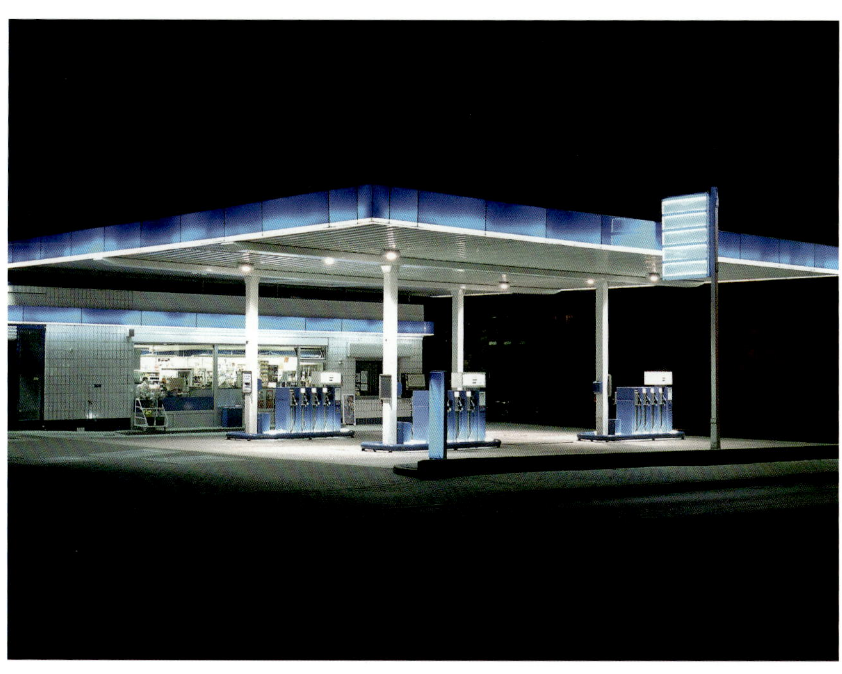 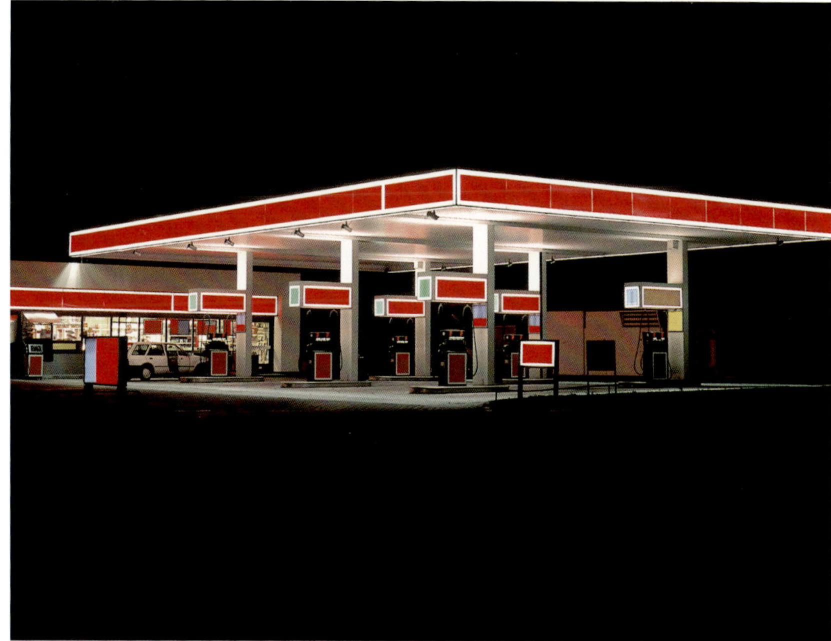

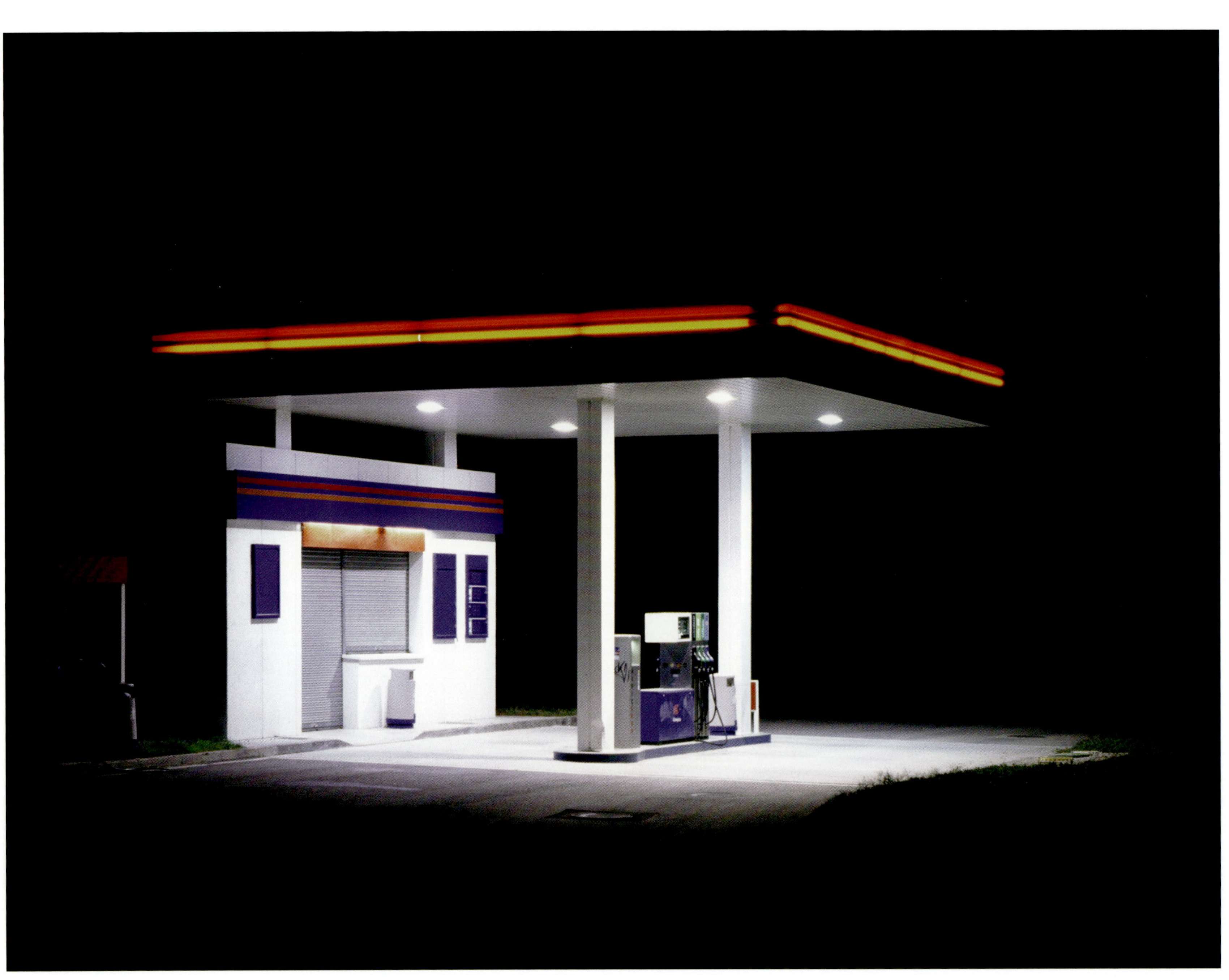

  BLAU/ROT/GELB / BLUE/RED/YELLOW 60 × 80 cm / 23.62 × 31.5 in.

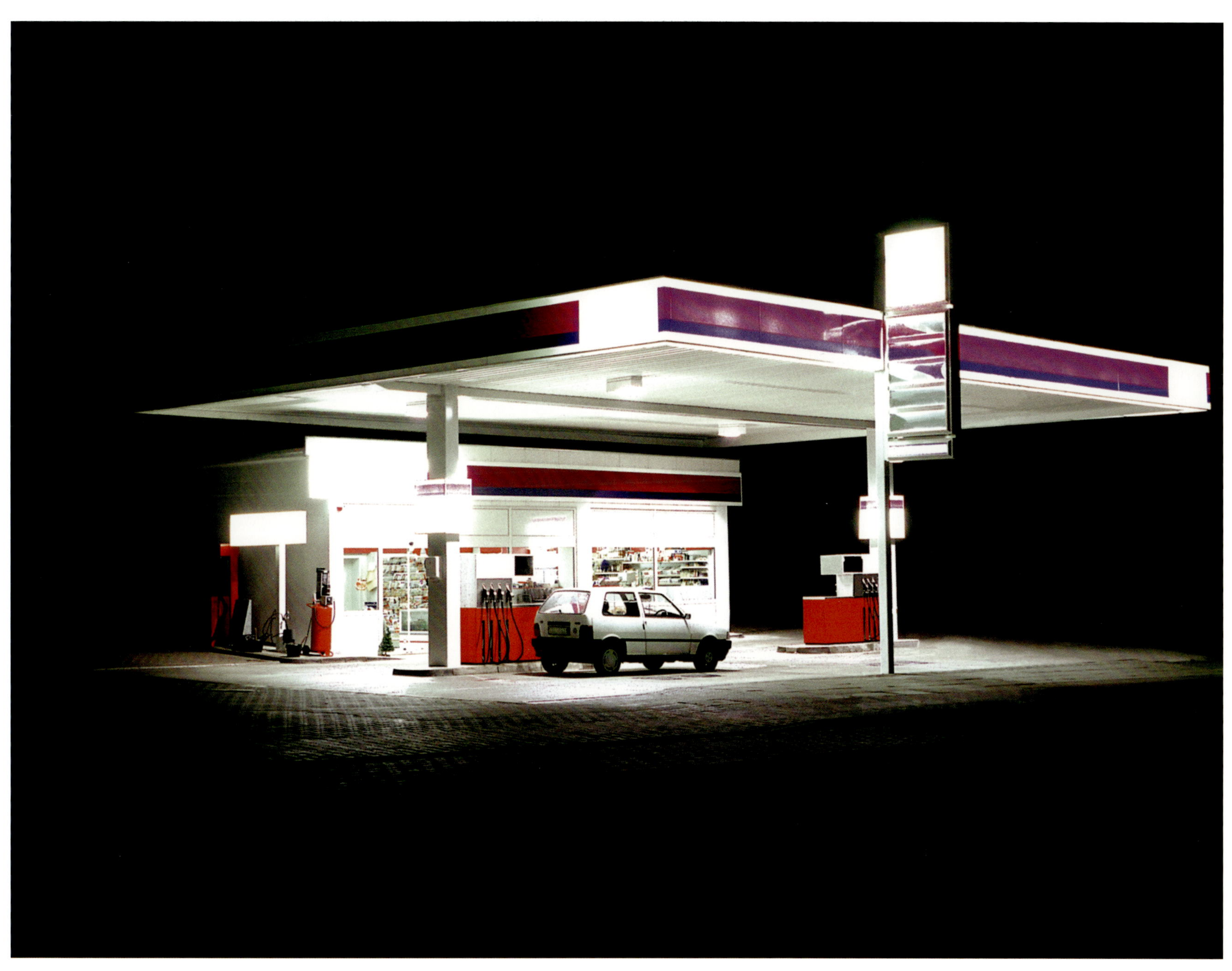

LILA / PURPLE 60 × 80 cm / 23.62 × 31.5 in.

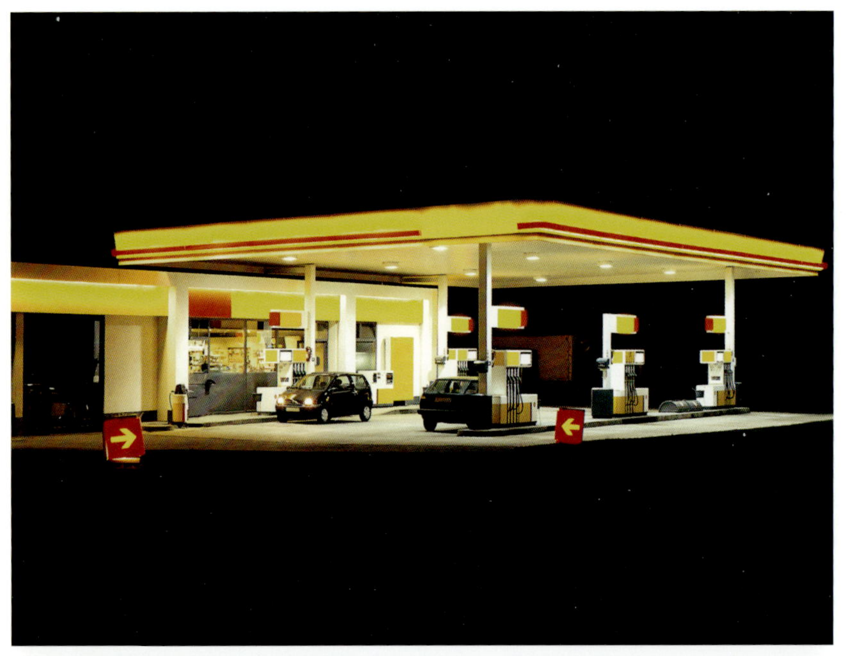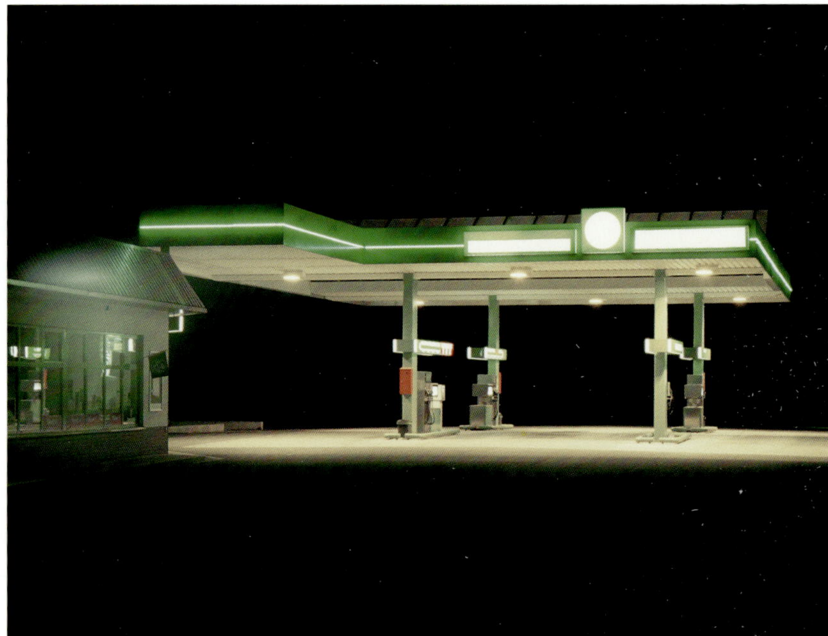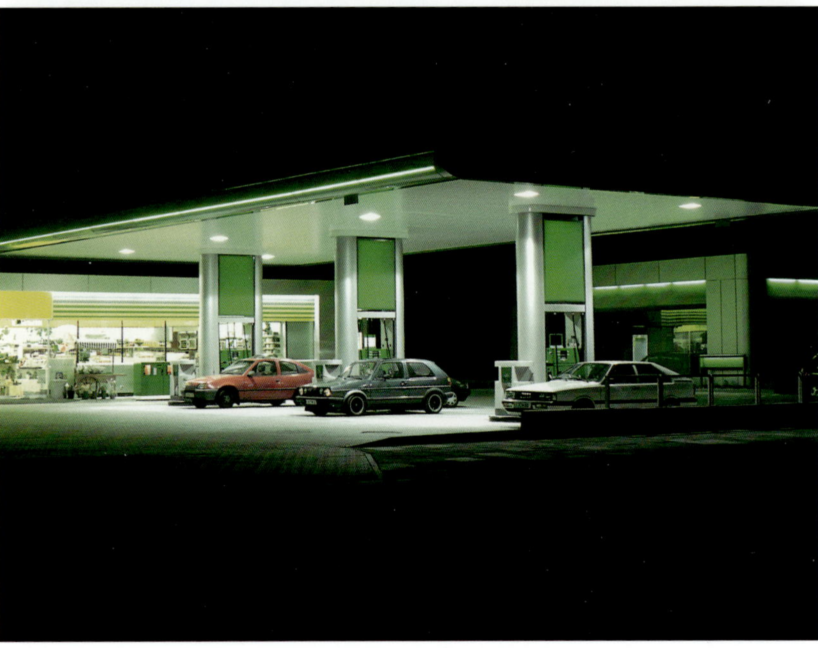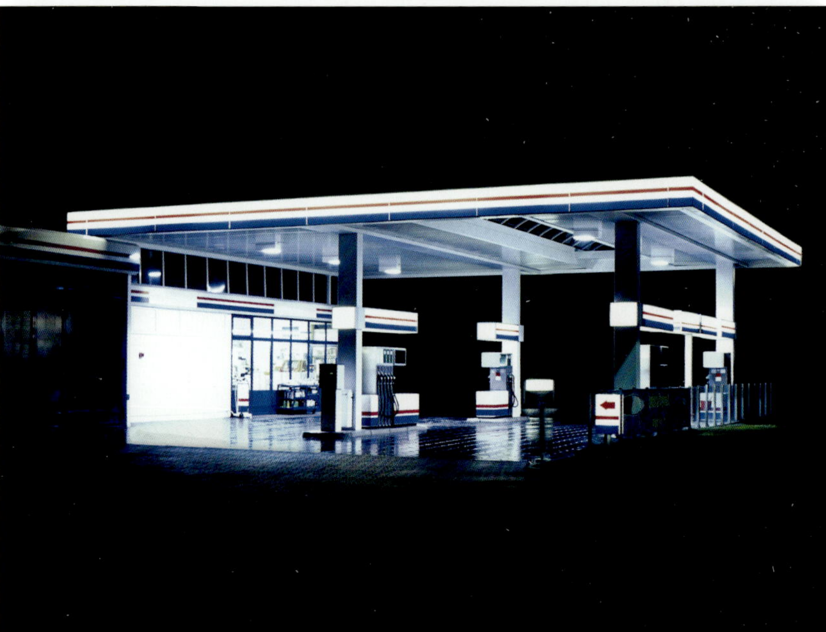

  GELB NEU / YELLOW NEW   GRÜN/WEISS/GRÜN / GREEN/WHITE/GREEN   GRÜN / GREEN   BLAU/ROT / BLUE/RED   60 × 80 cm / 23.62 × 31.5 in.

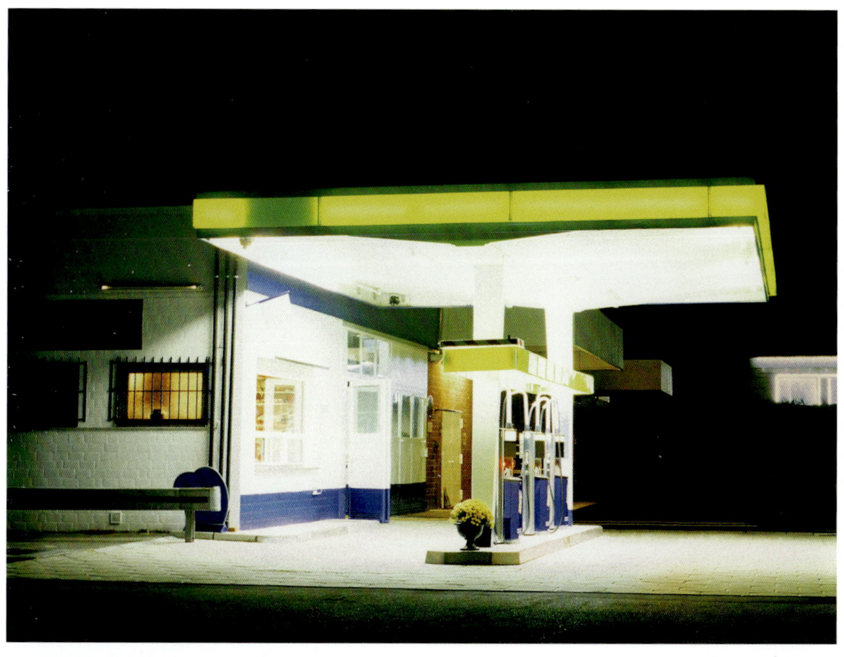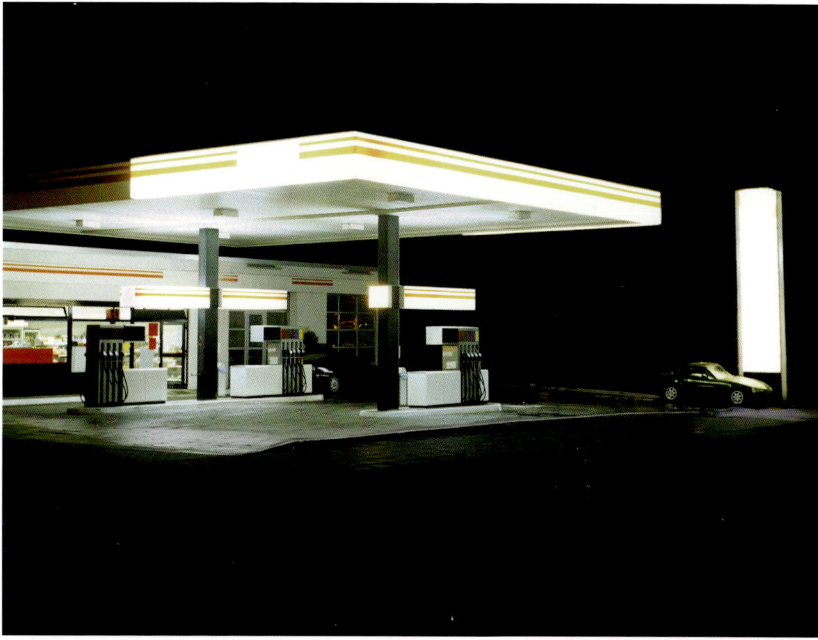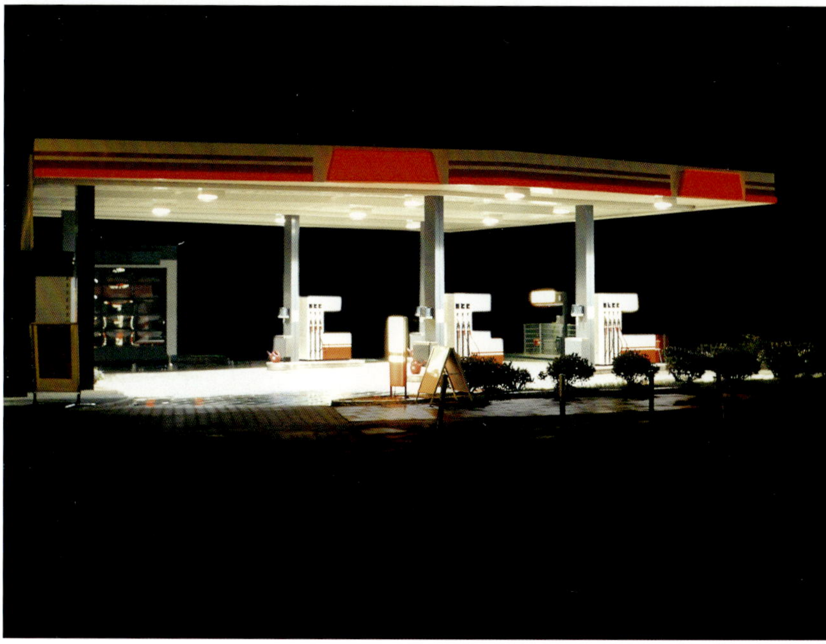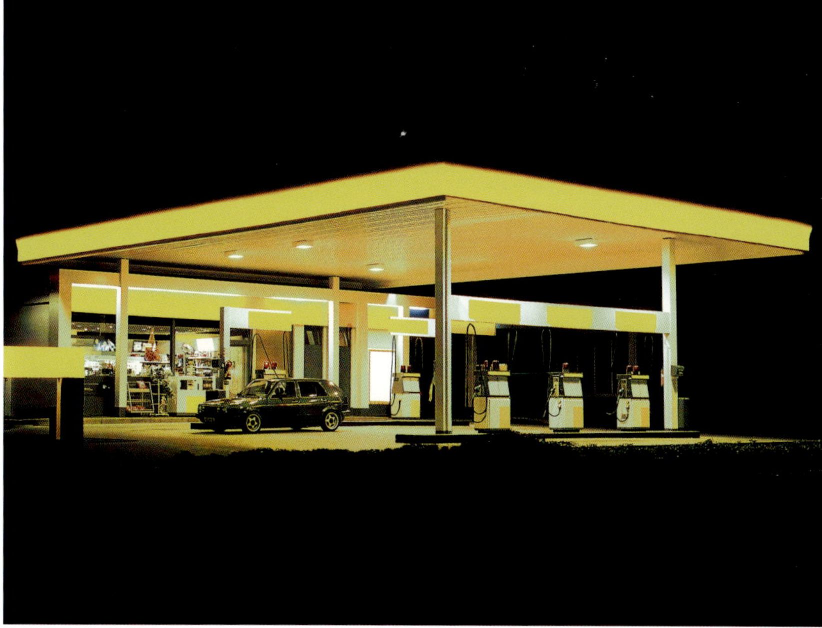

GRÜN/GELB / GREEN/YELLOW   ORANGE   SCHWARZ/ROT / BLACK/RED   GELB / YELLOW   60 × 80 cm / 23.62 × 31.5 in.

SUPERMÄRKTE / SUPERMARKETS 1998

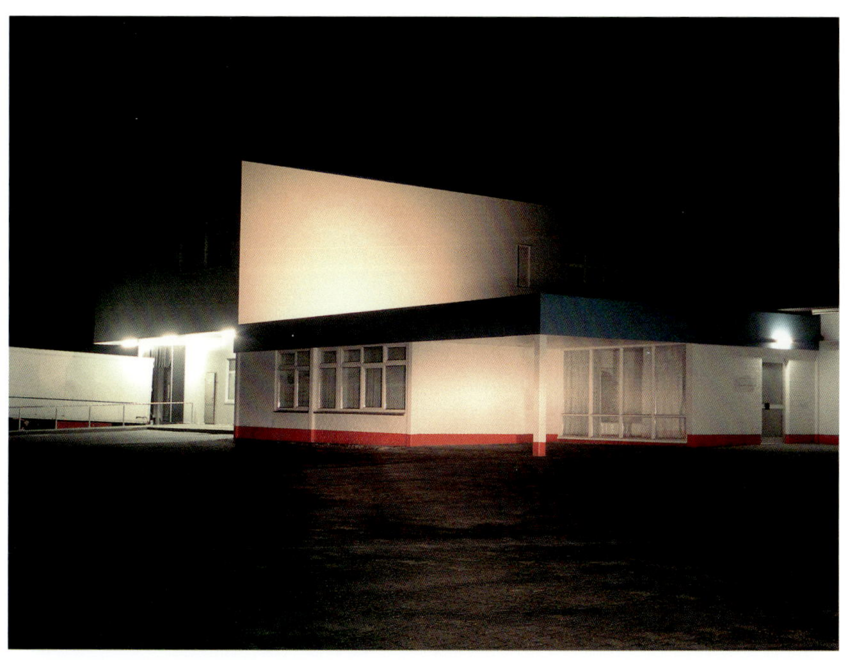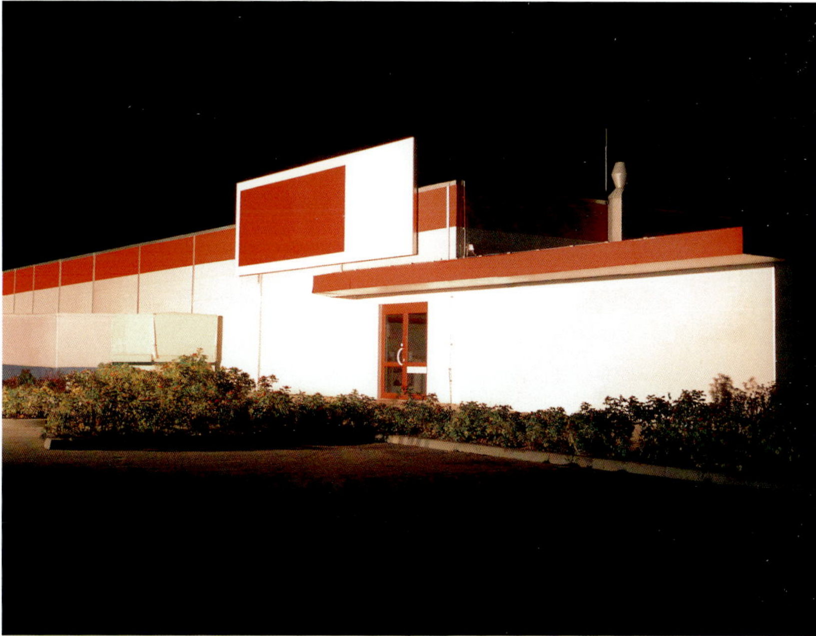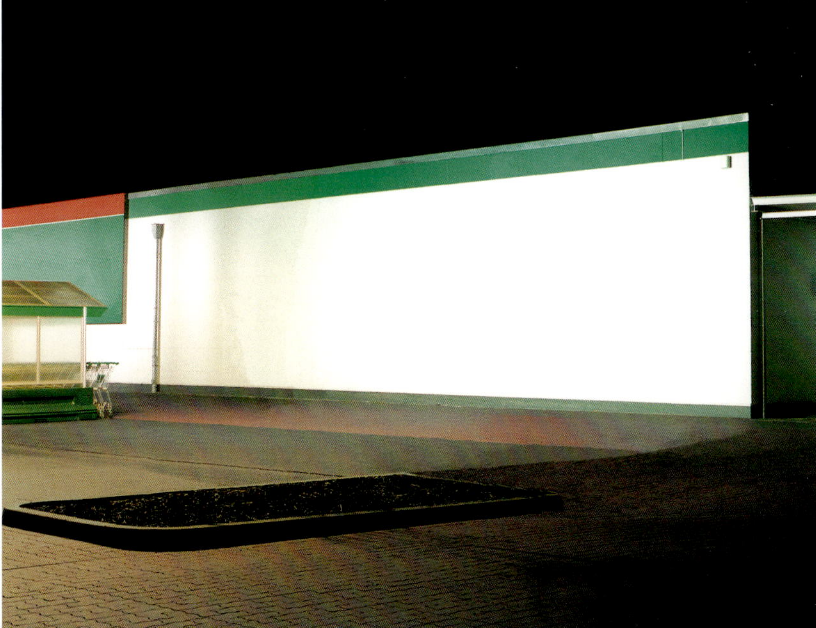

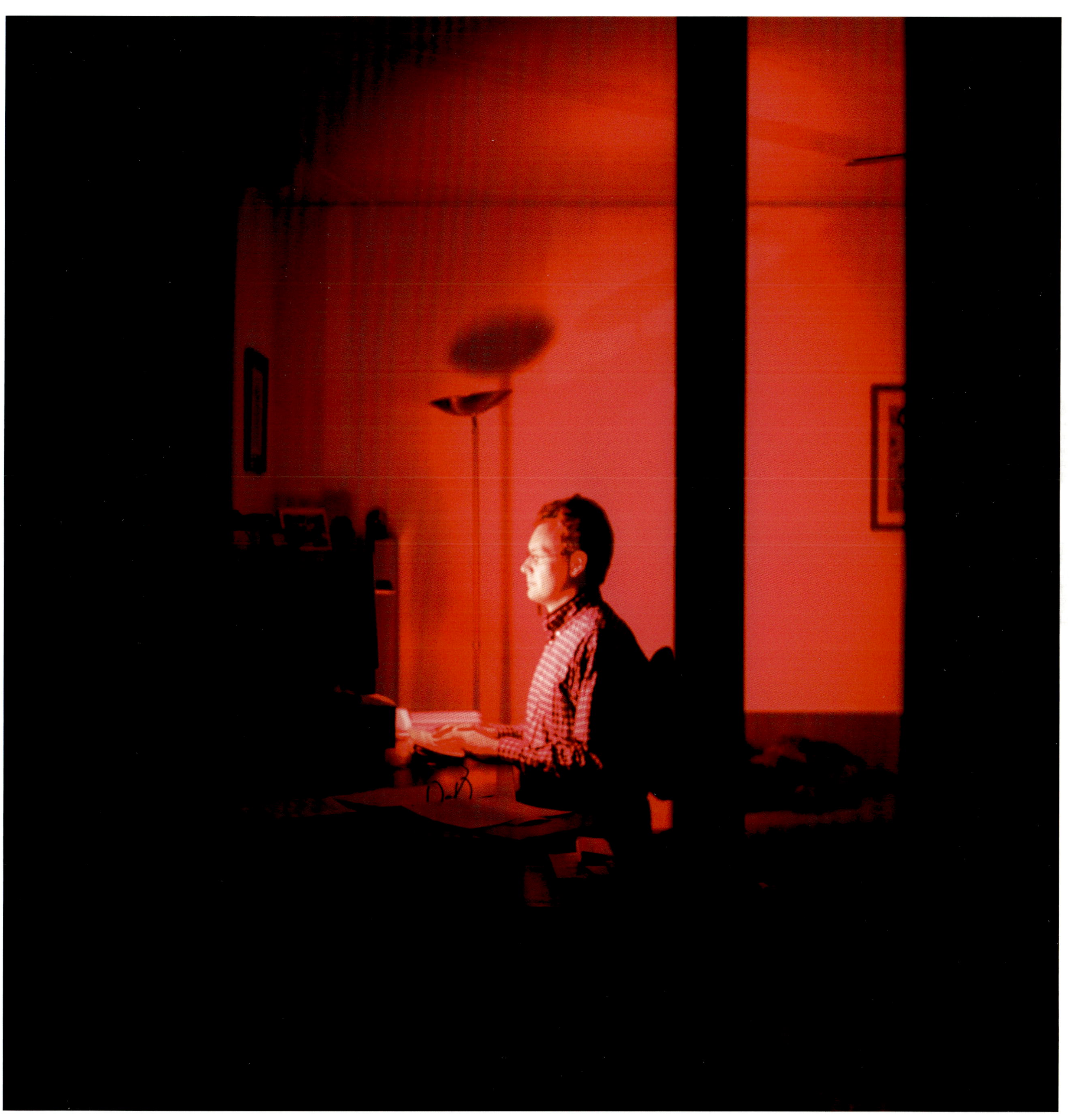

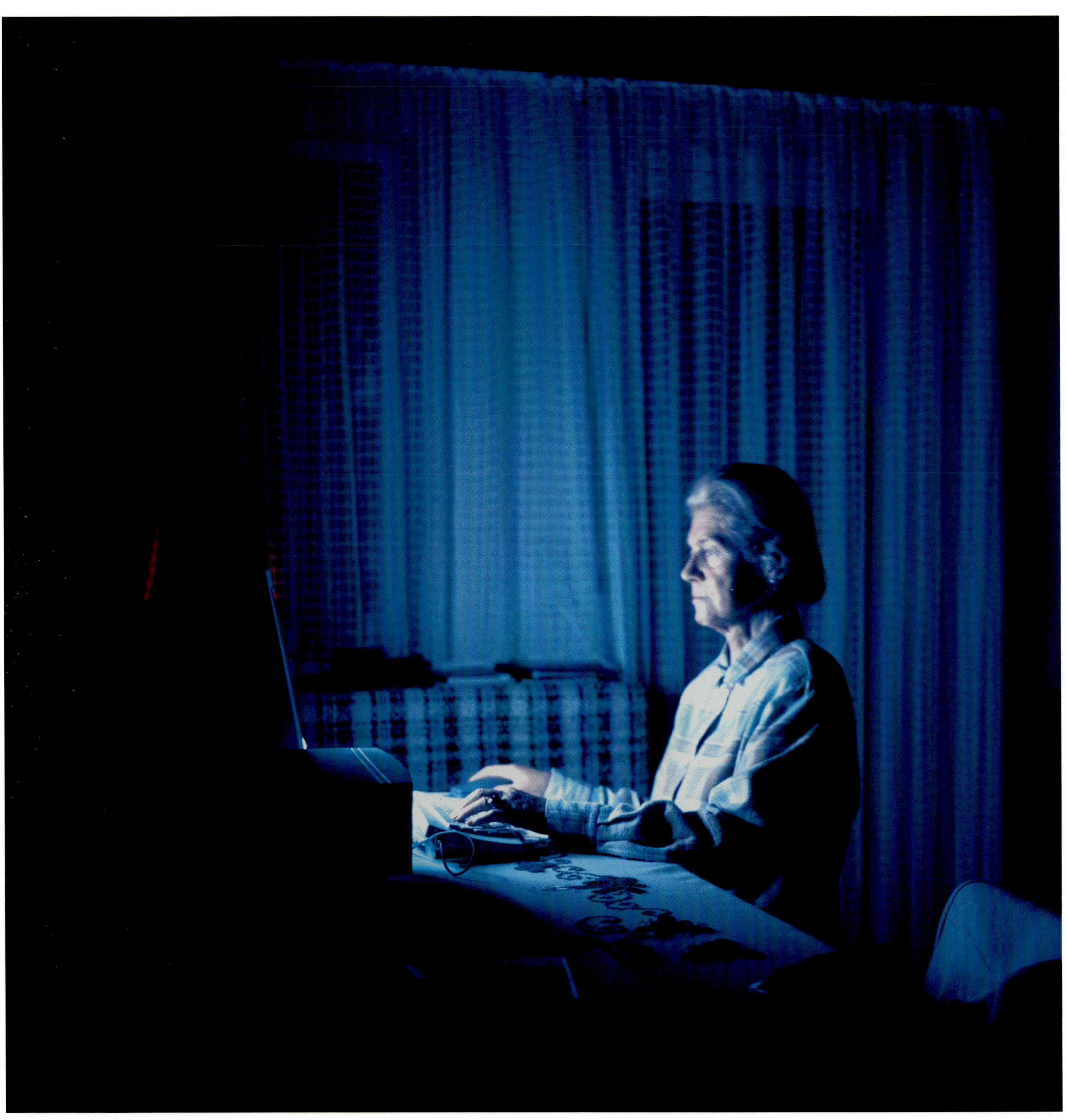

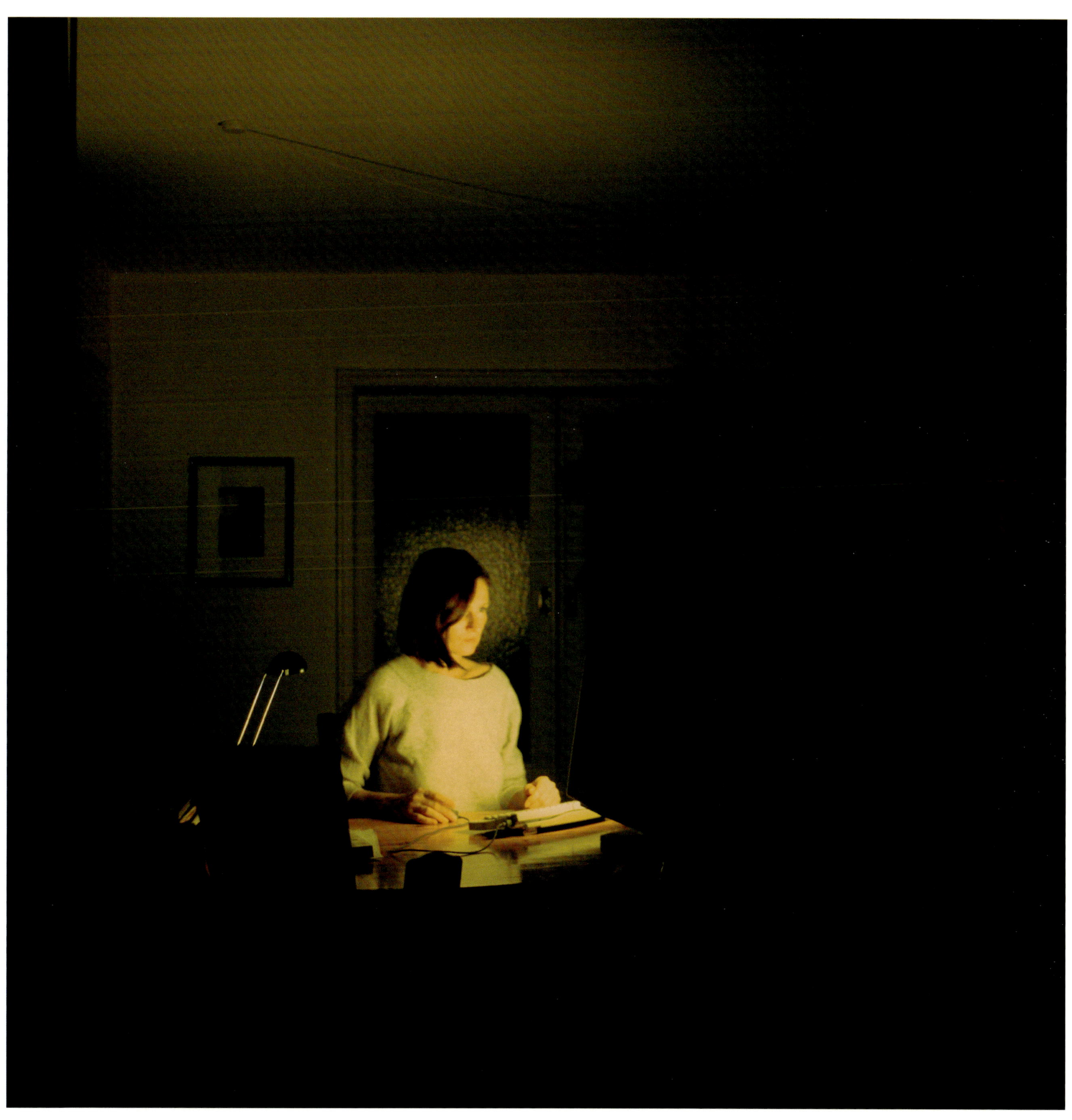

GELB / YELLOW 110 × 110 cm / 43.31 × 43.31 in.

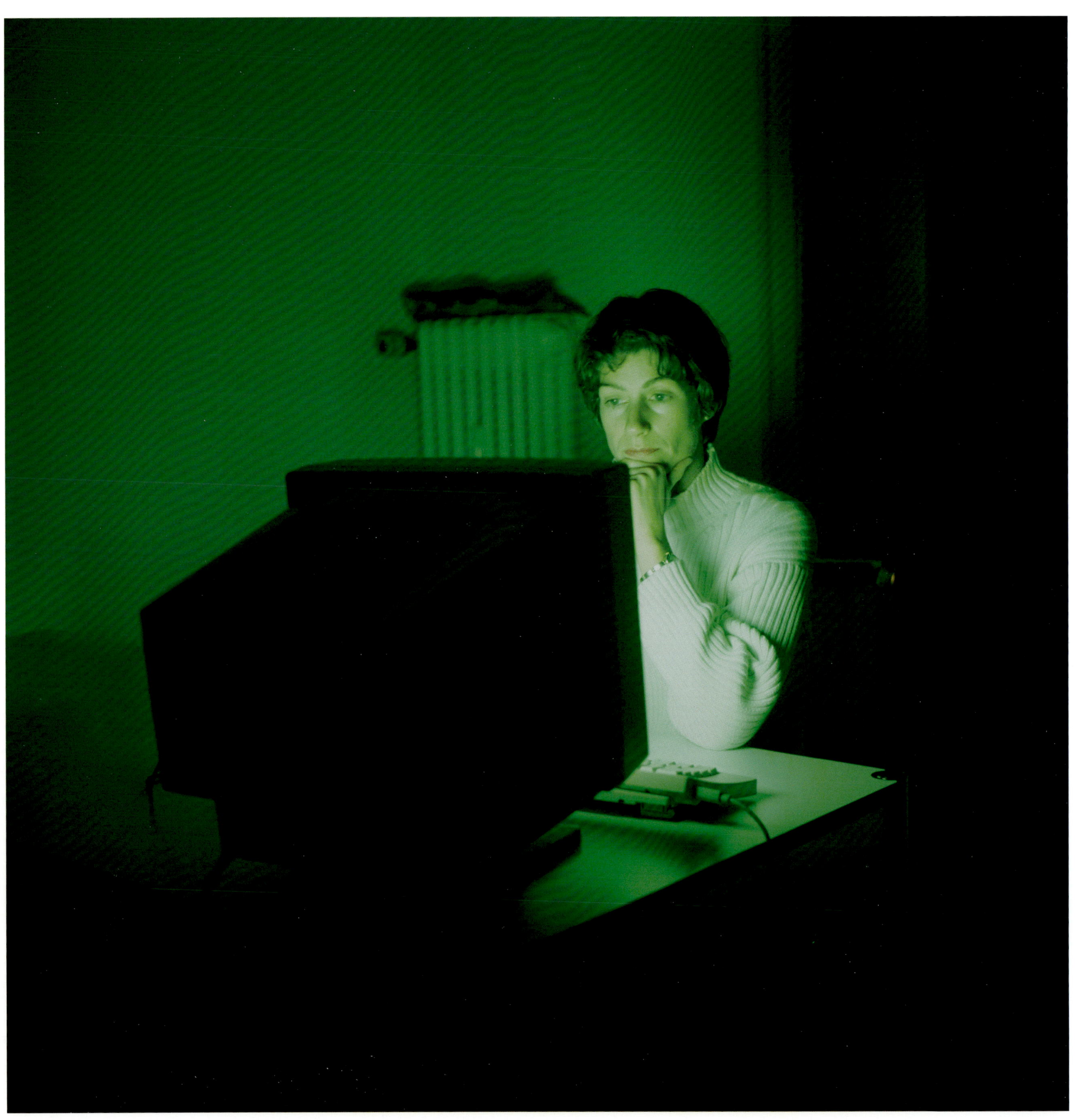

   GRÜN / GREEN 110 × 110 cm / 43.31 × 43.31 in.

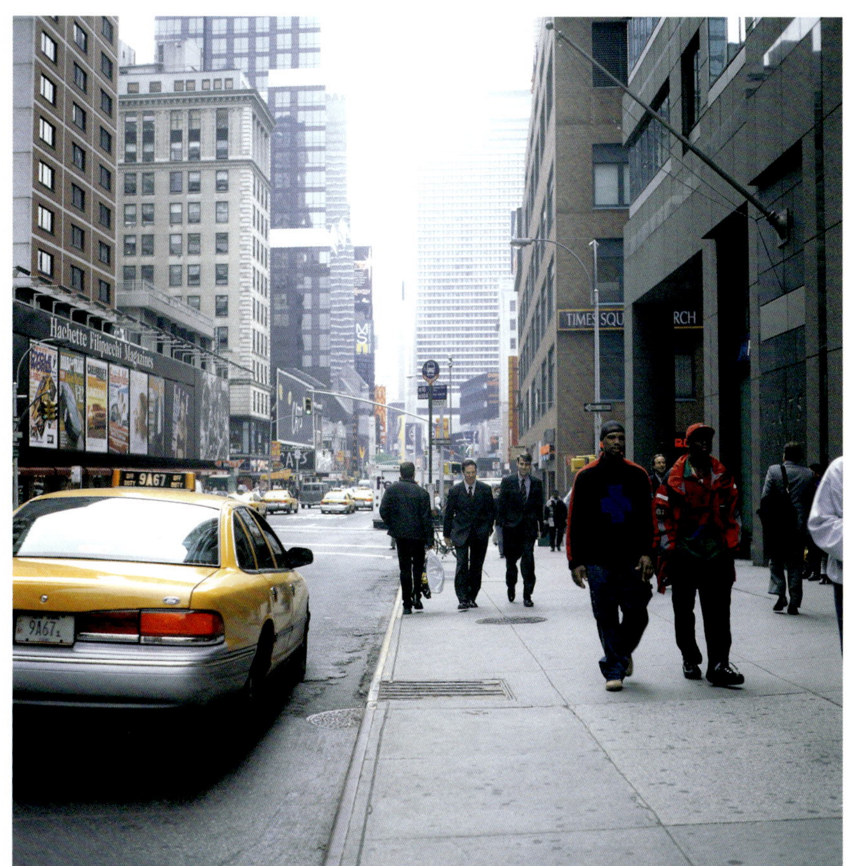
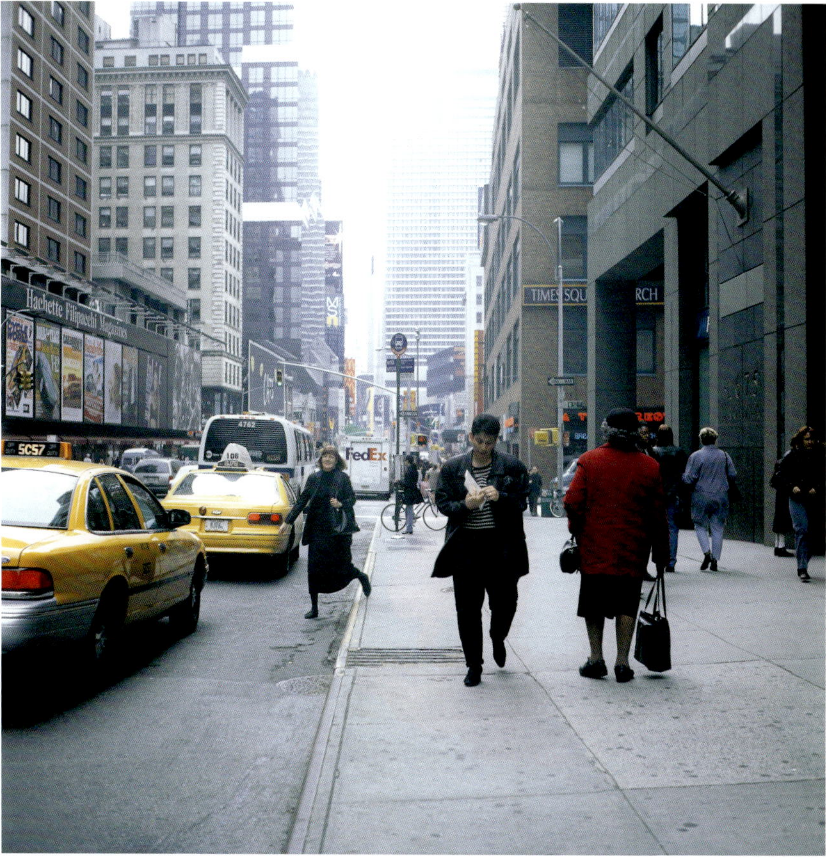
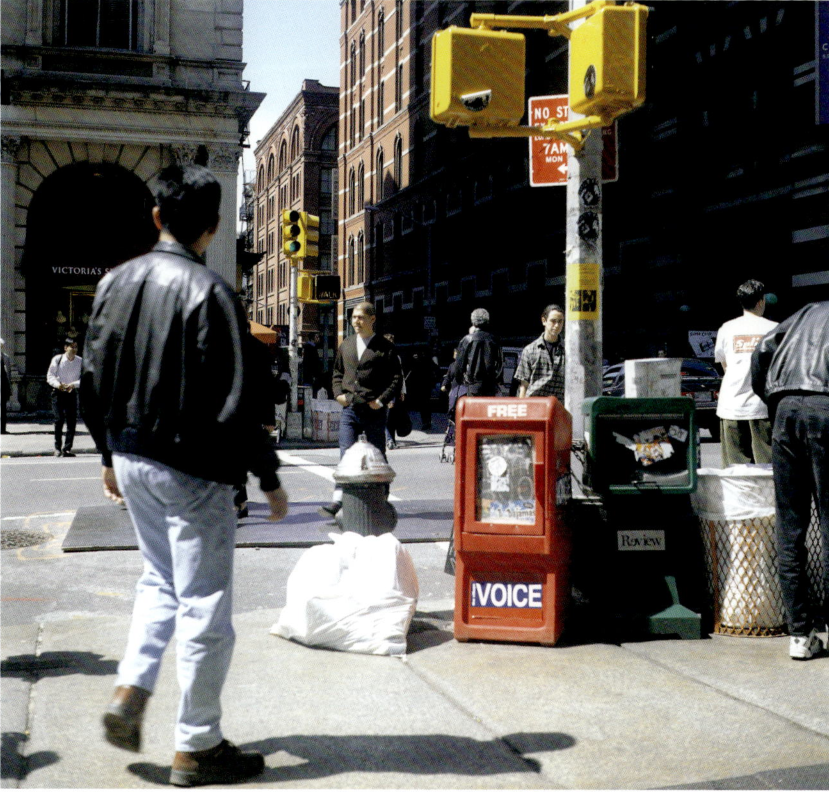
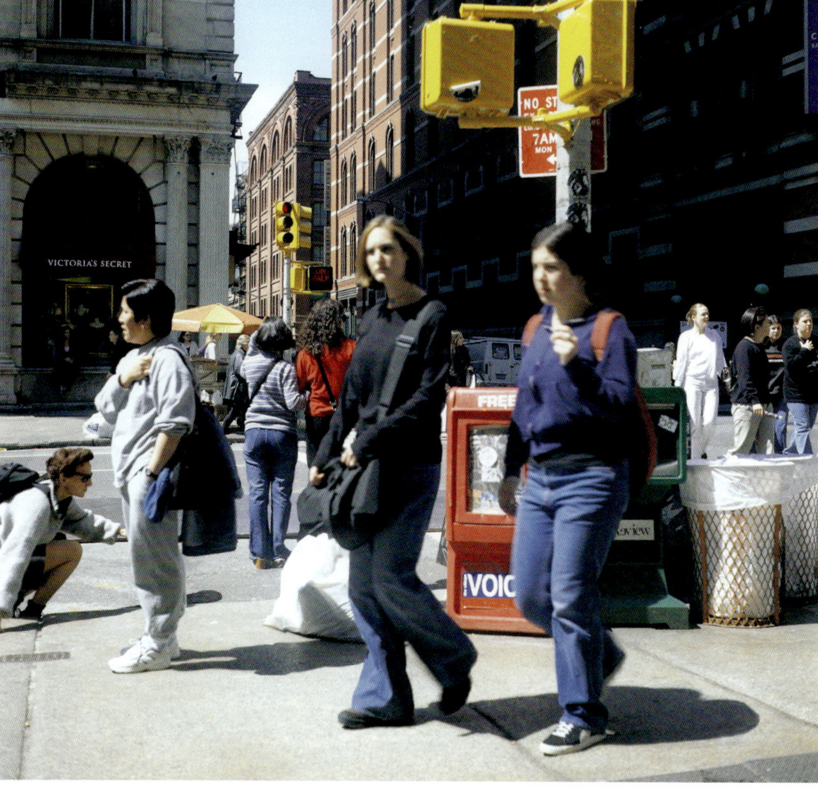

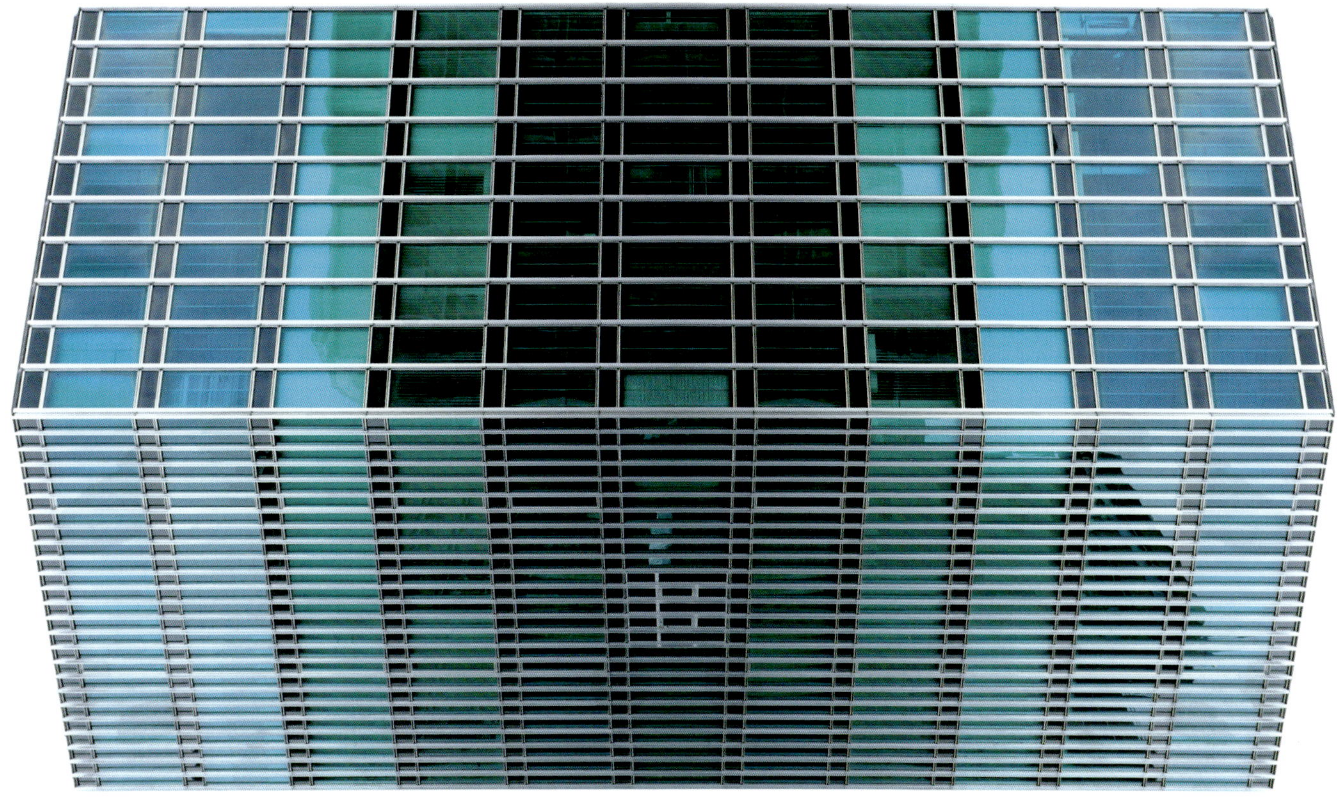

1 124 × 202 cm / 48.82 × 79.67 in.

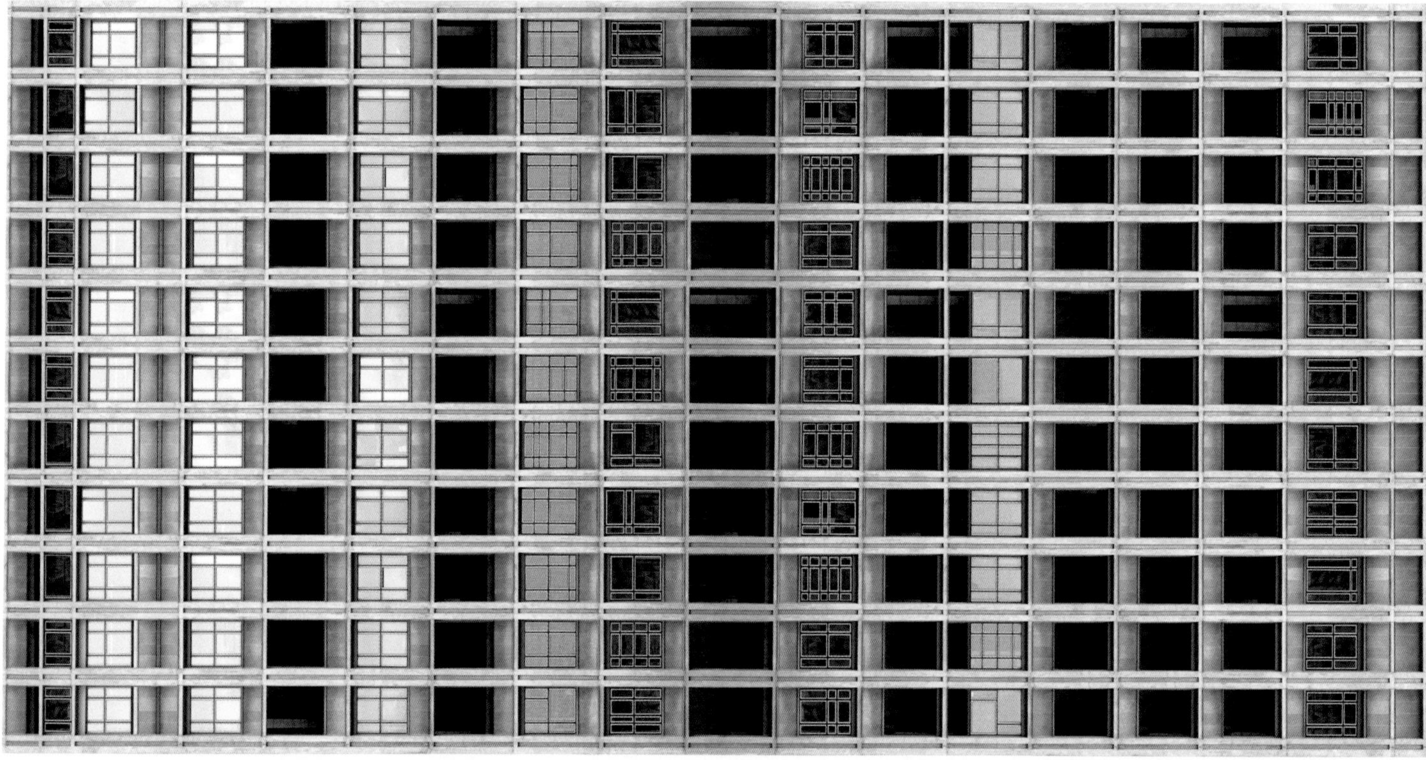

  # 6 124 × 223 cm / 48.82 × 87.84 in.

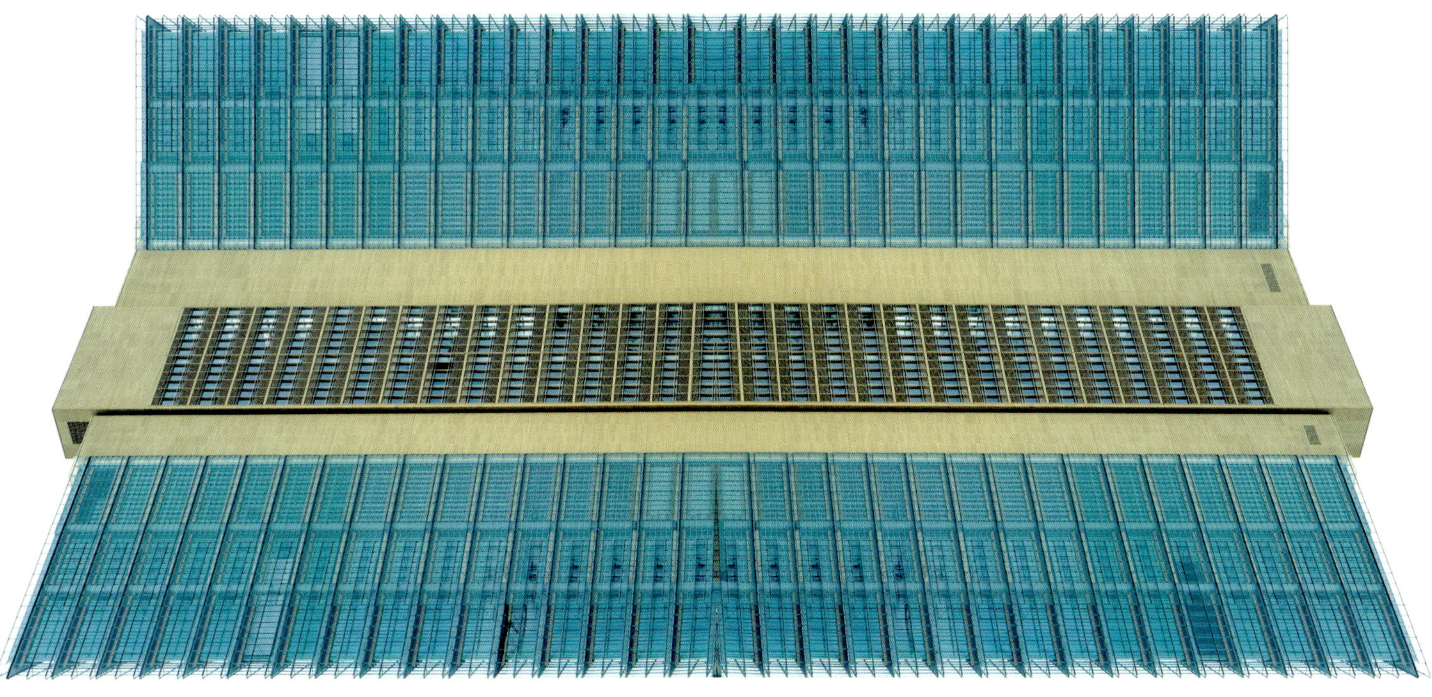

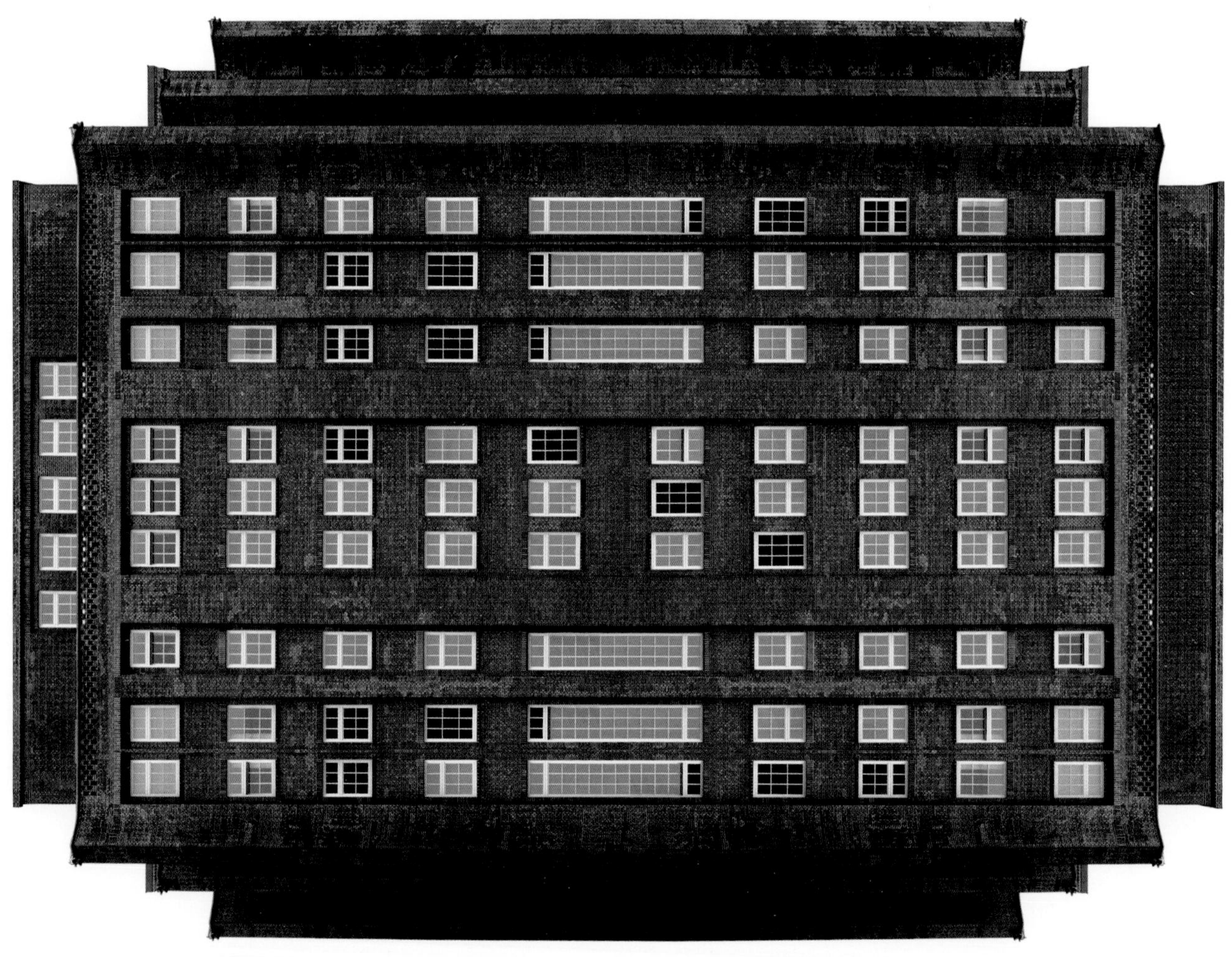

   # 5 124 × 181 cm / 48.82 × 71.3 in.

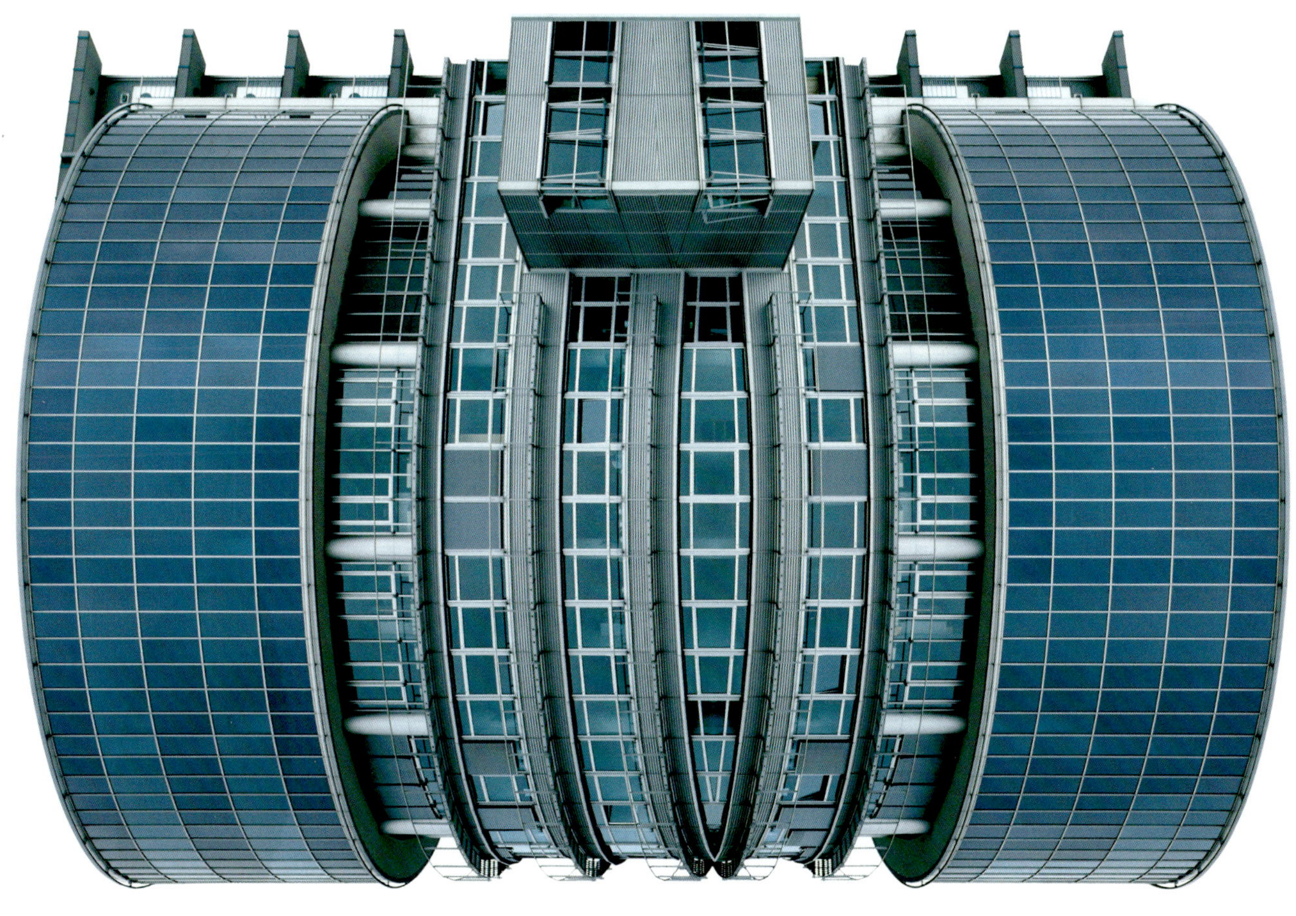

3 124 × 192 cm / 48.82 × 75.83 in.

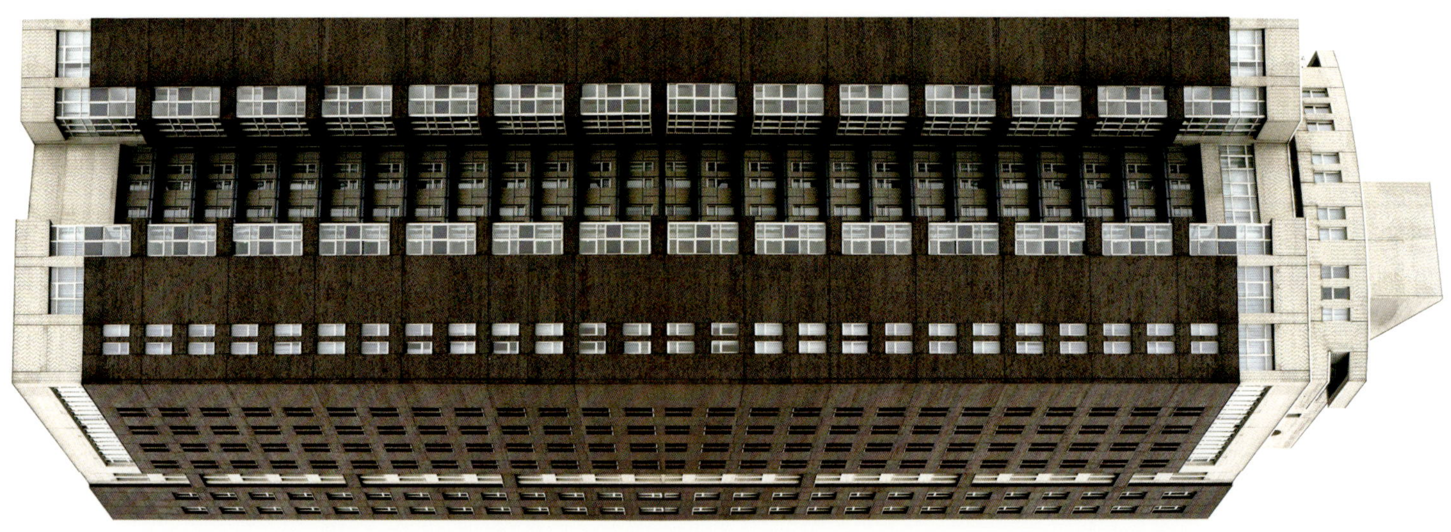

 # 4 124 × 282 cm / 48.82 × 111 in.

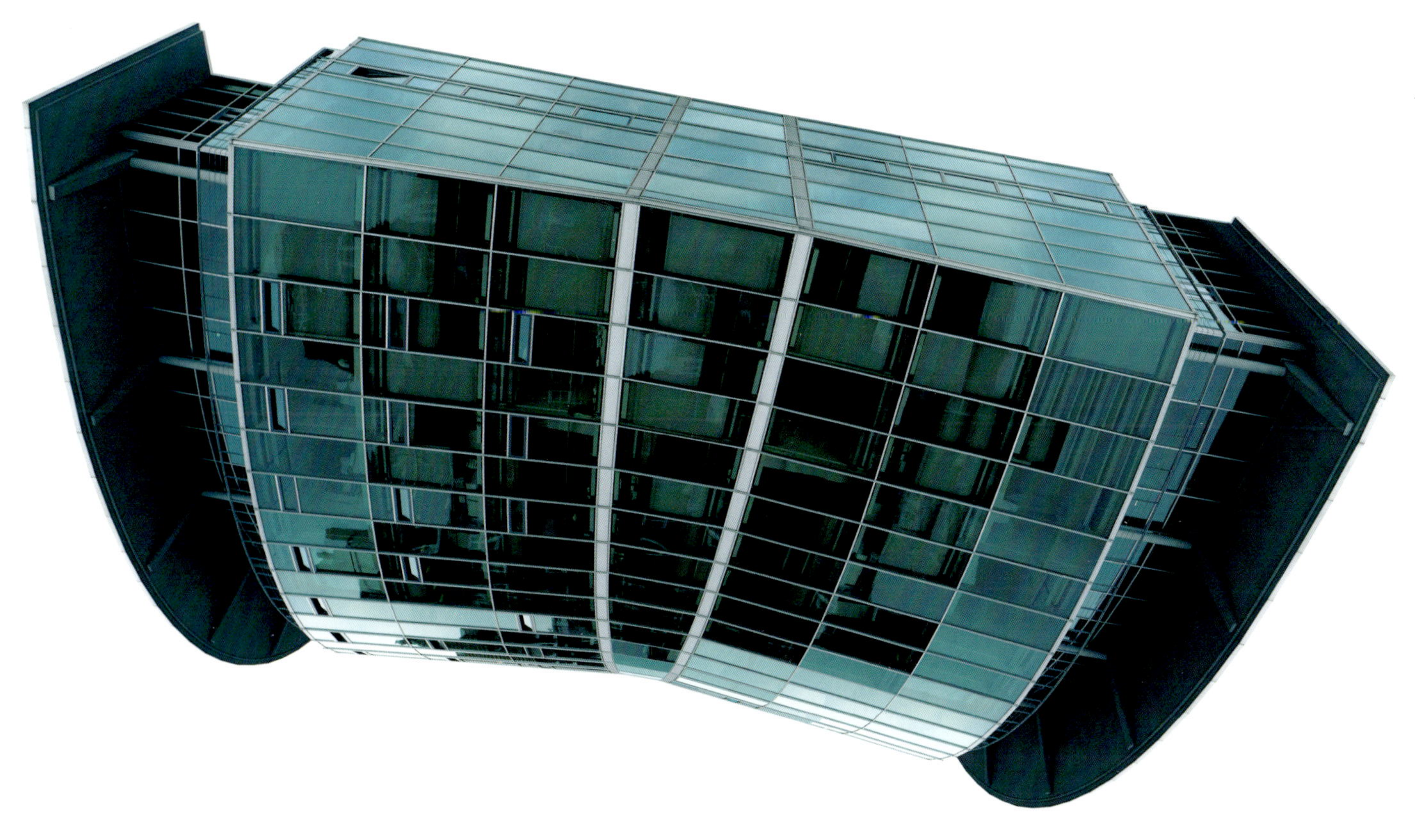

2 124 × 216 cm / 48.82 × 85.12 in.

MIX 2000/01

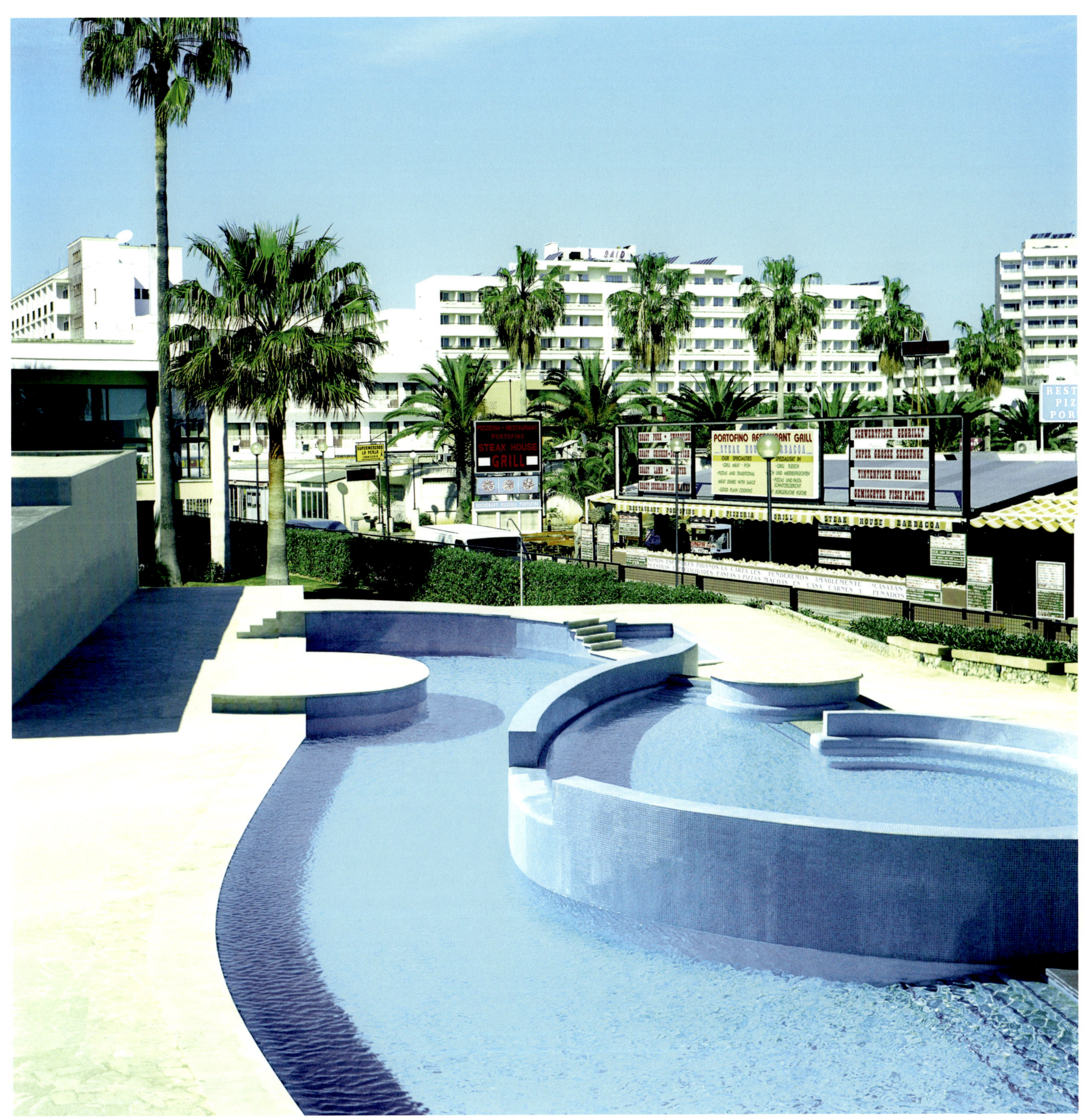

PIZZERIA - RESTAURANT
PORTOFINO
STEAK HOUSE
GRILL
PORTOFINO RESTAURANT GRILL
STEAK HOUSE BARBACOA
OUR SPECIALITIES
SPEZIALITÄT IN
SCHWERTFISCH GEGRILLT
SUPER GROSSE SEEZUNGE
TINTENFISCH GEGRILLT
GEMISCHTER FISCH PLATTE
RESTAURANT PORTOFINO PIZZERIA GRILL STEAK HOUSE BARBACOA

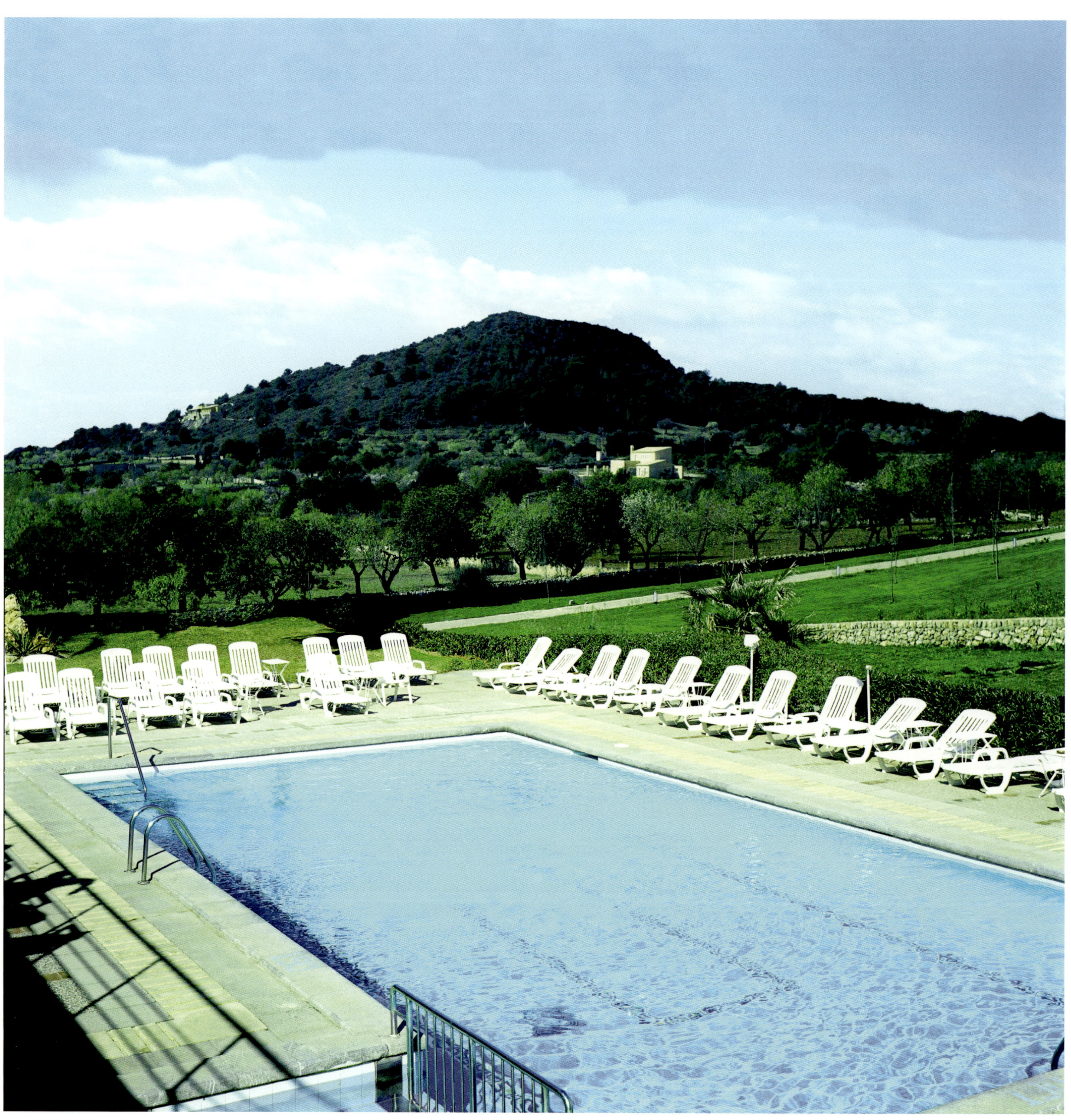

  TILJO 100 × 100 cm / 39.38 × 39.38 in.

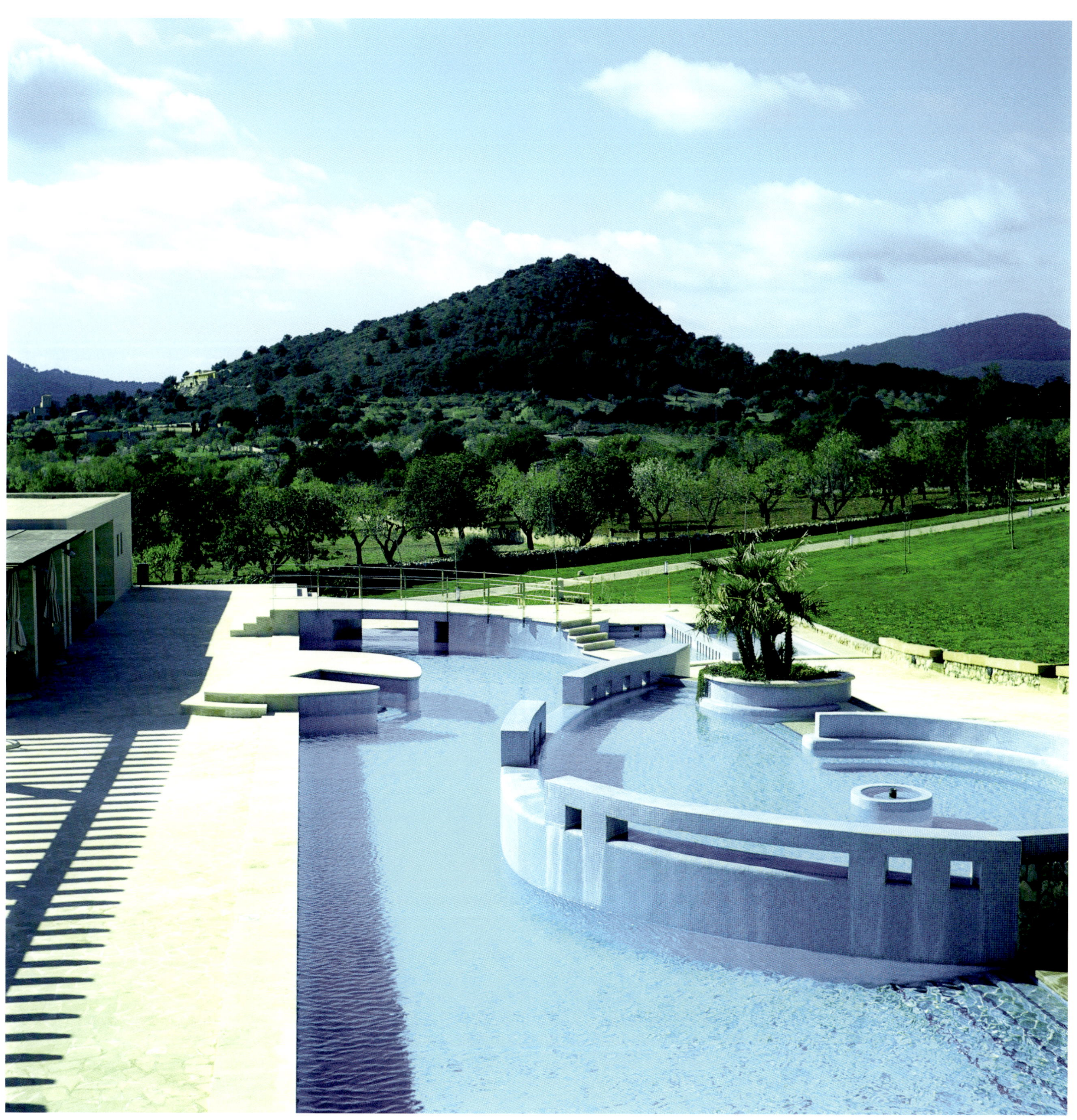

RAMANO 100 × 100 cm / 39.38 × 39.38 in.

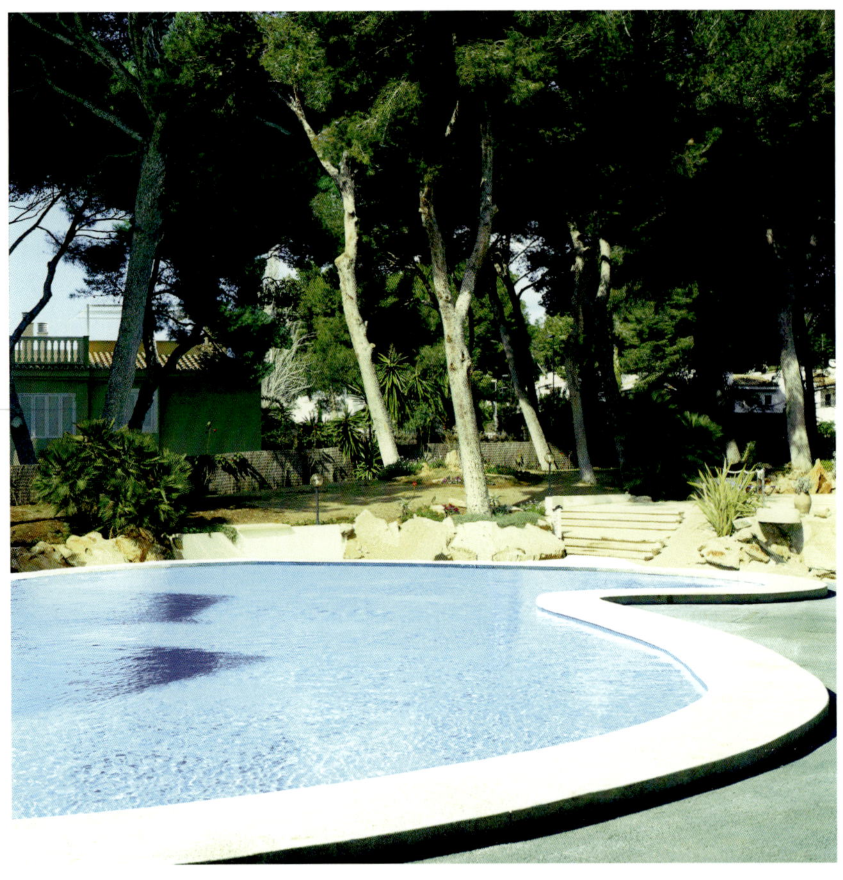
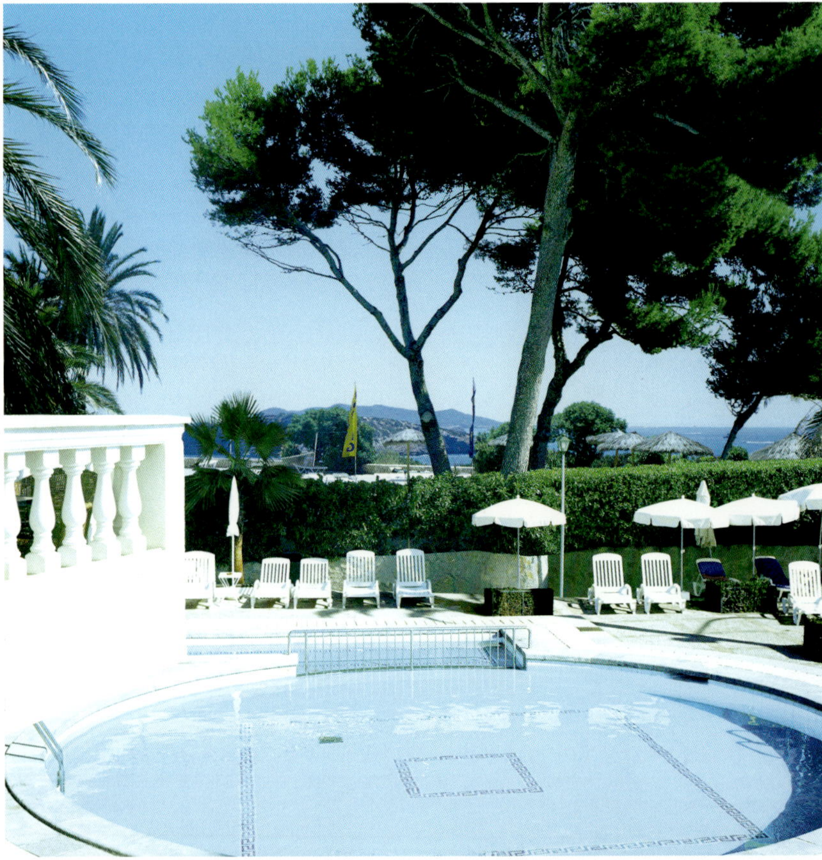
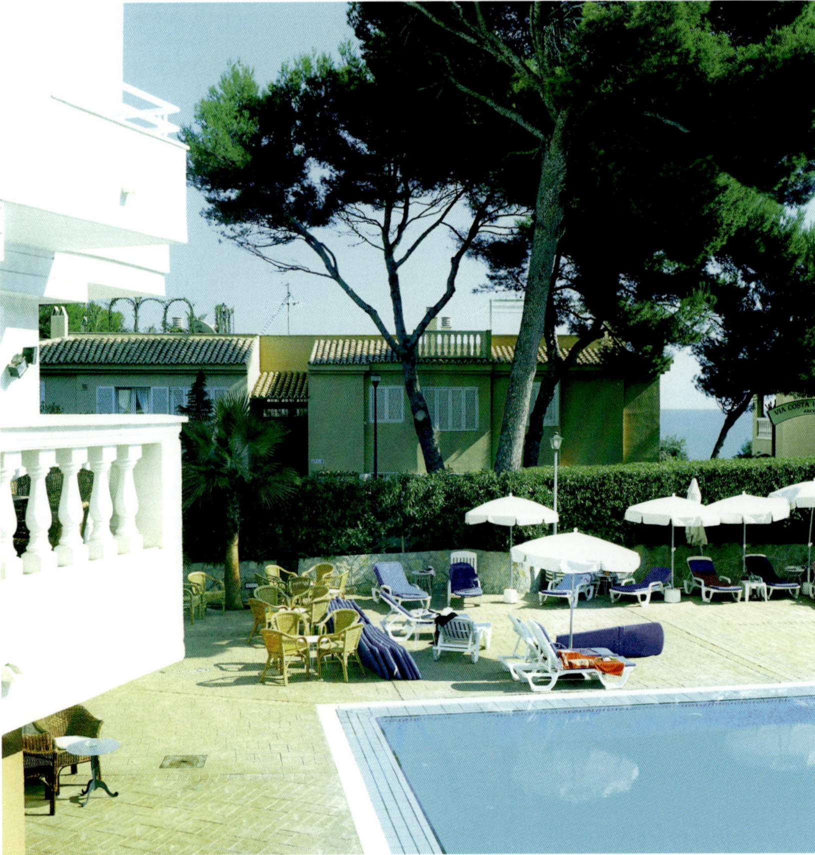
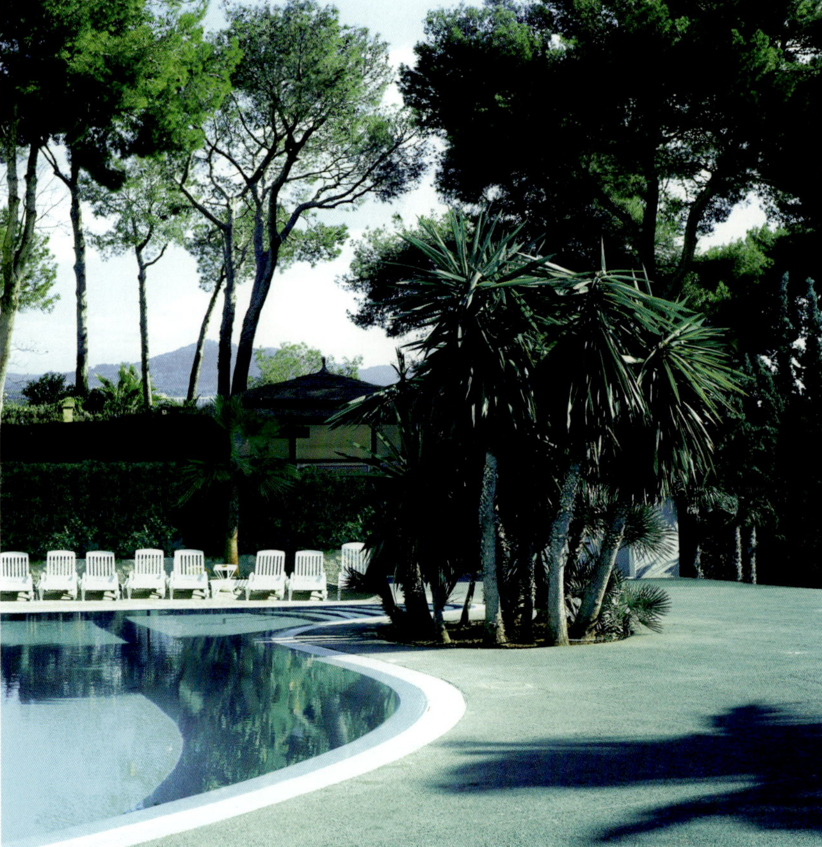

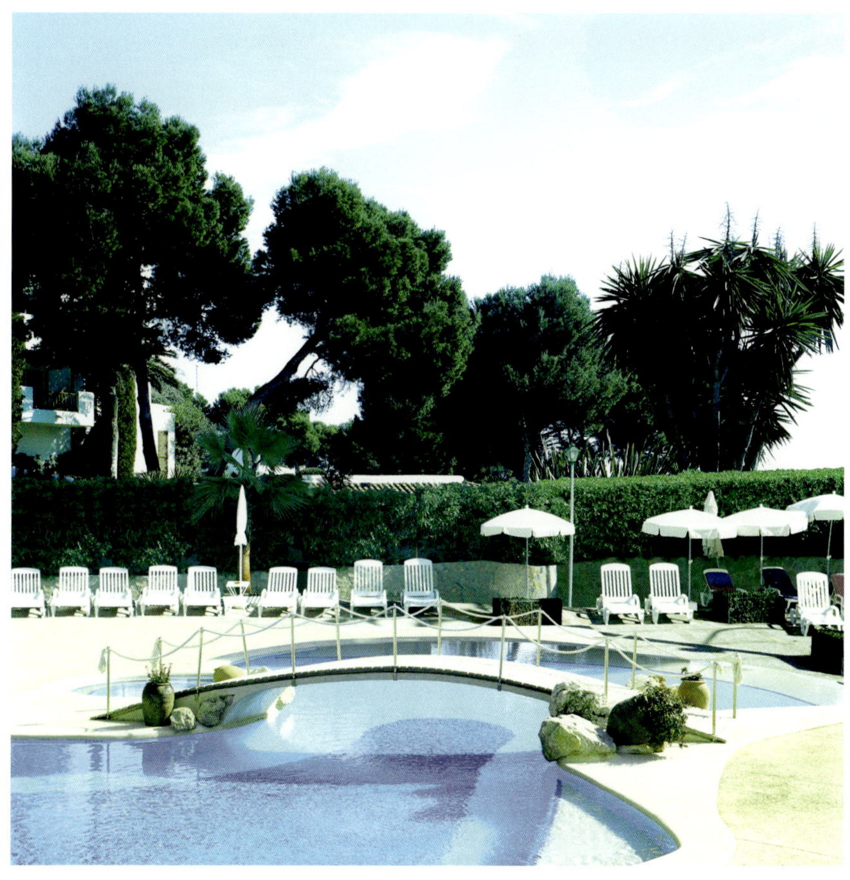
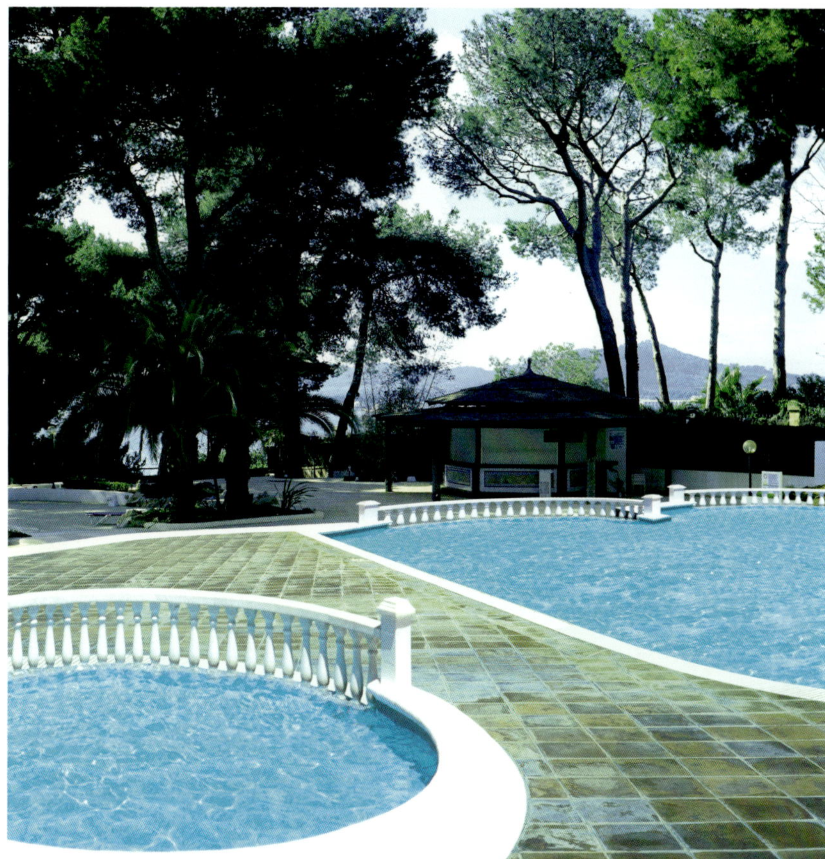
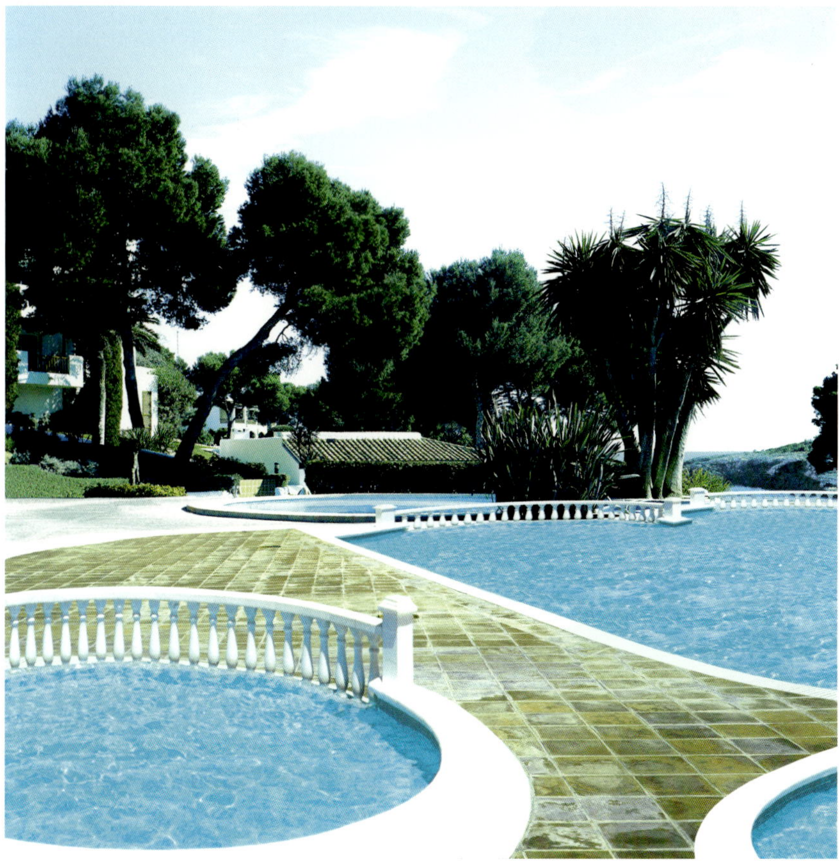
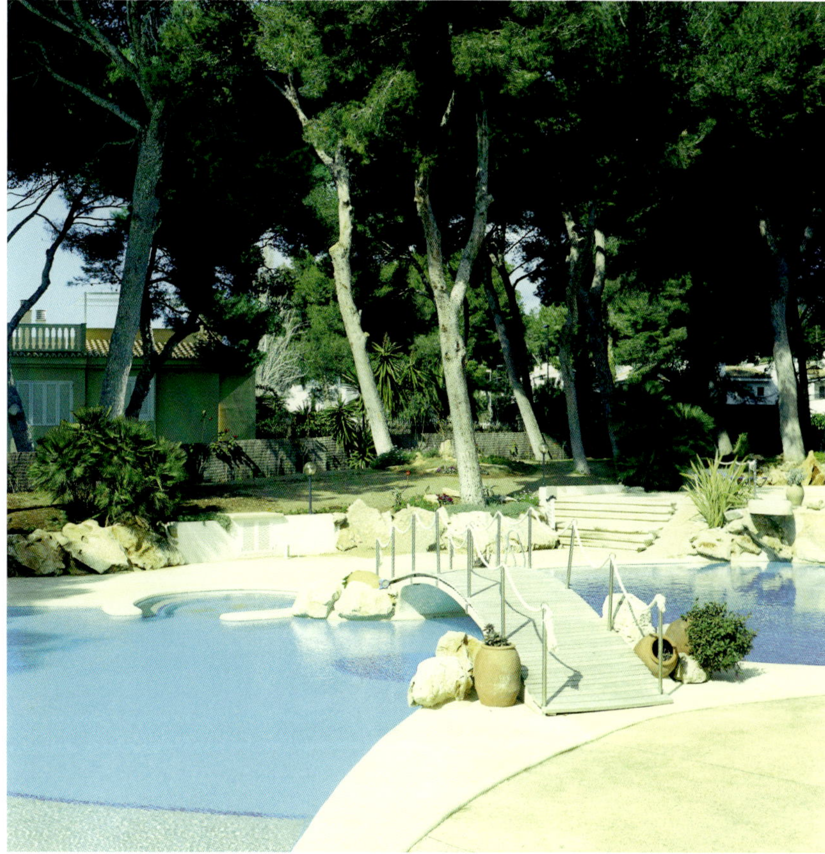

TUSAN   RALMARA   MASERA   ZINOLA   100 × 100 cm / 39.38 × 39.38 in.

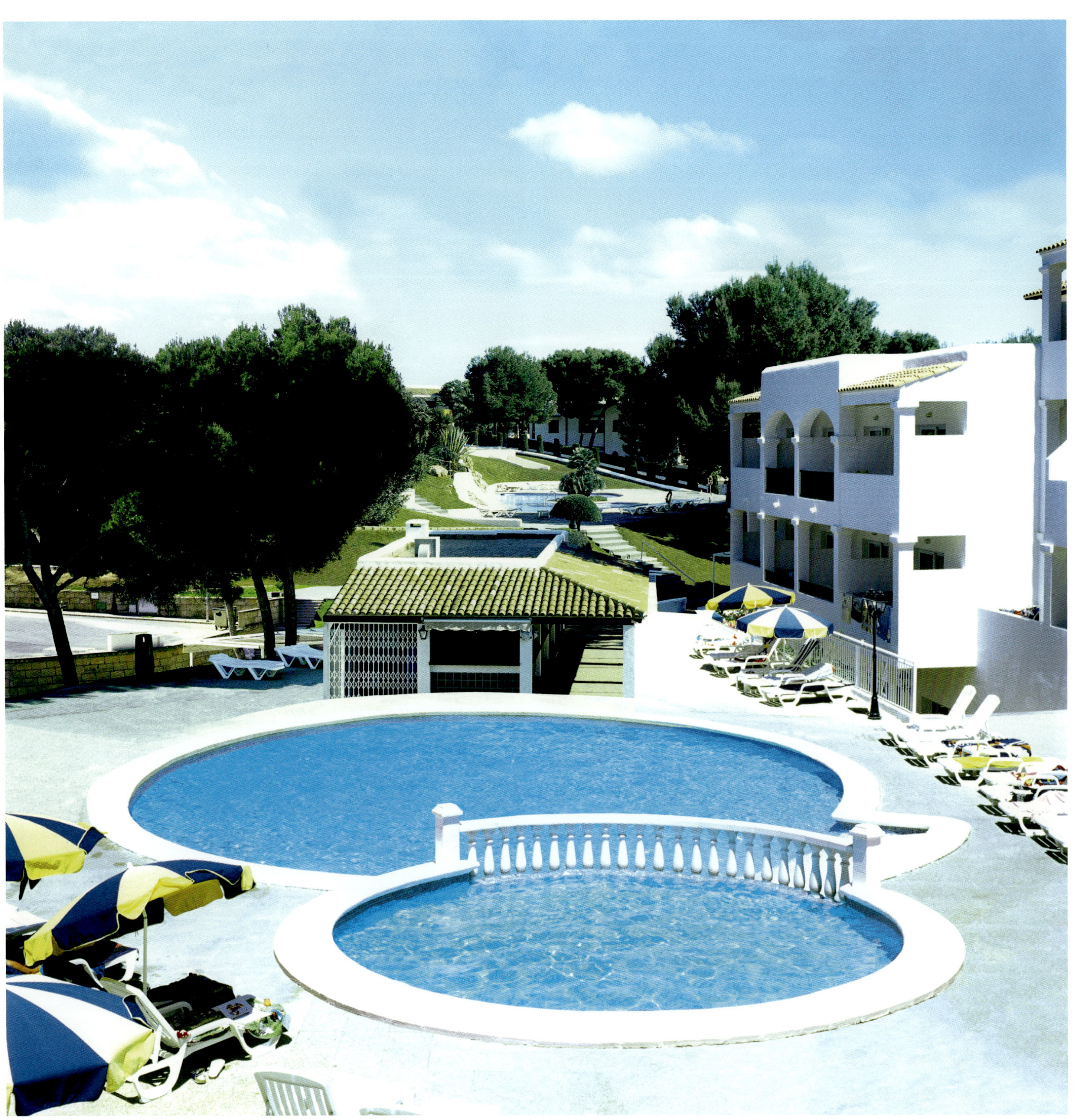

 TAMMARA 100 × 100 cm / 39.38 × 39.38 in.

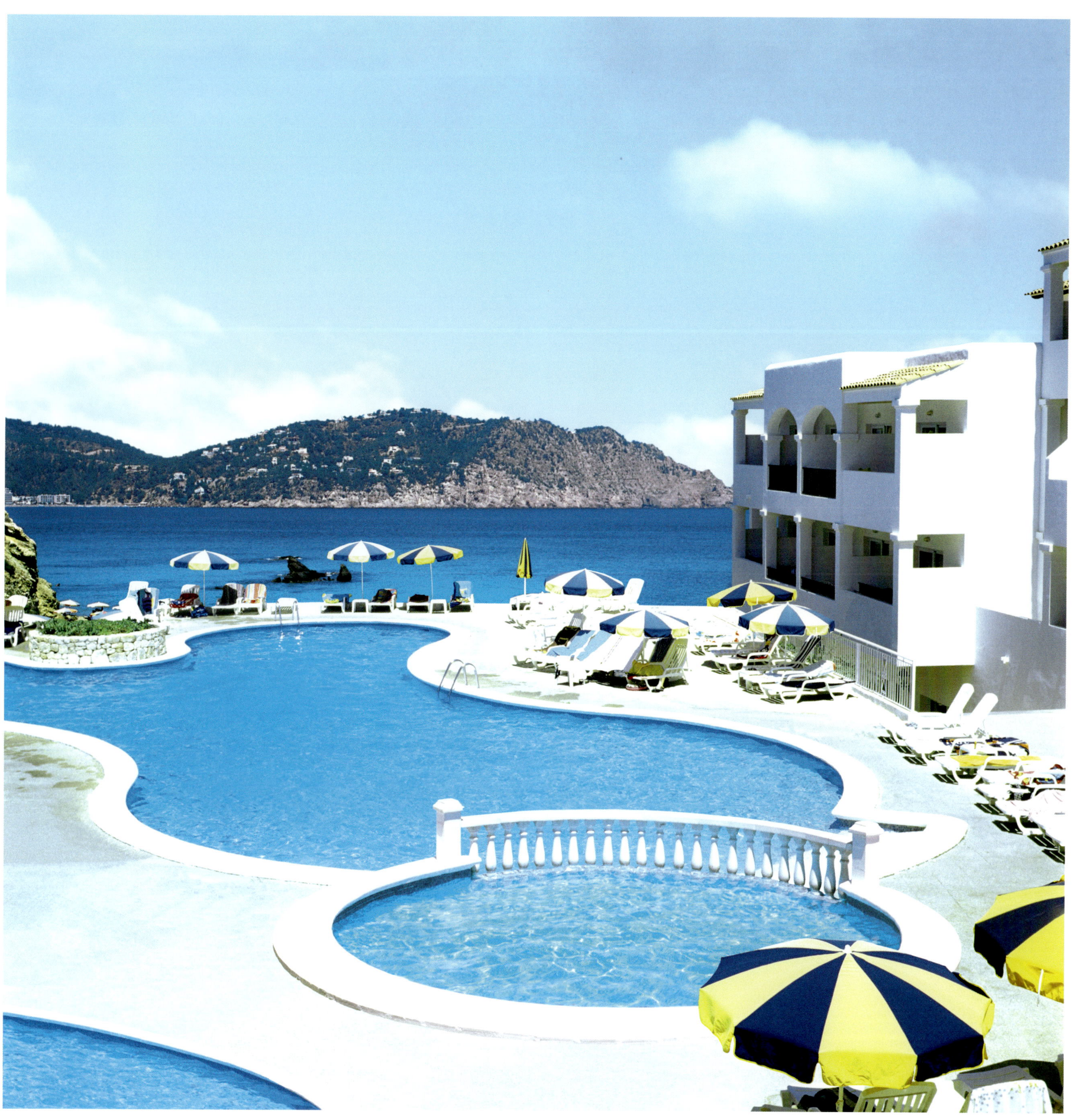

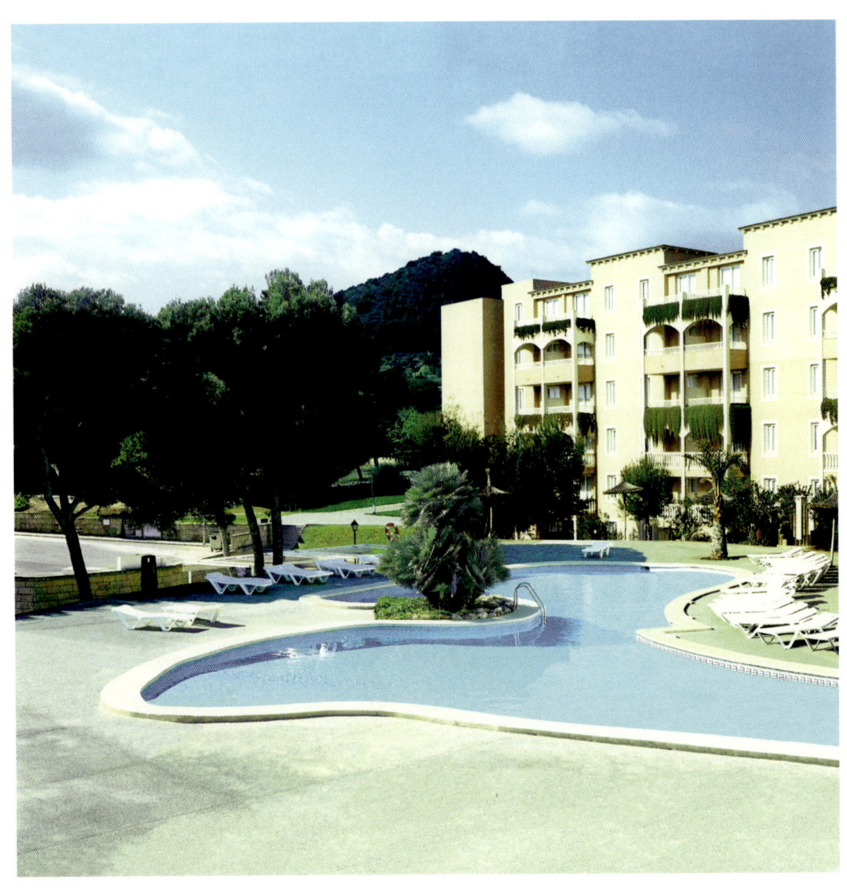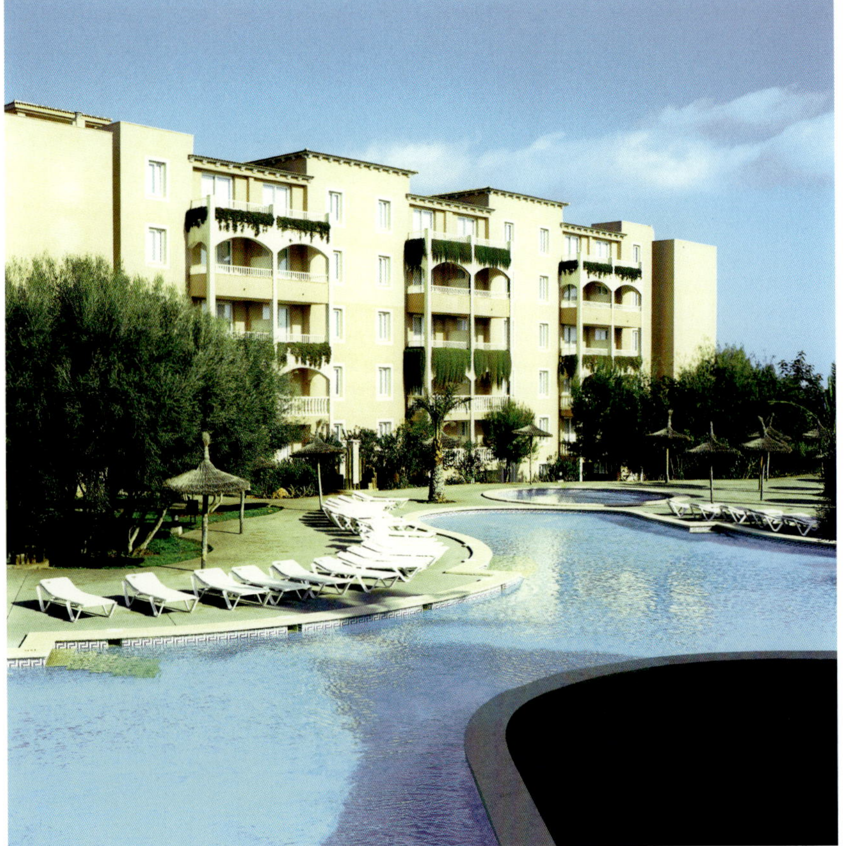

 MELANIE SONJA 100 × 100 cm / 39.38 × 39.38 in.

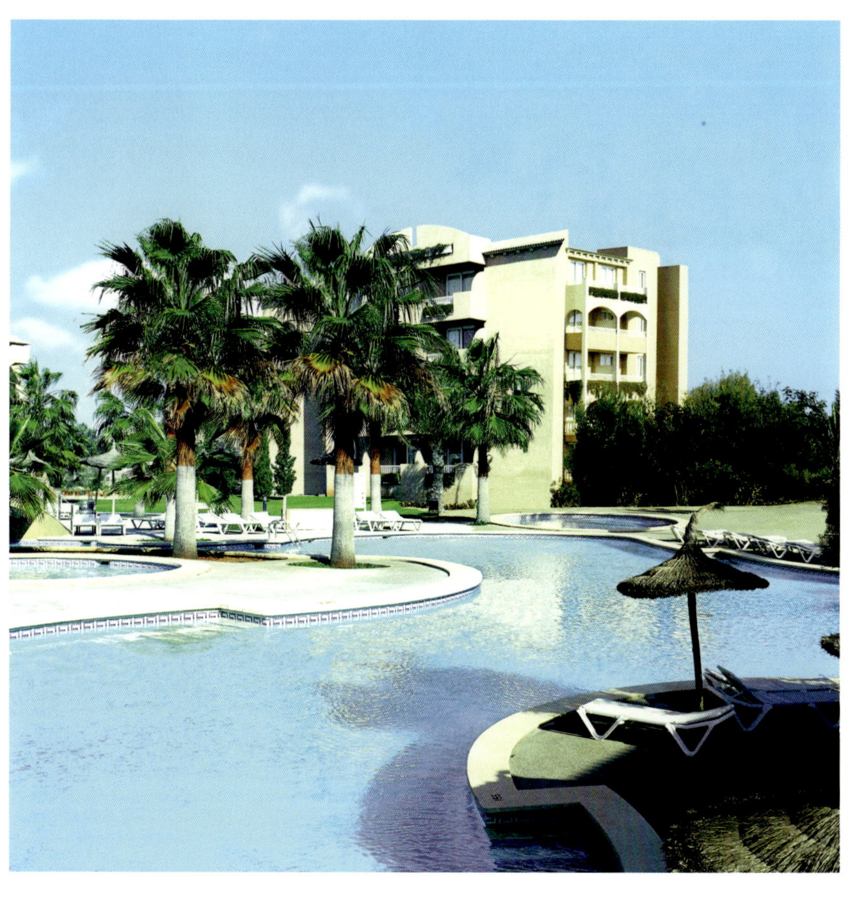 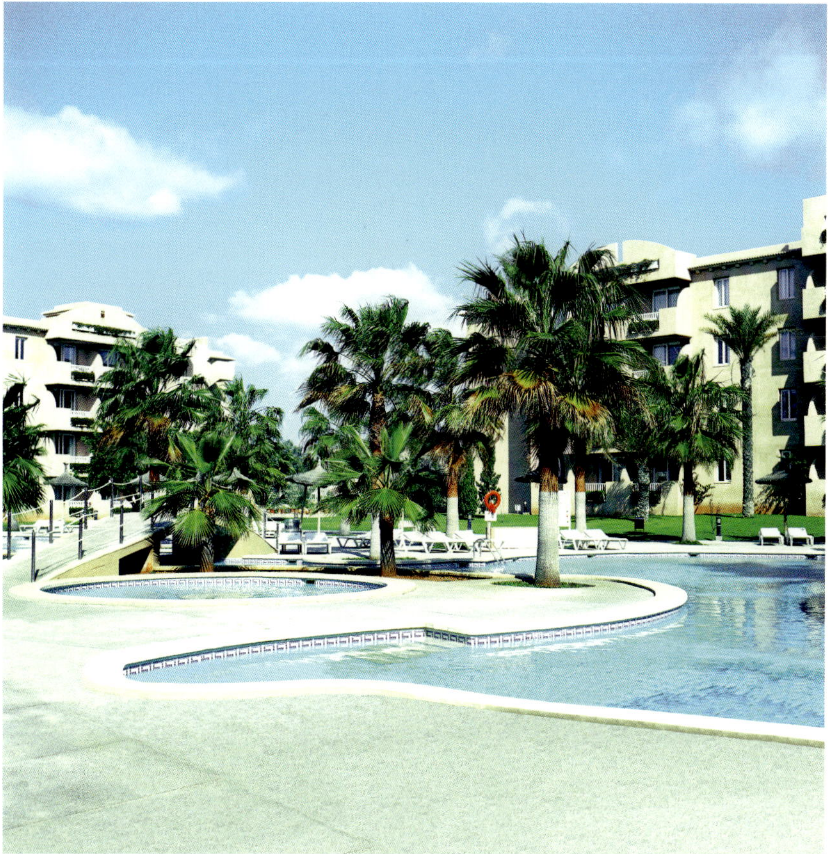

PORTRÄTS VON PORTRÄTS / PORTRAITS OF PORTRAITS 2001

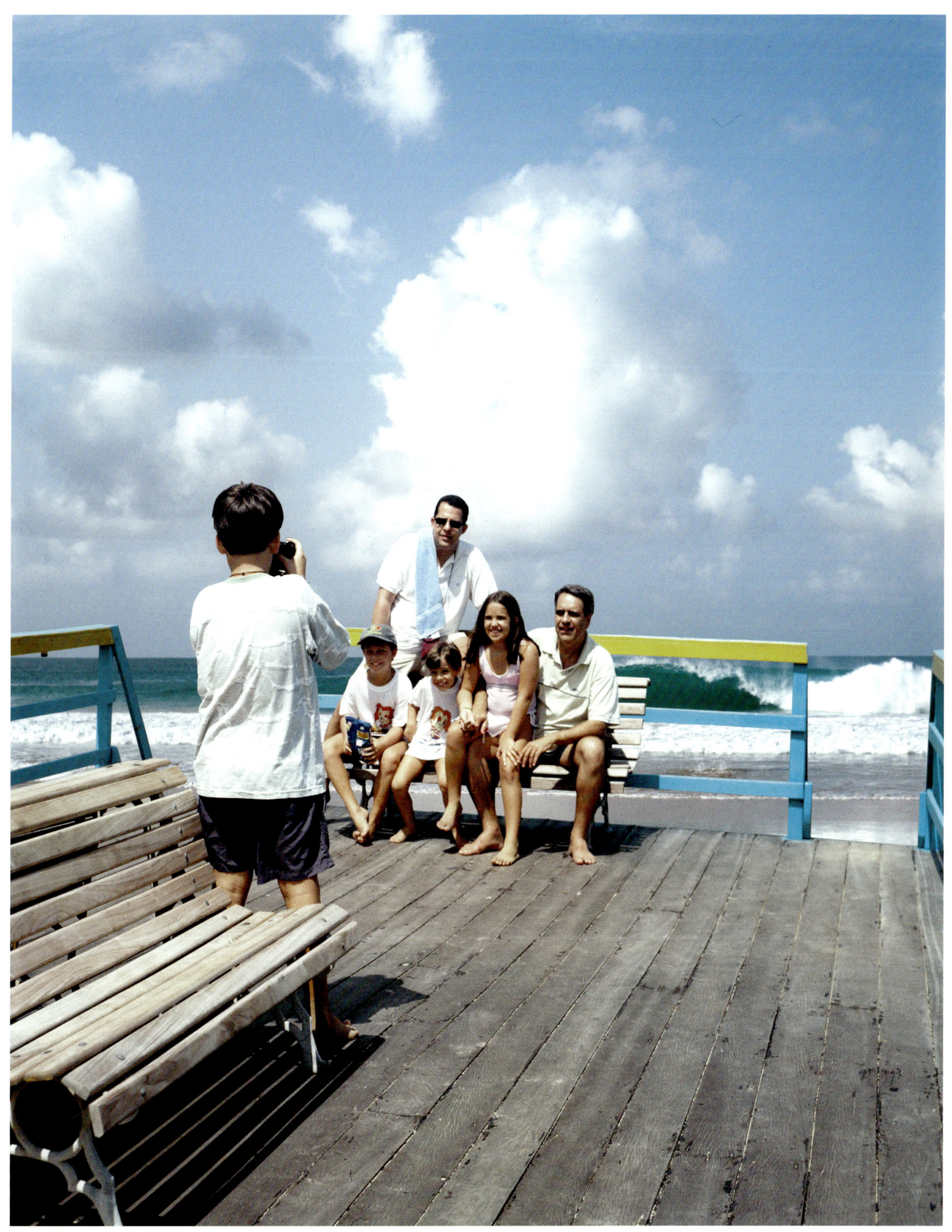

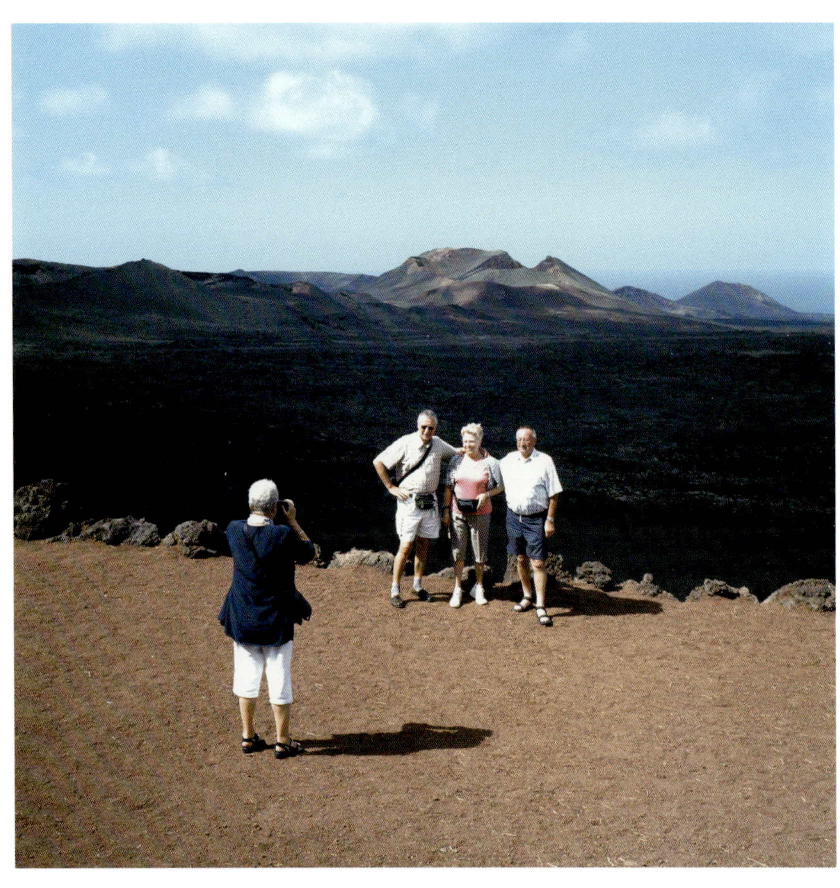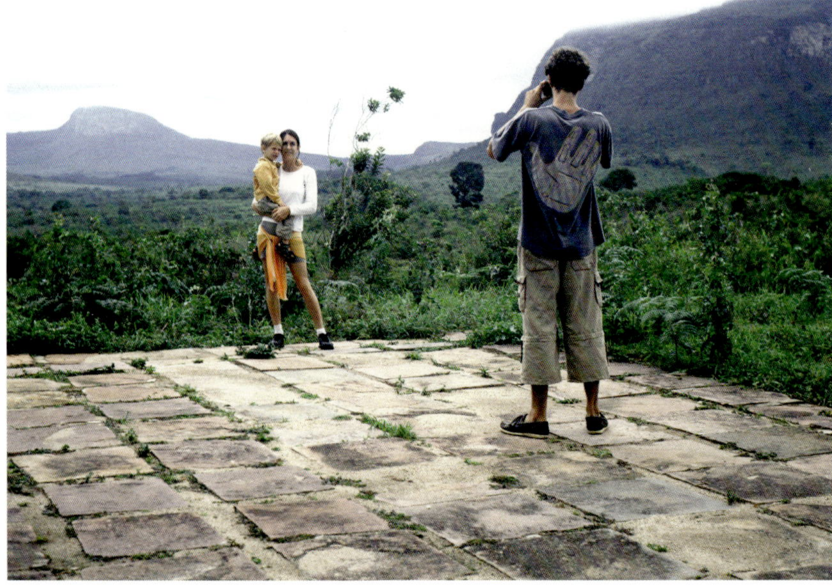

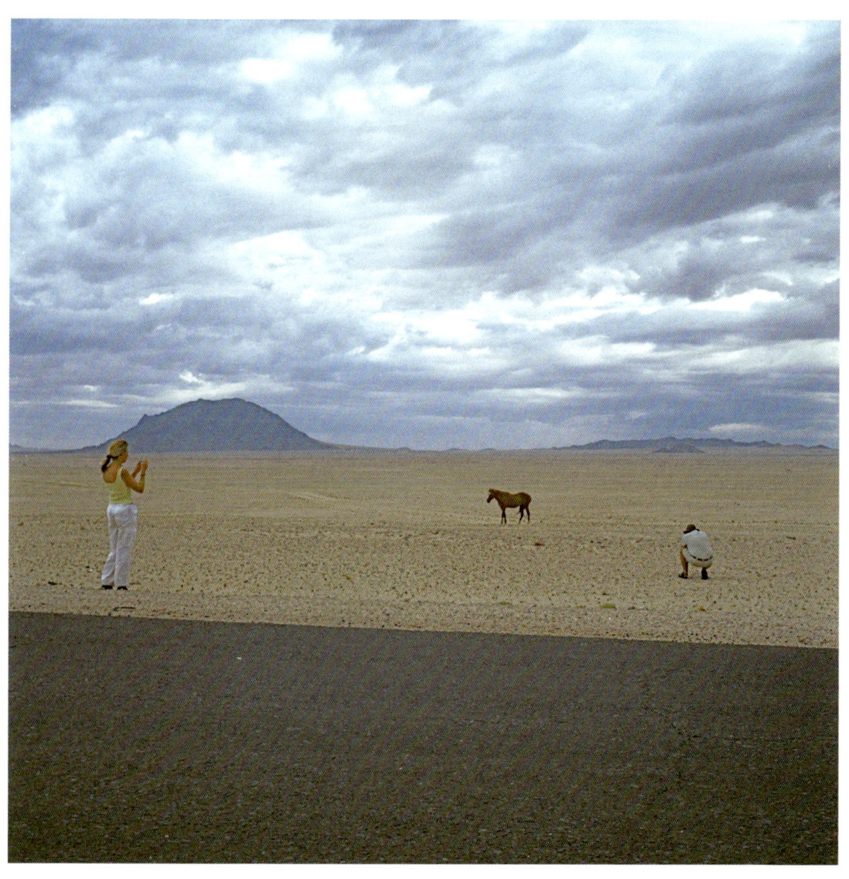 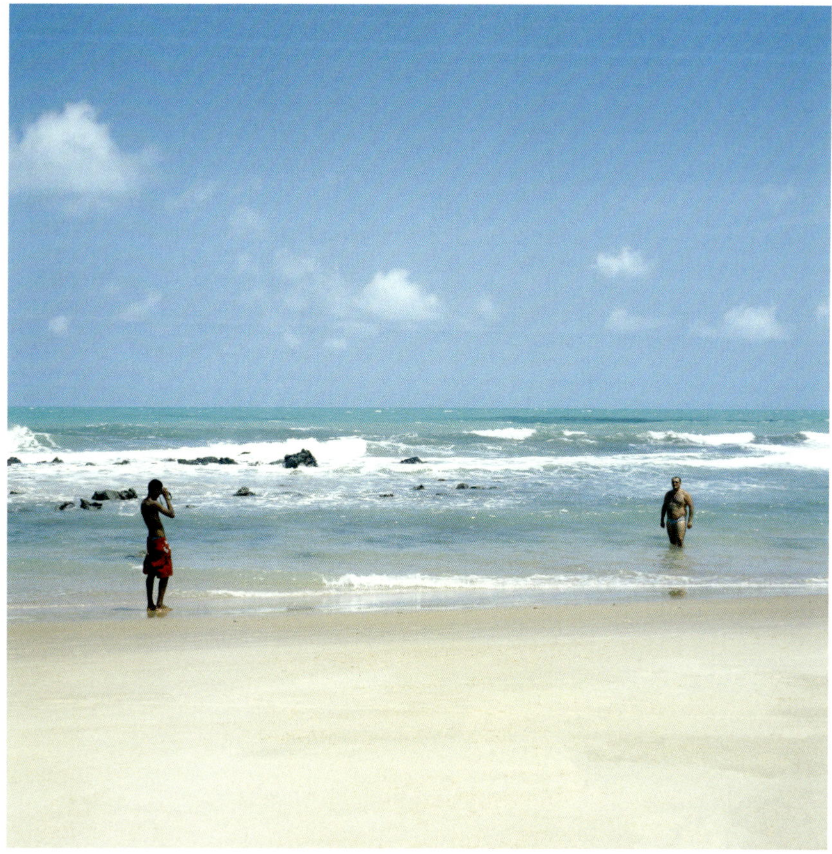

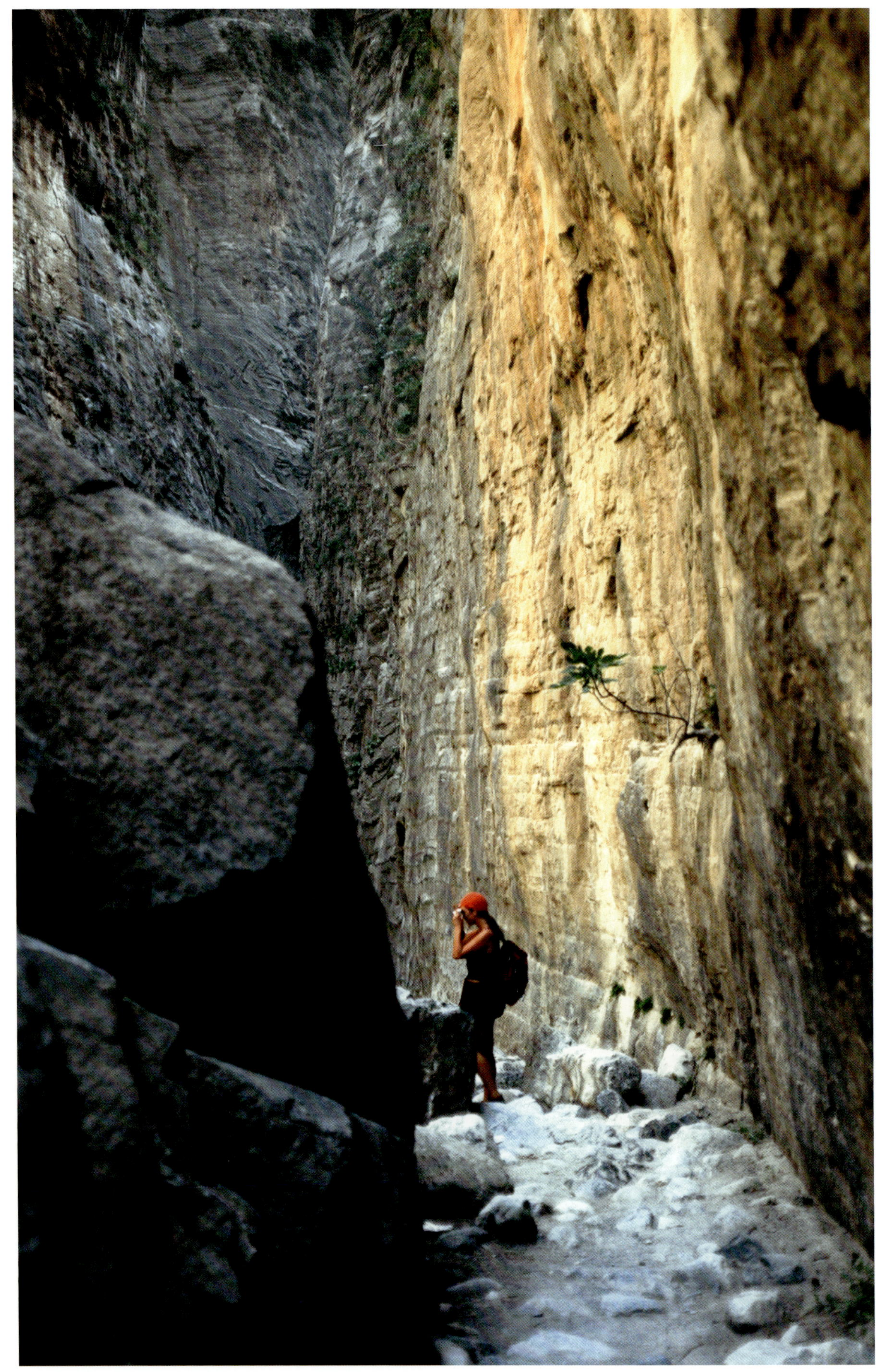

  ROTE KAPPE / RED CAP 100 × 65 cm / 39.38 × 25.59 in.

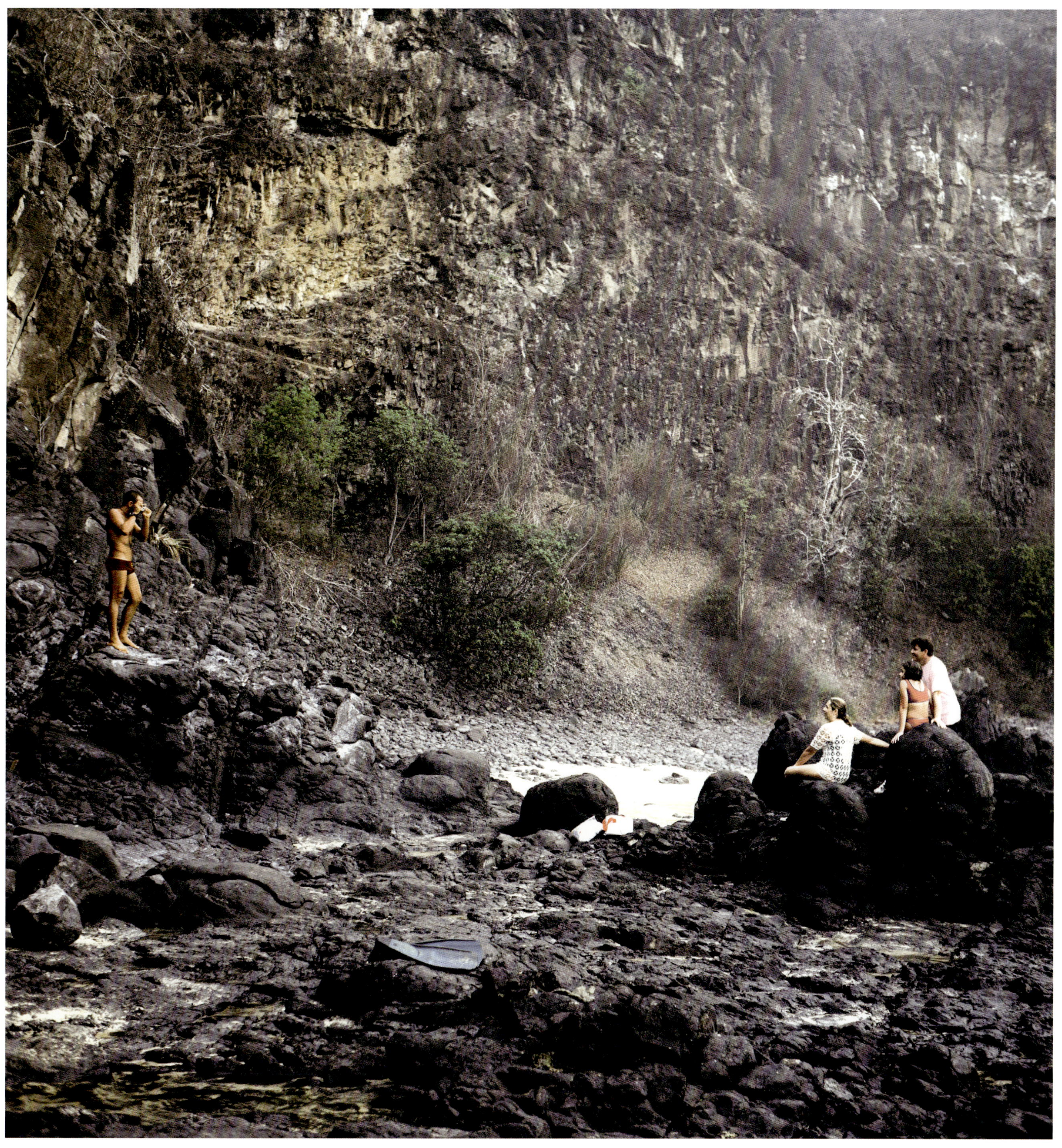

SCHLUCHT / GULLEY 100 × 100 cm / 39.38 × 39.38 in.

AUF DEM WEG ZUM ZYKLUS? /
TOWARDS AN AESTHETIC OF CYCLES? Renate Puvogel

Ralf Peters arbeitet fast ausschließlich in Serien. Das bedeutet nicht nur, dass er seine Fotografien im Nachhinein zu Serien zusammenstellt; vielmehr sind sie bereits im Stadium der Aufnahme als Serien konzipiert. Bekannt geworden ist er mit den Serien *Tankstellen, Skyline Tag, Skyline Nacht, Indoor, Porträts bei Nacht, Porträts von Porträts.* Diese Titel fassen die einzelnen Fotografien summarisch unter einer Überschrift zusammen, sie scheinen kein Geheimnis zu bergen, sondern schlicht Auskunft über die gewählten Motive zu geben. Die einzelnen Arbeiten innerhalb dieser Serien sind entweder mit fortlaufenden Nummern versehen, so etwa *Indoor 1, Indoor 2,* oder sie bezeichnen – ebenfalls sachlich und unverbrämt – das Motiv genauer; einem *Fluss* oder einer *Düne* begegnet man beispielsweise in der *Skyline*-Serie. Andere Arbeiten wiederum sind nach ihrer vorherrschenden Farbe benannt, so *Tankstelle blau* oder *Tankstelle gelb.* Die Bezeichnungen sind also wider Erwarten nicht einheitlich und nicht immer dem jeweiligen Sujet entsprechend gewählt. Damit geben sowohl Ober- als auch Einzeltitel bereits einen Hinweis darauf, dass jede Serie einen individuellen Charakter besitzt und der Künstler anhand besonderer Themen spezielle Probleme technischer, ästhetischer und inhaltlicher Art abhandelt.

Bei einer Serie mit Namen *Skyline* würde man Fotografien in Querformat erwarten, versteht man unter Skyline doch die Grenze zwischen dem Oben und dem Unten, genauer gesagt die sich gegen den Himmel abzeichnende, vornehmlich horizontale Kontur eines sich vor dem Auge ausbreitenden Wirklichkeitsausschnitts. Paradoxerweise erscheinen die Farbfotos aber im extrem schmalen Hochformat (S. 69–98). Überdies ist der normalerweise natürlich belebte Himmel, der hier teilweise mehr als zwei Drittel der Fläche einnimmt, zu einer neutral weißen, bei den nächtlichen Motiven zur schwarzen Fläche geronnen. Dabei ist bei Letzteren die Kontur selbst gar nicht zu erkennen, stattdessen erscheint eine Szenerie oder ein Objekt, etwa eine Fabrik oder ein Karussell, als farbig leuchtendes Faszinosum im schwarzen Umraum. Die Lichtquelle ist vielfach nicht auszumachen, wenn sie nicht von den blinkenden Kunstlichtern der Jahrmarktattraktionen herrührt.

Ralf Peters works almost exclusively in series. This doesn't merely mean that he later arranges the photographs he has taken in series; rather, they are already conceived as series when he takes them. He has become well known through his series *Petrol Stations, Skyline Day, Skyline Night, Indoor, Portraits by Night,* and *Portraits of Portraits.* These titles subsume the individual photographs beneath a single heading; they seem to conceal nothing, merely to give clear information about the chosen subject. The individual works within these series are either numbered consecutively, such as *Indoor 1, Indoor 2,* or offer a more precise—albeit factual and unadorned—description of the subject; for example, in the *Skyline* series one comes across both a *River* and a *Dune.* By contrast, other works are named after their prevailing color, such as *Blue Petrol Station* or *Yellow Petrol Station.* Thus, contrary to expectations, the descriptions are not consistent and are not always chosen to correspond with the subject. The titles both of groups and of individual works are used to show that each series possesses an individual character and that the artist is using specific subjects to address particular problems of technique, aesthetics, or content.

One might expect a series entitled *Skyline* to be composed of photographs taken in horizontal format, if by "skyline" one understands the dividing line between earth and sky, or more precisely, the largely horizontal contour of a section of reality extending before the viewer's gaze into the distance. But, paradoxically enough, the color photographs in *Skyline* are actually in an extremely narrow upright format (pp. 69–98). What is more, the sky, which in some photographs takes up slightly more than three-quarters of the picture, and which one would normally expect to find animated with clouds, has congealed into a neutral white expanse that appears black in the nocturnal pictures. In the latter images, the horizon itself cannot be made out; instead a scene or an object appears—such as a factory or a carousel—brightly colored and exuding a curious fascination against a dark expanse. Frequently the light source cannot be made out—at least, when it isn't coming from the shining decorative lights of the fairground attractions.

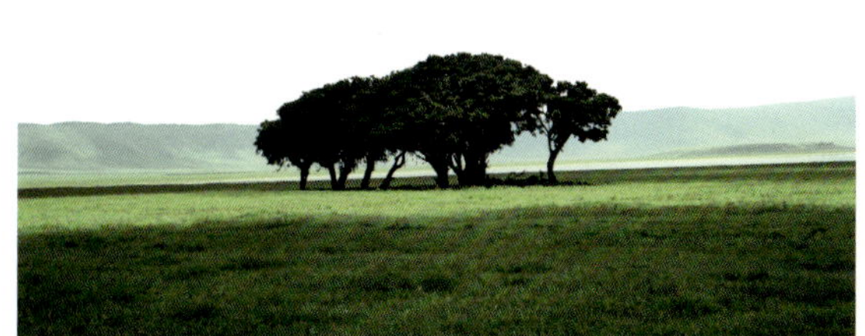

SKYLINE **BÄUME / TREES**
190 × 105 cm / 74.83 × 41.34 in.
2002–2009

SKYLINE **DÜNE / DUNE**
190 × 110 cm / 74.83 × 43.31 in.
2002–2009

Alle Arbeiten von Ralf Peters beruhen auf seinen eigenen Fotografien, aufgenommen mit unterschiedlichen Kameras, sie entspringen somit seinem persönlichen Erleben. Doch diese Fotos sind lediglich das Material, das der Künstler in der Folge digital bearbeitet. Aus diesem Grund versteht Peters sich auch nicht als Fotograf, er bedient sich der Fotografie, um mit ihr zu arbeiten: Er verändert die Fotos am Rechner, kombiniert einzelne Versatzstücke, wählt für jede Serie ein individuelles Format und eine dem Thema angemessene Größe. Wie immer entscheiden letztlich also ästhetische Werte über die endgültige Gestalt eines Kunstwerks. Zwar eignen sich seine Fotografien nicht zu Zwecken der Dokumentation, aber sie sagen dennoch auf dem Umweg über die künstlerische Anlage etwas über die Realität aus. Gerade das serielle Verfahren erleichtert den Zugang, denn das vergleichende Betrachten regt dazu an, zu reflektieren und nach einer Botschaft zu forschen.

Bei mehrteiligen Werken unterscheidet man die Serie von einer Folge und einem Zyklus, das gilt für alle künstlerischen Disziplinen. So unterliegt eine Serie im Gegensatz zu einer Folge keiner zeitlichen chronologischen Gliederung oder inhaltlich logischen Abwicklung. Die dargestellten Dinge ereignen sich gewissermaßen gleichzeitig oder sind gänzlich aus der Zeit genommen; obendrein sind die einzelnen Teile keiner Hierarchie unterworfen, sondern gleichrangig und gleichwertig; sie lassen sich austauschen, etwa bei der Hängung, und es kann auch jedes Teil unabhängig von den anderen bestehen. Durch Vergleiche untereinander treten Besonderheiten wie auch Ähnlichkeiten zutage. Ein Thema lässt sich anhand mehrerer sich ergänzender Teile anders, unter Umständen sogar tiefer ausloten als an einem einzigen Beispiel. Peters beweist, dass dies gelingen kann, ohne das dokumentarische Potenzial bemühen zu müssen. Skepsis an einer authentischen Aussage über die Wirklichkeit ist ja ohnehin längst angesagt. Selbst wenn man dem Wirklichen nicht direkt näherkommt, so bringt die Serie einen Mehrwert an Erkenntnis.

Anschaulich stellt Peters beispielsweise heraus und zur Diskussion, welch unverwechselbare und zugleich symptomatische Eigenschaften einer Düne

All Peters's works are based on his own photographs, taken with different cameras; they therefore have their origins in personal experience. Yet these photographs are only the material that the artist subsequently works on digitally. This is also why Peters doesn't think of himself as a photographer; rather, he uses photography to work with: he alters the photographs on the computer, combining individual elements, choosing for every series an individual format and a suitable size for its subject. Thus aesthetic principles always determine the final form of the artwork. Although his photographs aren't really forms of documentation, in the process of pursuing their artistic aims they do still express something about reality. And it is precisely their existence as series that helps them to achieve this, for the process of looking at and comparing the different pictures encourages the viewer to reflect and to look for a meaning.

In all artistic disciplines, multi-part works tend to fall into several different categories: a series, a sequence, and a cycle. What distinguishes a series from a sequence, for example, is that the former is not arranged in any chronological order, and there is no inherently logical development to its content. In a sense, a series shows things that either occur simultaneously or exist outside time altogether. What is more, its individual parts are not arranged hierarchically, but given equal importance and value; they are interchangeable, for instance in how they are hung, but they can also exist independently. Comparisons between them reveal peculiarities specific to individual images as well as similarities. In some circumstances a subject can be explored more profoundly through works composed of many different parts, each complementing the other, than through those consisting of a single image. Peters proves that this can be done without the work having to necessarily document anything. Skepticism about making any authentic statements about reality has, of course, long been around. Even if a series doesn't aim to approach reality directly, it can provide new insights.

Peters clearly highlights and explores what the unmistakable and symptomatic qualities of a dune might be (pp. 87, 89, 91, 97); or how similar, or indeed indistinguishable, the architecture of petrol stations

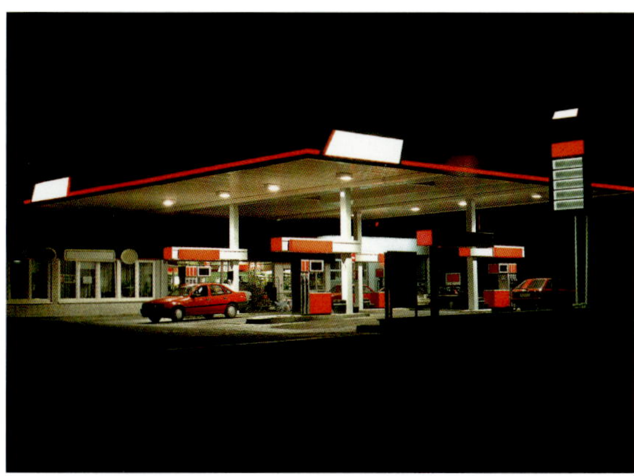

TANKSTELLEN / PETROL STATIONS **ROT/SCHWARZ / RED/BLACK** 60 × 80 cm / 23.62 × 31.5 in. 1998

TANKSTELLEN / PETROL STATIONS **GRÜN/SCHWARZ / GREEN/BLACK** 60 × 80 cm / 23.62 × 31.5 in. 1998

zukommen (S. 87, 89, 91, 97) oder wie gleichgeartet, ja ununterscheidbar die architektonischen Anlagen von Tankstellen sind (S. 13–25). Peters arbeitet an der Serie *Tankstellen* jenes langweilige, zugleich raffiniert kalkulierte Grundmuster heraus: Aus gleicher Perspektive gezeigt, fragt man sich, wie der Kunde empfangen wird, wohin sein erster Blick gerichtet ist, wohin er strebt. Nur durch die jeweilige Farbgebung unterschieden, geht angesichts dieser Uniformität alles Individuelle weitgehend verloren. Die Fotos nehmen emotional ein und bleiben dennoch in besonderer Weise distanziert – eine ambivalente Befindlichkeit, wie man sie auch bei Gemälden von Edward Hopper erfahren kann. Grundsätzlich aber unterscheiden sich die Zielsetzungen beider Künstler. Finden sich auf Hoppers Bildern nur vereinzelte Menschen, anhand derer die Einsamkeit und Verlorenheit in einer urbanen Welt eingefangen wird, so verzichtet Peters ganz auf das Publikum einer Tankstelle oder eines Supermarkts und eliminiert zudem sämtliche individuellen Zeichen und Daten. Damit kann er demonstrieren, wie austauschbar die konkurrierenden Unternehmen und in welchem Maße die Verbraucher von ihnen abhängig sind. Ist doch im Gegensatz zu Peters' Fiktionen realiter der Markt auf nur wenige Unternehmen geschrumpft.

Ähnlich wie bei der Serie *Tankstellen* greift Peters stets Symptome des Zeitgeistes auf. Und gerade in der seriellen Form lassen sich Fragen nach dem uniformen Leben, der Globalisierung und dem Verlust von Identität stellen. Dieser Mangel an selbstbestimmtem Leben, der bis an die Anonymität heranreicht, spielt in Peters' Arbeiten wiederholt eine Rolle. Die *Porträts bei Nacht* kommen den hopperschen Vorstellungen wiederum von anderer Seite nahe (S. 29–32). Man sieht jeweils eine Person vor ihrem Rechner sitzen, alleine und konzentriert, ihr Antlitz ist ausschließlich vom Licht des Bildschirms erleuchtet, jede Figur in einer anderen Farbe, in Rot, Blau, Grün und Gelb. Dadurch, dass Peters die Serie auf vier Fotos mit vier Farben angelegt hat, hebelt er die Frage nach dem Unterschied zwischen den Lichtfarben und den Körperfarben, den additiven und subtraktiven Farben aus. Auch der gesamte Raum ist in das Licht getaucht, das vom Bildschirm ausgeht, sodass der

is (pp. 13–25). In the series *Petrol Stations*, Peters explores their dreary yet ingenious underlying design. By showing these from the same perspective, the photograph prompts the viewer to consider how customers approach the station, where their gaze is directed, and where they find themselves heading. Distinguished only by their different color schemes, everything individual about the stations is largely lost beneath this uniformity. The photographs approach their subjects sympathetically, while at the same time remaining distanced in a particular way—an ambivalent attitude, and one that can also be found in certain paintings by Edward Hopper. Nevertheless, the aims of the two artists are fundamentally different. While Hopper's pictures show only isolated individuals, expressive either of the loneliness or forlornness of city life, Peters's do without the gas station or supermarket customers altogether, while at the same time eliminating all individual signs and data. This enables him to show how interchangeable the competing businesses are, and the degree to which the people using them have become dependent on them. In contrast to Peters's fictional images, in reality the market has shrunk to only a few businesses.

The series *Petrol Stations* is an instance of how Peters is constantly examining symptoms of the Zeitgeist. And the serial form is particularly suited to posing questions about the standardization of daily life, globalization, and the loss of identity. The sense that we have lost control over our lives, that they have been reduced to a kind of anonymity, repeatedly features in Peters's work. *Portraits by Night,* however, approaches this rather Hopperian theme from a different perspective (pp. 29–32). Each of the works shows a person sitting in front of their computer, alone and lost in concentration. Their face is illuminated only by the light of the screen, which bathes each figure in a different color: red, blue, green, and yellow. By creating the series from four photographs in four different colors, Peters raises the question of the difference between the color of the light and the color of his subjects' bodies, between additive and subtractive colors. The entire room is also bathed in the light coming from the screen, so that the natural colors of both the objects and the person are lost,

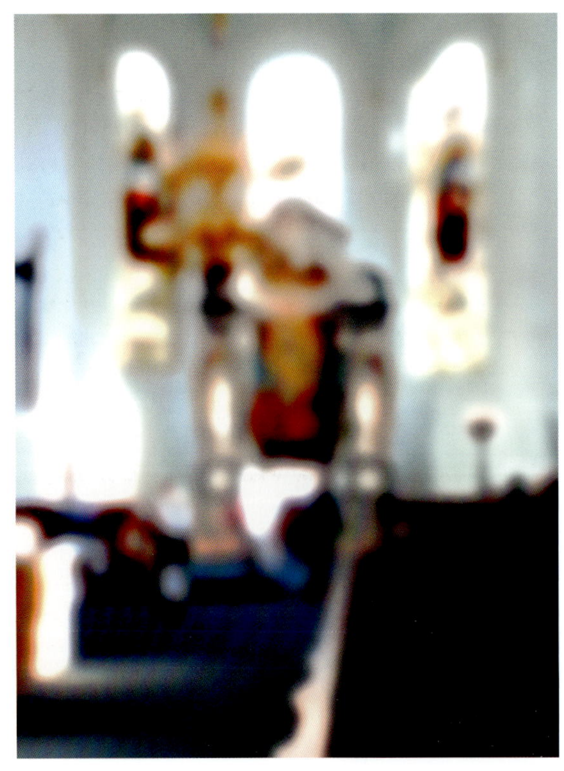

CANDIES **# 37** 100 × 70 cm /
39.38 × 27.56 in. 2002/03

farbige Eigenwert der Gegenstände wie auch des angestrahlten Menschen als wesentlicher Ausdruck seiner Persönlichkeit verloren geht. Durch die Position des Monitors im Raum ist die Quelle des Lichts für den Betrachter nicht direkt sichtbar. Man kann die Kunst der Caravaggisten heranziehen; sie haben die Möglichkeiten eines raffinierten Bildlichts ausgekostet, dabei allerdings ihr Interesse insbesondere dem harten Chiaroscuro gezollt und damit im Gegensatz zu Peters die beleuchteten Figuren plastisch modelliert. Stattdessen entsteht in dem geschlossenen Ambiente auf Peters' Fotografien eine Atmosphäre ruhiger versonnener Abgeschiedenheit, sodass ganz von Ferne Gemälde von Jan Vermeer van Delft vor das innere Auge treten.

Mit den vier Bildern ist für Peters das Thema *Porträts bei Nacht* ausgereizt – es scheint, als verlange jedes Sujet eine bestimmte Anzahl von Varianten. In der Serie *Männer/Frauen* hat Peters beispielsweise bei zwei nahezu identischen Straßenszenen die männlichen und weiblichen Passanten jeweils in das eine beziehungsweise andere Foto verschoben und mit dieser Konstellation ein reichlich unnatürliches Alltagsszenario geschaffen (S. 35). Dieses Thema braucht demnach lediglich an einem oder zwei Beispielen durchgespielt zu werden. Demgegenüber ließe sich die Serie der *Candies* prinzipiell beliebig erweitern, weil die vielfältigsten Motive der Idee, Konturen aufzuweichen und Plastizität verschwinden zu lassen, zur Verfügung stehen (S. 104–118).

Neben den Serien finden sich in Ralf Peters' Werk aber auch Einzelarbeiten, etwa das Foto einer Badeanstalt, eines Strandhäuschens am Meer, einer Treppe im Innenraum (S. 164, 169). Selbst bei Peter Piller, der sein Fotomaterial unendlich vielen Sammlungsgebieten zuordnet, gibt es einige »ungeklärte Fälle«. Doch Piller greift für sein Archiv auf in Zeitungen gefundene Abbildungen zurück, während Peters ohne Weiteres den erwähnten Motiven eigene vergleichbare Fotos an die Seite stellen könnte. Allerdings sind die Einzelarbeiten besonders reich an individuellen Details, welche, in die serielle Form gefasst, wohl ein wenig verringert werden müssten. Generell eignet sich, so auch die Meinung des Künstlers, jedes Motiv grundsätzlich dazu, seriell ausgestaltet zu werden.

in so far as they are an expression of his personality. The position of the monitor in the room means that the light source is not directly visible to the viewer. This device is reminiscent of the art of the Caravaggists, who creatively explored the various ways pictorial light might be used, and in so doing developed an interest in stark chiaroscuro, using it, unlike Peters, to model the form of the illuminated figure. In Peters's photographs, by contrast, an atmosphere of quiet, thoughtful solitude emerges, which at a distance makes them reminiscent of paintings by Jan Vermeer.

With these four pictures, Peters found he had exhausted the subject of *Portraits by Night*—and it does seem that every theme requires a quite specific number of variations. For example, in the series *Men/Women* Peters has taken almost identical street scenes and moved the male and female passers-by in them from one photograph to the other, thereby creating an everyday scene that is also thoroughly unnatural (p. 35). This means he only need treat this subject in one or two examples to explore it thoroughly. By contrast, the series *Candies* can be extended at will, because it offers almost unlimited variations on the idea of dissolving outlines and allowing three-dimensional form to disappear (pp. 104–118).

Along with series, Peters's work also includes individual photographs, such as those of a swimming pool, of a beach hut by the sea, or of a flight of stairs inside a building (pp. 164, 169). Even Peter Piller's collection of photographic material, which he has classified into a vast number of categories, holds several "unsolved cases." Yet Piller's archive draws on photographs found in newspapers, while Peters could always easily come up with similar photographs of his own on the same subject. It is true, though, that individual works are particularly rich in individual details and that these always tend to become somewhat diminished in serial form. But in general, the artist believes, every subject lends itself to being developed as a series.

The photographs from the new series *Indoor*, and still more so those from *Salta*, *Seoul*, and *Sar*, lack almost any characteristic elements; the differences between the photographs are limited to a few inconspicuous details. The photographs of the four series all have

Die Fotos der neueren Serien *Indoor* und noch stärker die von *Salta, Seoul* und *Sar* entbehren nahezu sämtlicher charakteristischer Einzelheiten, Unterschiede zwischen den Arbeiten sind auf unscheinbare Kleinigkeiten begrenzt. Gemeinsam ist den Fotos der vier Serien, dass sie in Flughäfen entstanden und aus der Empfangshalle heraus einen Ausblick auf die Landschaft bieten. Peters hat sich also nicht gescheut, die Fotos durch reflektierende Fensterscheiben hindurch aufzunehmen – für einen Laienfotografen stets eine lästige Beeinträchtigung. Nichts von irgendwelchen Lichtbrechungen oder Unschärfen ist jedoch auf Peters' Fotografien zu entdecken, umso reizvoller zeichnet sich das Raster der Fensterrahmen auf dem blanken Boden im Vordergrund ab. Diese Gitterstruktur bildet die Koordinaten der Darstellung, gliedert sie und enthebt sie der Wirklichkeit, um sie in die Nähe der Abstraktion zu führen. Über diese vergleichbaren Elemente hinaus kommen jeder Serie besondere Eigenschaften zu. So hat Peters zwei Fotografien im Nachhinein zu *Sar 1* und *Sar 2* zusammengestellt, weil die Warteräume zweier Flughäfen ähnliche architektonische Details aufweisen (S. 156, 157). Da sowohl das Foto mit dem stabilen wie auch das mit dem gekippten Fensterskelett mit einem weißen Rand umgeben ist, verselbstständigen sich die Fenstersprossen und schweben gleichsam frei im Raum.

Die Serie *Salta 1–4* beruht auf einzelnen Aufnahmen an ein und demselben Ort, die Peters kaum verändern musste (S. 154, 155). Ihn hat die verblüffende Farbkonstellation und die lineare Schichtung der Flächen inspiriert. Der blaue Himmel, die Grünfläche, das beige Rollfeld und der weinrote Fußbodenbelag fügen sich in das Koordinatensystem der schwarzen Fensterrahmen in einer Weise ein, dass ein nahezu gegenstandsloses Bild entsteht. Die Komposition lässt durchaus an Künstler des Konstruktivismus oder des De Stijl denken (wenn auch Piet Mondrian zum Beispiel das Grün generell gemieden hat). Bei dieser Serie wird besonders deutlich, dass das Einzelfoto zwar bestehen kann, dass aber die Serie eine Grundidee noch besser zur Geltung bringt. Mit seiner Methode der seriellen Fertigung nähert sich Peters erstaunlicherweise den Kriterien eines Zyklus an;

in common that they were taken in airports and offer views from the arrivals hall of the surrounding countryside. They show that Peters is not afraid to take photographs through reflective window panes—a difficult obstacle for most amateur photographers. Peters's photographs, however, show no signs of light refraction or blurring of focus; the result is that the grid formed by the window frames becomes especially fascinating, dominating the foreground and standing out against the shiny floor. These grid structures form the coordinates of the image, both structuring it and stripping it of its realism, thereby bringing it closer to abstraction. Beyond these common elements, each series has its own specific qualities. Thus, for example, in *Sar 1* and *Sar 2* Peters put together two photographs he had taken separately, because the departure lounges of the two airports showed similar architectural details (pp. 156, 157). Since both the photographs with the upright and the tilting window frames are surrounded by a white edge, the glazing bars look natural and seem almost to float in space.

The series *Salta 1–4* is based on individual photographs all taken in the same place, which Peters barely had to change (pp. 154, 155). He was inspired by the extraordinary constellation of colors and the linear layering of planes. The blue sky, the green lawn, the beige runway, and the wine-red surface of the floor fit into the black window frames' system of coordinates in a way that produces an almost objectless image. The composition makes one think immediately of the artists of Constructivism or De Stijl (despite the fact that Piet Mondrian, for example, generally avoided green). In this series it becomes particularly clear that although an individual photograph can work by itself, a series is a better way of developing a basic idea. Astonishingly, Peters's method of serial production comes close to meeting the definition of a cycle; a cycle being distinguished by the fact that its individual works revolve around a central theme, and its whole is more than the sum of its parts.

In the series *Seoul,* finally, Peters brings to a culmination the idea of photography that overcomes the factual object (pp. 158, 159). Here, too, he took photographs through window panes set in brown

dieser zeichnet sich dadurch aus, dass die Einzelarbeiten ein zentrales Thema umkreisen und das
Ganze mehr ist als die Summe seiner Teile.
In der Serie *Seoul* schließlich treibt Peters die Idee
einer den realen Gegenstand überwindenden Fotografie zu einem Höhepunkt (S. 158, 159). Auch hier hat
er durch das in braune Rahmen gefasste Fensterglas
fotografiert, dabei hat er aber die ferne Landschaft
gleichsam als ein abstraktes, nicht zu ortendes Gitter-
muster an die Fensterrahmen herangeholt. Das Muster setzt sich an den rechten und linken Seiten fort
und erreicht dort durch die Intensivierung der Farbe
sogar einen höheren Realitätsgrad. Damit scheint es
über den Bildrahmen hinaus fortsetzbar. Plastizität,
Tiefe oder gar Räumlichkeit sind gänzlich ausge-
schaltet. Andererseits verleiht der Kunstgriff, in die
Fotos Abbildungen von Kirschblüten einzuschleusen,
der Gesamtinszenierung einen besonderen Charme.
Und dies, obgleich sich die Blüten zu undeutbaren,
formlosen weißen Flächen zu verflüchtigen scheinen.
Aber sie geben ein zusätzliches Indiz, dass die in
beigebraunen Tönen gehaltenen Arbeiten als Inkar-
nation des Asiatischen wahrzunehmen sind.
Das Fernöstliche kann man bei dieser Serie als die
thematische und geistige Mitte bezeichnen. Die
Fotos als zyklische Komposition zu werten scheitert
allerdings daran, dass das Thema lediglich unter
einem Aspekt beleuchtet wird. Dennoch sei ab-
schließend die Frage gestellt, ob sich die Arbeit von
Ralf Peters insgesamt mehr oder weniger auf ein
zyklisches Gestaltungsprinzip hinbewegt.

frames, but in so doing he brought the distant land-
scape up against the window frame, turning it into an
abstract grid pattern that cannot be located in space.
The pattern extends from the left- and right-hand
sides of the image, where its more intense colors
actually cause it to achieve a higher degree of realism.
The result is that it looks like it might continue beyond
the picture frame. Three-dimensional form, depth,
or space are entirely eliminated. On the other hand,
the clever trick of smuggling photographs of cherry
blossoms into the picture lends the entire composition a special charm. And it does so despite the fact
that the blossoms seem to evaporate into indistinct,
formless white surfaces. They offer, though, an addi-
tional indication that these works captured in tones
of beige brown are to be understood as symbolizing
the Asiatic world.
The Far East can be described as the thematic and
intellectual focal point of this series. However, the
photographs cannot be considered part of a cyclical
composition because their subject is only illuminated
from one perspective. For all that, the question may
be raised in conclusion of whether Peters's work when
taken as a whole is more or less moving towards a
principle of cyclical development.

SKYLINE 2002–2009

CONTAINER / CONTAINERS 190 × 108 cm / 74.83 × 42.52 in.

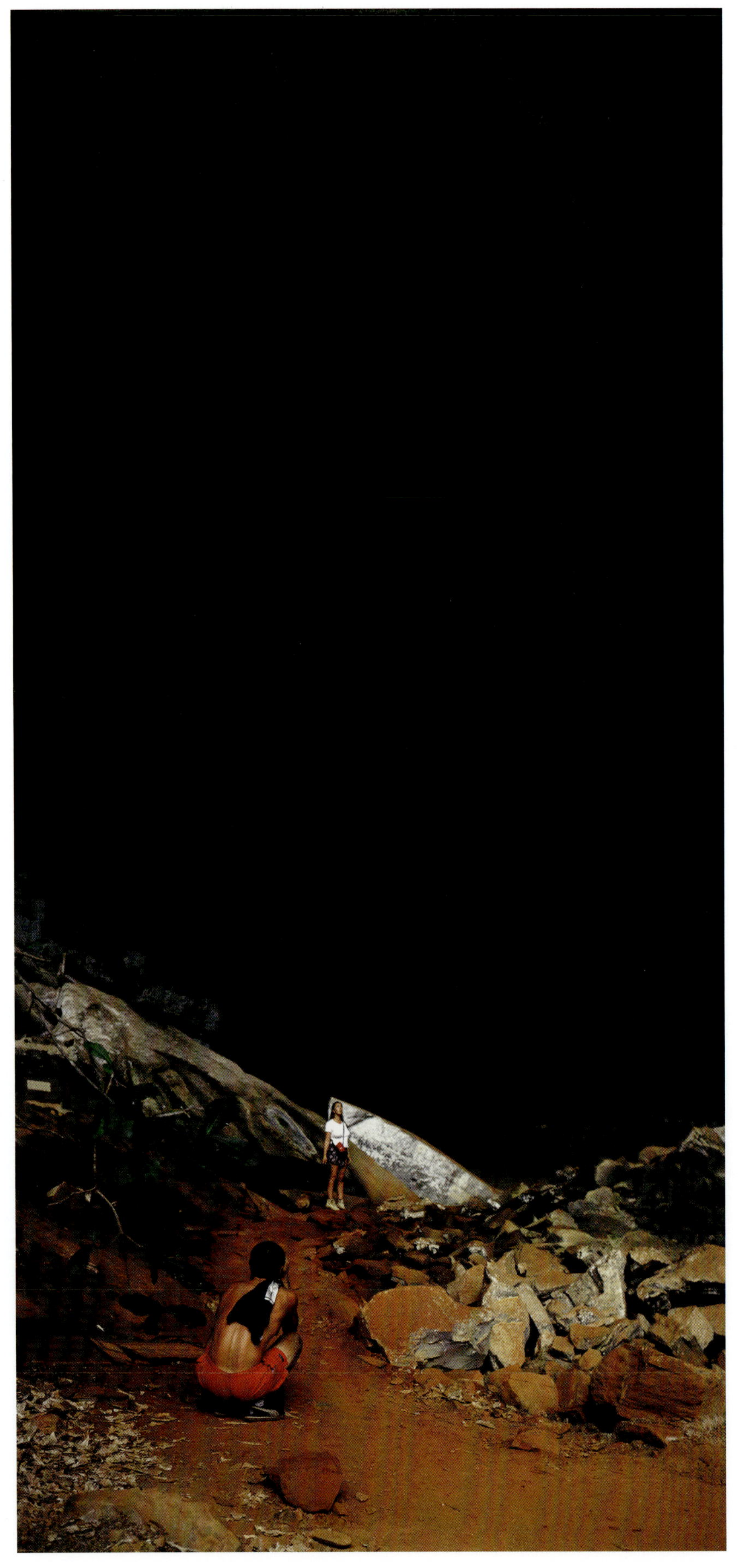

GROTTE / GROTTO 190 × 90 cm / 74.83 × 35.43 in.

SCHNORCHEL / SNORKEL 190 × 90 cm / 74.83 × 35.43 in.

SAL 190 × 81 cm / 74.83 × 32 in.

HAFEN / PORT 190 × 70 cm / 74.83 × 27.55 in.

  STREIFEN / LINES 190 × 90 cm / 74.83 × 35.43 in.

KARUSSELL / CAROUSEL 190 × 95 cm / 74.83 × 37.4 in.

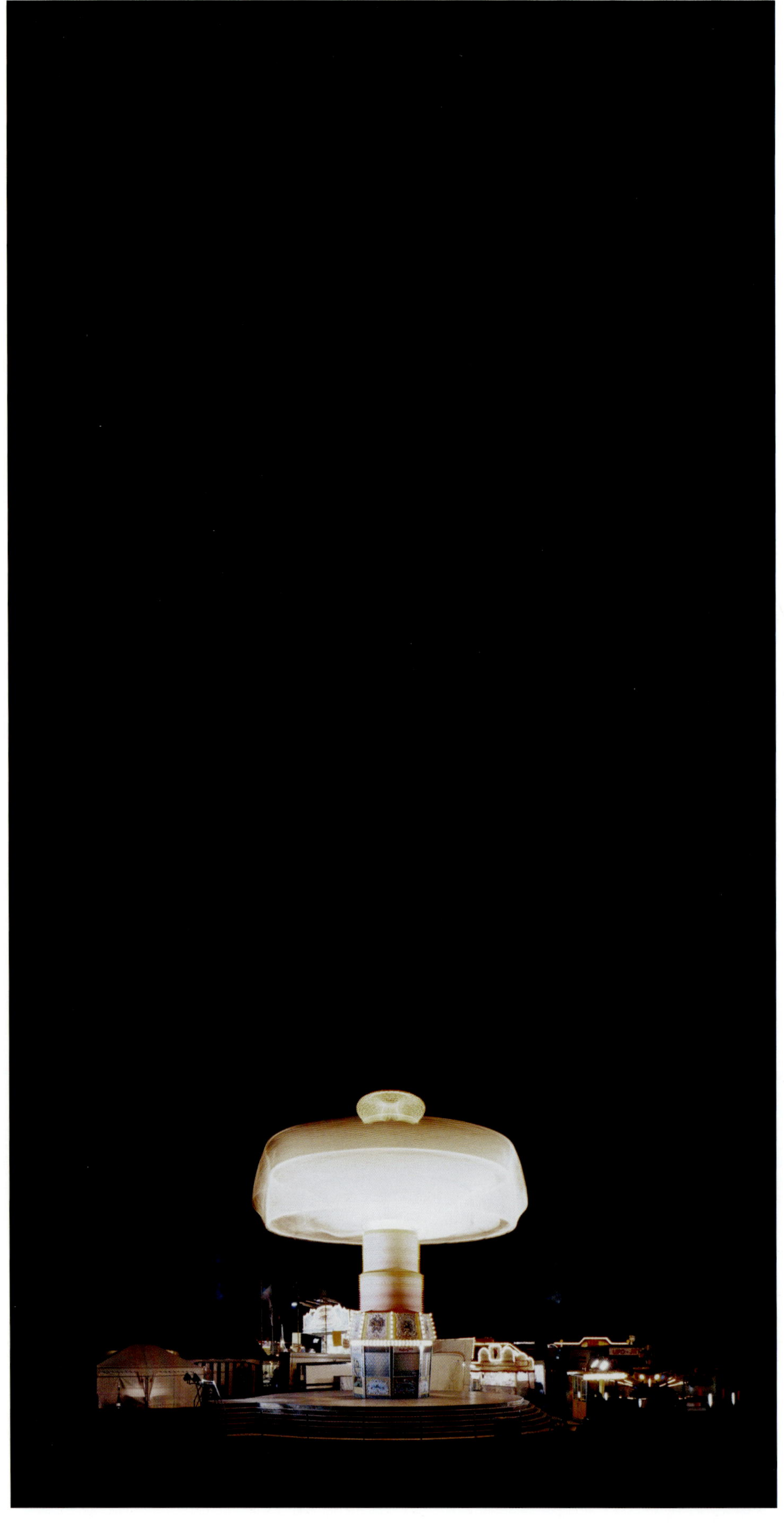

TRUDEL / **SPIN** 190 × 100 cm / 74.83 × 39.38 in.

FEUERWERK / FIREWORKS 190 × 105 cm / 74.83 × 41.33 in.

TERMINAL 190 × 90 cm / 74.83 × 35.43 in.

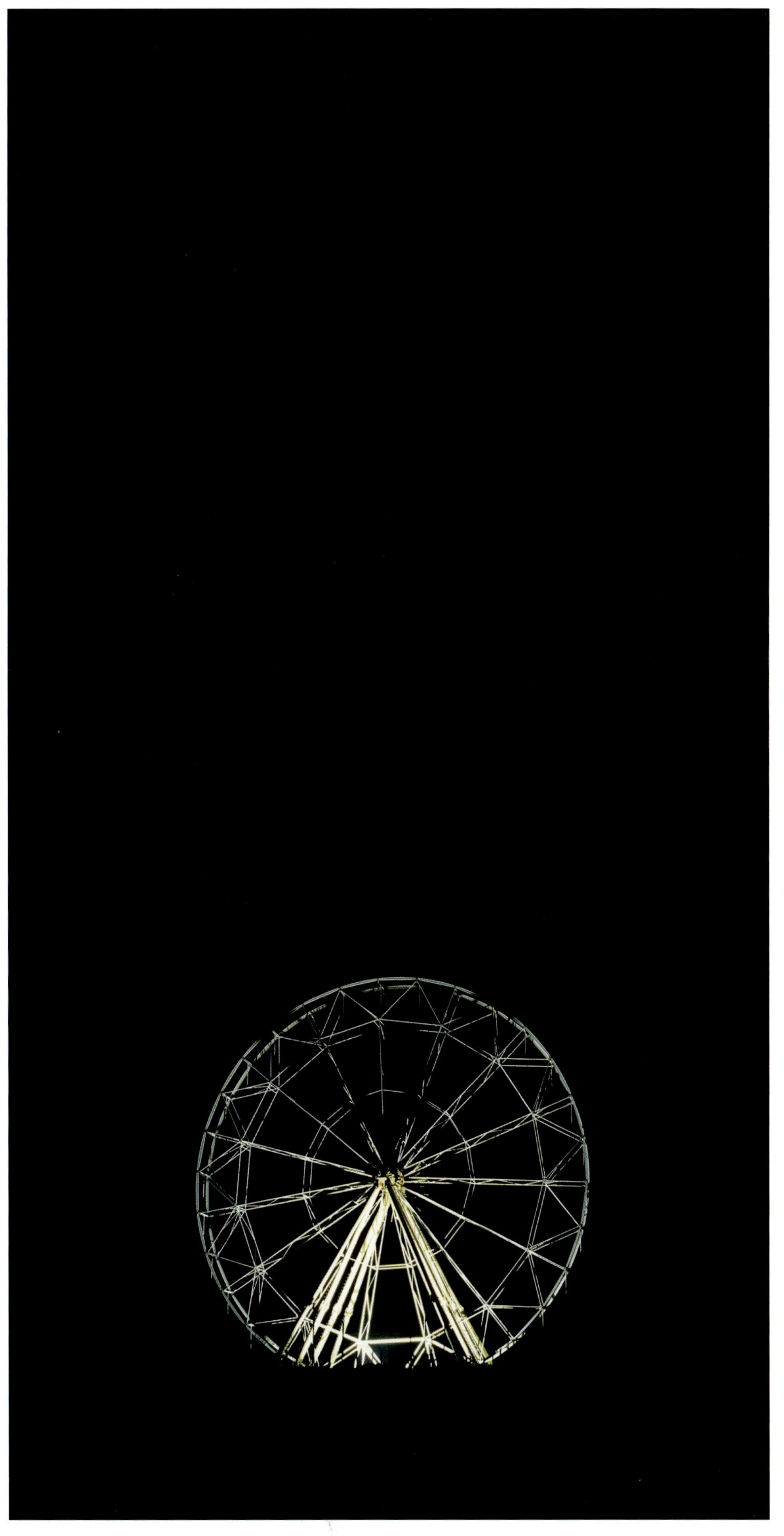

RAD / WHEEL 190 × 98 cm / 74.83 × 38.58 in.

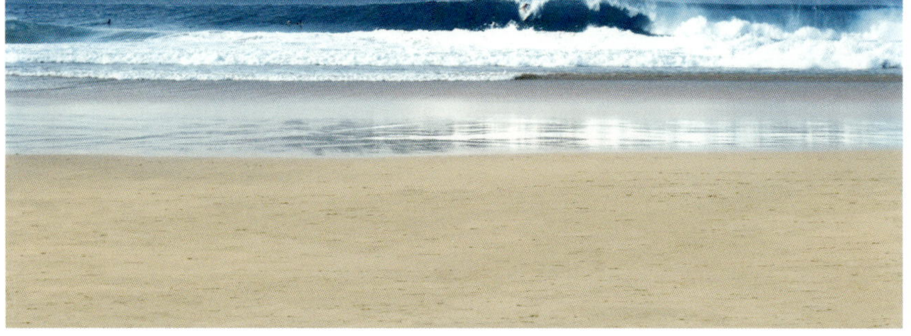

WELLE / WAVE 190 × 90 cm / 74.83 × 35.43 in.

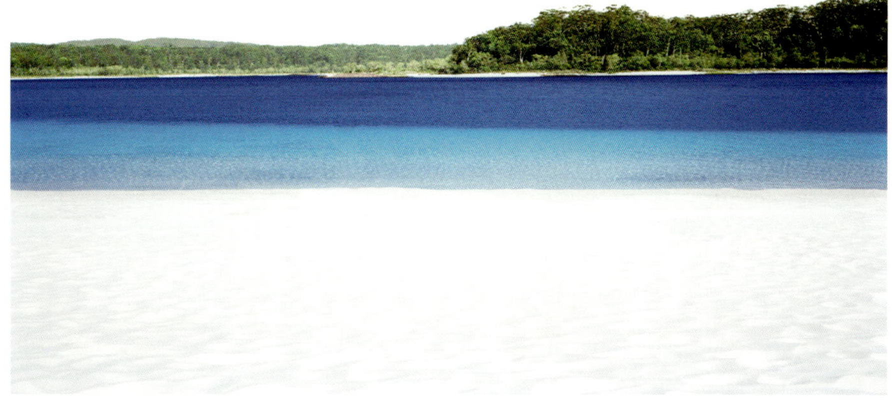

FRASER 190 × 95 cm / 74.83 × 37.4 in.

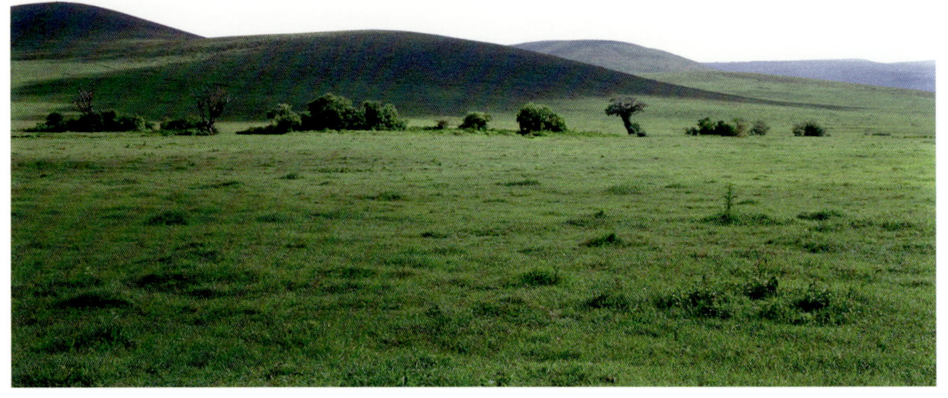

HÜGEL / HILL 190 × 100 cm / 74.83 × 39.38 in.

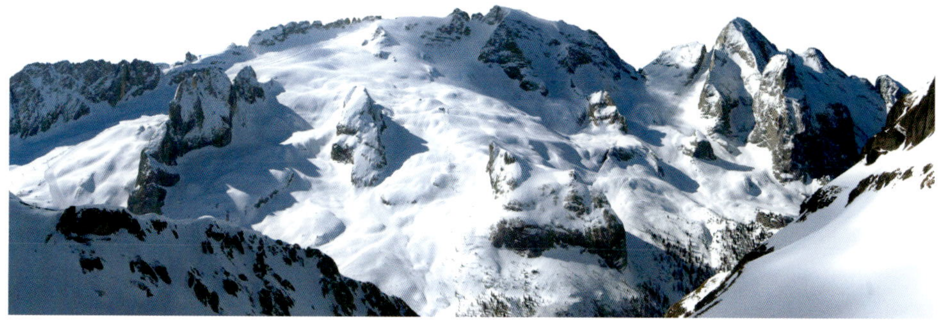

MARMOLADA 190 × 100 cm / 74.83 × 39.38 in.

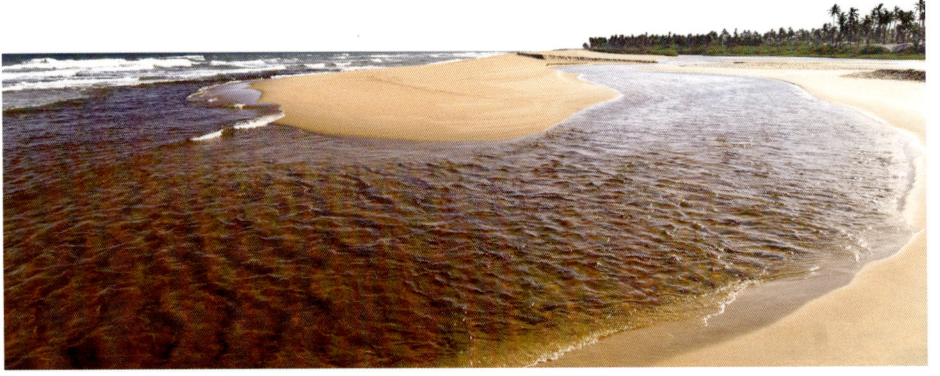

  FLUSS/MEER / RIVER/SEA 190 × 100 cm / 74.83 × 39.38 in.

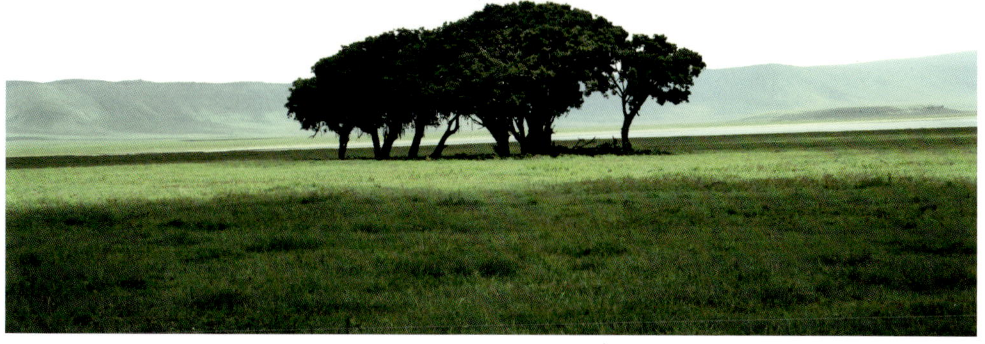

BÄUME / TREES 190 × 105 cm / 74.83 × 41.34 in.

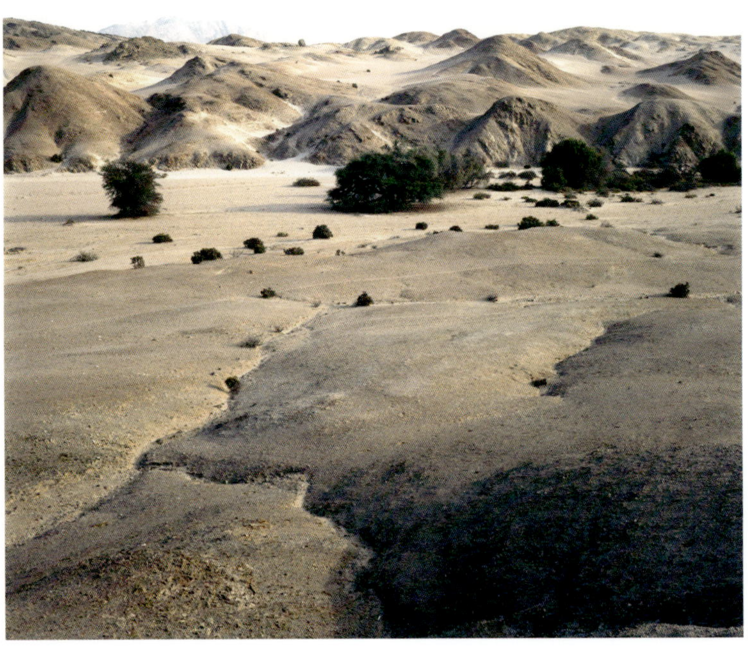

TRAUM / DREAM 190 × 80 cm / 74.83 × 31.5 in.

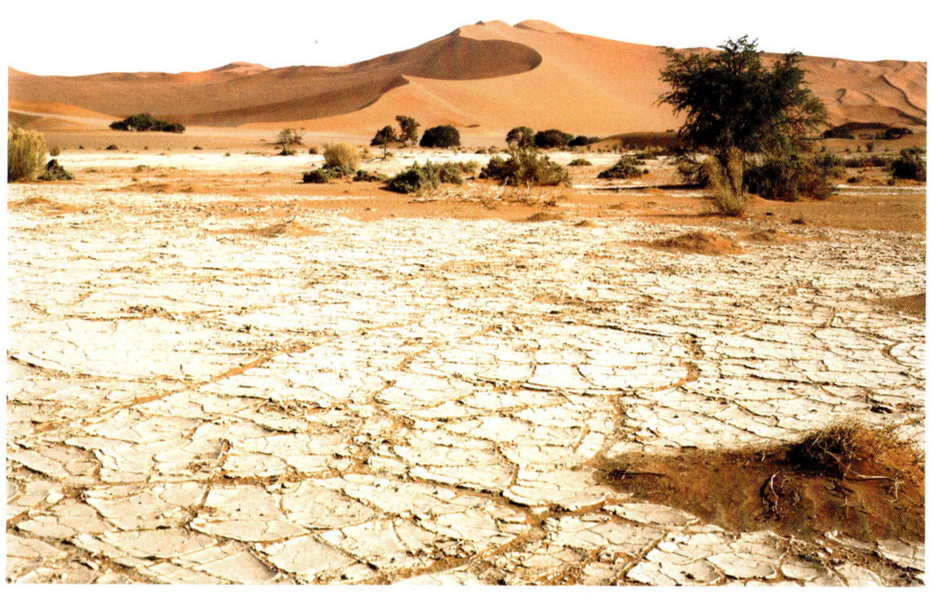

KRUSTE / CRUST 190 × 100 cm / 74.83 × 39.38 in.

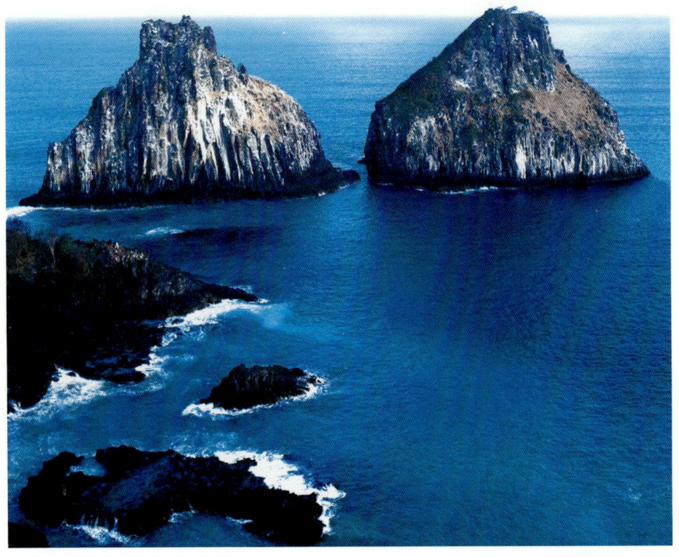

FERNANDO 190 × 72 cm / 74.83 × 28.35 in.

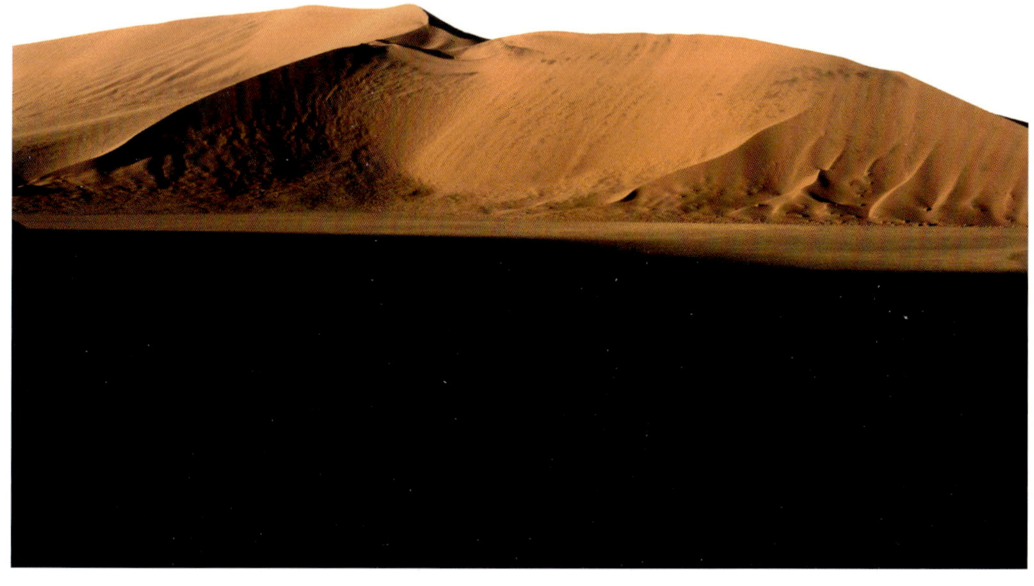

DÜNE / DUNE 190 × 110 cm / 74.83 × 43.31 in.

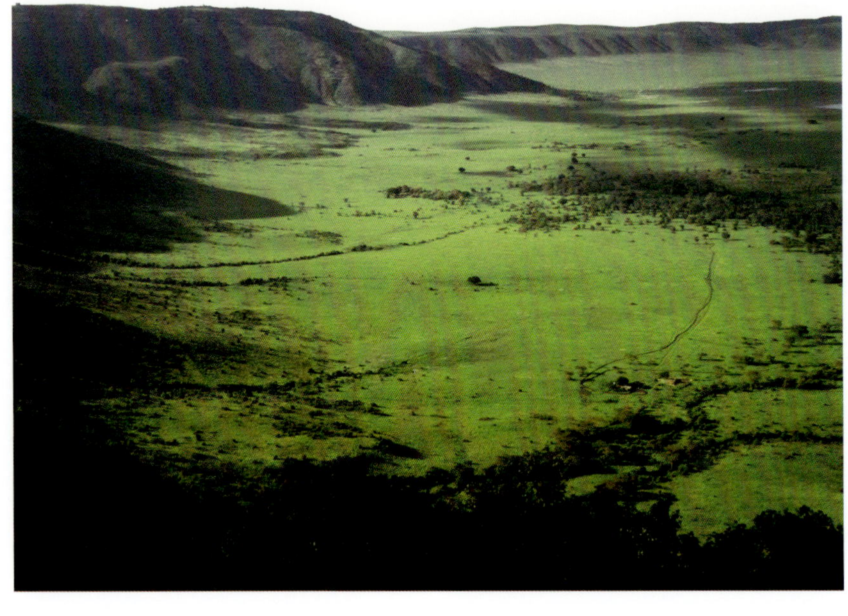

NGORONGORO 190 × 90 cm / 74.83 × 35.43 in.

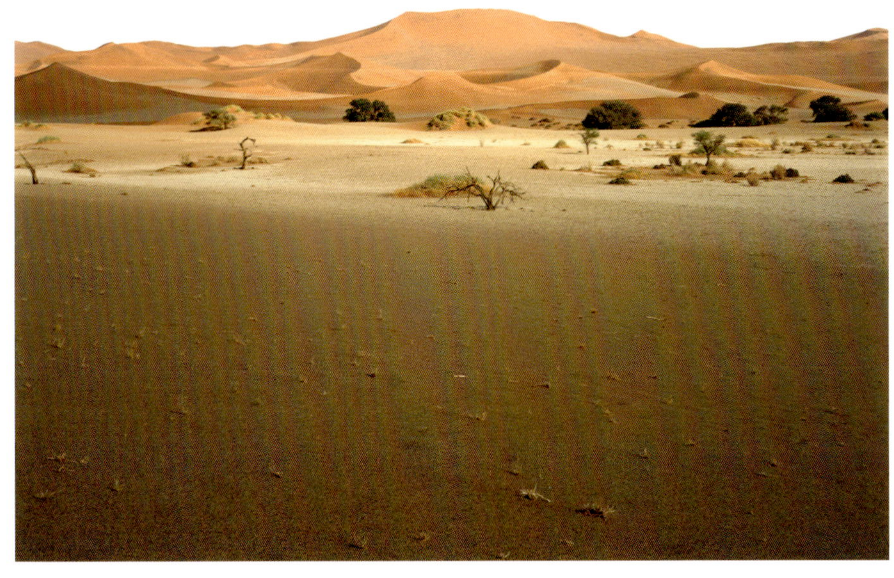

SSUSS 190 × 95 cm / 74.83 × 37.4 in.

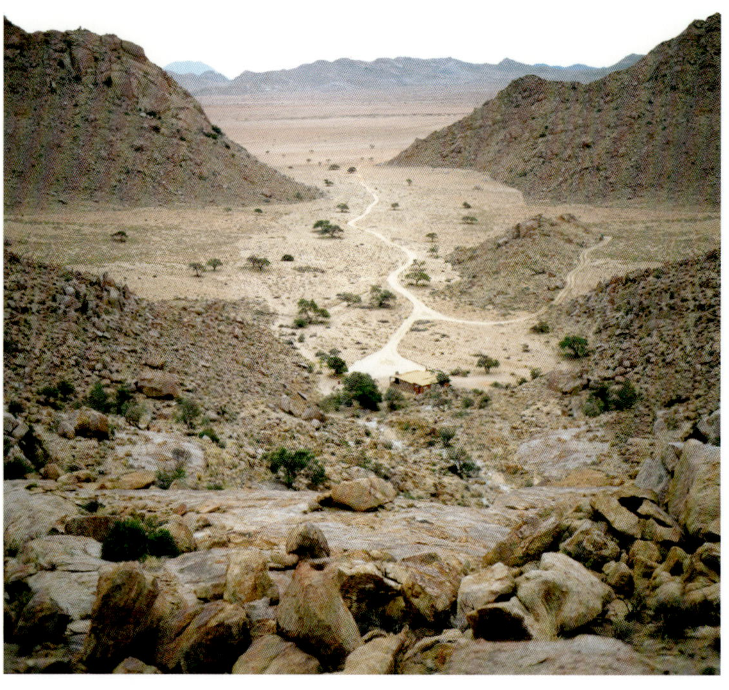

     TAL / VALLEY 190 × 78 cm / 74.83 × 30.71 in.

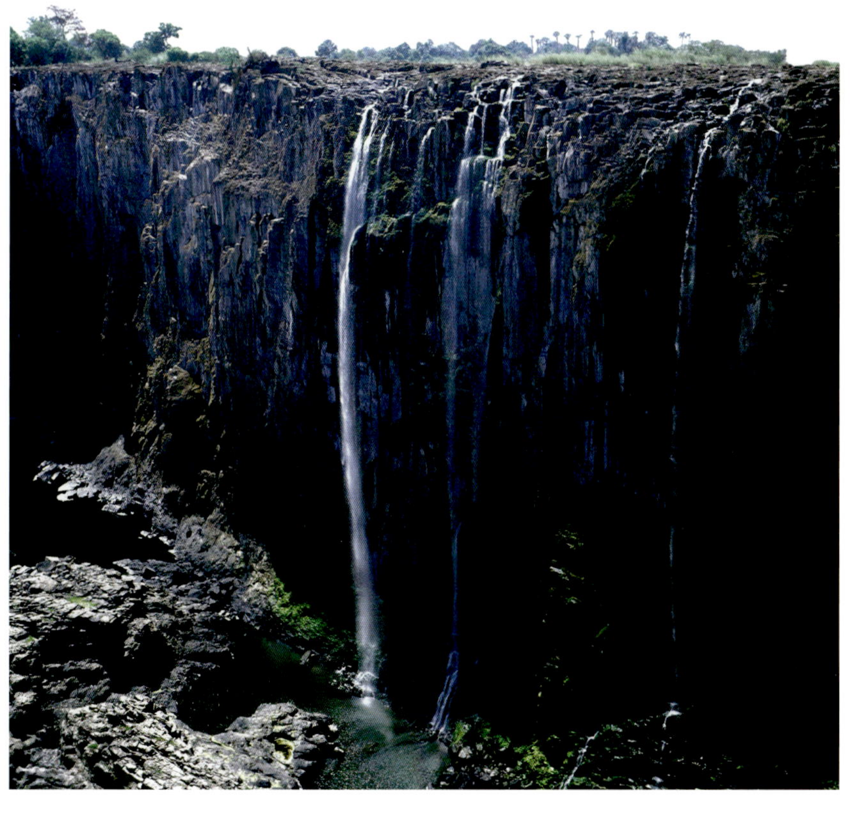

VIC FALLS 190 × 90 cm / 74.83 × 35.43 in.

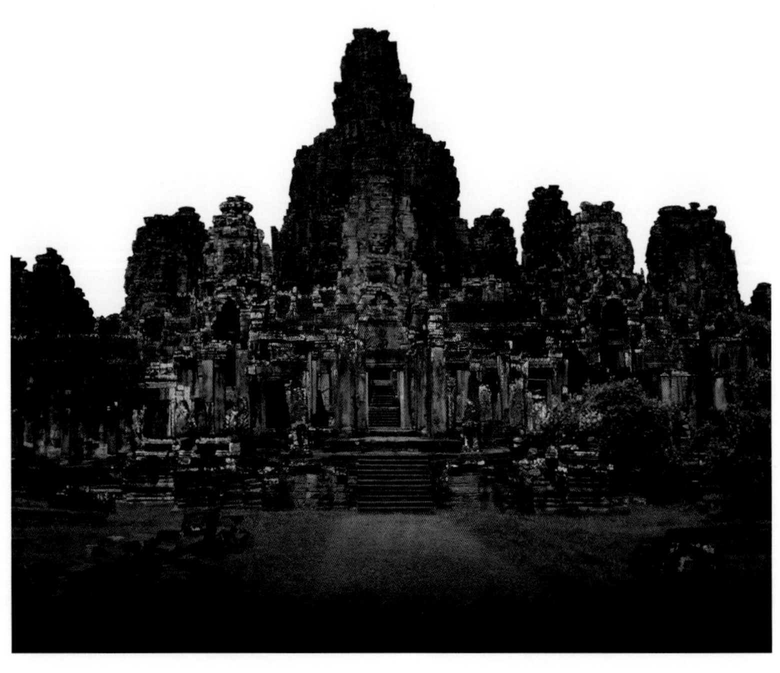

 TEMPEL MITTE / TEMPLE CENTER 190 × 83 cm / 74.83 × 32.68 in.

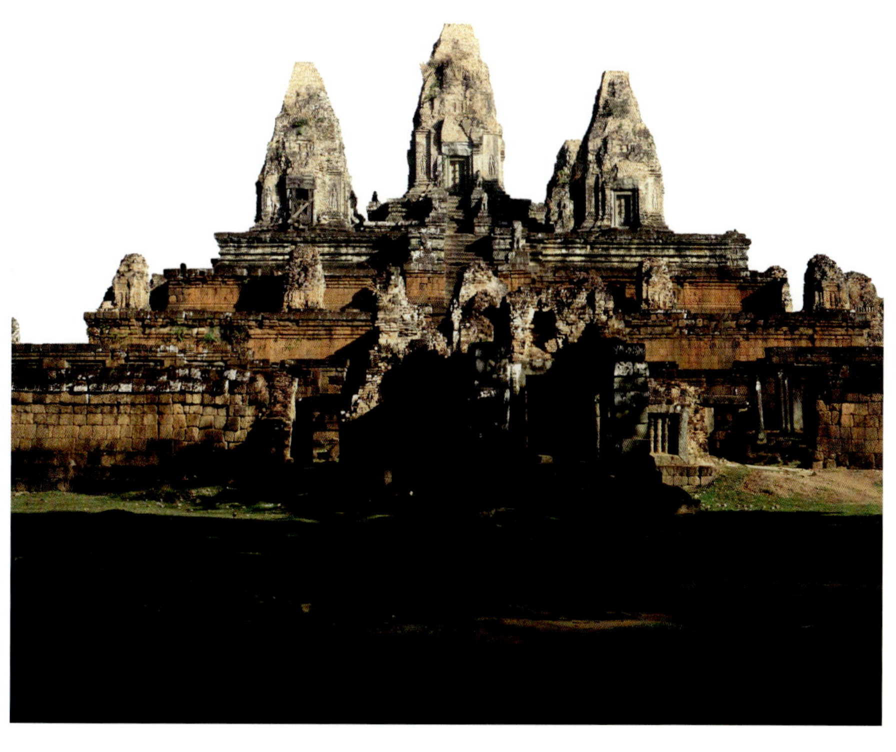

SEAM MITTE / SEAM CENTER 190 × 94 cm / 74.83 × 37 in.

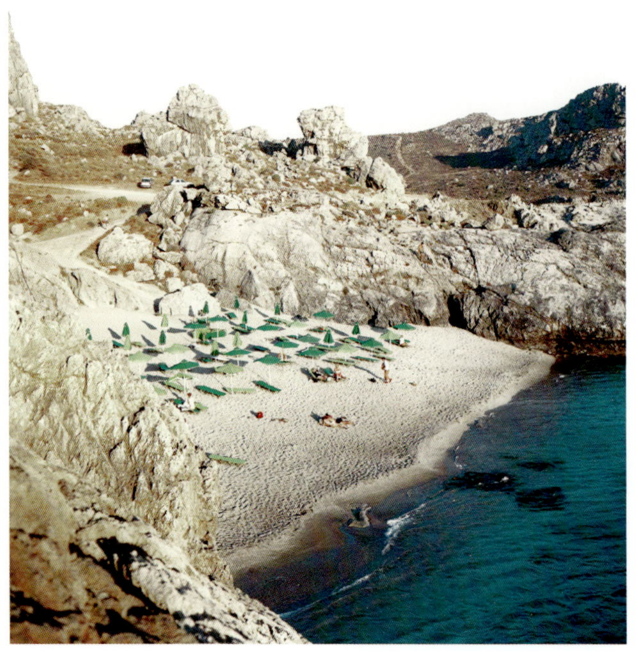

 KRETA / CRETE 190 × 67 cm / 74.83 × 26.38 in.

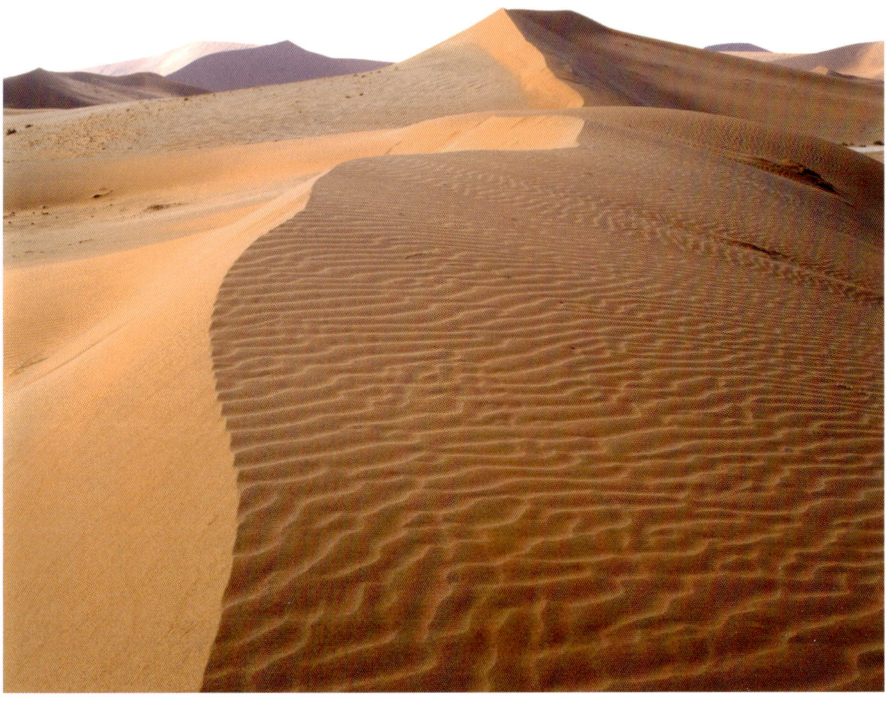

MITTE / CENTER 190 × 95 cm / 74.83 × 37.4 in.

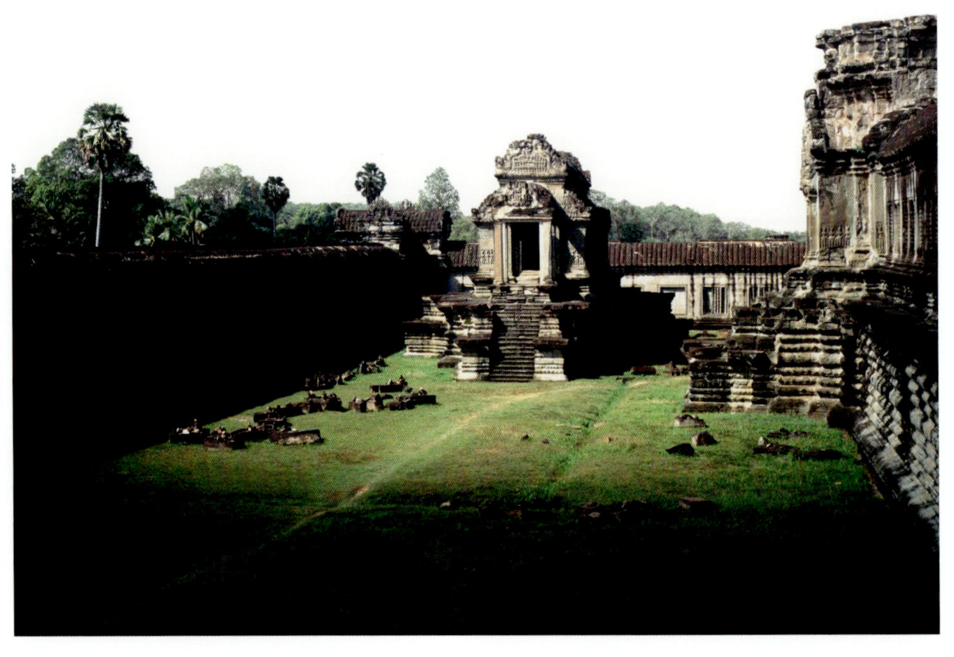

TEMPEL KLEIN / TEMPLE SMALL 190 × 100 cm / 74.83 × 39.38 in.

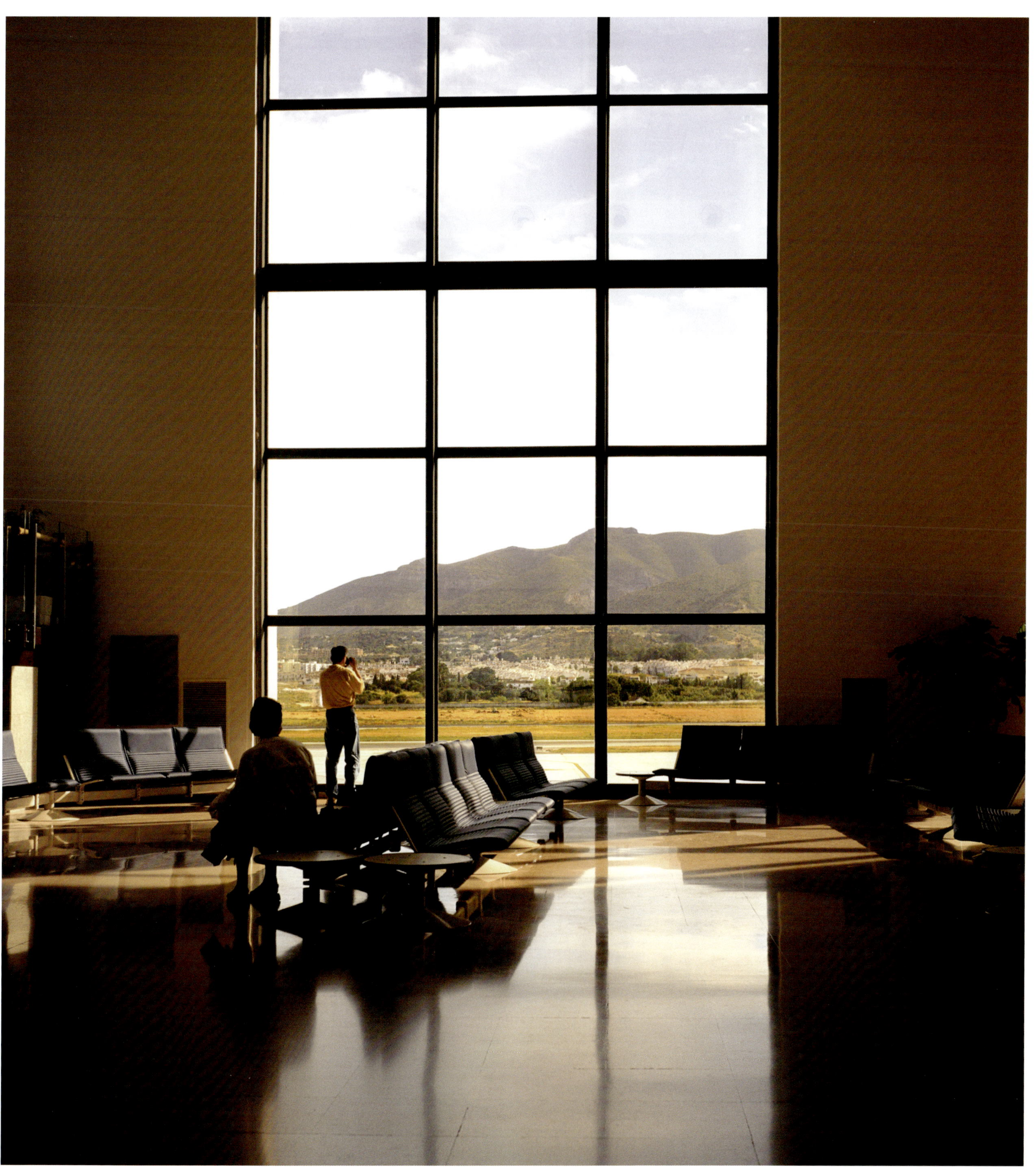

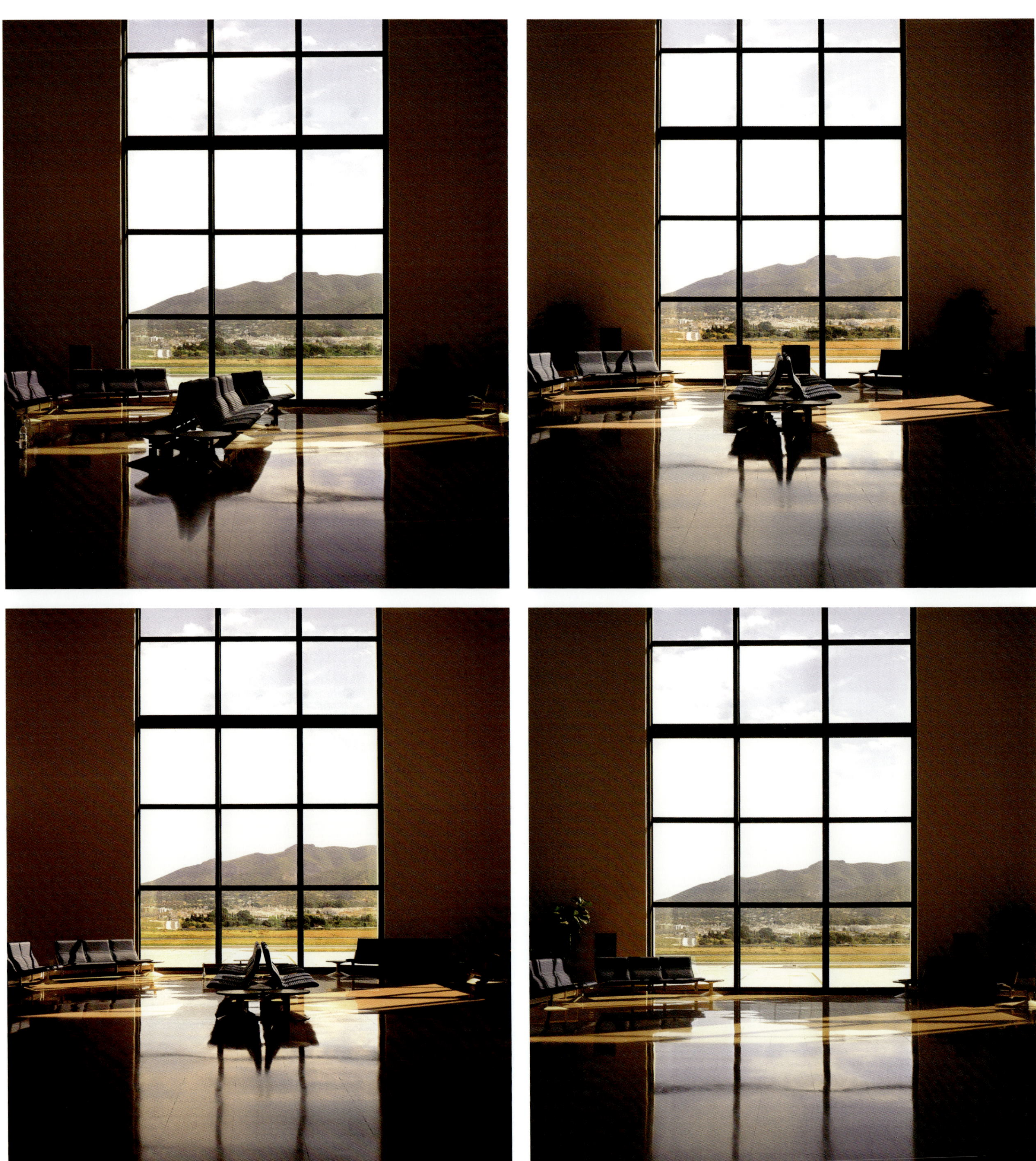

 # 4 **# 2** **# 6** **# 5** 120 × 110 cm / 47.24 × 43.31 in.

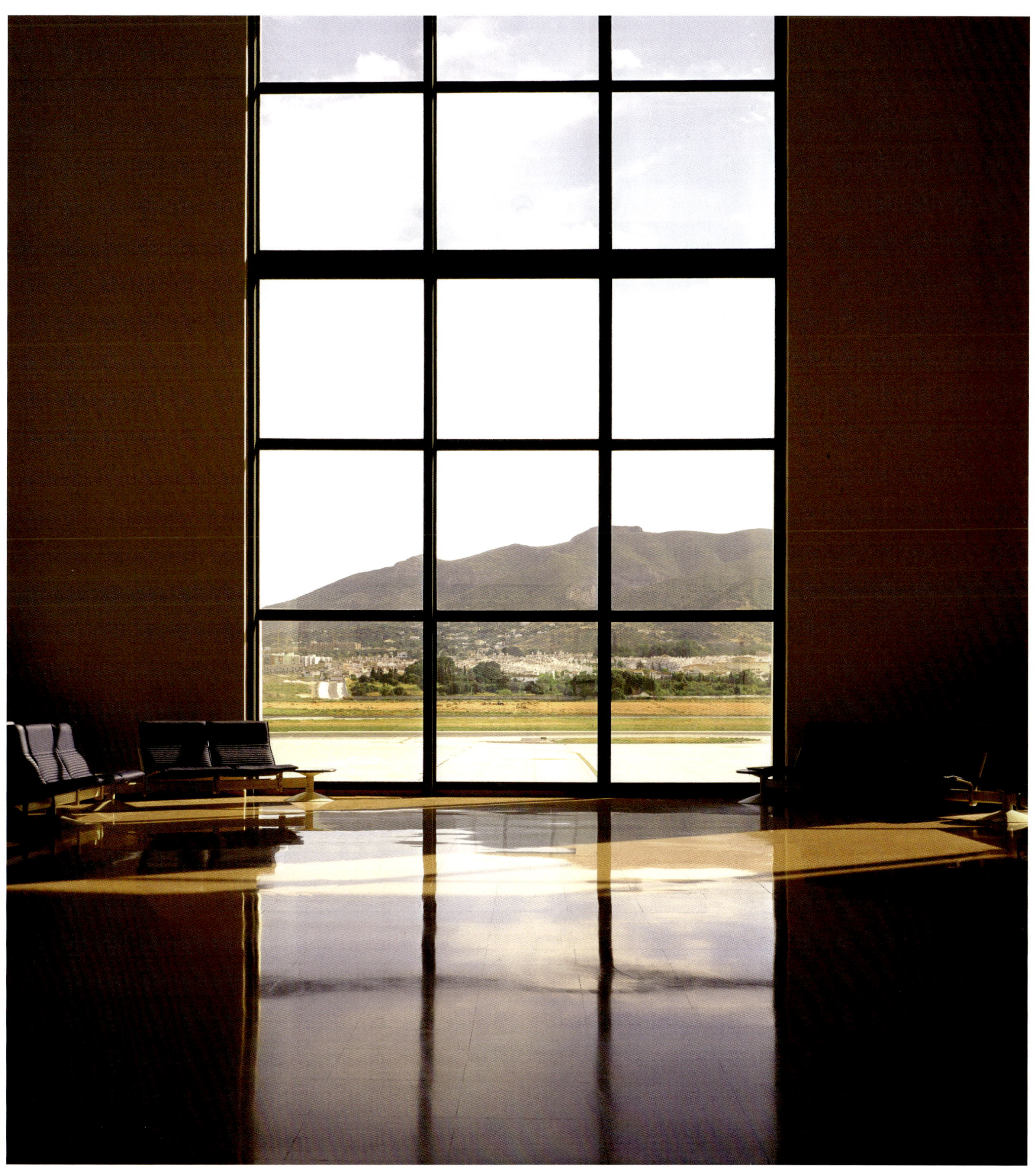

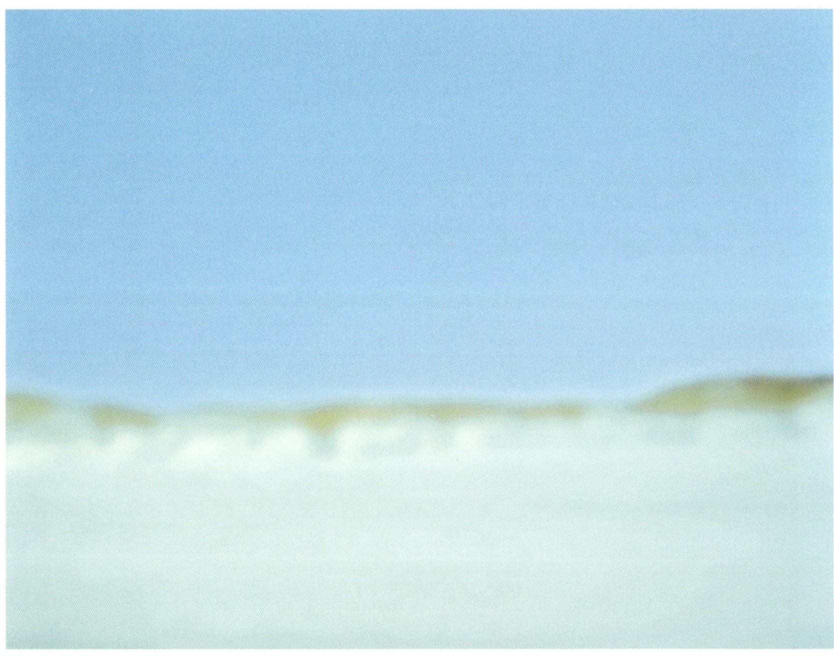

16   # 18   # 17   70 × 100 cm / 27.56 × 39.38 in.

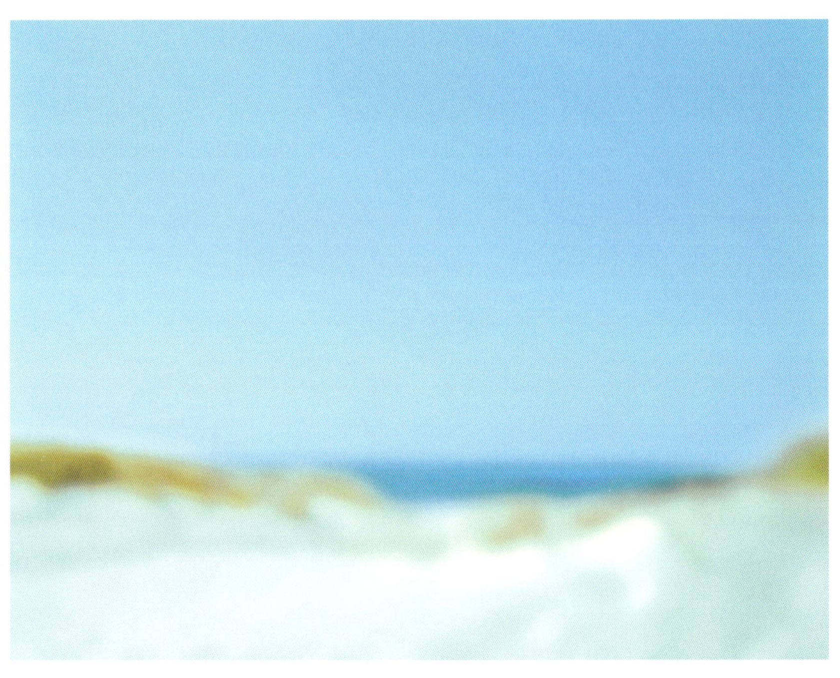 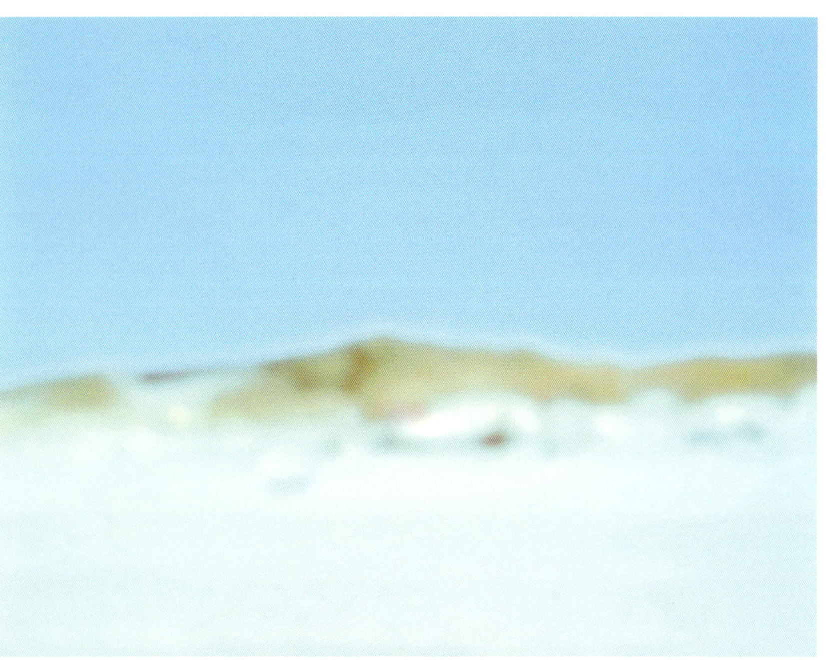

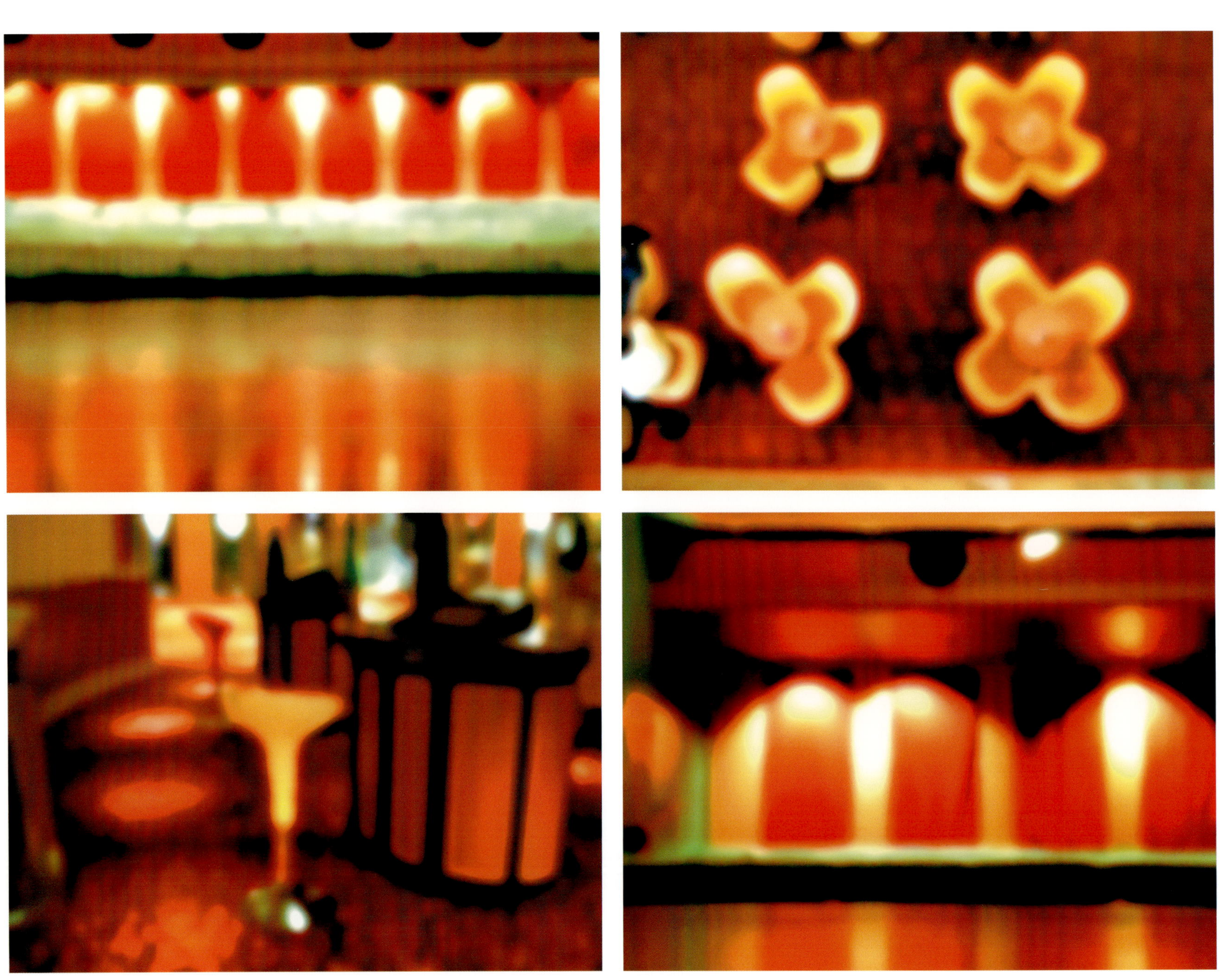

106   **# 35**   **# 10**   **# 6**   **# 54**   70 × 100 cm / 27.56 × 39.38 in.

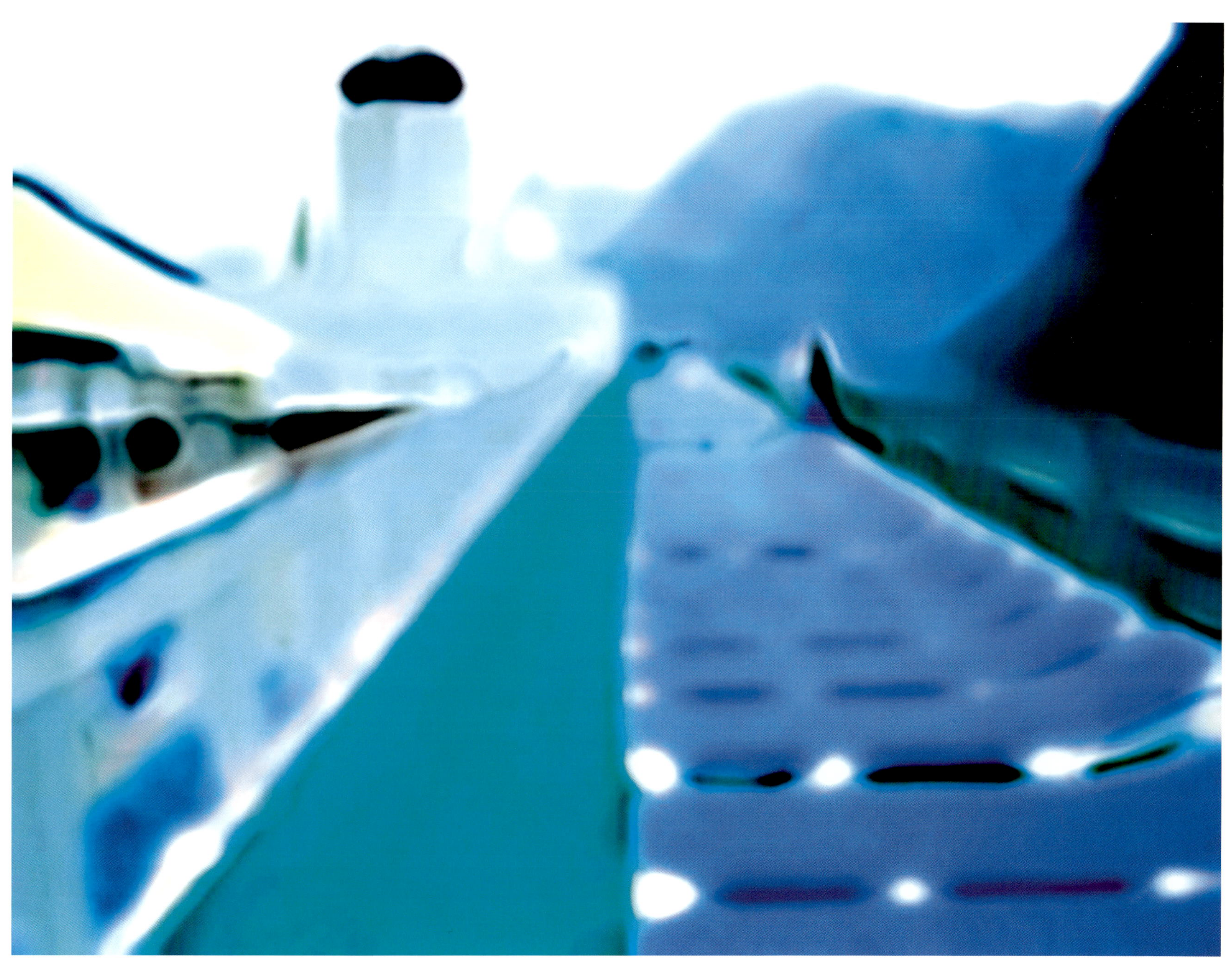

14 70 × 100 cm / 27.56 × 39.38 in.

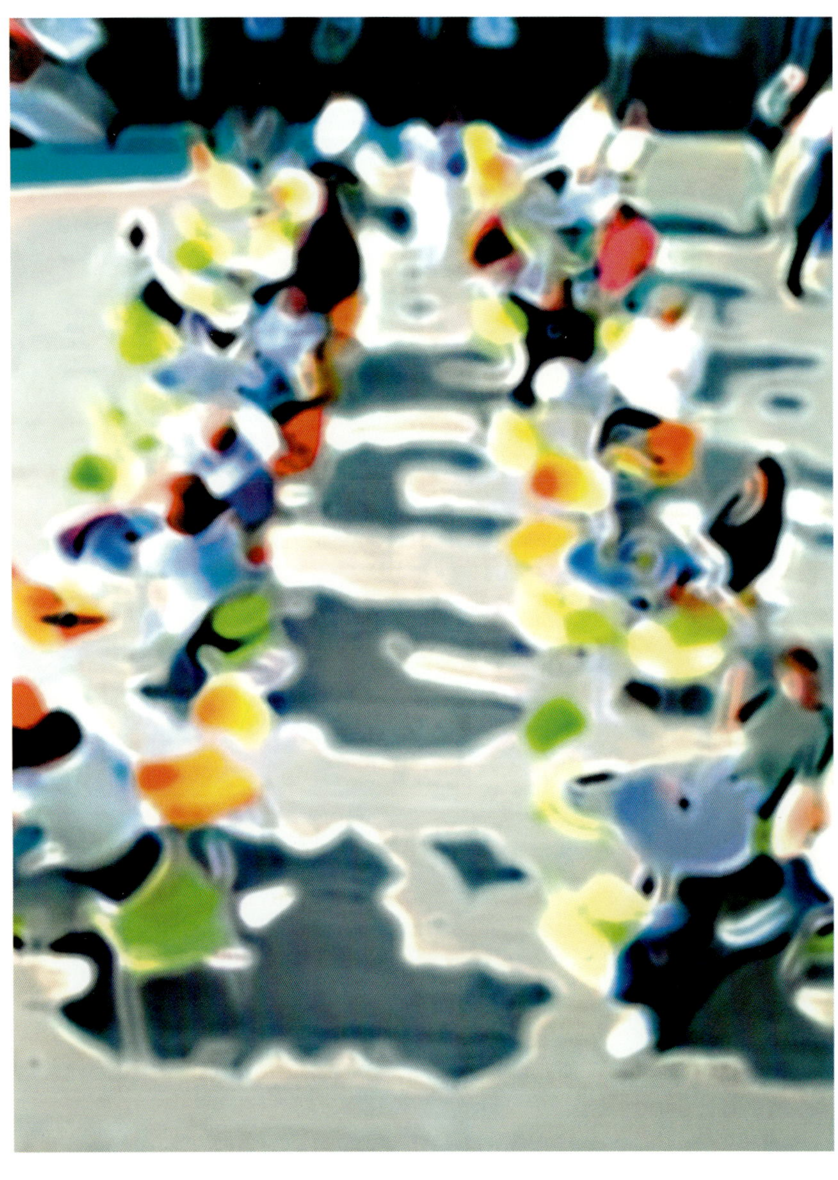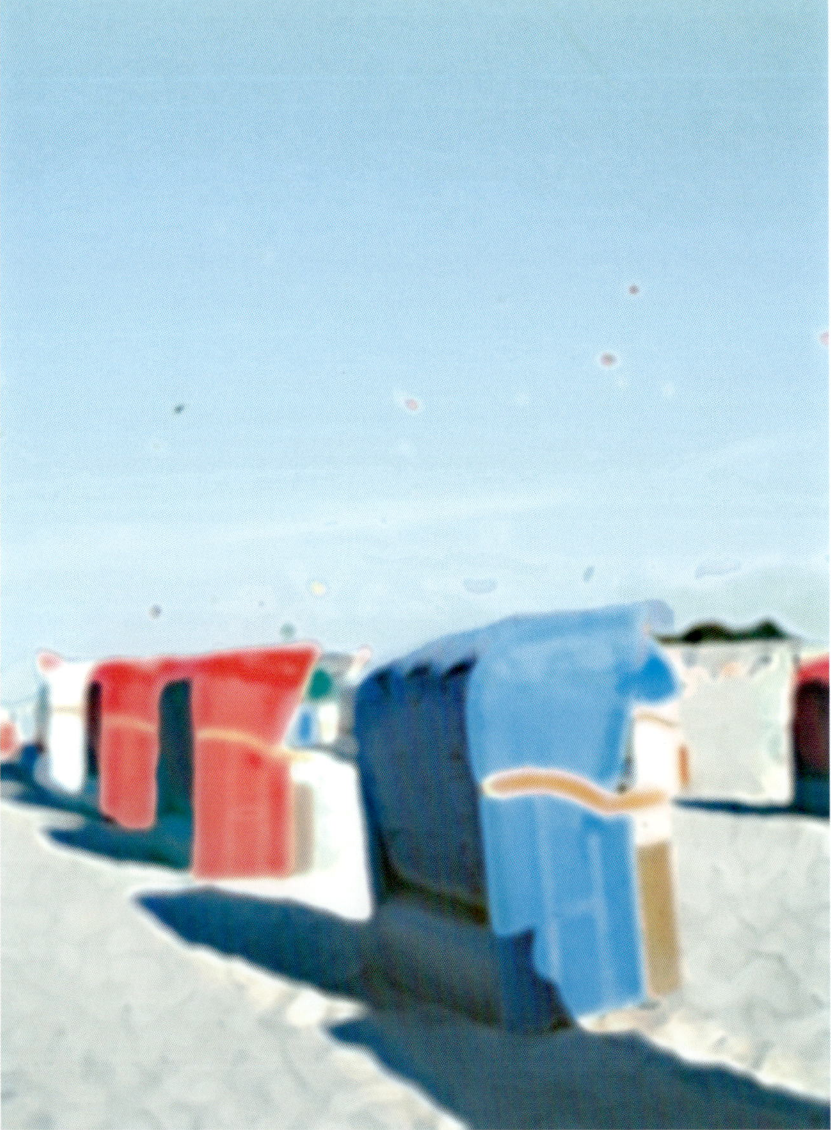

  # 36 **# 30** 100 × 70 cm / 39.38 × 27.56 in.

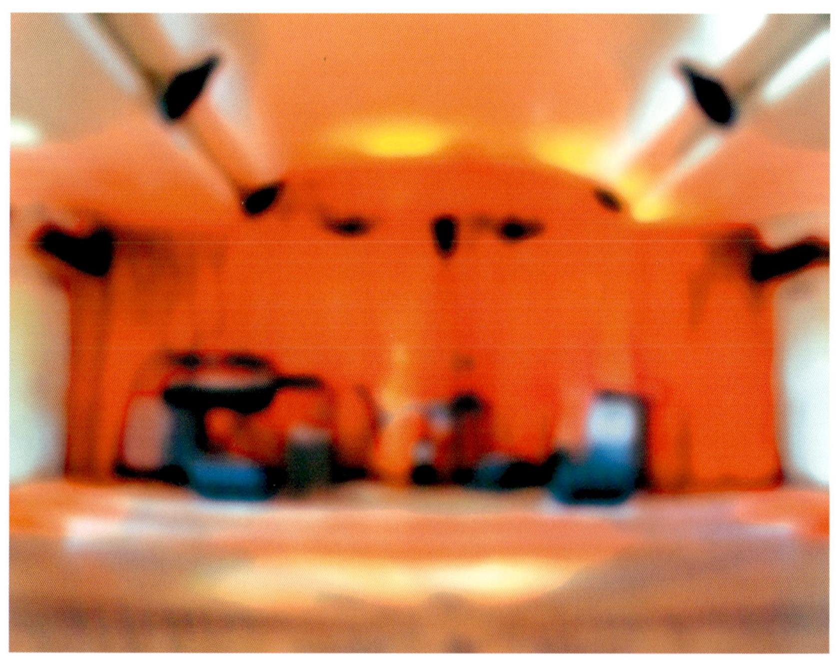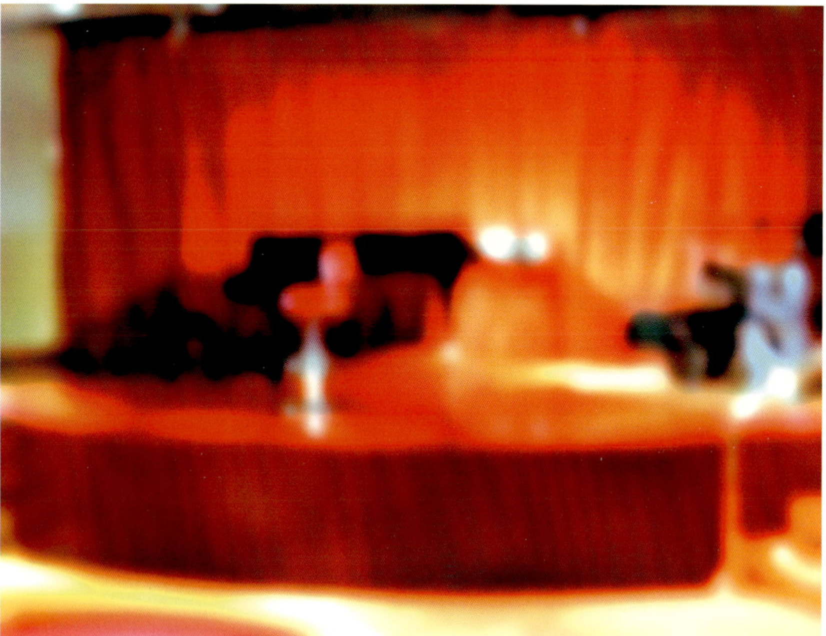

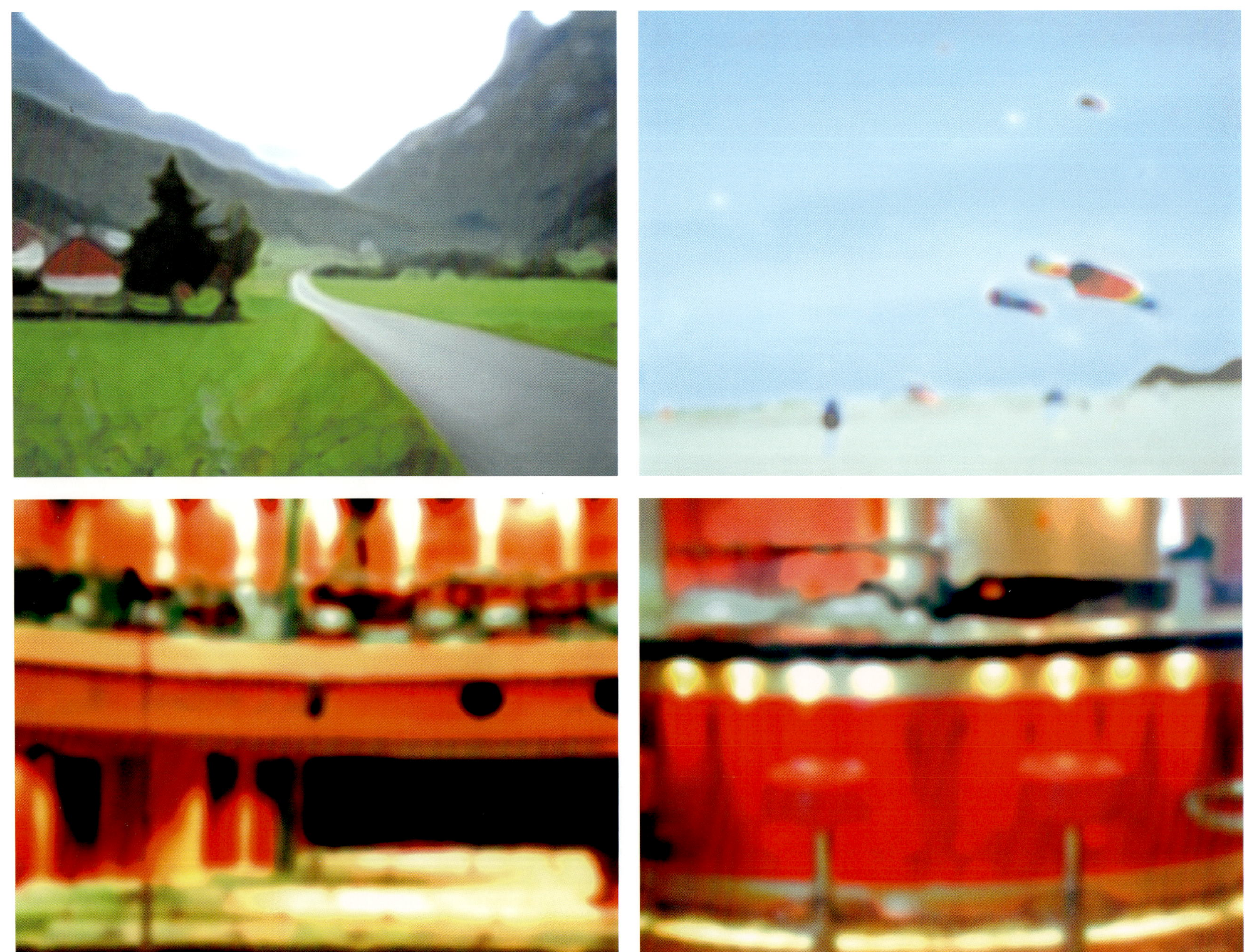

110 **#48 #25 #46 #45** 70 × 100 cm / 27.56 × 39.38 in.

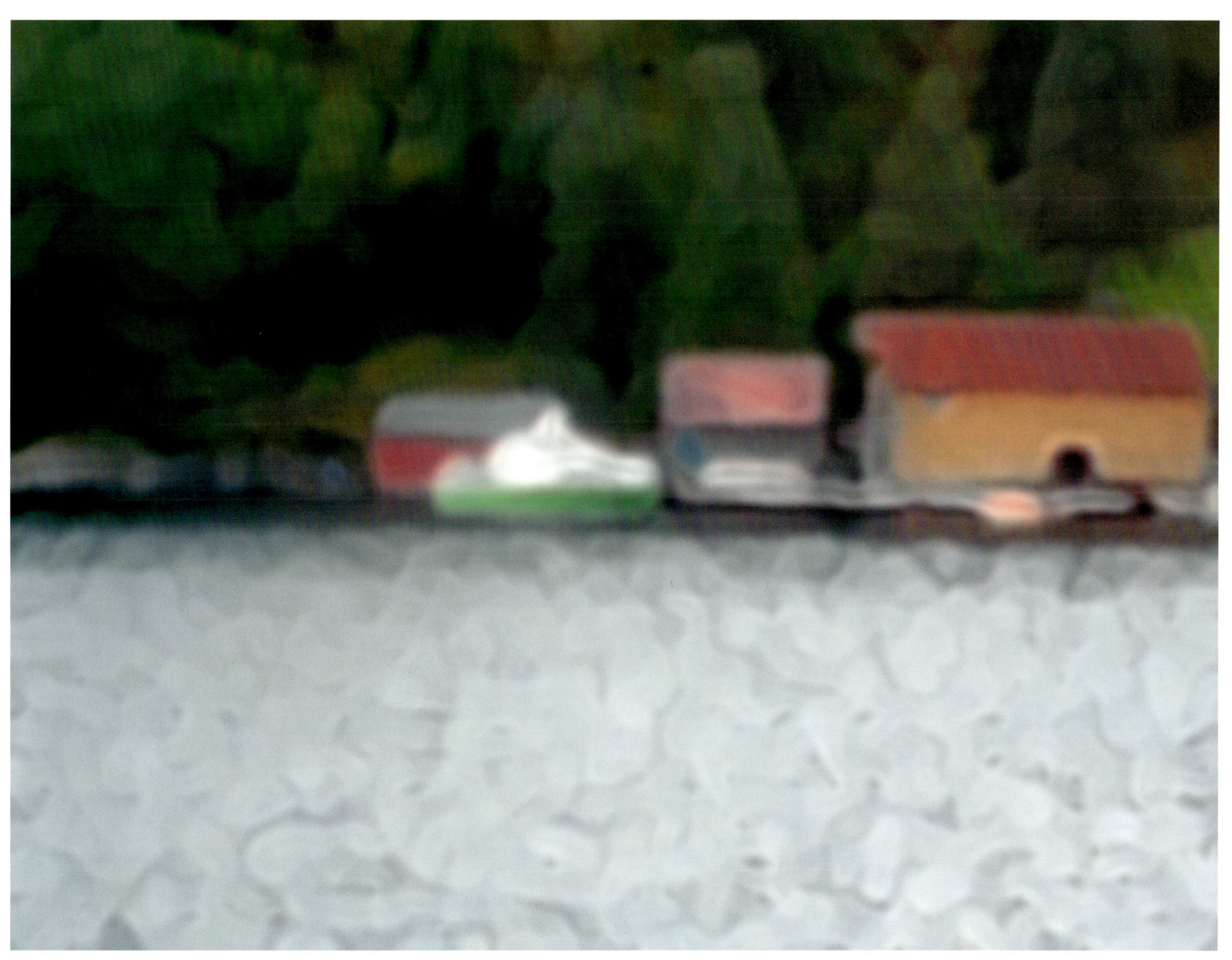

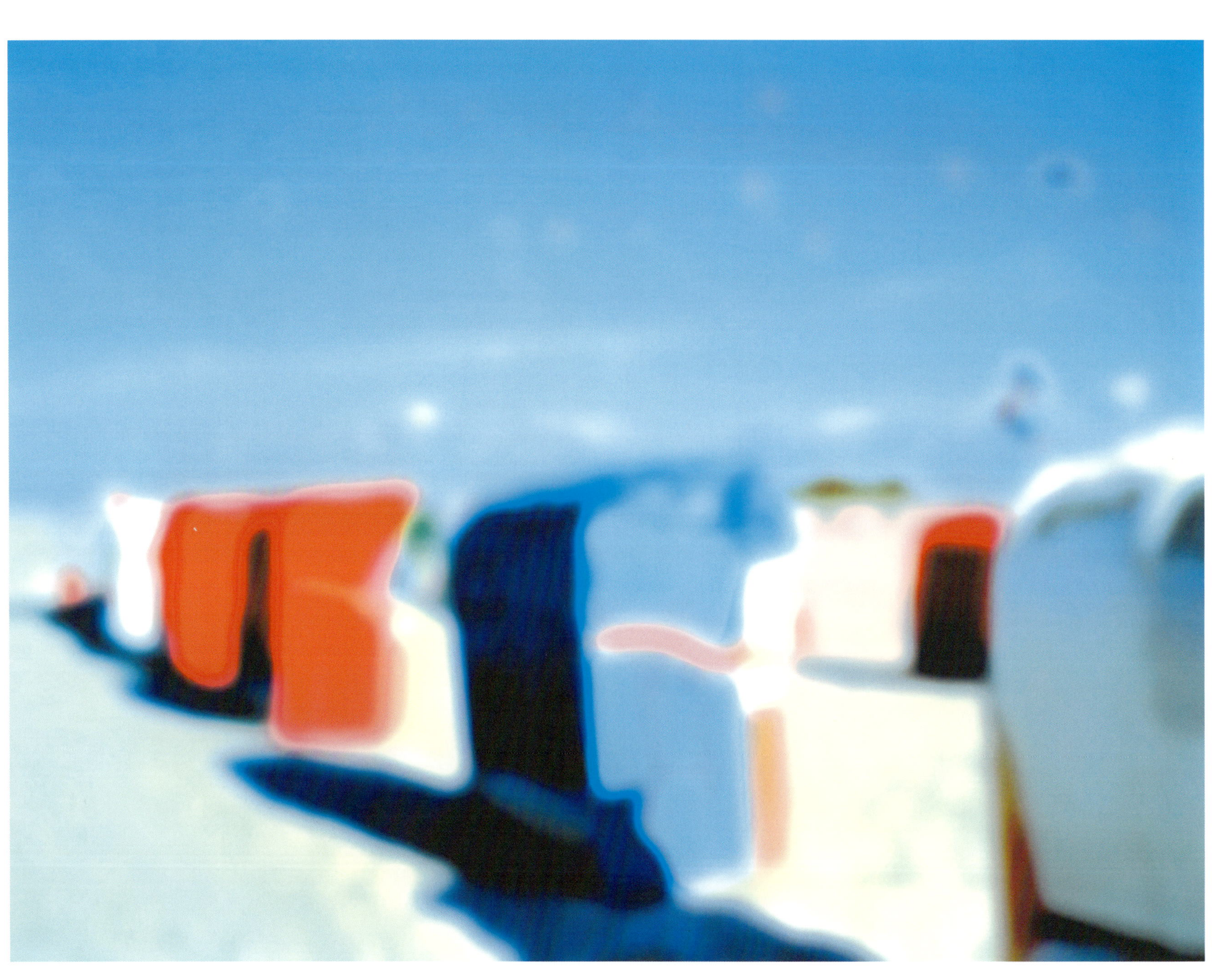

  # 24 70 × 100 cm / 27.56 × 39.38 in.

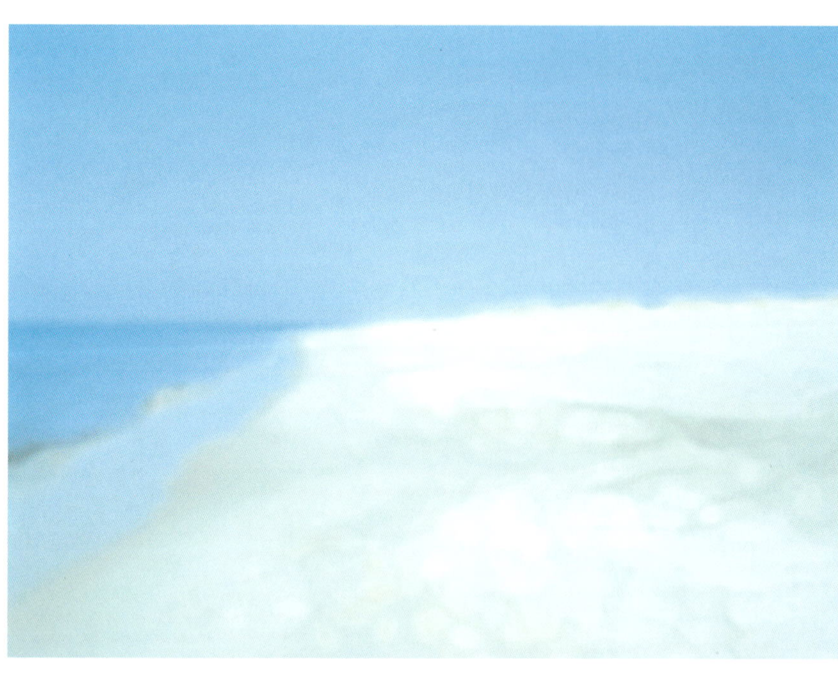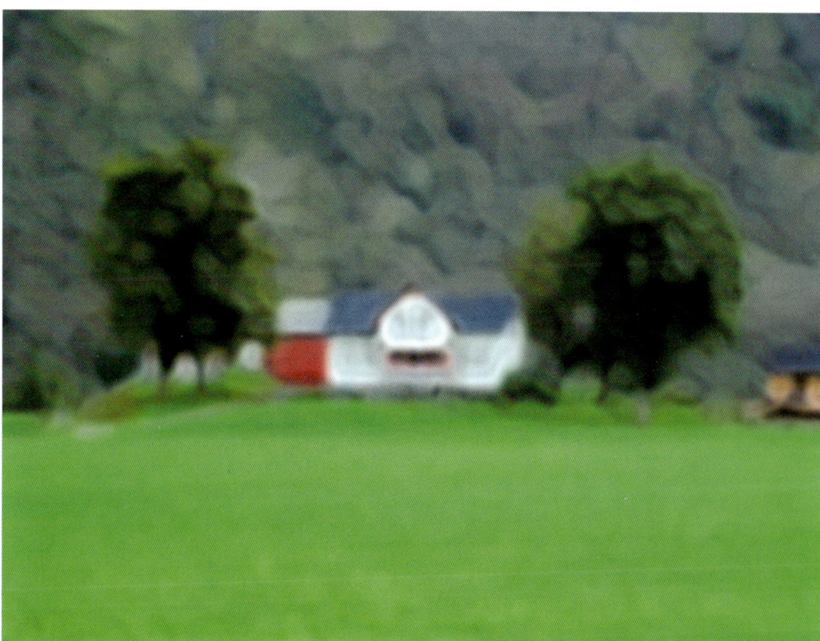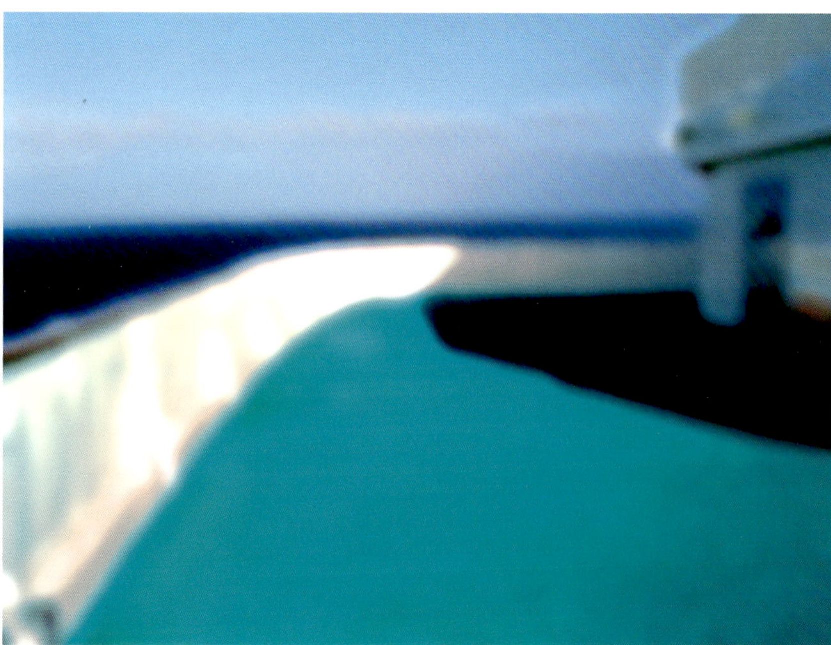

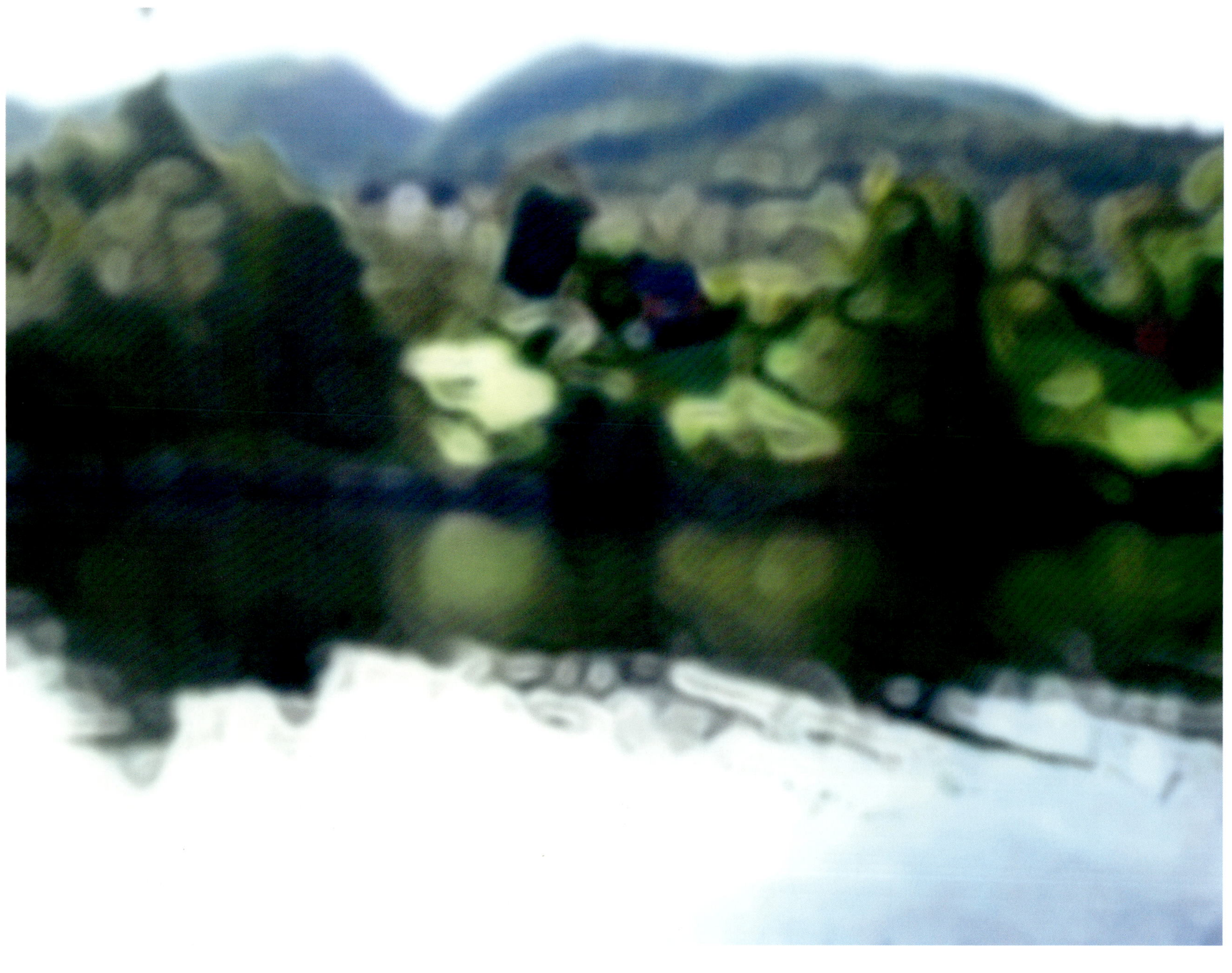

  # 12 70 × 100 cm / 27.56 × 39.38 in.

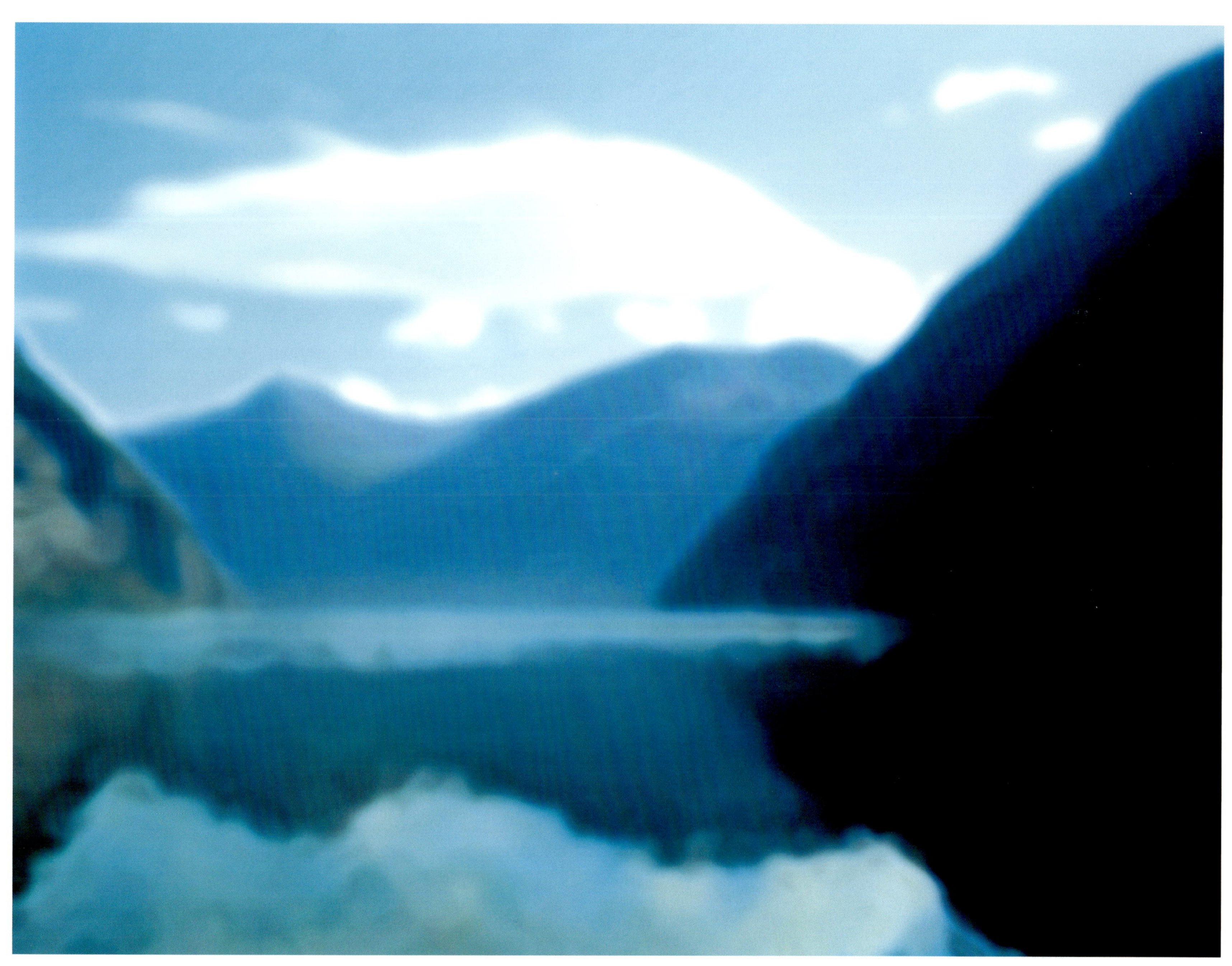

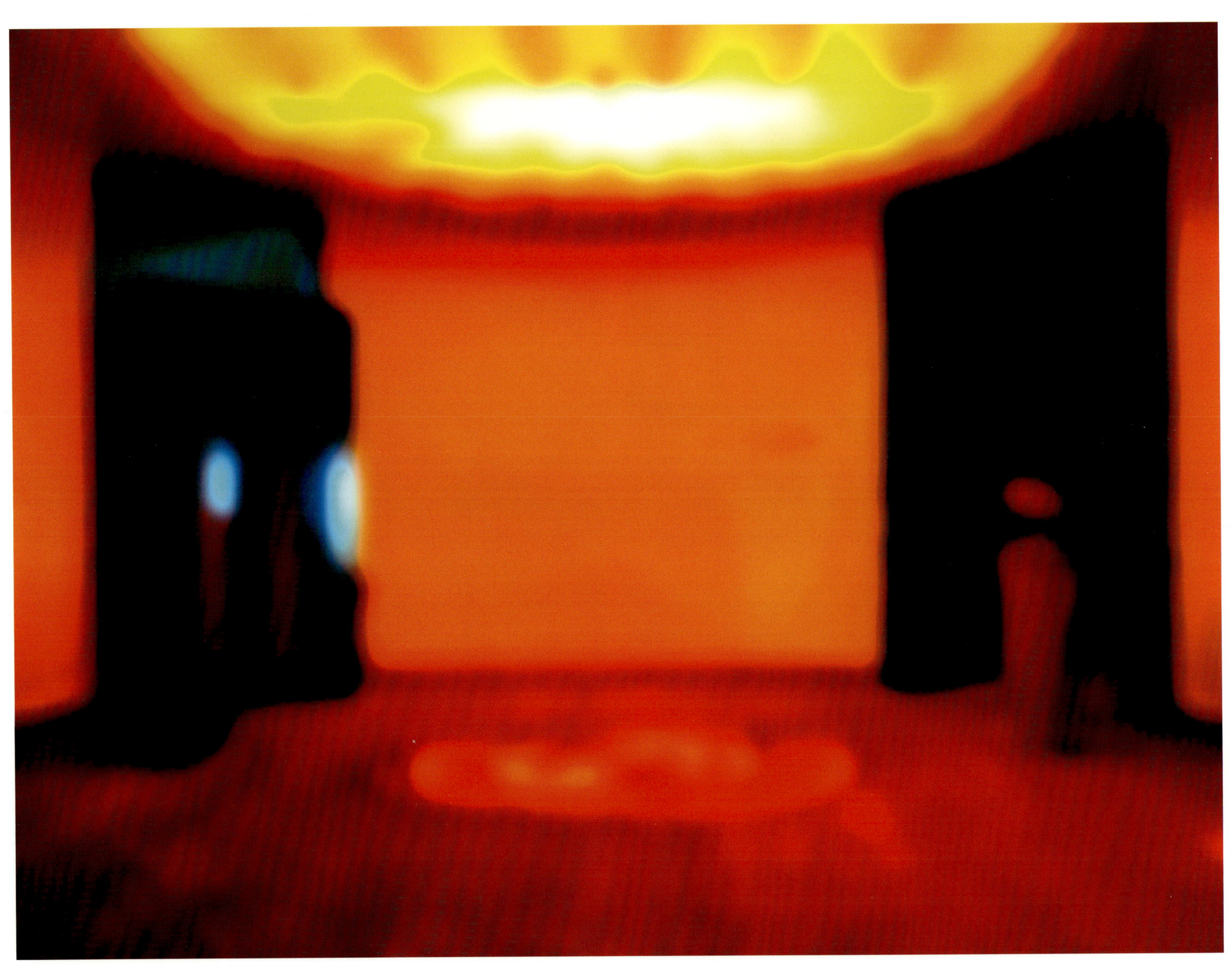

  # 8 70 × 100 cm / 27.56 × 39.38 in.

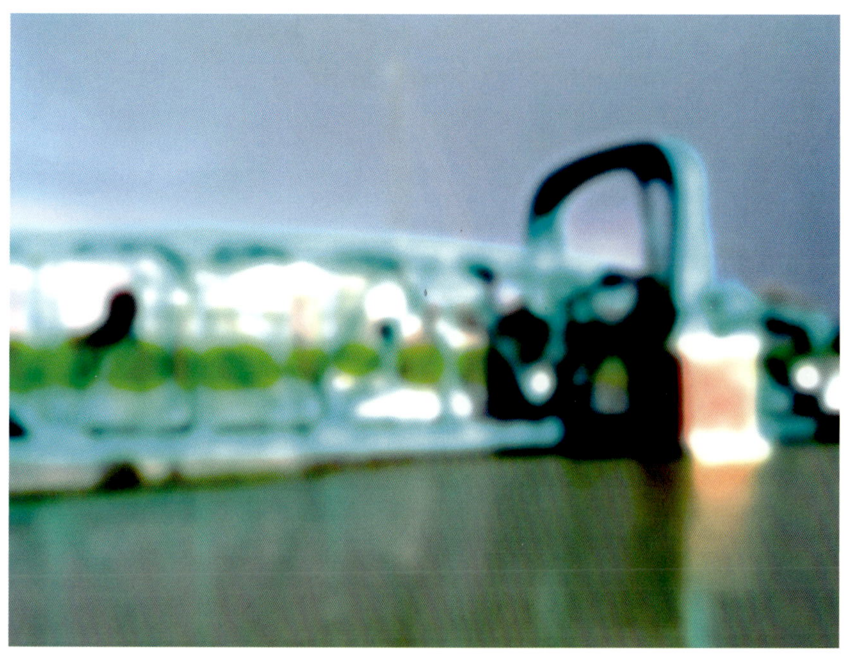
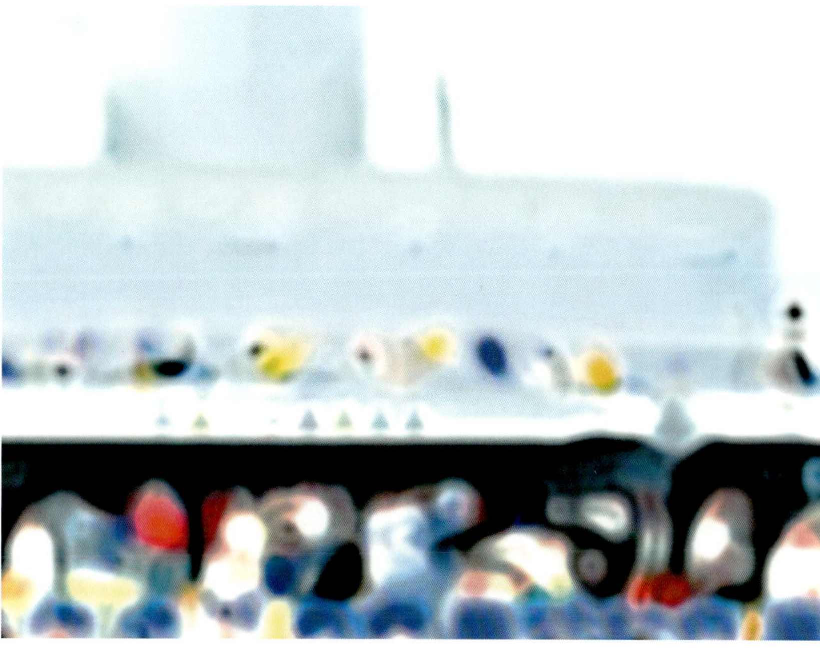
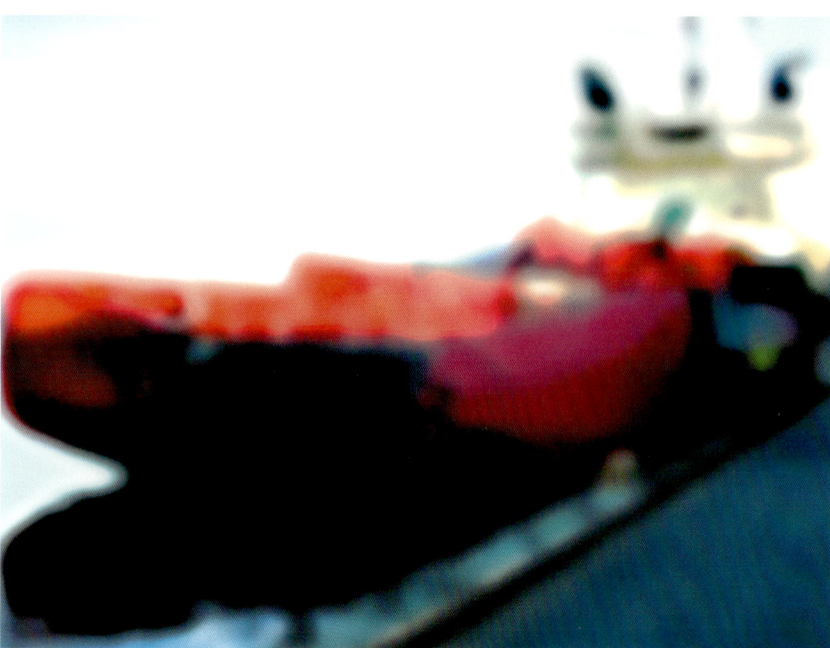
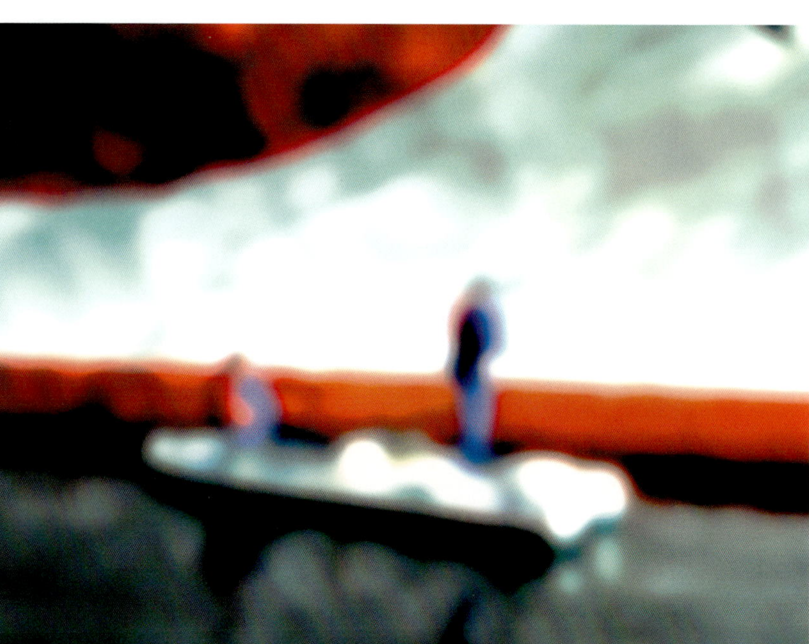

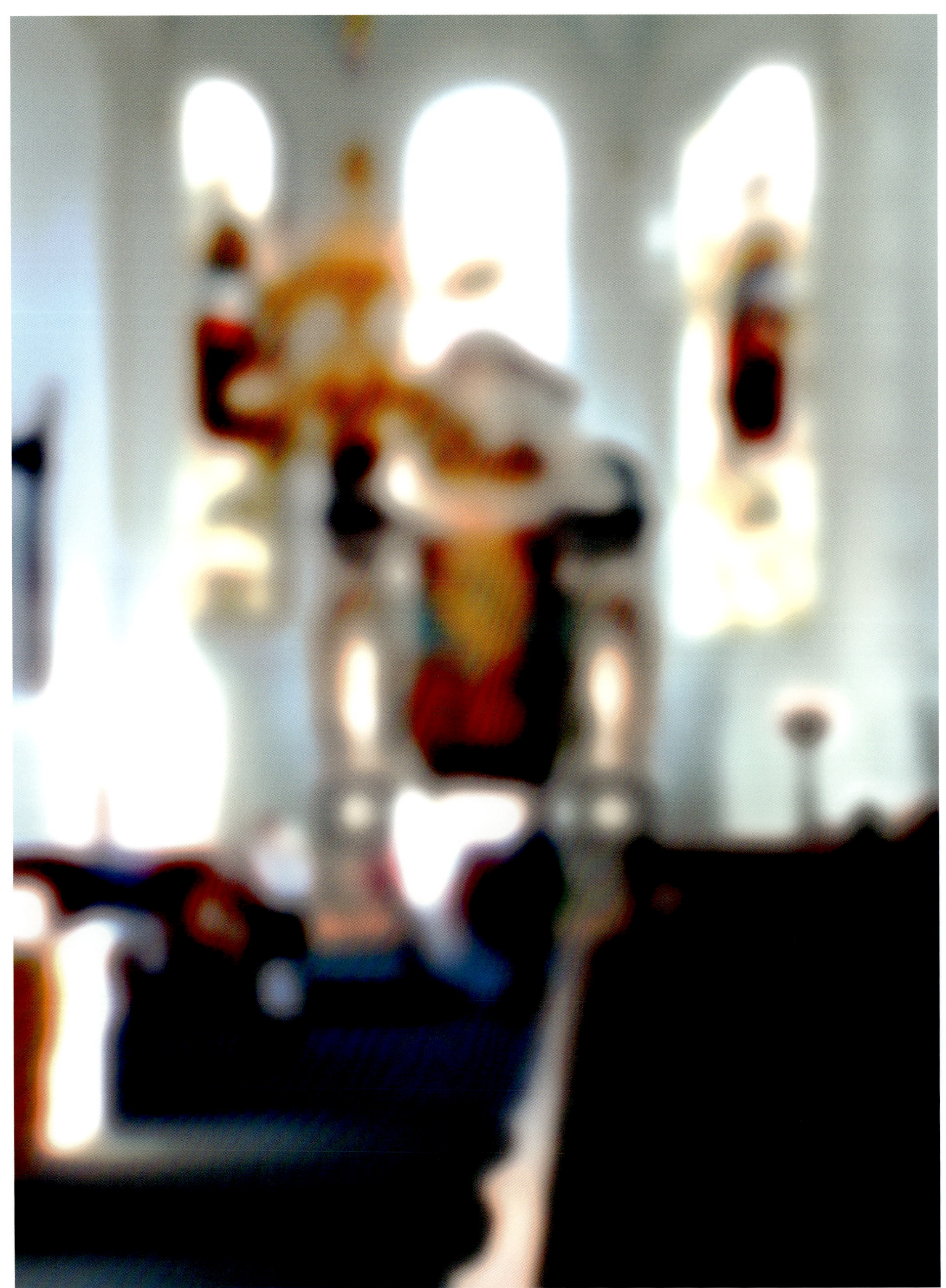

  # 37 100 × 70 cm / 39.38 × 27.56 in.

DIFFERENT PICTURES ÜBERLEGUNGEN ZUR KÜNSTLERISCHEN ARBEIT VON RALF PETERS / REFLECTIONS ON THE ART OF RALF PETERS Raimar Stange

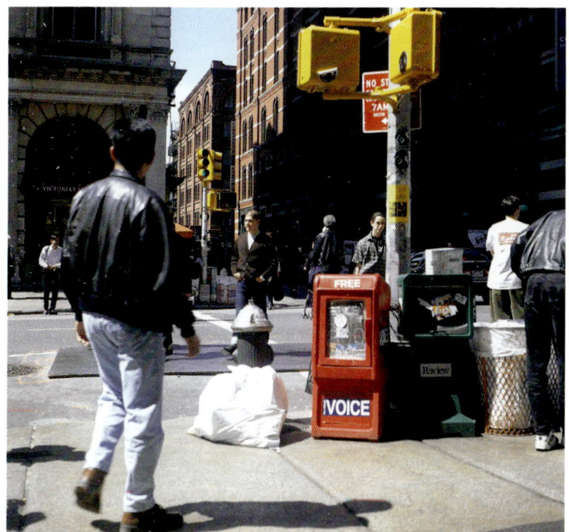

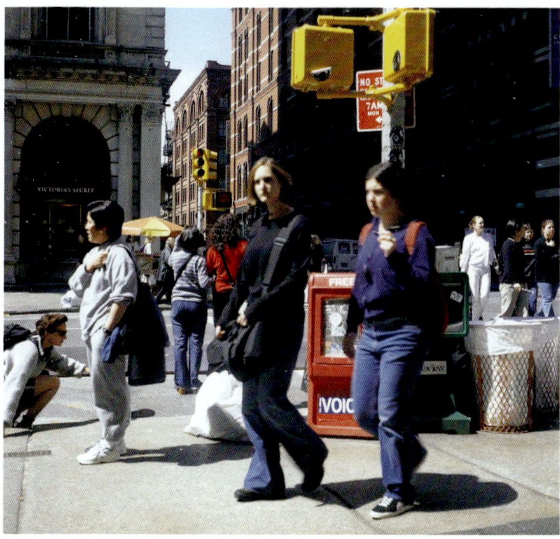

MÄNNER/FRAUEN /
MEN/WOMEN **BROADWAY**
102 × 110 cm / 40.16 × 43.31 in.
1998/99

I Von Männern und Frauen?

Die Bilder von Ralf Peters verraten meist erst auf den zweiten Blick ihr prekäres Moment. Das gilt auch für seine Serie *Männer/Frauen* von 1998/99, in der der Künstler urbane Szenen aus New York City vorstellt (S. 35). Bei einer flüchtigen Wahrnehmung erinnern die Fotos ein wenig an Arbeiten von Beat Streuli, doch eine genauere Betrachtung erkennt schnell, dass es Ralf Peters um gänzlich anderes geht als dem Schweizer Fotokünstler. Also der Reihe nach: Zunächst suchte Peters aus zehn Originalaufnahmen von »Big Apple« zwei Bilder aus. Beide zeigen Passanten auf einem Fußweg, einmal sind sie aus einer eher nahen Position, das andere Mal aus einer größeren Distanz abgelichtet. Diese beiden Bilder wurden nun, und dies ist das Entscheidende, am Computer so »manipuliert«, dass jeweils nur Männer beziehungsweise Frauen auf ihnen zu sehen sind. Als Diptychon werden diese gleichsam »geschlechtergetrennten Stadtporträts« dann unter dem Titel *Broadway* und *9th Avenue* gehängt, links jeweils die »Stadt der Männer«, rechts, der italienische Regisseur Federico Fellini lässt grüßen, die »Stadt der Frauen«.

Sicherlich können diese Arbeiten als eine Art »Gender Studies« interpretiert werden, etwa in der Form von: »Wem gehört die Stadt?«. Ist doch ein männlich dominiertes Stadtbild viel weniger irritierend als eines, in dem nur Frauen auftreten. Auch Fragen nach atmosphärischen Veränderungen, die sich auf solchen »geschlechtergetrennten« Bildern möglicherweise ereignen, liegen nahe.[1] Spannender jedoch erscheint mir hier das Problem der codierten Wahrnehmung von Bildern, das in den *Männern/Frauen* so subtil wie präzise im doppelten Sinne des Wortes »vorgeführt« ist, also demonstriert und demontiert zugleich wird. Es beginnt schon mit der Auswahl der zwei Motive: der Broadway und die 9th Avenue – klar, das ist New York! Oder vielleicht doch nur das Klischee dieser Metropole, das uns sofort die Stadt als »Big Apple« erkennen lässt?! Und es ist das Klischee, das den besagten ersten Blick so einfängt, dass ihm die Bildmanipulationen des Künstlers zunächst gar nicht auffallen. Die Codiertheit unseres Blicks wird aber vor allem auch durch die hier simulierte Geschlechtertrennung problematisiert, denn prompt tritt die

I Of Men and Women?

The disconcerting nature of Ralf Peters's pictures generally only betrays itself at second glance. This is certainly the case for his series *Men/Women* from 1998–99, in which the artist shows scenes from New York City (p. 35). At first glance the photographs are slightly reminiscent of work by Beat Streuli; on closer inspection, however, we quickly realize that Peters has a quite different set of concerns to the Swiss photographer. To briefly explain: for this work, Peters first selected two pictures from ten original photographs of the "Big Apple." Both show passersby on a sidewalk; in one they are photographed at relatively close range, in the other from a greater distance. Both the pictures were then—and this is what is distinctive about them—"manipulated" on a computer so that in each picture we see either only men or only women. These, as it were, "gender-segregated city portraits" were then exhibited under the titles *Broadway* and *9th Avenue,* with in each case the "city of men" on the left-hand side, and—in a nod to the Italian film director Federico Fellini—the "city of women" on the right.

No doubt these works could be interpreted as an instance of visual "gender studies," something along the lines of "who does the city belong to?" And indeed, a male-dominated image of the city is much less jarring than one in which only women appear. Also relevant here is how such "gender-segregated" images can change the atmosphere of the scenes they show.[1] However, what seems more interesting in them to me is the issue of how our perception of images is coded, something *Men/Women* subtly and precisely does in both senses of the German word "vorführen"—to show and to make a fool of—at the same time. It begins with his selection of the two motifs Broadway and Ninth Avenue, clearly showing us that this is New York. Or perhaps what they rather show is just the cliché of the city, enabling us to recognize it at once as the "Big Apple." And the cliché engages our first glance so completely that initially we don't notice the artist has manipulated the image at all. Nevertheless, it is primarily the gender segregation it simulates that forces us to confront the way in which our perception is coded, raising questions

Frage nach so etwas wie »Geschlechtsspezifischem« auf den Plan: Gehen DIE Frauen wirklich anders als DIE Männer durch die Stadt? (Und was ist mit Lesben und Schwulen?) DER Mann bewegt sich wohl eher ziel-strebig und geschäftig, DIE Frauen dagegen gehen schlendernd zum Shopping? Die Antwort von Peters' *Männer/Frauen* ist da eindeutig: Selbstverständlich ist es so einfach nicht, ein Unterschied zwischen Frau-en und Männern ist kaum zu entdecken, selbst die Kleidung ist ähnlich. So sind geschlechterspezifische Rollenzuschreibungen dann auch nicht zuletzt medi-ale Konstruktionen,[2] die genau deshalb von medialen Formulierungen wie den *Männern/Frauen* treffend entlarvt werden können.

II Auf Urlaub

Auch in *Mix* (2000/01) steht die mediale Konstruk-tion von Realität im Mittelpunkt der Kunst von Ralf Peters (S. 45–53). In dieser Werkgruppe arbeitete Peters mit gut 80 Fotos, genauer: mit Fotos von »paradiesischen« Hotelanlagen. Aus diesen suchte er sich acht Hotels aus und mischte sie dann, ein wenig wie ein Hip-Hop-DJ am Mischpult seine Musik sam-pelt, am Computer zu neuen, wahrlich fantastischen Hotelanlagen zusammen. Swimmingpools gehören auf den 17 Bildern genauso zu den wiederkehren-den Elementen wie schmucke Grünanlagen und der ewig blaue Himmel. Zudem tauchen verschiedene architektonische Versatzstücke, etwa eine geschwun-gene Bassinmauer, gleich auf mehreren Bildern auf. Auch verwundert es, dass diese künstlichen Anlagen menschenleer sind, es fehlt sogar jedwede Spur von Benutzung wie herumliegende Handtücher oder Ver-gleichbares. So verraten sich die Bilder dann doch als komponierte Artefakte, auch wenn ihr Sampling so »täuschend echt« gelungen ist, dass die artistischen Eingriffe zumindest auf technisch-formaler Ebene kaum auszumachen sind.

Wie so oft im Werk von Peters geht es dem Künstler in *Mix* nicht um eine »wirklichkeitsgetreue« Wieder-gabe von Vorhandenem, sondern um eine kalku-lierte Ästhetisierung, die dezidiert den Anspruch an einen konventionellen »Realismus« zurückweist und paradoxerweise genau deswegen »realistisch« wird. »Realistisch« nämlich sind diese Bilder in dem Sinne,

of "gender-specificity": do women really walk around the city in a different way to men? (And what about lesbians and gays?) Do men typically move more purposefully and busily, while women stroll around shopping? Peters's *Men/Women* offers a very clear answer: namely, that of course it isn't that simple. There is actually hardly any difference between men and women; even their clothes are similar. The gender-specific allocation of roles is revealed as be-ing not least of all a media construction,[2] and for just this reason can be effectively unmasked as such by media creations like *Men/Women*.

II On Holiday

A concern with the media construction of reality is also to be found in Peters's *Mix* (2000–01, pp. 45–53). In this group of works, the artist worked with about eighty photographs of "idyllic" hotel complexes. From these he selected eight hotels and then mixed them together on a computer to produce genuinely fantastical buildings, rather in the way that a hip-hop DJ samples his music at a mixing desk. Swimming pools feature prominently in the seventeen images, while other recurrent elements include carefully tended lawns and eternally blue skies. A number of architectural clichés also appear in several pictures, such as swimming pools with curved walls. The other surprising thing about these artificial spaces is that they are deserted; they show no trace of human presence, not even such things as discarded towels. In this way, the images reveal themselves as con-structed artifacts, even though their sampling has been executed with such "deceptive realism" that, at the technical and formal level at least, the artist's interventions can barely be made out.

As is so often the case in Peters's work, in *Mix* the artist is not concerned with producing a representa-tion of the world that is "true to reality," but rather with a calculated aestheticization of it, one that firmly rejects the claims of conventional "realism" and thereby becomes, paradoxically enough, "realistic" for just this reason. In other words, these pictures are "realistic" in the sense that they correspond to a real-ity that is increasingly becoming "a reproduction of its own images," as the philosopher Günther Anders

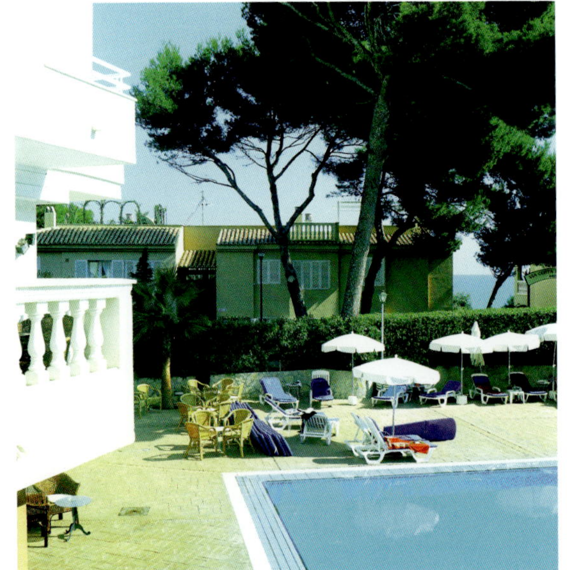

MIX **OLAN** 100 × 100 cm / 39.38 × 39.38 in. 2000/01

dass sie einem Wirklichen entsprechen, das immer mehr »zum Abbild seiner Bilder wird«, wie der Philosoph Günther Anders bereits 1956 in seinem medienkritischen Kapitel »Die Welt als Phantom und Matrize« seines Buches *Die Antiquiertheit des Menschen* prophetisch formulierte.[3] Gerade an der Architektur moderner Ferienanlagen ist dieser Prozess unserer Zivilisation ablesbar. So schrieb der Schriftsteller J. G. Ballard einmal über ein solches »Ressort«, dass es »nordafrikanische Charakteristika« besäße, sich aber auf »ein von jemandem erfundenes Nordafrika« beziehe.[4] Diese Konstruktion nach einer Konstruktion von Exotik, die das Klischee als Vorbild nutzt, wird von den computerbearbeiteten Fotos der *Mix*-Serie noch einmal gedoppelt und damit lustvoll und kritisch zugleich offenbart.[5]

III Vorspiel

»Fotografieren heißt, sich das fotografierte Objekt aneignen«, schrieb Susan Sontag.[6] Kaum ein Foto versucht dies – wenn auch unfreiwillig, wurde es doch zu einem anderen Zweck gemacht – so konkret wie ein Fahndungsfoto. Und hat das Fahndungsfoto seine Schuldigkeit einmal getan, dann wird es nicht weiter verbreitet, es hat somit eine begrenzte Auflage. Also nannte Peters sein frühes, 1990 entstandenes kastenförmiges Objekt mit dem schwarz-weißen Fahndungsfoto der Ex-Terroristen Susanne Albrecht links (!) neben einem roten Teppichbodenstoff, in den vier Sterne geschnitten sind, zu Recht *Edition Albrecht*. 15-mal gibt es diese Edition, die die gerade von mir beschriebene Assemblage hinter schusssicherem Panzerglas präsentiert. Gleichsam eine Parallelaktion, diesmal lässt Robert Musil grüßen, wurde hier vom Künstler konstruiert, eine Parallelaktion, die binäre Realitätskonstruktionen in die ebenfalls widersprüchliche Konstruktion des Kunstwerks überführt. Da fallen vor allem zwei binäre Konstruktionen auf: der Gegensatz zwischen der suggerierten »idyllischen« Privatheit des roten Teppichstoffs und der glasharten Sterilität des Panzerglases, der stellvertretend für die Sicherheitsbemühungen der Staatskräfte steht. Der zweite Dualismus ist der von Bürgerlichkeit und revolutionärem Kampf, also der von Teppich und Susanne Albrecht, ein Gegensatz,

prophetically put it in "Die Welt als Phantom und Matrize" ("The World as Phantom and Matrix"), the chapter on media in his 1956 book *Die Antiquiertheit des Menschen* (The Outdatedness of Human Beings).[3] The architecture of modern holiday complexes seems to be particularly expressive of this tendency within our civilization. The writer J.G. Ballard, for example, once wrote of just such a "resort" that it possessed "North African characteristics," but that these derived from "a North Africa that someone had invented."[4] This construction based on a construction of the exotic, which uses a cliché as a model, is doubled yet again by the computer-generated photographs of the *Mix* series, which thereby playfully and critically reveal it.[5]

III Prologue

Susan Sontag once wrote that "To photograph is to appropriate the thing photographed."[6] Hardly any other type of photograph attempts to do this quite as literally as the police mug shot (albeit not deliberately, since it is taken for quite a different purpose). Once the mug shot has served its purpose it is taken out of circulation: it is therefore always produced in a limited edition. Thus Peters was quite right to give the title *Edition Albrecht* to his early box-shaped object from 1990, which shows a black-and-white mug shot of the former terrorist Susanne Albrecht alongside a piece of red carpeting with four stars cut in it. The edition runs to fifteen copies, and the entire assemblage is exhibited behind bullet-proof glass. In a nod to Robert Musil, the artist here creates a "parallel action" that takes binary constructions of reality and transfers them into the similarly contradictory construction of a work of art. Two binary constructions above all stand out in the work. The first is the opposition between the idyllic private world suggested by the red carpeting, and the hard sterility of the armor-plated glass, which represents the efforts of the state authorities to ensure public security. The second is the dualism between the bourgeois way of life and revolutionary struggle, that is, between the carpet and Susanne Albrecht, an opposition that is emphasized by the "anarcho-Marxist" stars, which gape through the carpet like a wound.

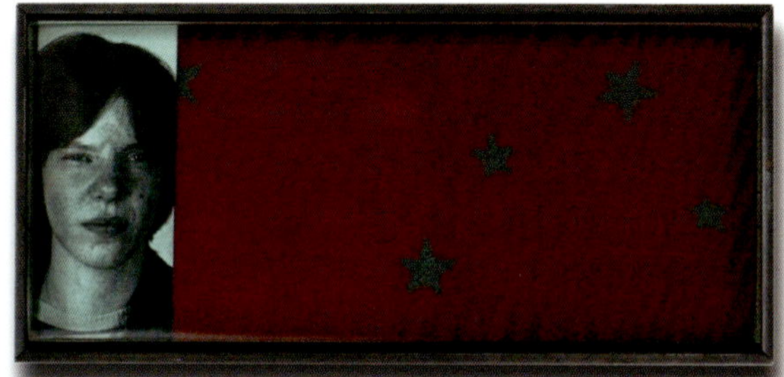

EDITION ALBRECHT
16 × 36 × 6 cm /
6.30 × 14.17 × 2.36 in. 1990

der noch verstärkt wird durch die »anarchistisch-marxistischen« Sterne, die in dem Teppich (wie eine Wunde) klaffen. Exakt dies waren rund um den »deutschen Herbst« Ende der 1970er-Jahre die zentralen Themen, mit denen das Feld »Terrorismus« medial beackert wurde: der starke Staat, die bedrohte Privatheit, der die Gesellschaft verlassende Terrorist und die marxistische Gefahr.

In dieser relativ frühen Arbeit deutet sich in der beschriebenen Parallelität von Kunst und »realem Leben« bereits der oben entwickelte Prozess des »Wirklichen, das zum Abbild seiner Bilder wird«, an. Die mediale Konstruktion von Realität jedenfalls ist schon hier Thema, später wird Peters sie in immer wieder neuen bildlichen Formulierungen in Angriff nehmen.

IV   Different Persons

Wie sich die Gesichter gleichen: Zwölf weibliche Gesichter sind da auf je einer, einem Passfoto ähnlichen Aufnahme zu sehen (S. 127–138). Alle Frauen haben blonde kurze Haare, blaue Augen, volle Lippen und eine vergleichbare Kopfform – sie sehen sich also sehr ähnlich. Handelt sich hier aber um ein Gesicht, das dann am Computer leicht bearbeitet wurde – solche Arbeiten von Thomas Ruff zum Beispiel haben wir alle in unserem imaginären Museum abgespeichert –, oder tatsächlich, wie der Titel *Different Persons* nahelegt, um zwölf verschiedene Frauen? Letzteres ist der Fall: Für die Fotoserie aus dem Jahr 2006 wurden Originalaufnahmen von zwölf Frauen verwendet, die der Künstler mithilfe von Modellagenturen gefunden oder die er zufällig auf der Straße gesehen und fotografiert hatte.

So spielt Peters in *Different Persons* einerseits mit unseren Rezeptionserwartungen, denn, wie eben angedeutet, das Manipulieren von Bildern am Computer ist längst zu einer Konvention geworden, die heute beinahe wahrscheinlicher erscheint als die Übernahme einer sogenannten »Originalaufnahme«. Andererseits stellt der Künstler die Frage nach der Qualität des Einzelbildes: Wie »individuell« ist es wirklich, was sagt seine Visualität über das Dargestellte aus? Wohlgemerkt: Diesmal stellt sich diese Frage nicht nur hinsichtlich des medialen Konstruktes »Bild« oder »Foto«, sondern direkt hinsichtlich des

It is precisely these that formed the central themes of the "German Autumn" of the late nineteen-seventies, and characterized the contemporary media treatment of "terrorism": the strong state, the threat to the private domestic world, the terrorist who had turned against society, and the danger of Marxism.

In this relatively early work, one can interpret this parallelism of art and "real life" as an instance of the process described above of "reality becoming a reproduction of its images." It is certainly already concerned with the media construction of reality, and Peters would later repeatedly return to it in new visual formulations.

IV   Different Persons

The faces are remarkably similar: a series of passport-like photographs show twelve female faces (p. 127–138). All the women have short blonde hair, blue eyes, full lips, and similarly shaped heads—they look, in fact, very much like one another. Do the images show a single face that has been slightly altered on a computer, like those in the works by Thomas Ruff that we now have stored in our collective imagination? Or do they really show twelve different women, as the title *Different Persons* suggests? It seems the latter is the case: for this photoseries from 2006, original photographs of twelve women were used, taken by the artist, who found them either through modeling agencies or happened to catch sight of them on the street.

Thus Peters's *Different Persons* plays with ideas about what we expect to see, for, as has been suggested, the manipulation of images on computers has long since become a convention that an artist today would almost be more likely to use than so-called "original photographs." At the same time, the artist poses questions about the value we ascribe to the unique image: how "unique" is it really, what does its visual quality say about what it represents? We should bear in mind, however, that this time the question arises not only in relation to media constructions such as "image" or "photograph," but directly in relation to reality, that is, in relation to the image of the woman in each photograph. We needn't believe in physiognomy, which claims that the character of a person

Wirklichen, nämlich hinsichtlich des Erscheinungsbildes der abgelichteten Frau. Ohne gleich ein Anhänger der Physiognomik zu sein, der von der äußeren Erscheinung eines Menschen auf dessen Charakter schließt, so glauben wir doch alle mehr oder weniger an die Ausdrucksfähigkeit des Körpers und sind daran gewöhnt, dem Menschen ein einzigartiges Gesicht zuzuschreiben,[7] eben deswegen erscheint es ja auf dem Passfoto. Beide Annahmen irritiert die Arbeit *Different Persons* nachhaltig und erschüttert damit unser Vertrauen in die »Wahrhaftigkeit« von Visualität überhaupt. Genau deshalb bezeichnet sich Ralf Peters auch zu Recht als »Konzeptkünstler«[8] und weniger als Fotograf.

Anmerkungen

1 Eine solche Interpretationen schlägt etwa Justin Hoffmann vor; »Sie hier, er dort«, in: *Süddeutsche Zeitung*, 6.8.1998.

2 In diesem Zusammenhang ist immer noch lesenswert: Camille Paglia, *Vamps & Tramps*, New York 1994.

3 Günther Anders, *Die Antiquiertheit des Menschen*, Bd. 1, München 1988, S. 179.

4 J. G. Ballard, *Weißes Feuer*, München 1998, S. 36.

5 Lesenswert ist auch Daniel Spankes Analyse von *Mix*, in: *Plastische Fotografie – Ralf Peters*, Ausst.-Kat. Kunsthalle Wilhelmshaven, Mannheim 2004, S. 13 ff.

6 Susan Sontag, *Über Fotografie*, Frankfurt am Main 1980, S. 10.

7 Doppelgänger, Zwillinge oder gar Drillinge sind daher stets ein Kuriosum. In einigen archaischen Gesellschaften werden Zwillinge sogar direkt nach der Geburt getötet.

8 Ralf Peters, in: *Kopf an Kopf*, Ausst.-Kat. Kunsthalle Tübingen, Heidelberg 2007, S. 154.

can be inferred from their physical appearance, to more or less have faith in the expressive potential of the body; and all of us are in the habit of imagining that each individual human being has a face that is unique[7] (precisely the assumption behind passport photographs). *Different Persons* profoundly upsets both these assumptions, shaking our confidence in the "truthfulness" of the visual image itself. It is for just this reason that Peters rightly describes himself as more a "conceptual artist"[8] than a photographer.

Notes

1 Justin Hoffmann offers just such an interpretation in his article "Sie hier, er dort," *Süddeutsche Zeitung*, August 6, 1998.

2 Camille Paglia's *Vamps & Tramps* (New York, 1994) is still worth reading in relation to this.

3 Günther Anders, *Die Antiquiertheit des Menschen*, vol. 1 (Munich, 1988), p. 179.

4 J.G. Ballard, *Cocaine Nights* (London, 1996).

5 It is worth reading Daniel Spanke's analysis of *Mix* in *Plastische Fotographie—Ralf Peters*, exh. cat. Kunsthalle Wilhelmshaven (Mannheim, 2004), pp. 13ff.

6 Susan Sontag, *On Photography* (New York, 1977), p. 4.

7 As a result, doppelgängers, twins or triplets have always been objects of curiosity. In some archaic societies twins were even killed immediately after they were born.

8 Ralf Peters in *Kopf an Kopf*, exh. cat. Kunsthalle Tübingen (Heidelberg, 2007), p. 154.

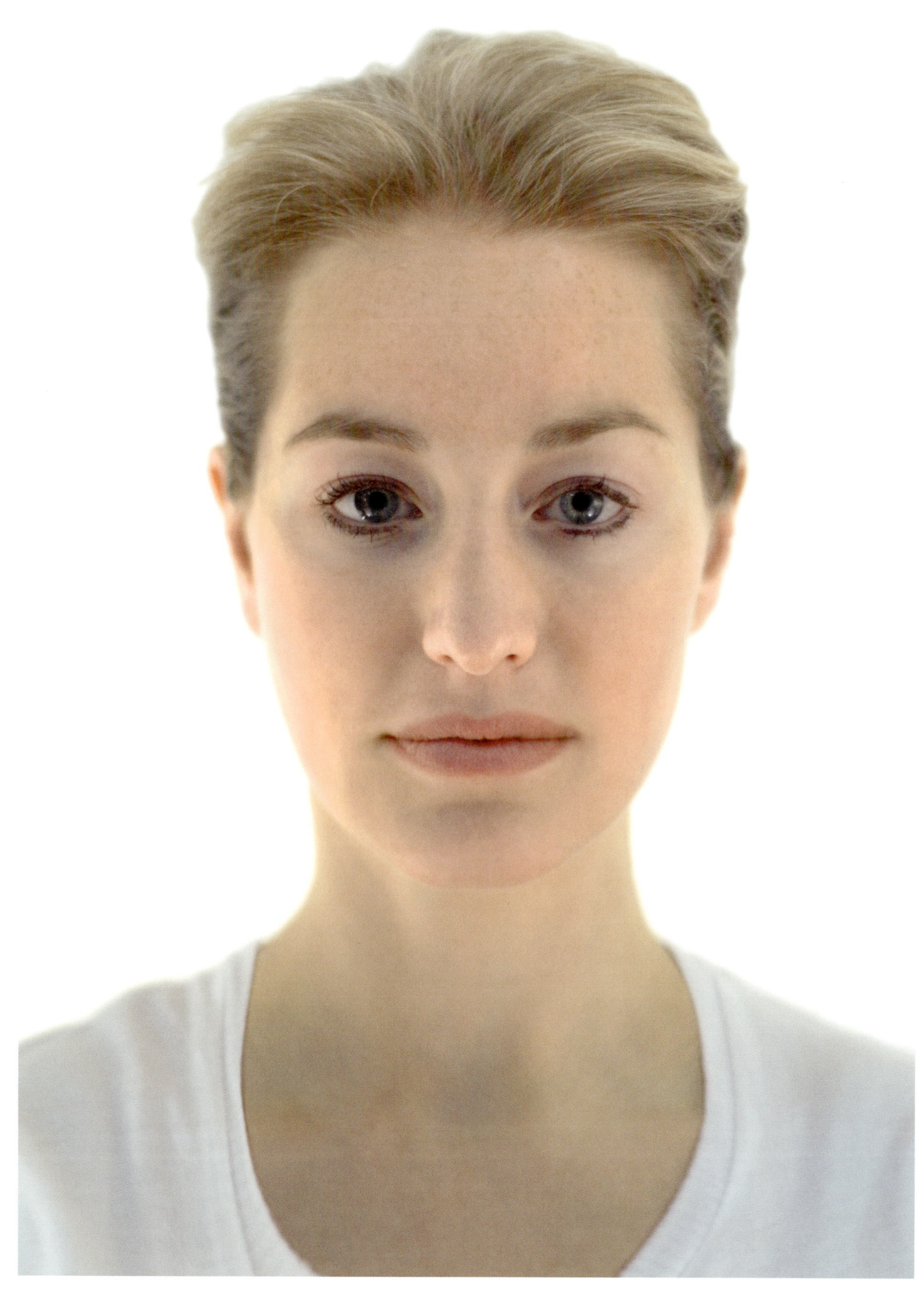

SUSANNE 76 × 52 cm / 29.92 × 20.47 in.

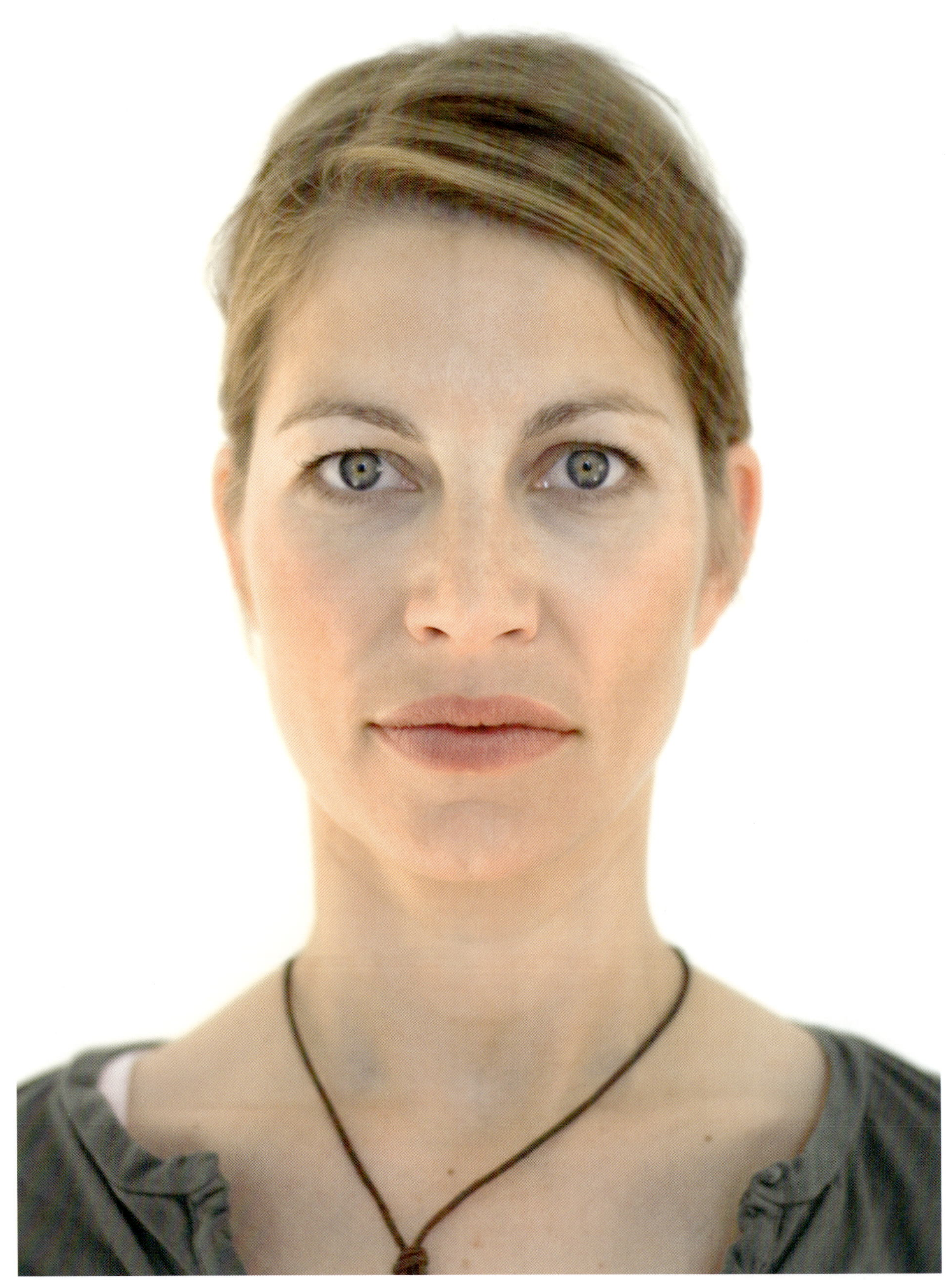

  TINA 76 × 52 cm / 29.92 × 20.47 in.

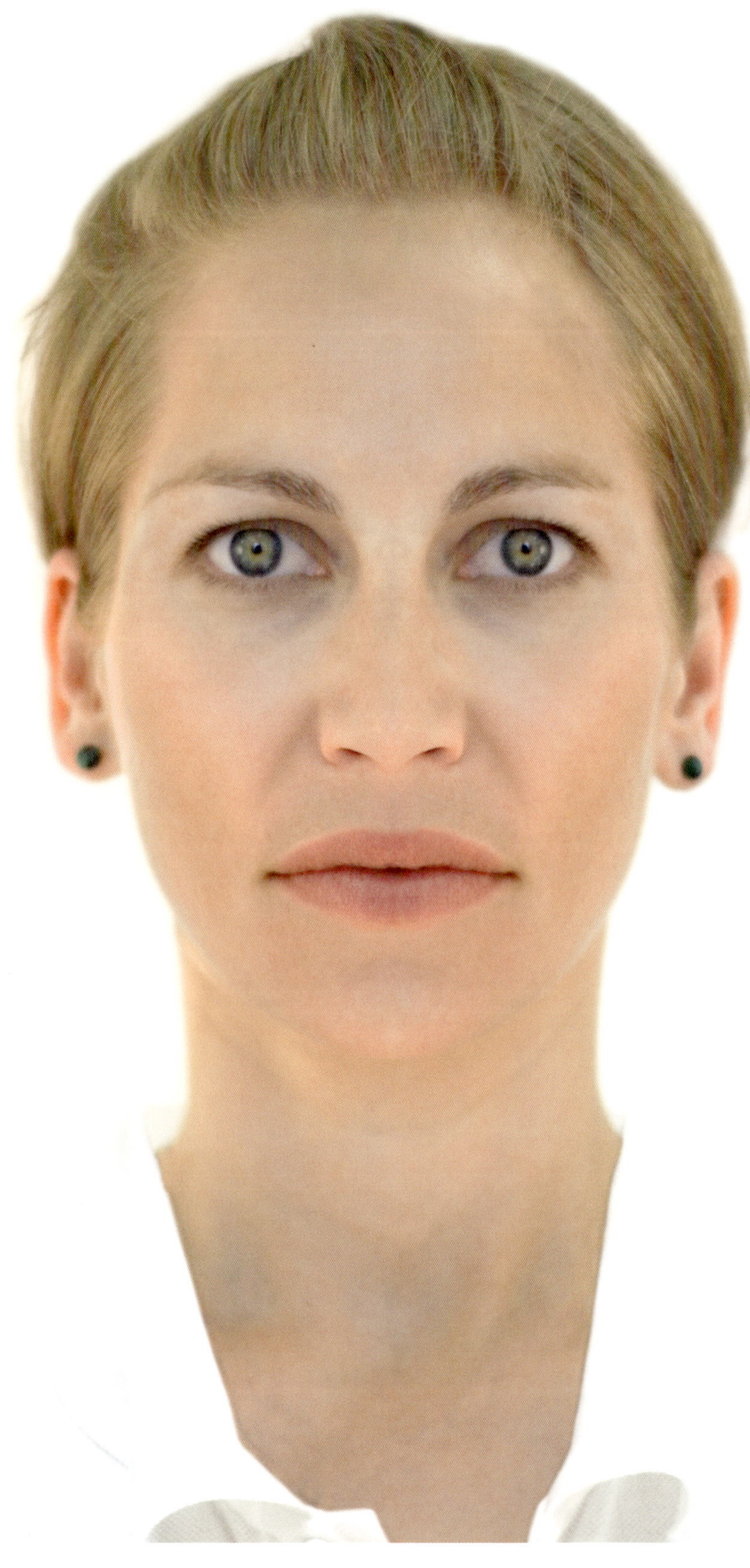

ANETTE 76 × 52 cm / 29.92 × 20.47 in.

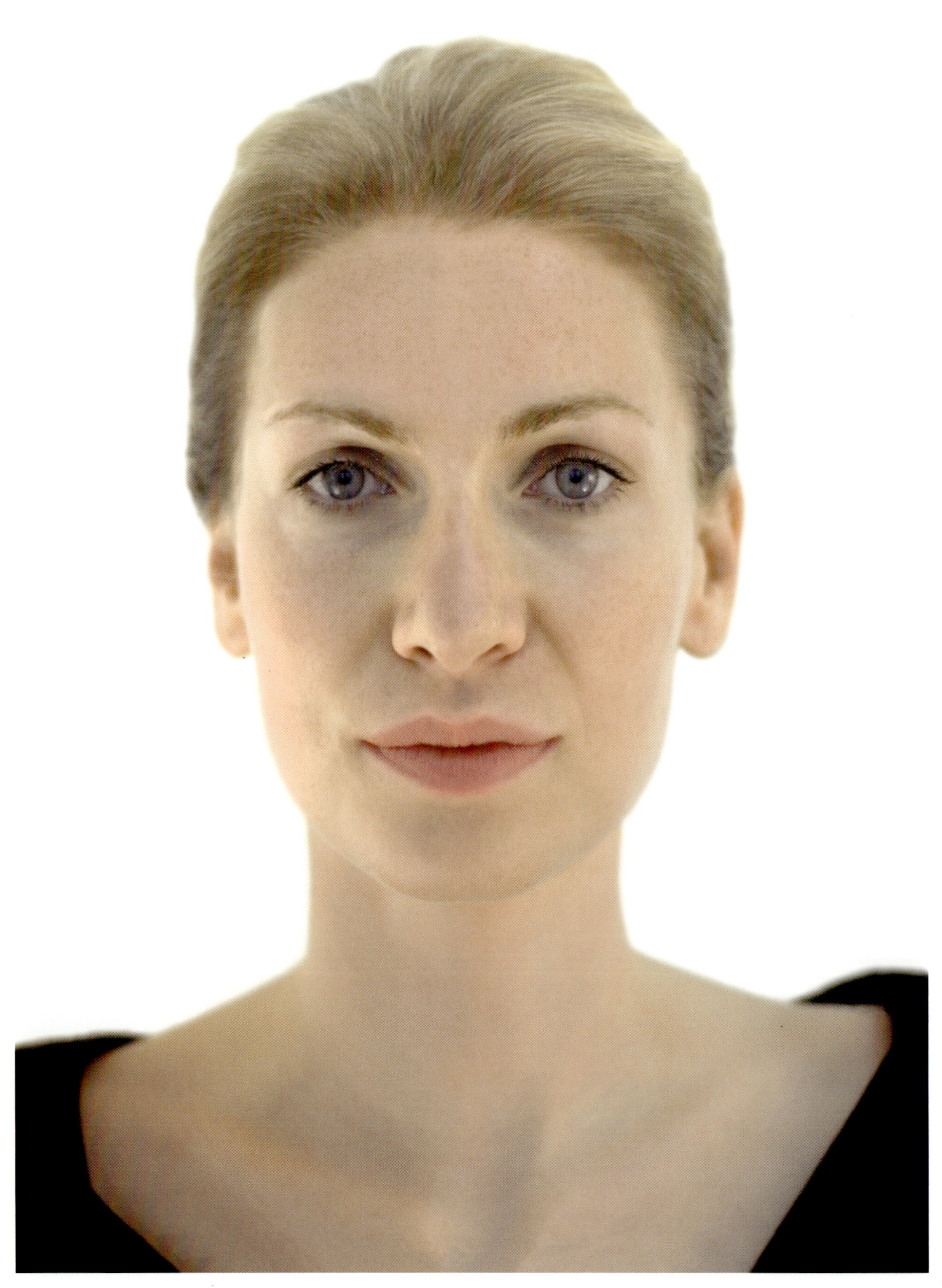

  STEFFI 76 × 52 cm / 29.92 × 20.47 in.

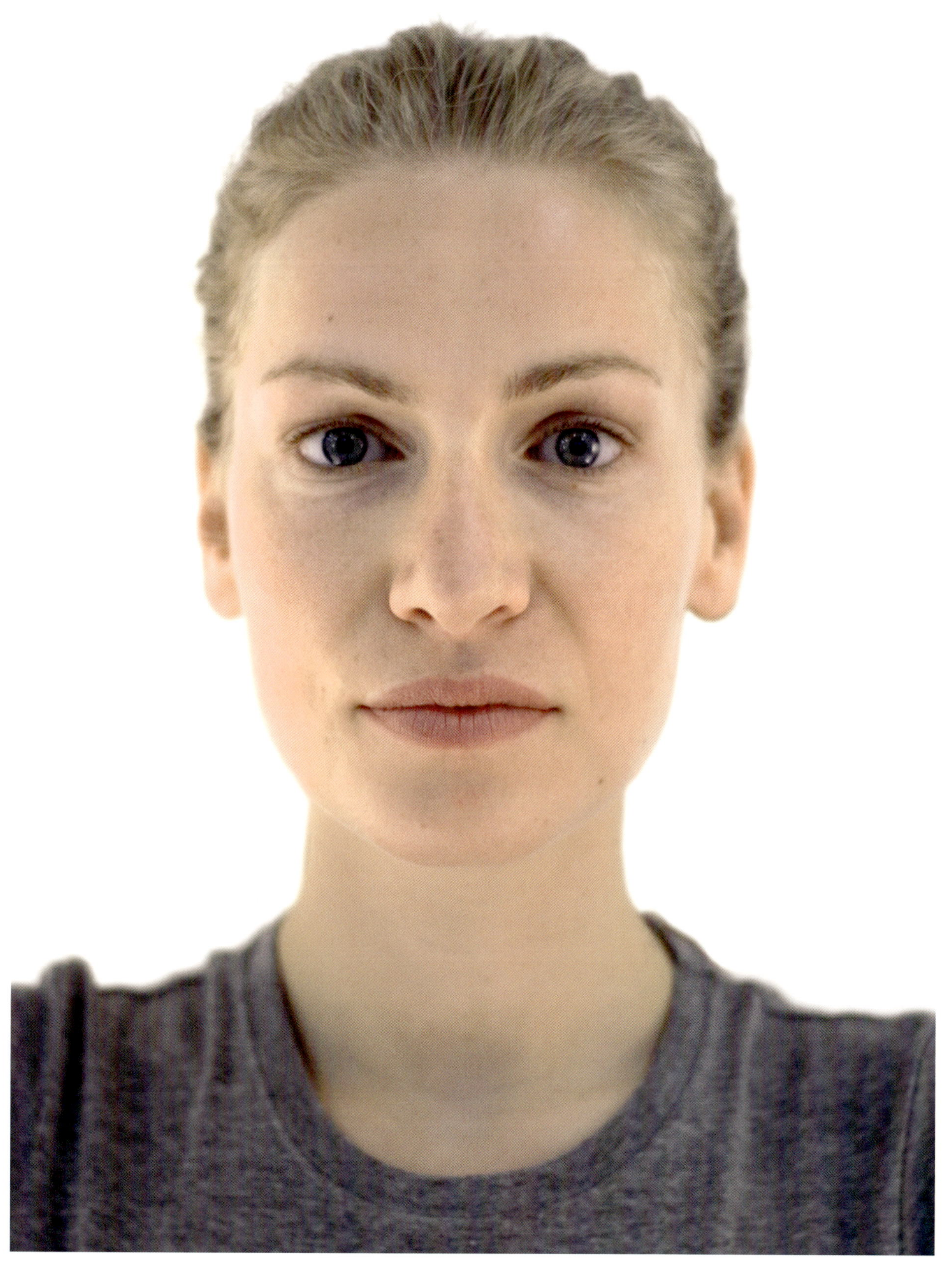

KONSTANZE 76 × 52 cm / 29.92 × 20.47 in.

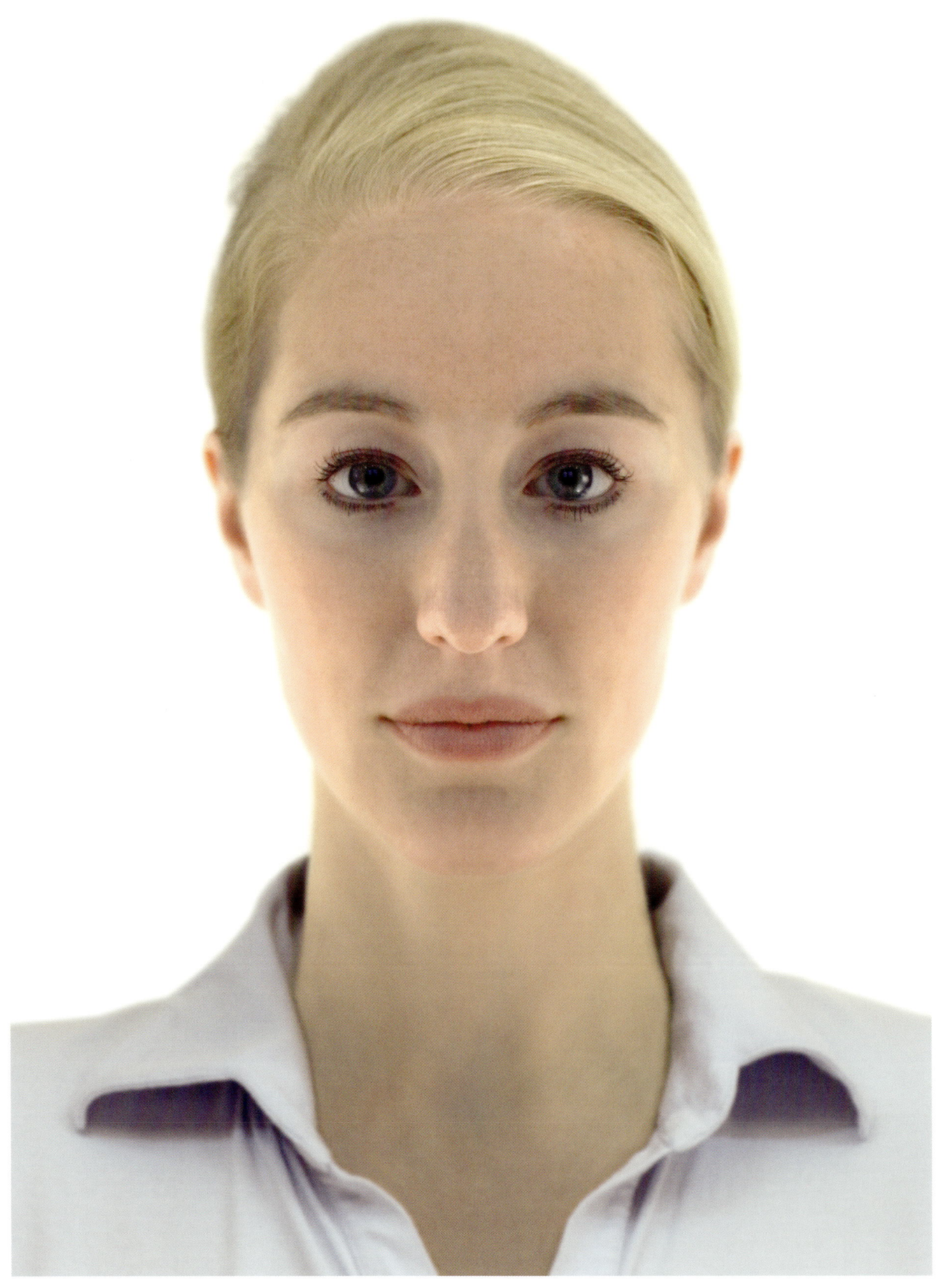

  CAROLL 76 × 52 cm / 29.92 × 20.47 in.

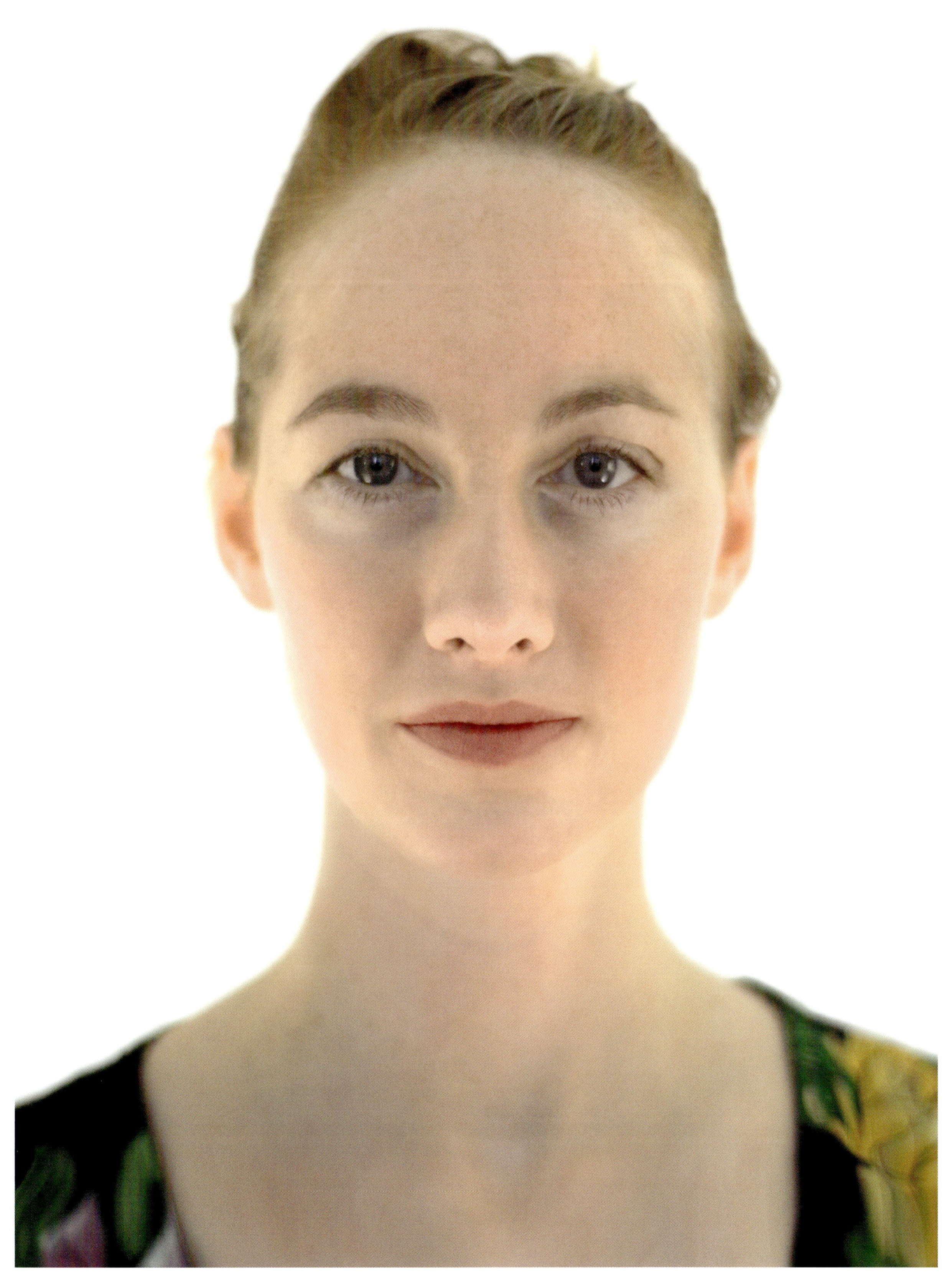

MARION 76 × 52 cm / 29.92 × 20.47 in.

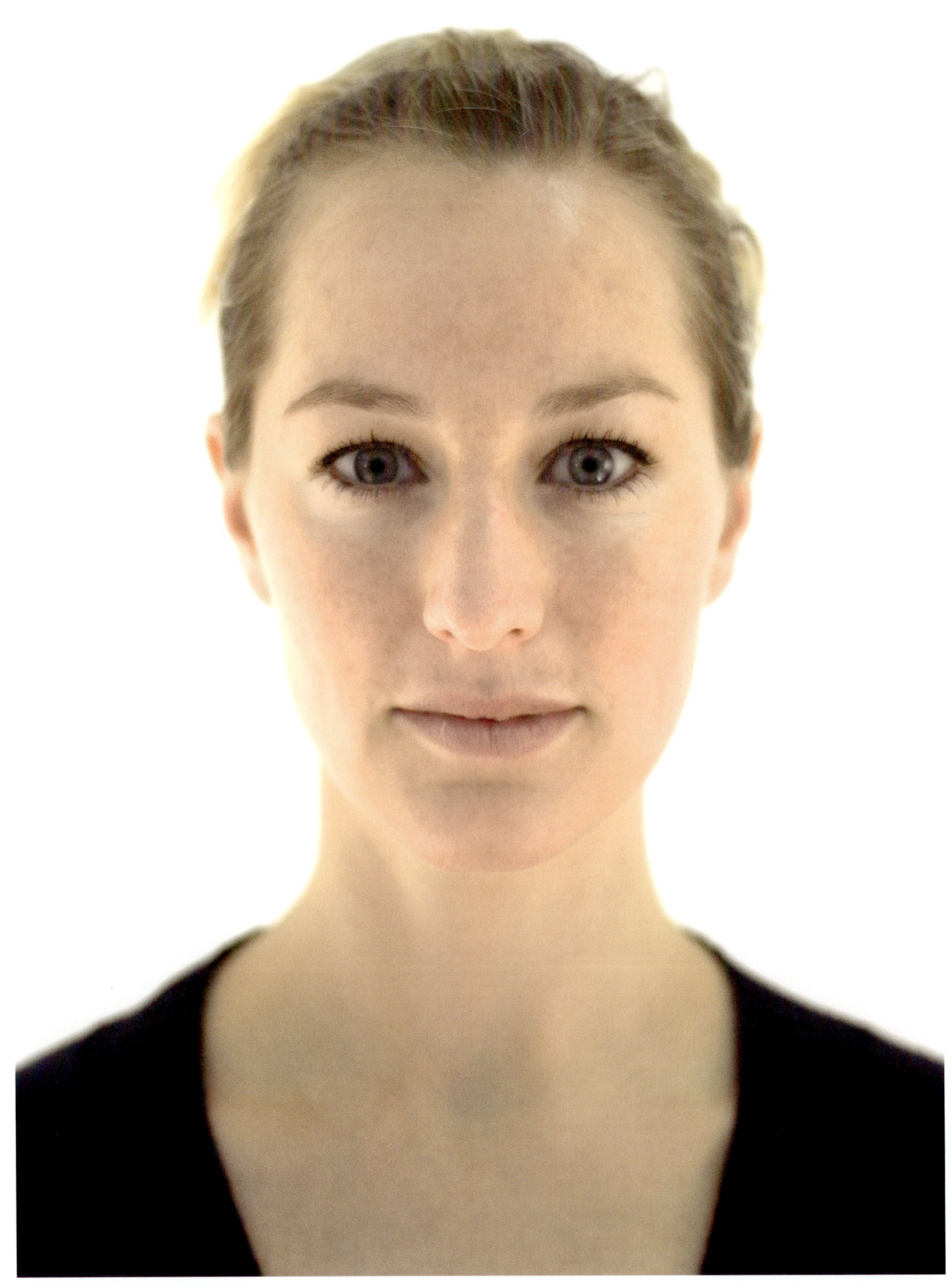

134 **INSA** 76 × 52 cm / 29.92 × 20.47 in.

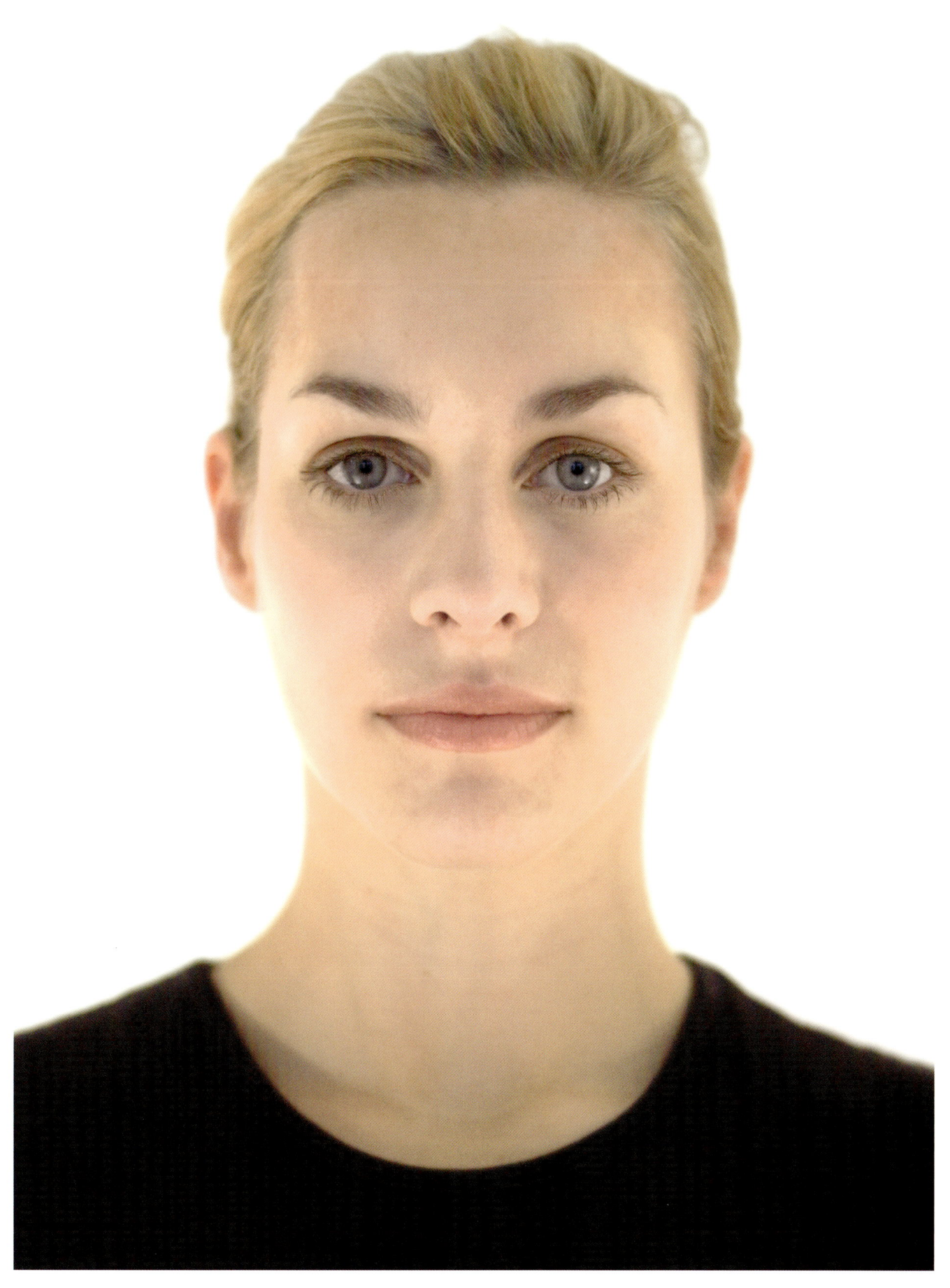

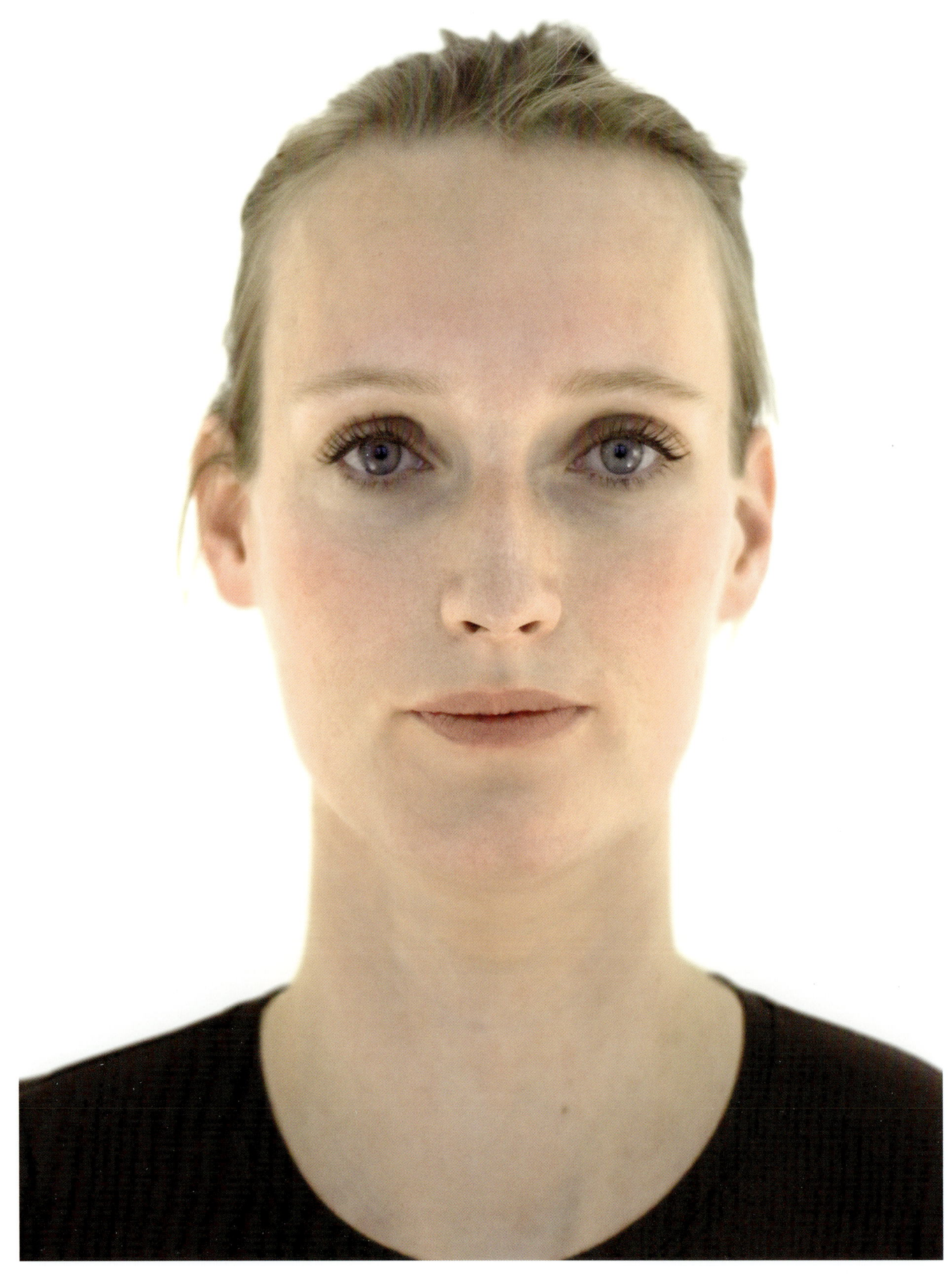

SASKIA 76 × 52 cm / 29.92 × 20.47 in.

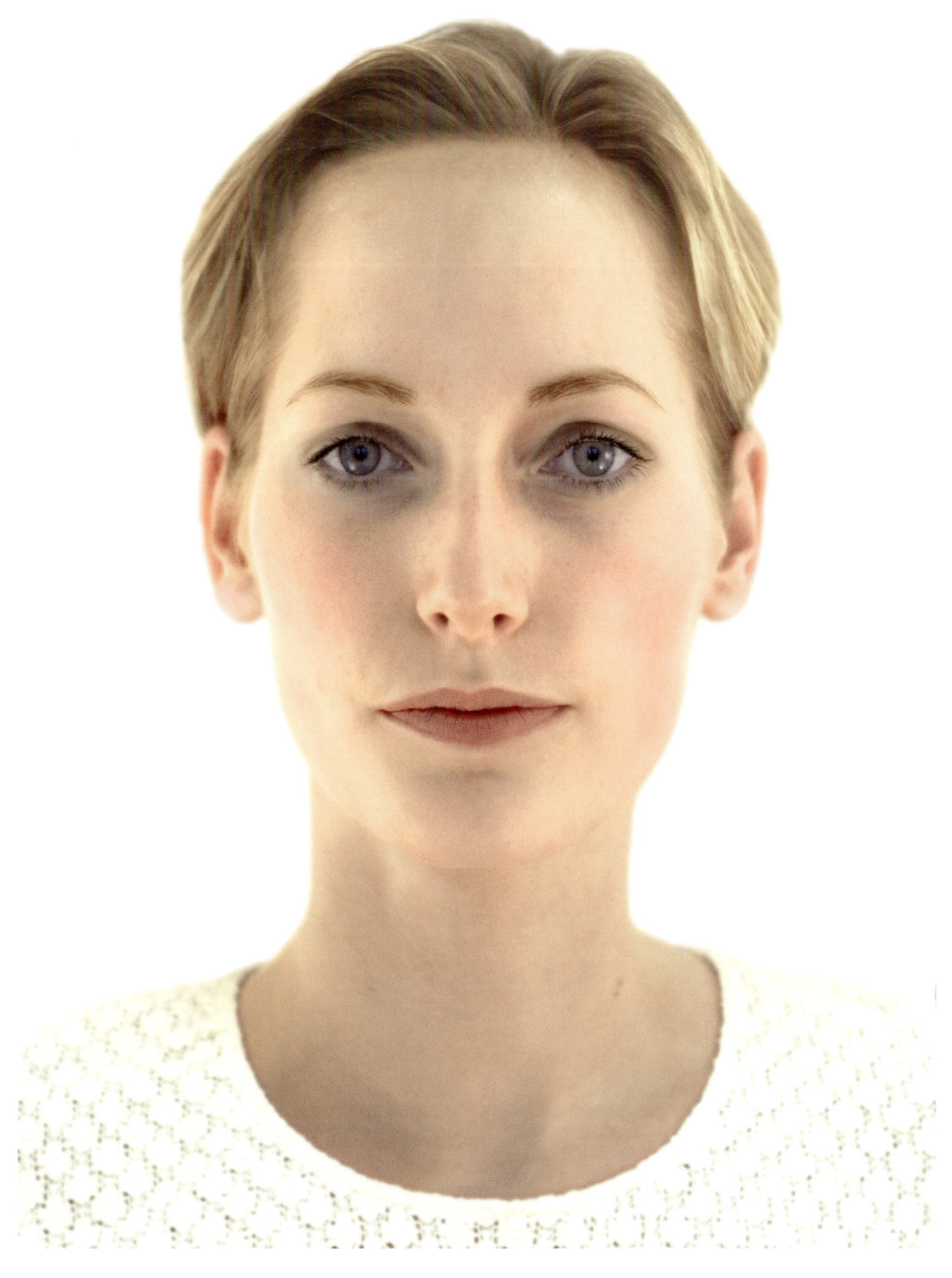

SABINE 76 × 52 cm / 29.92 × 20.47 in.

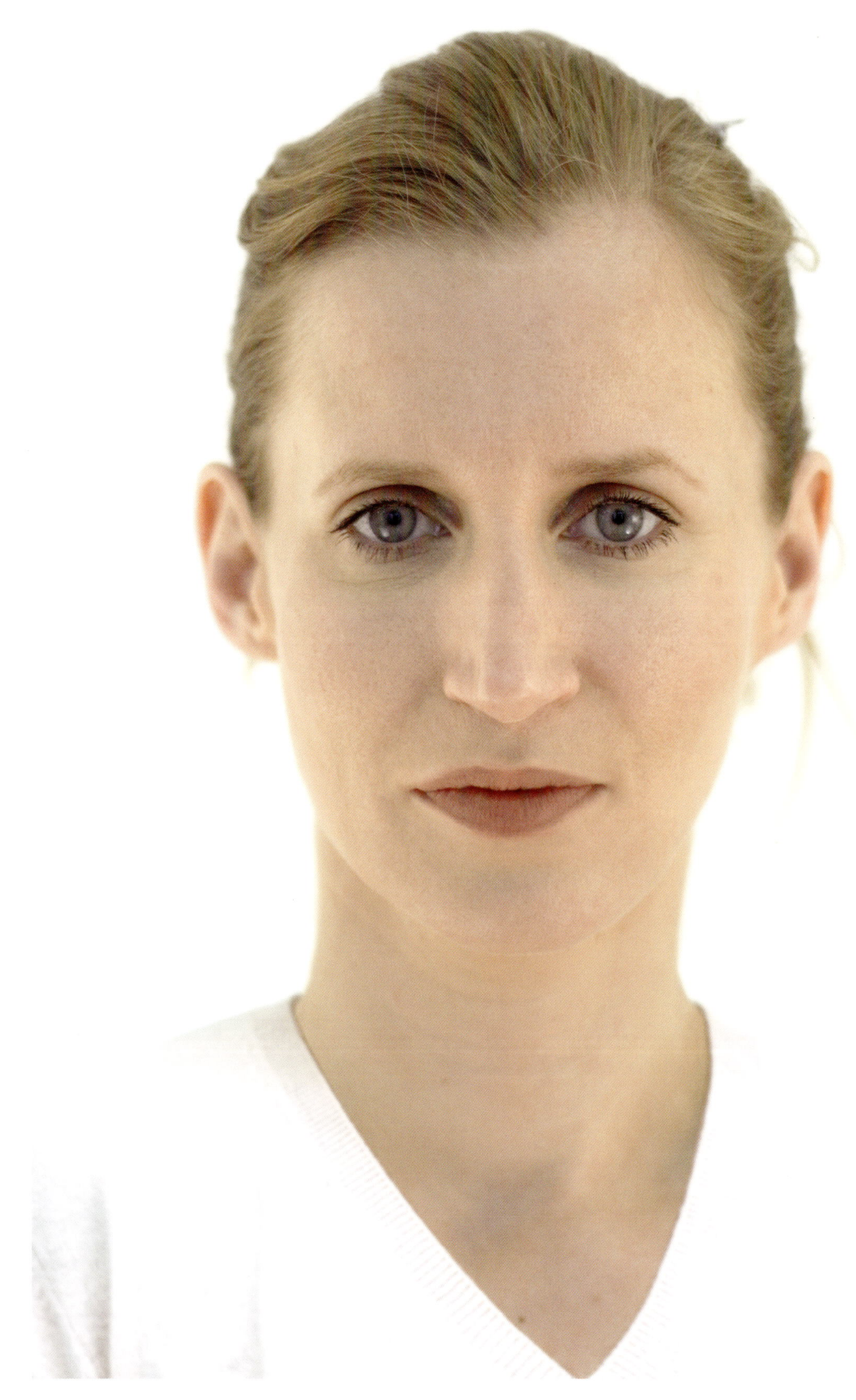

SYBILLE 76 × 52 cm / 29.92 × 20.47 in.

24 HOURS 2008

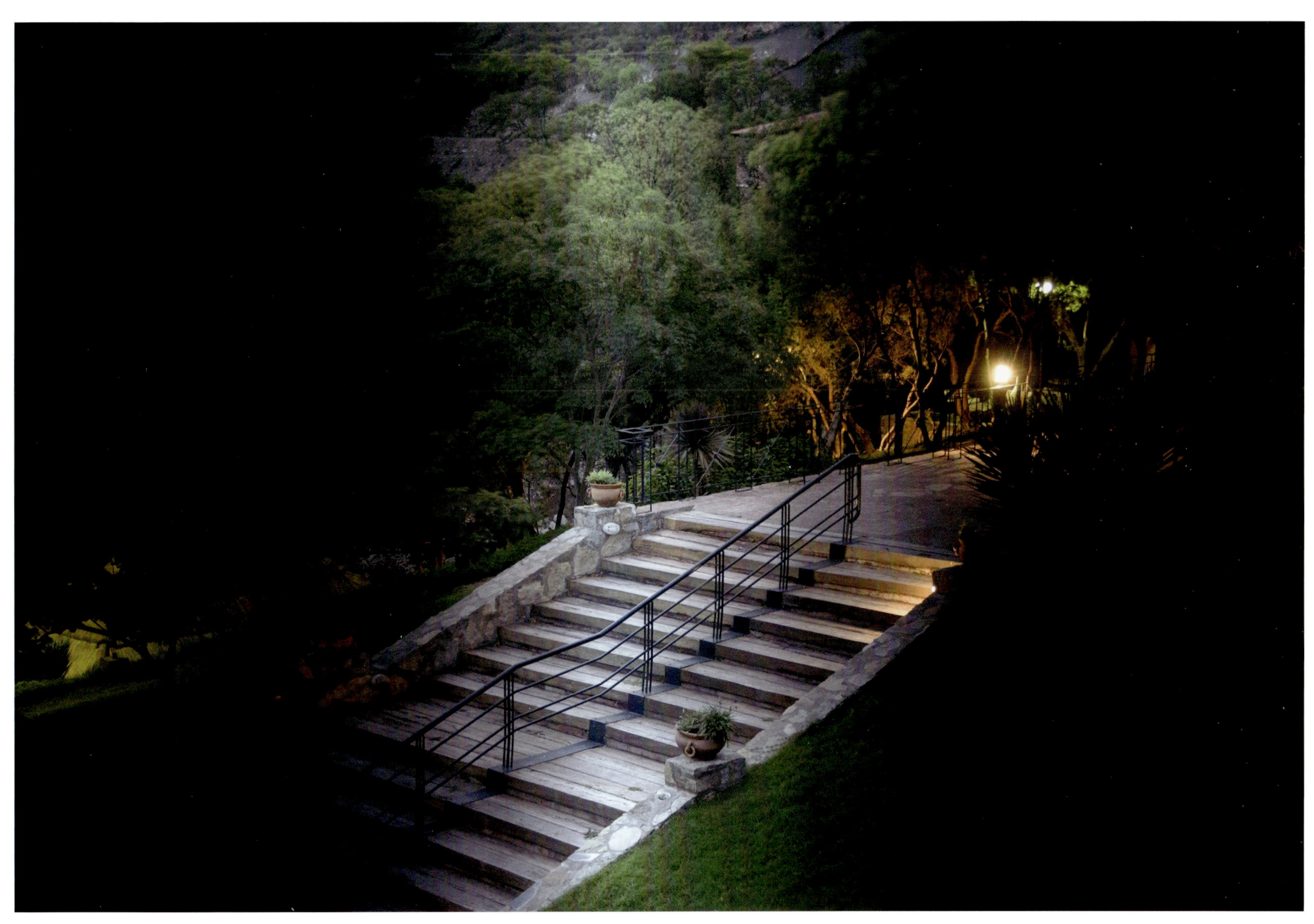

TREPPE / STAIRS 70 × 100 cm / 27.56 × 39.38 in.

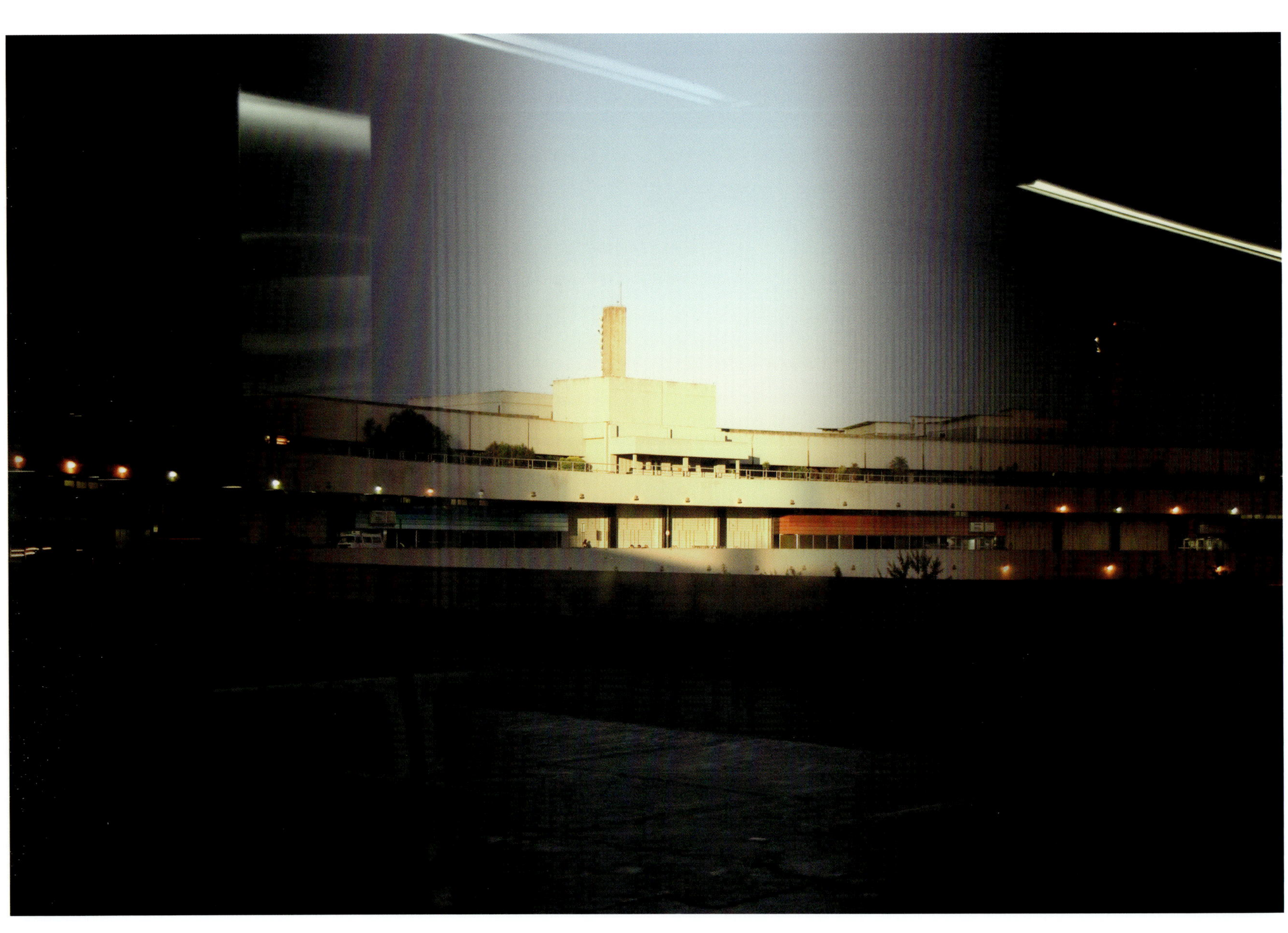

142 **FLUGHAFEN / AIRPORT** 70 × 100 cm / 27.56 × 39.38 in.

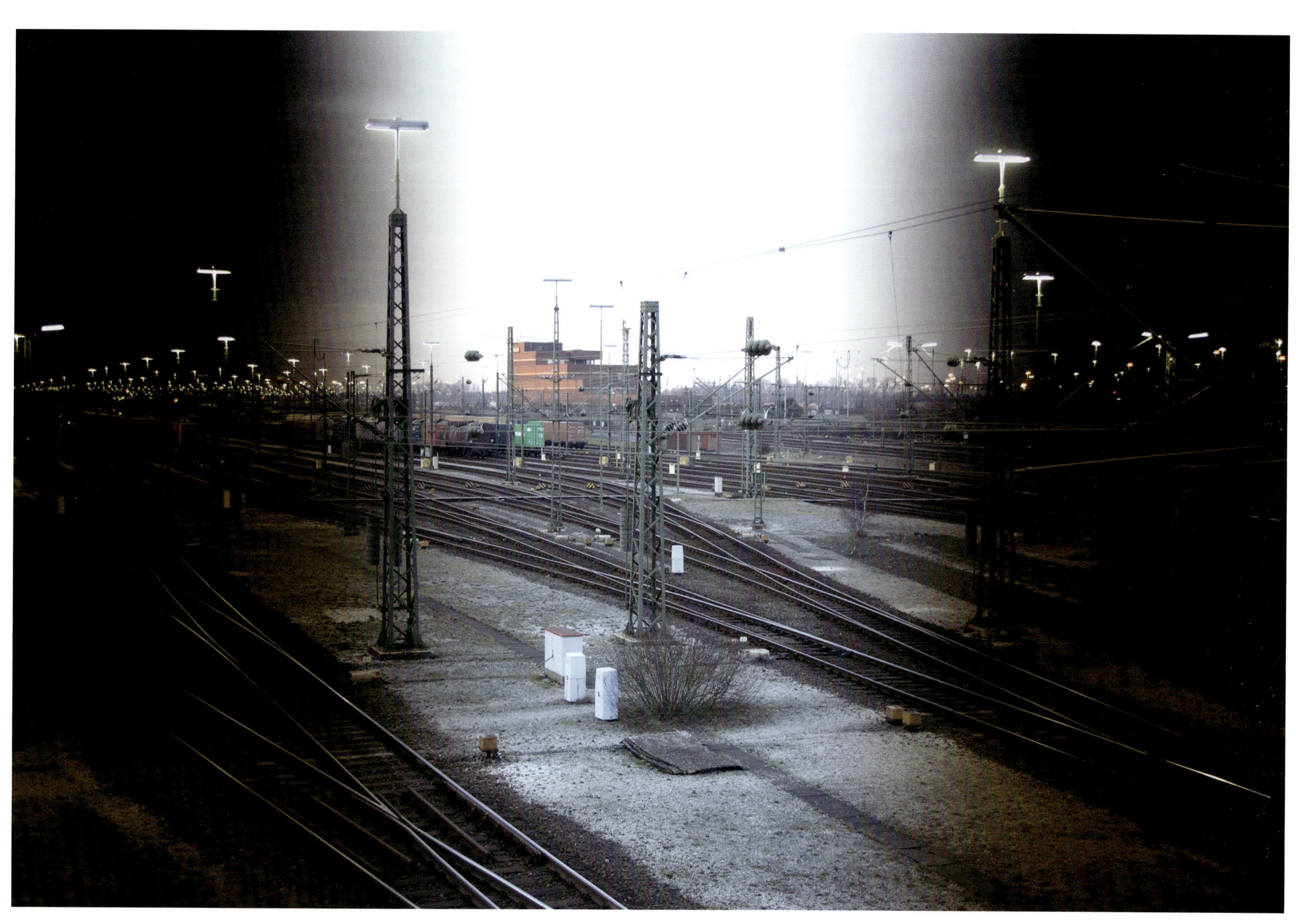

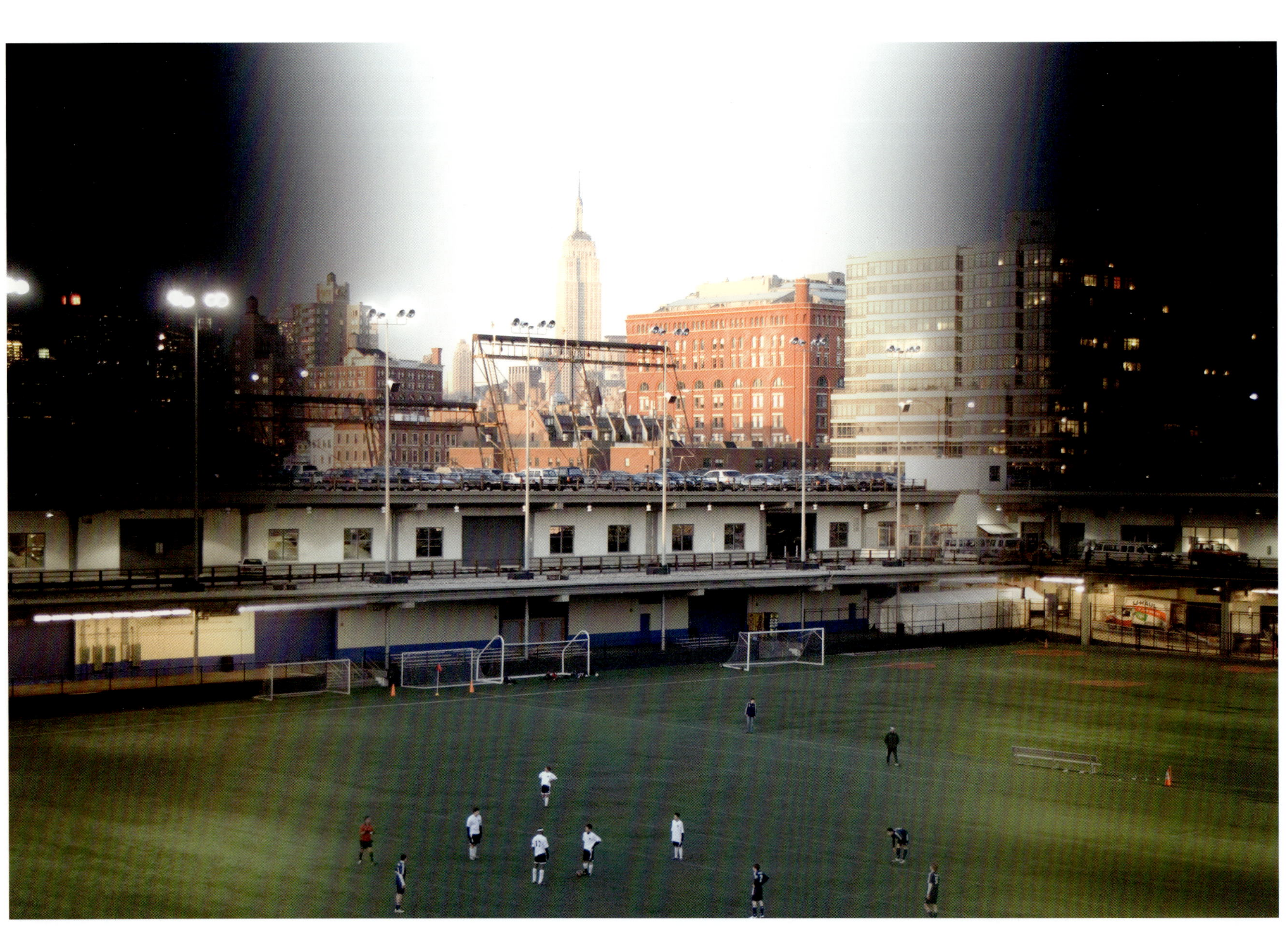

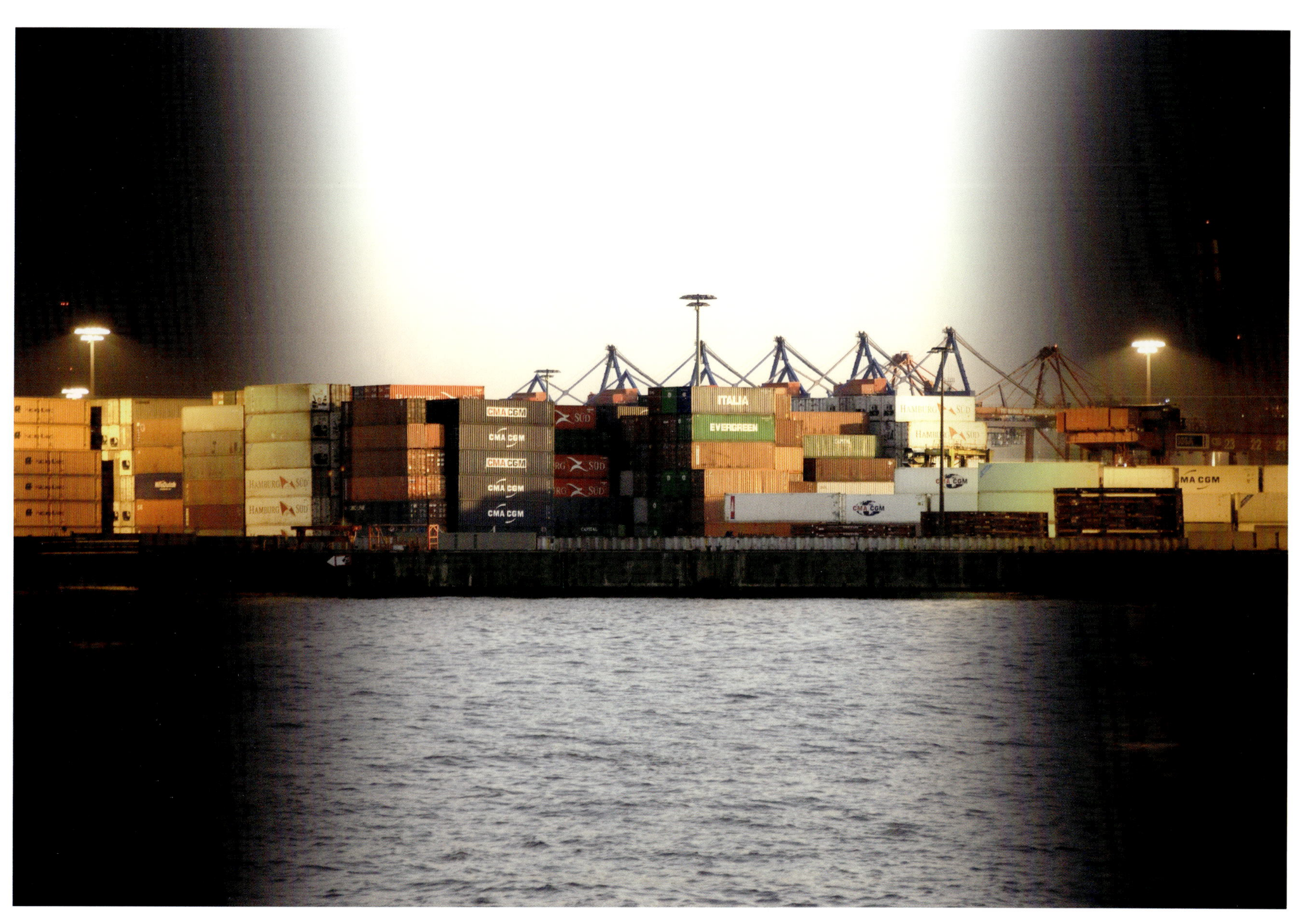

CMA CGM
CMA CGM
CMA CGM
CMA CGM
CMA CGM
SÜD
SÜD
SÜD
HAMBURG SÜD
HAMBURG SÜD
ITALIA
EVERGREEN
HAMBURG SÜD
HAMBURG SÜD
CMA CGM
CMA CGM

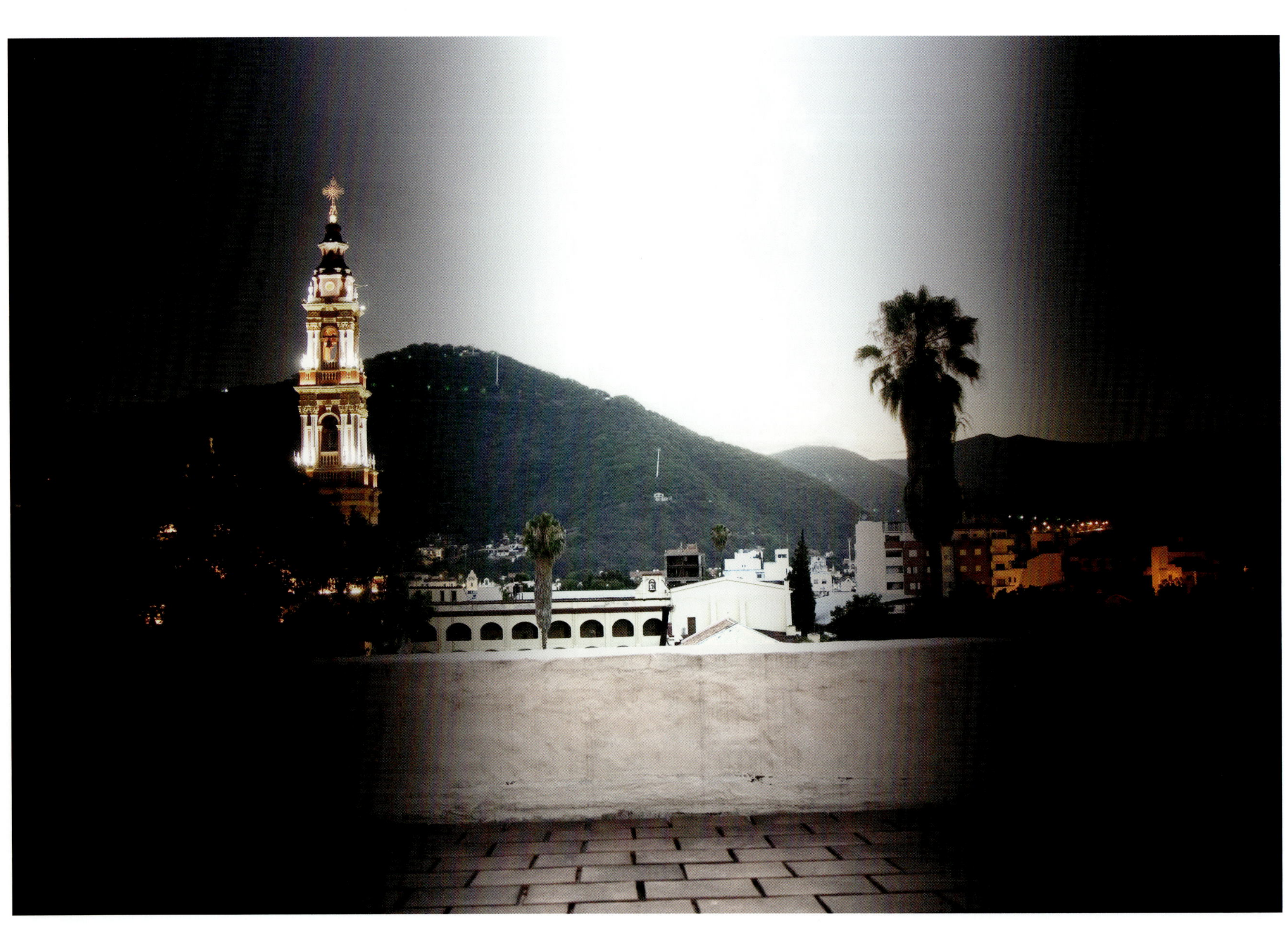

 KIRCHTURM / CHURCH TOWER 70 × 100 cm / 27.56 × 39.38 in.

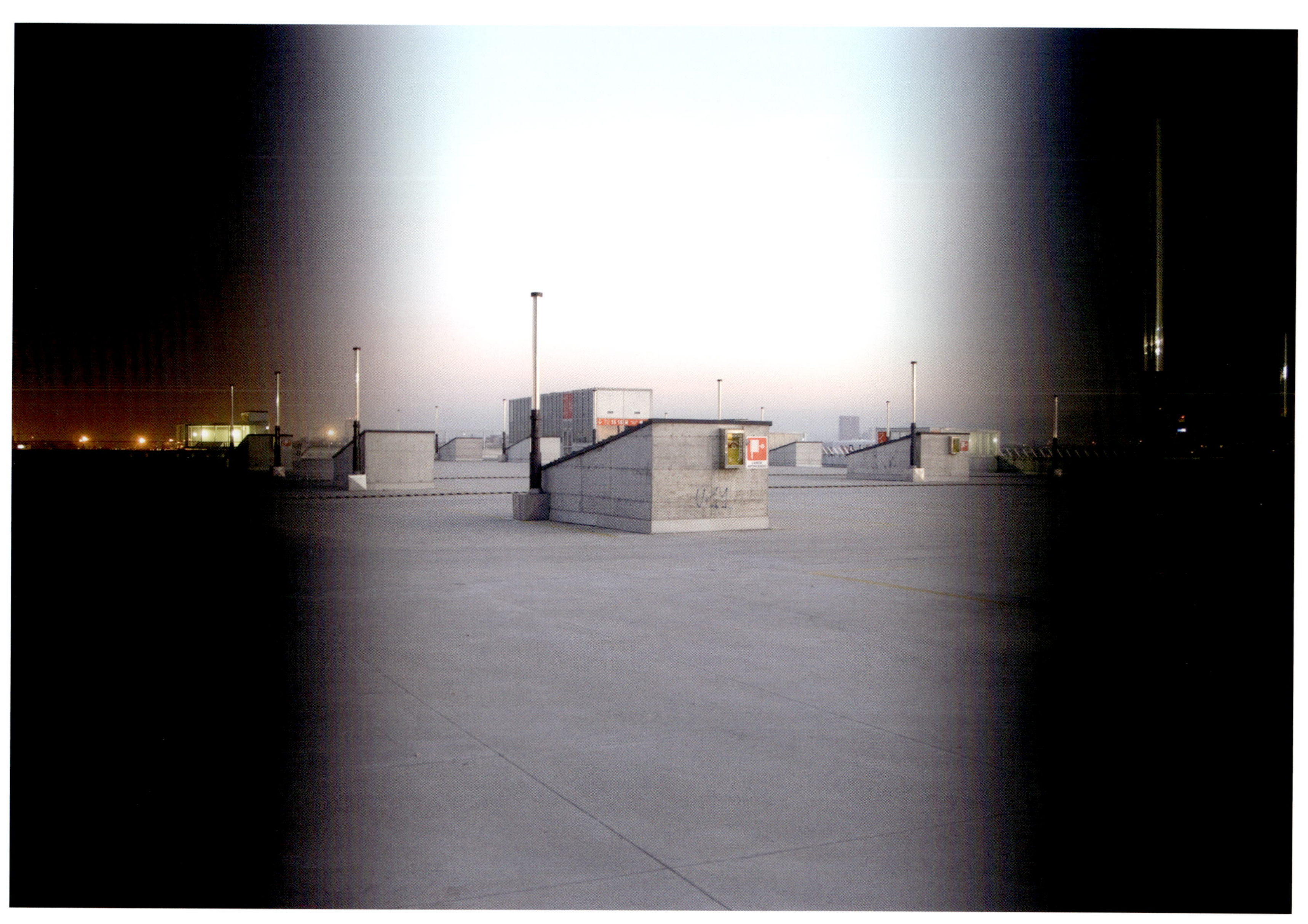

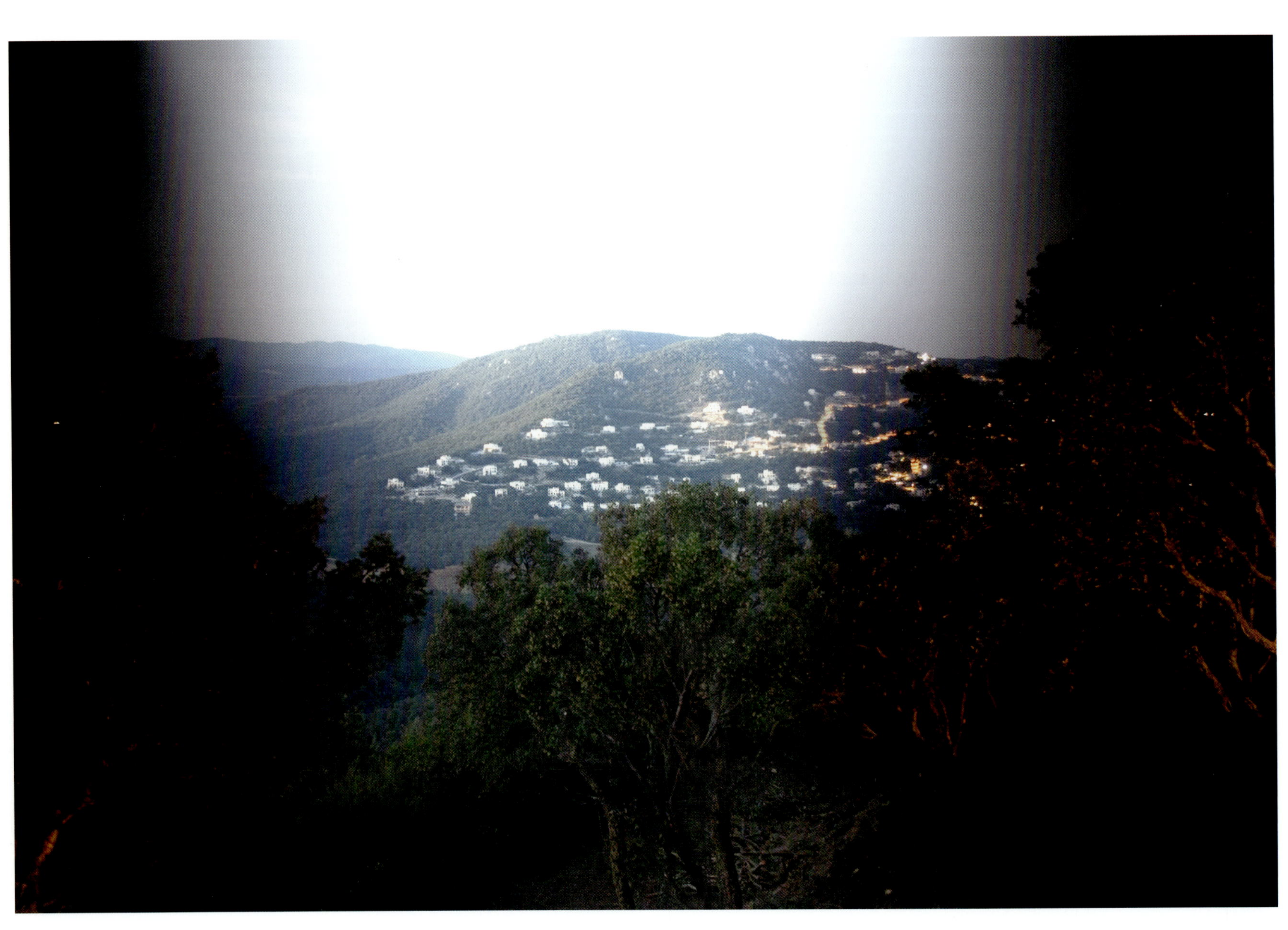

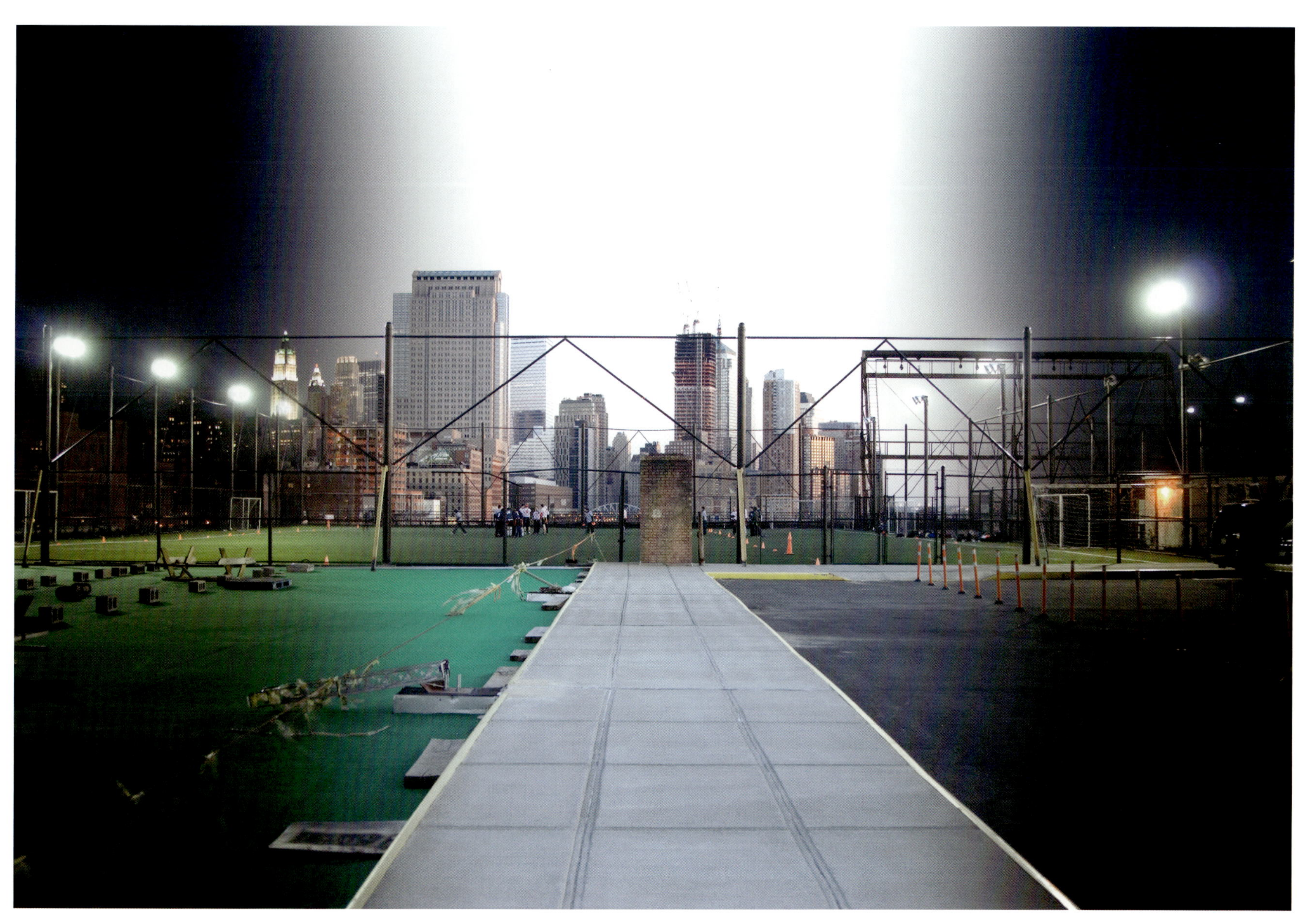

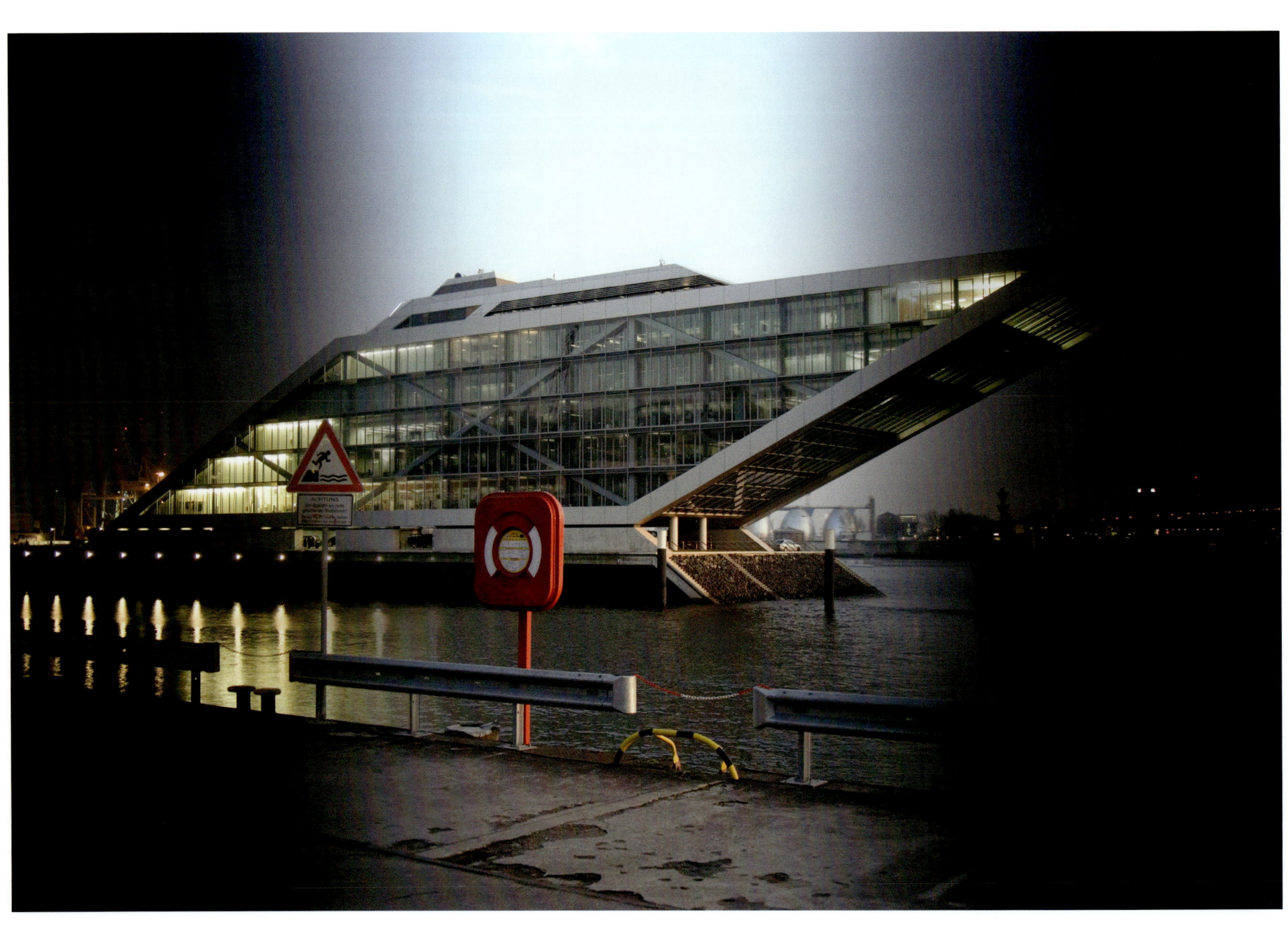

 HAFENHAUS / HARBOR BUILDING 70 × 100 cm / 27.56 × 39.38 in.

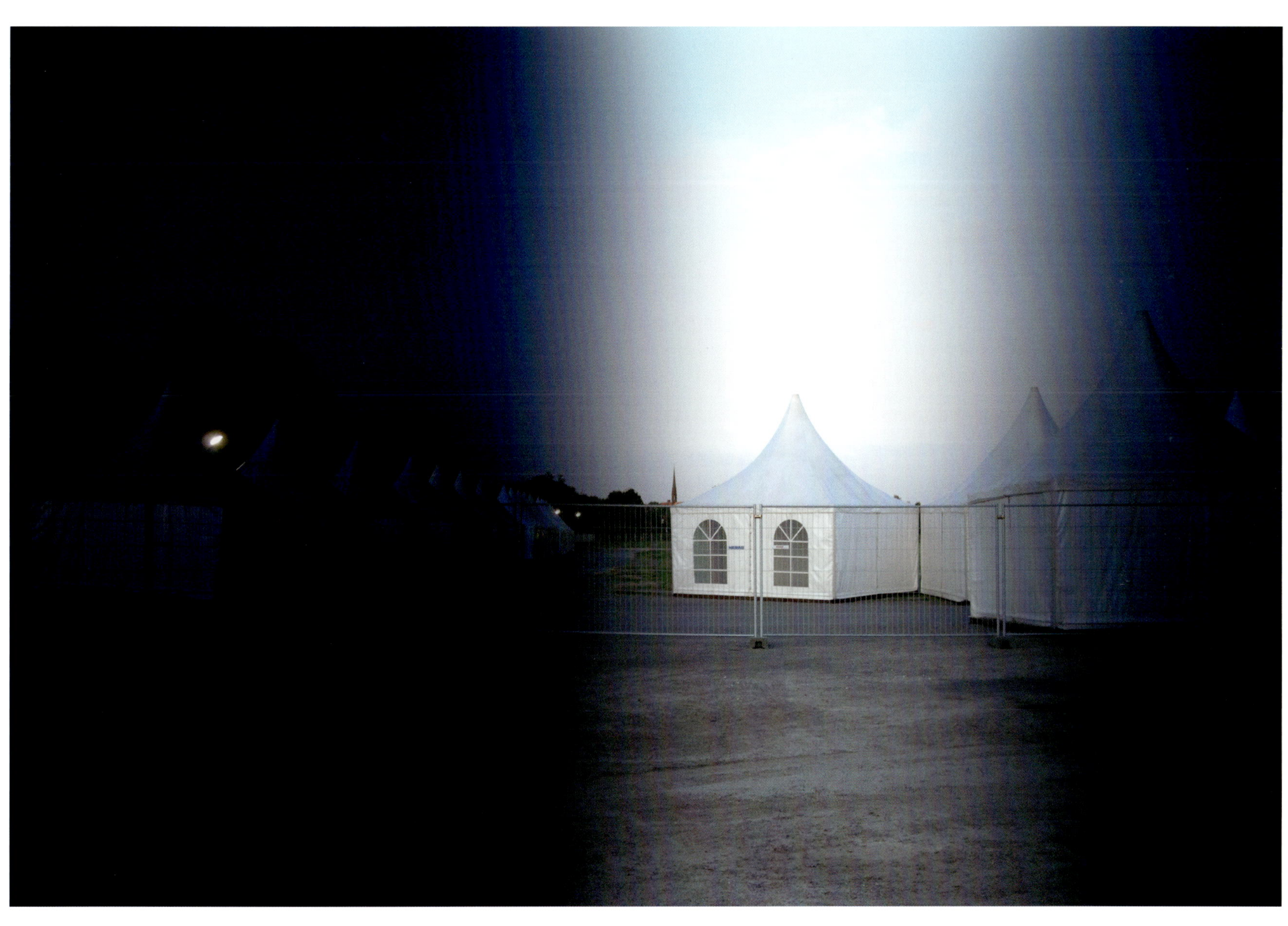

ZELTE / TENTS 70 × 100 cm / 27.56 × 39.38 in.

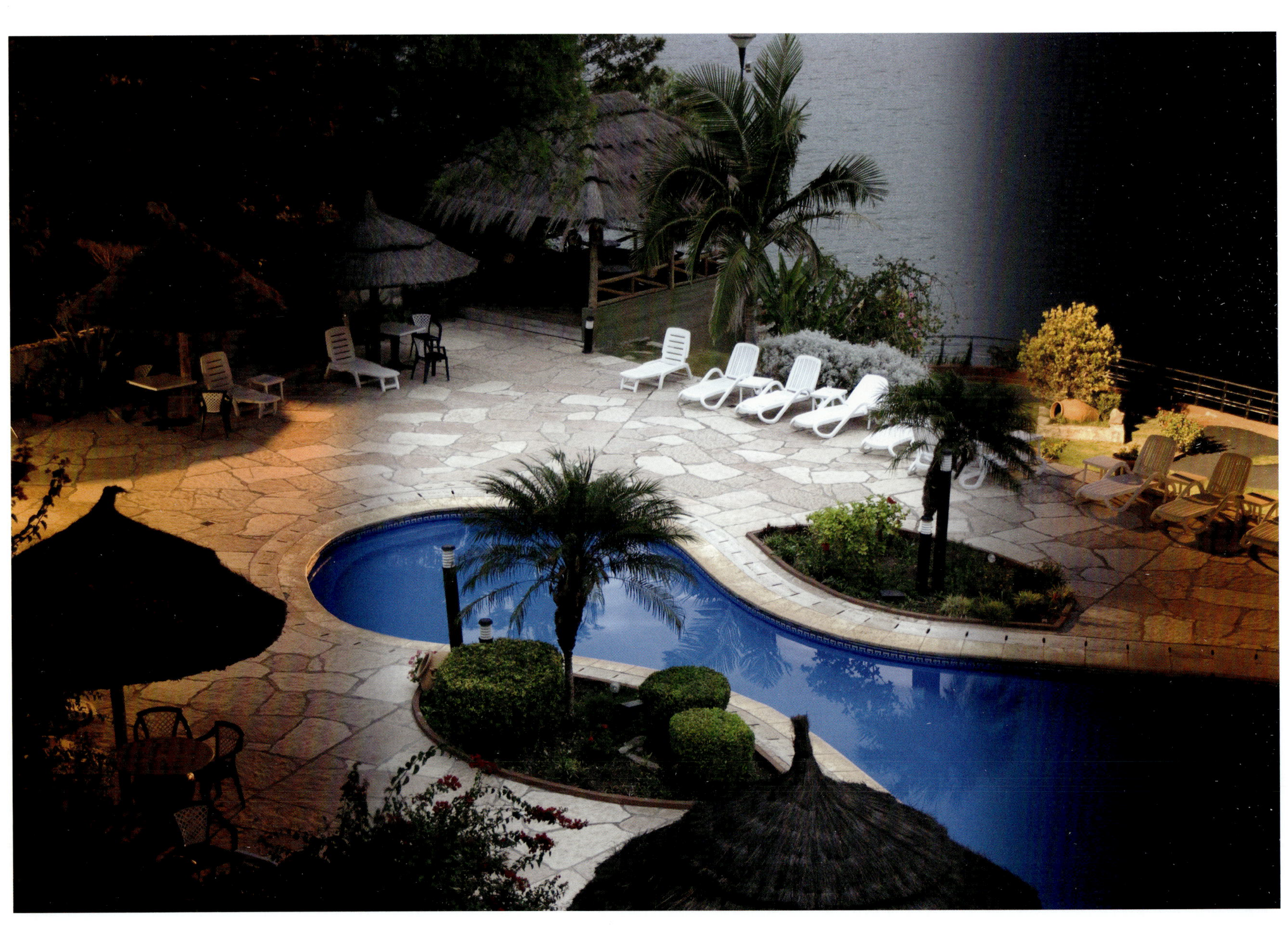

 HOTEL 70 × 100 cm / 27.56 × 39.38 in.

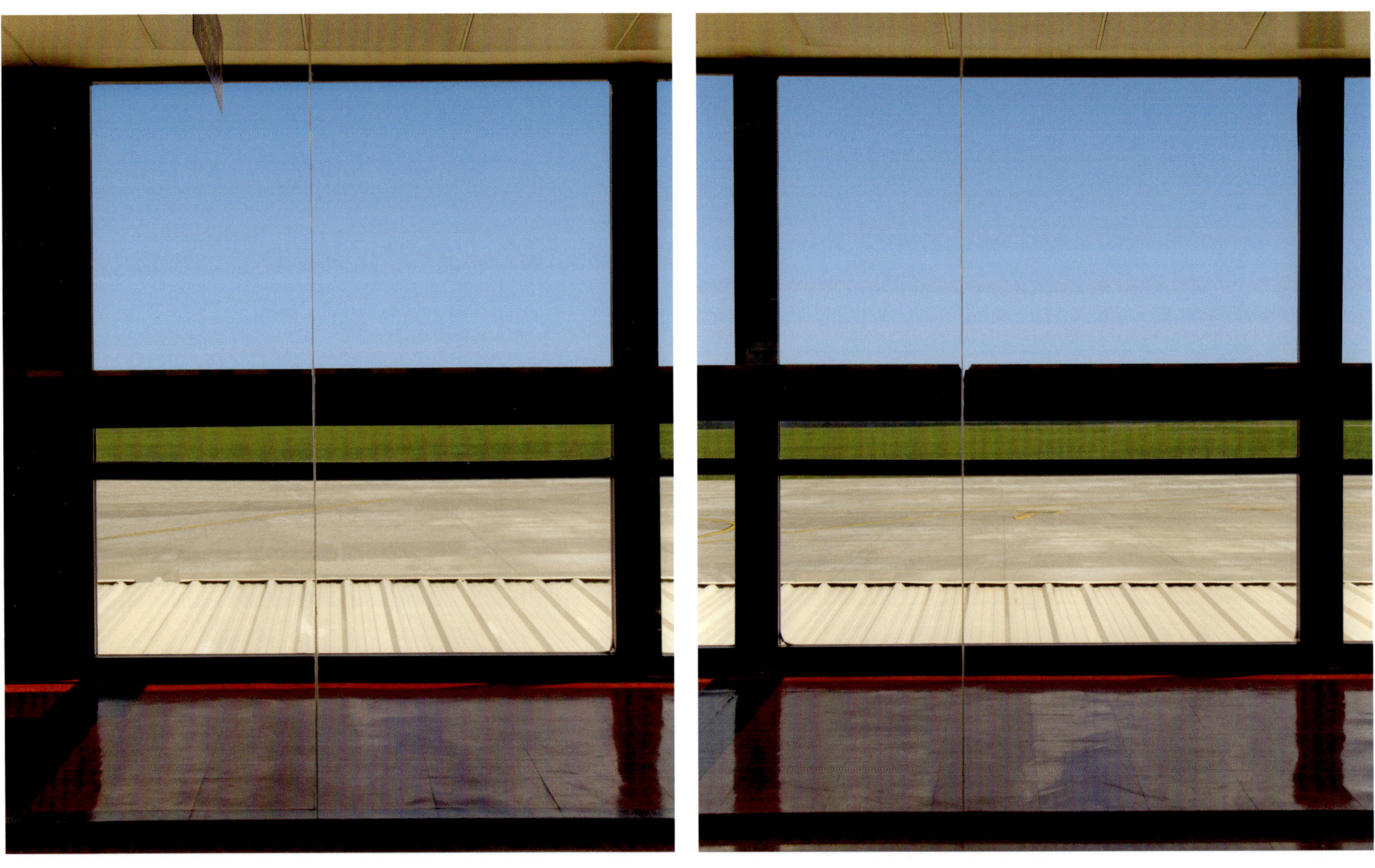

154 **#1 #2 #3 #4** 110 × 91 cm / 43.31 × 35.83 in.

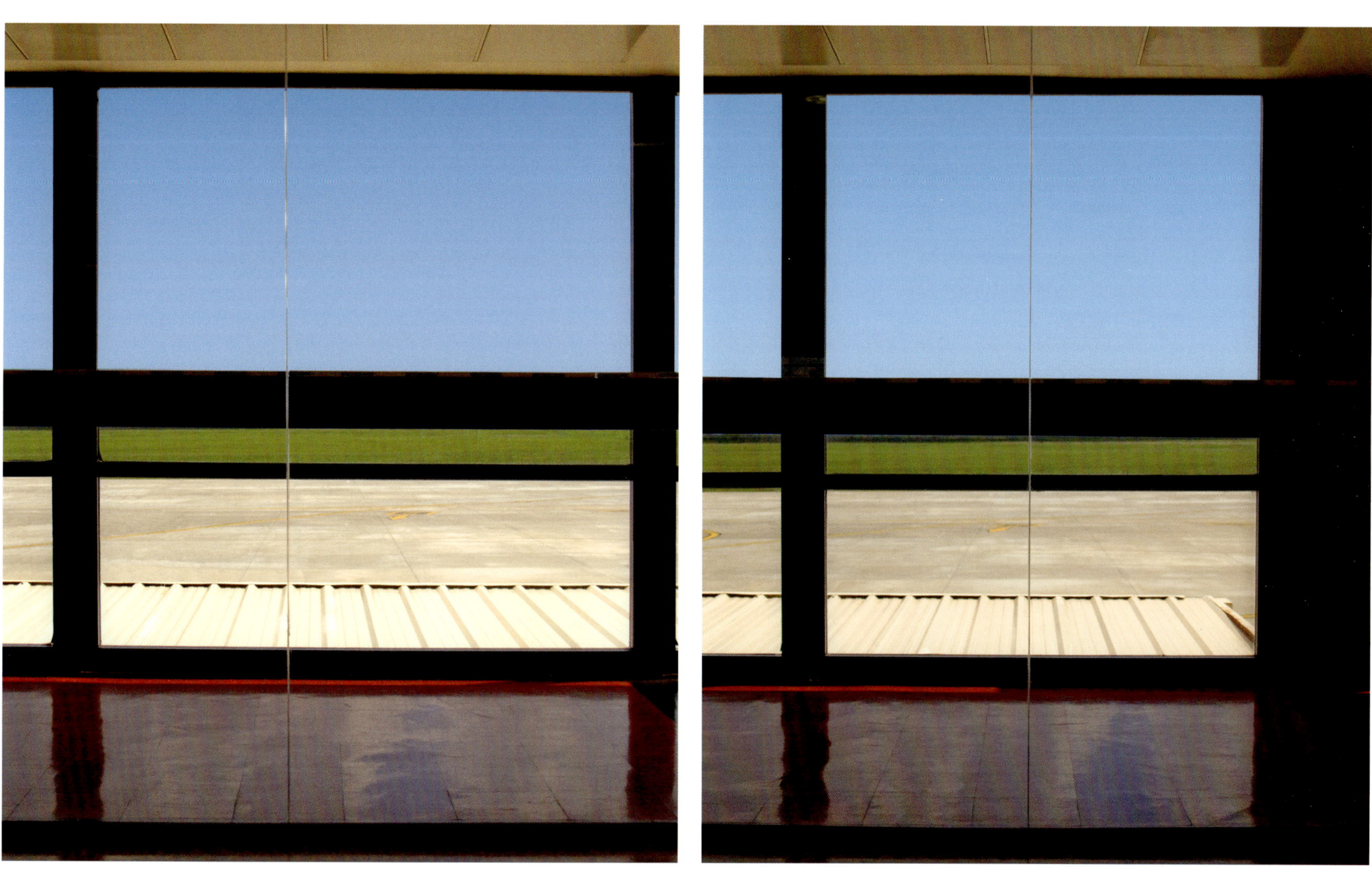

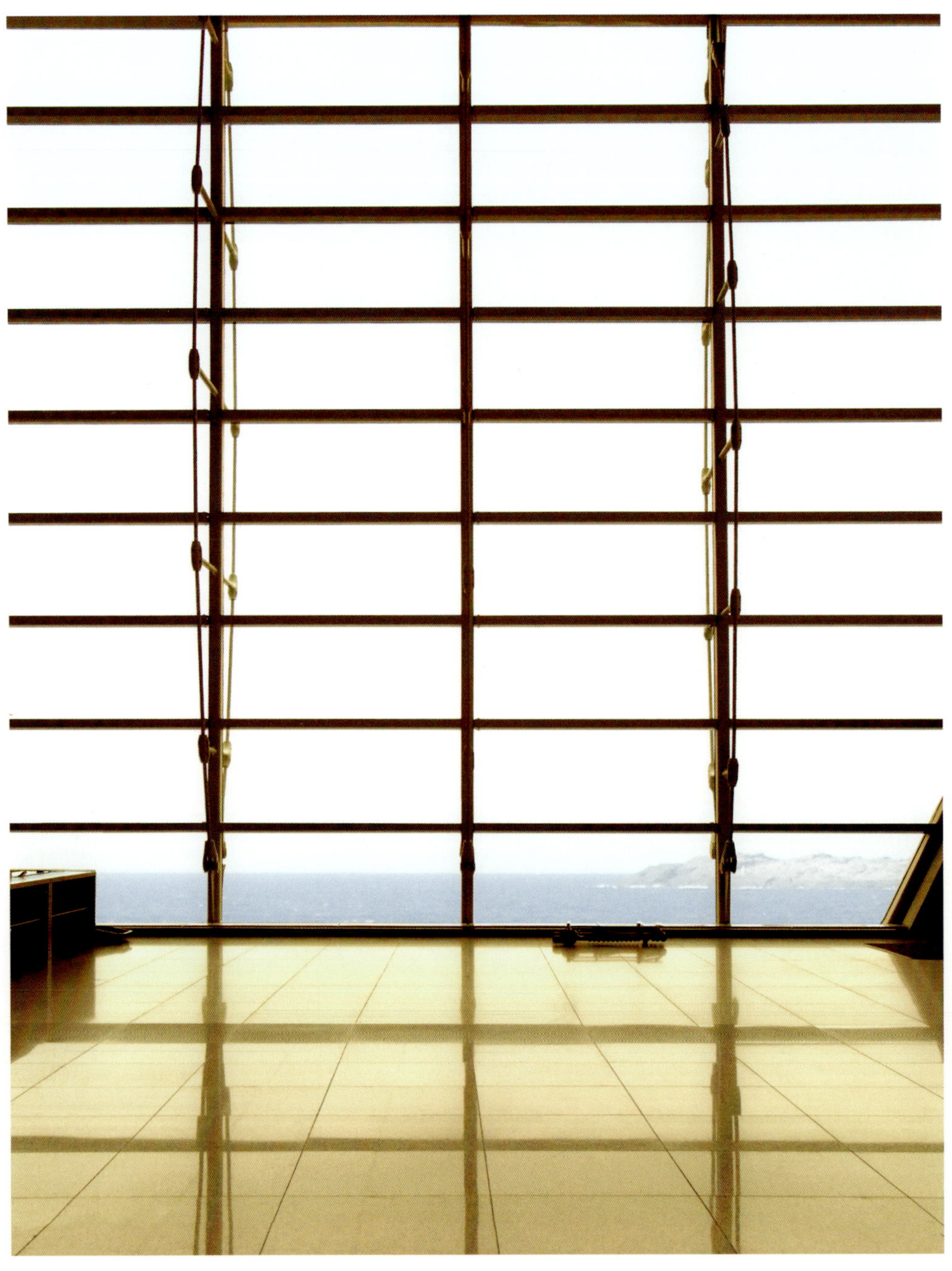

 # 1   # 2   100 × 80 cm / 39.38 × 31.5 in.

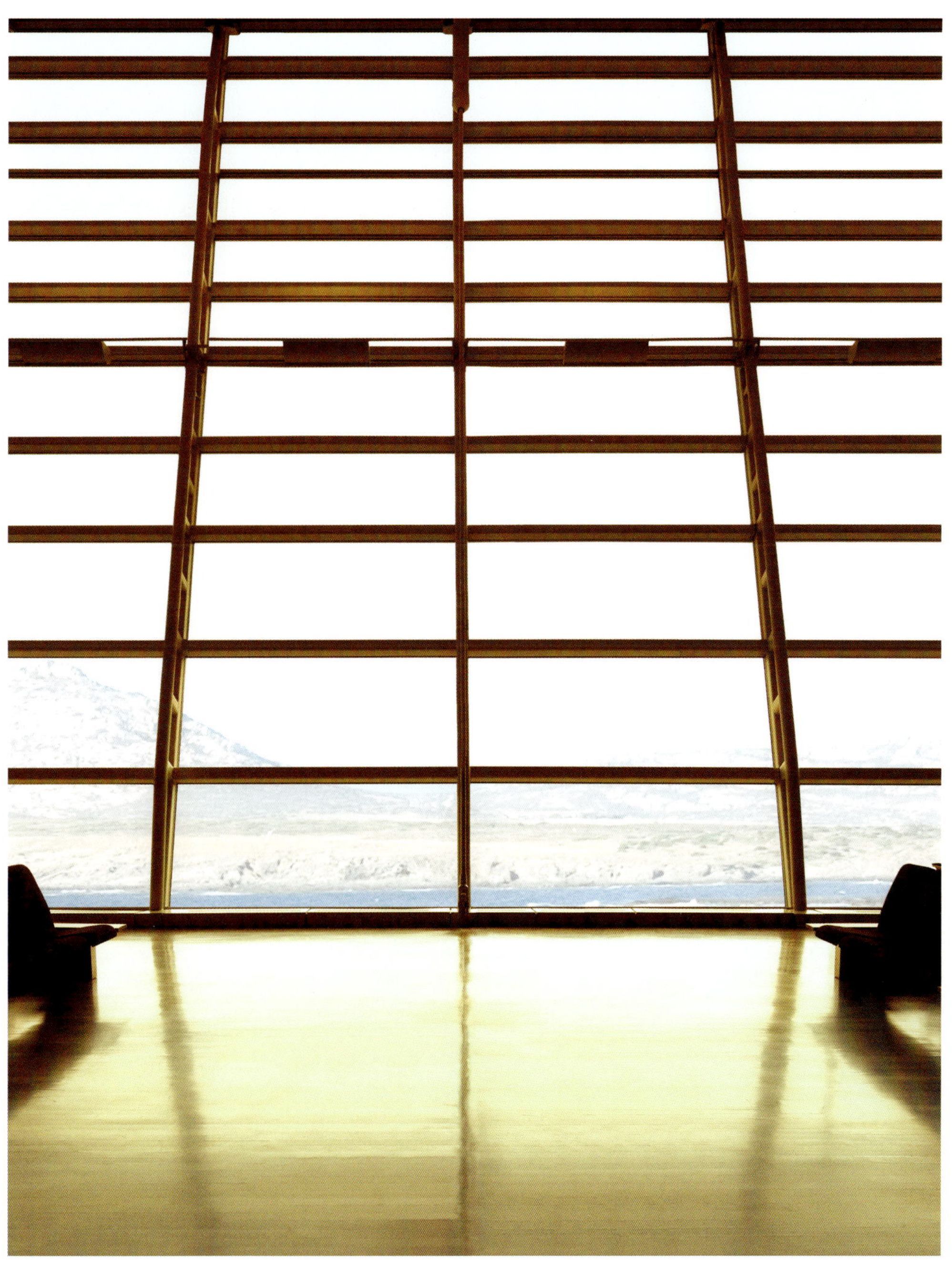

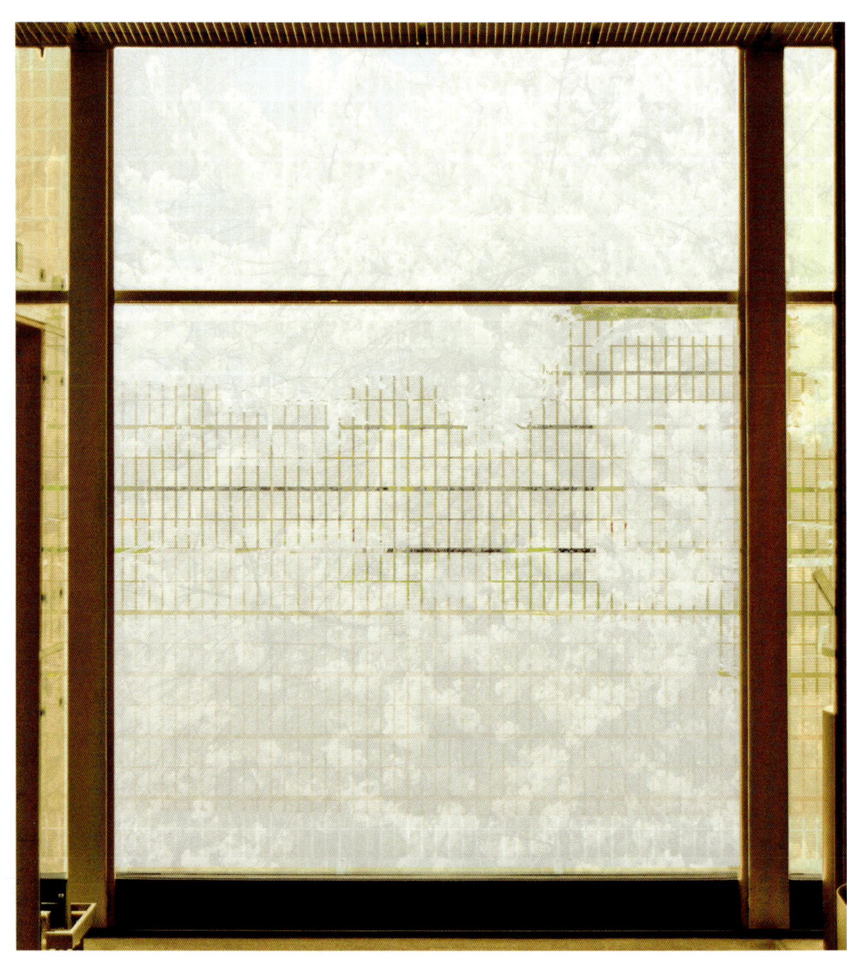

     # 1   # 2   # 3   90 × 82.6 cm / 35.43 × 32.52 in.

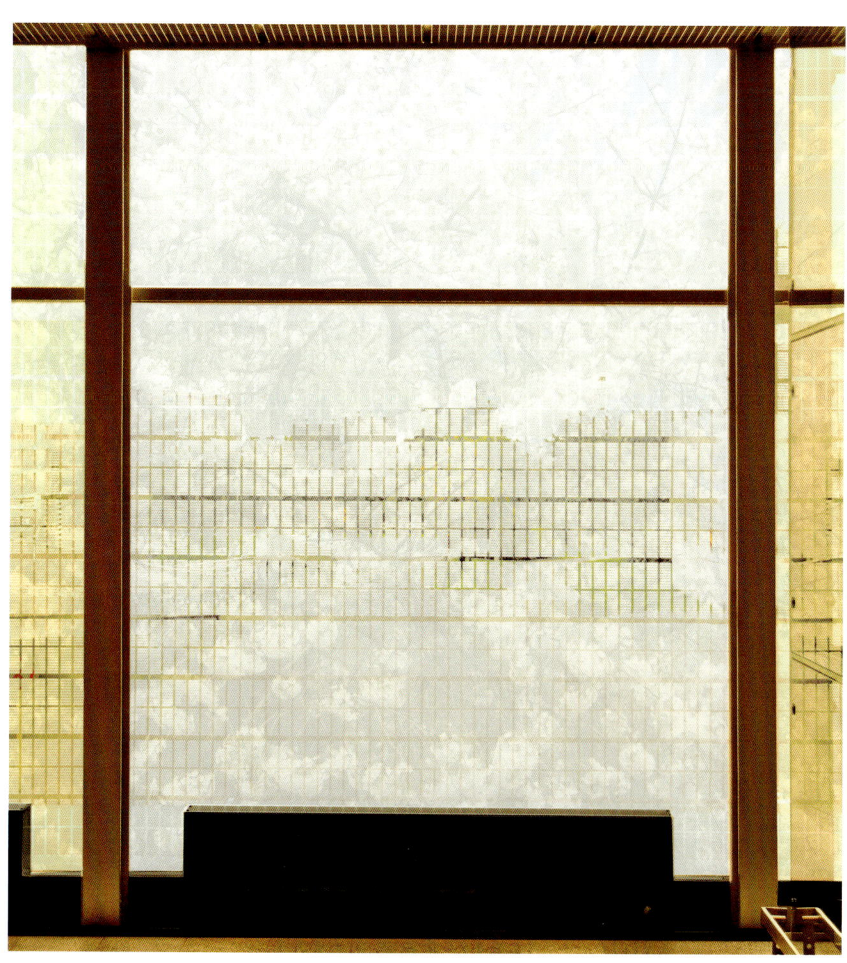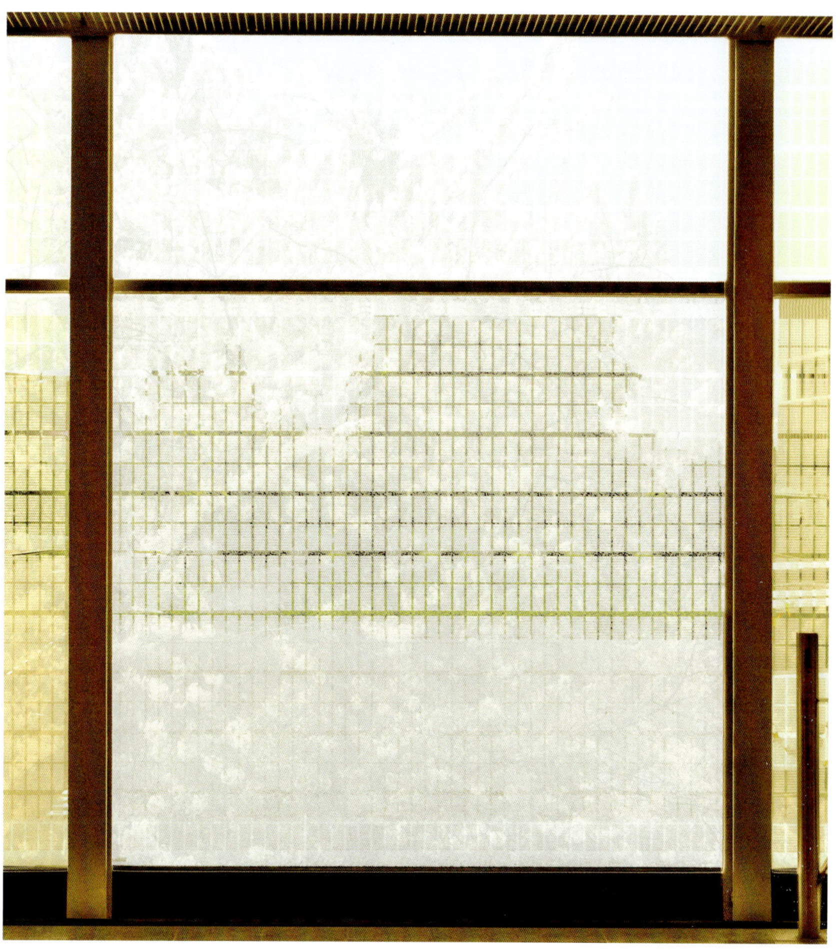

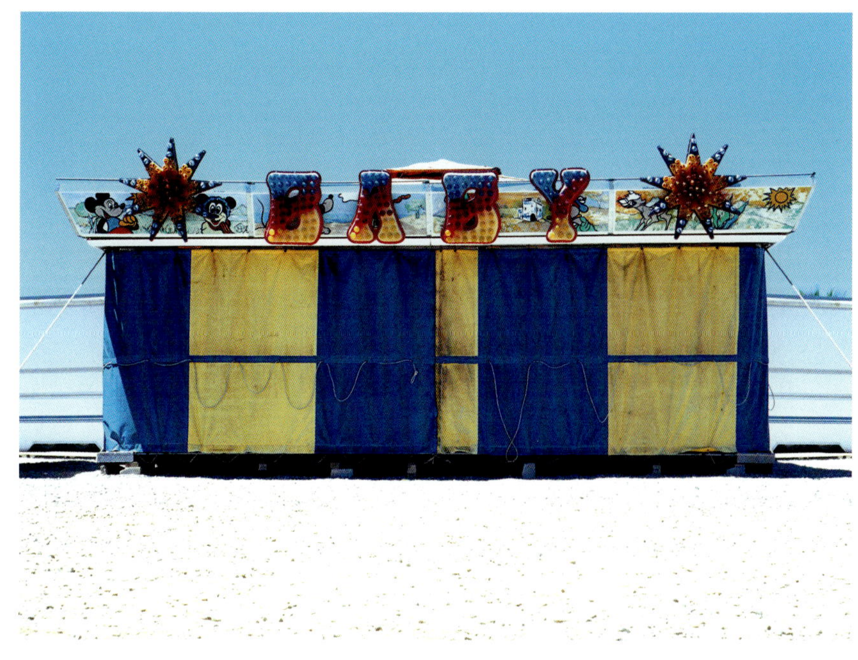
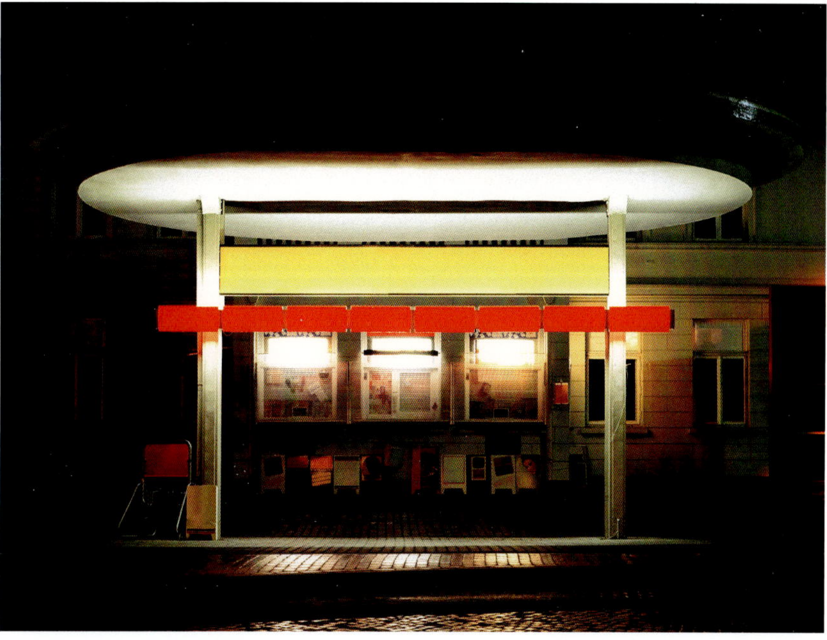
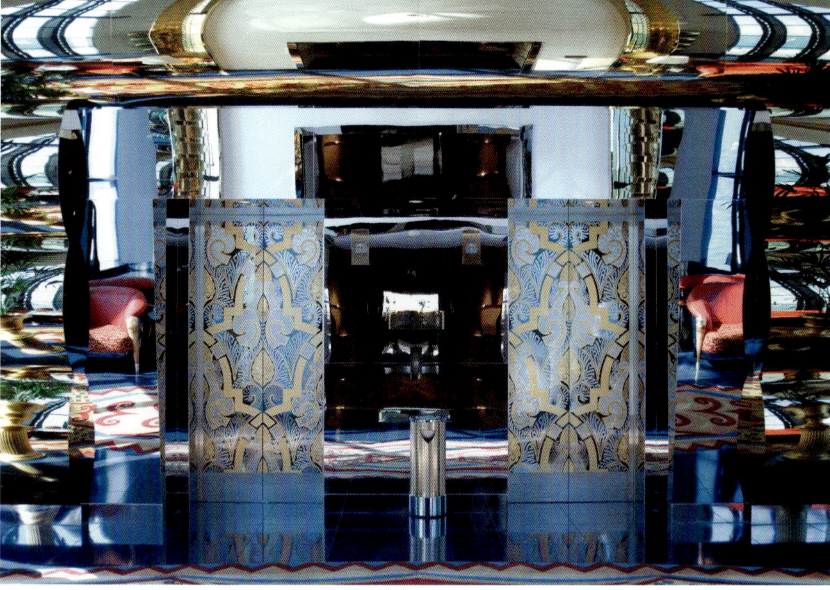
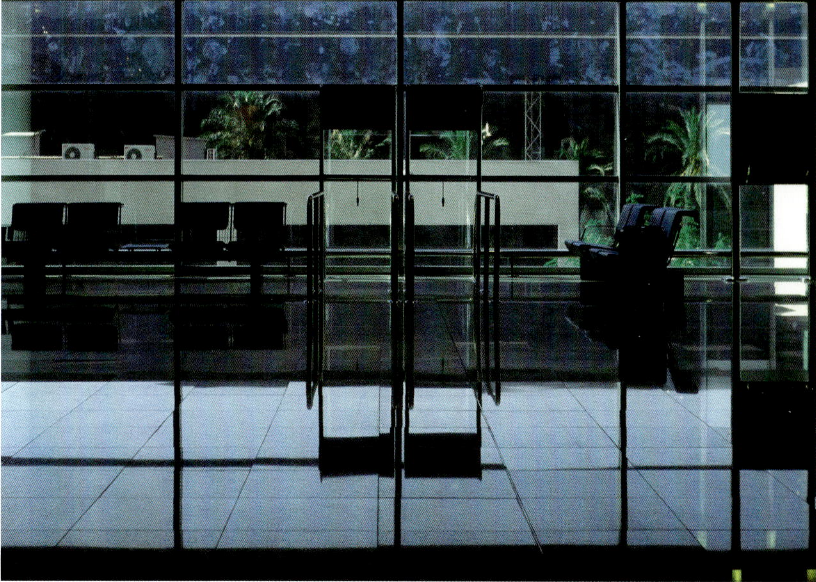

BABY 65.5 × 90.5 cm / 25.79 × 35.63 in. **UELZEN** 61.5 × 83.5 cm / 24.21 × 32.87 in. **BUR** 50 × 70 cm / 19.69 × 27.56 in. **FENSTER / WINDOW** 21 × 30 cm / 8.27 × 11.81 in.

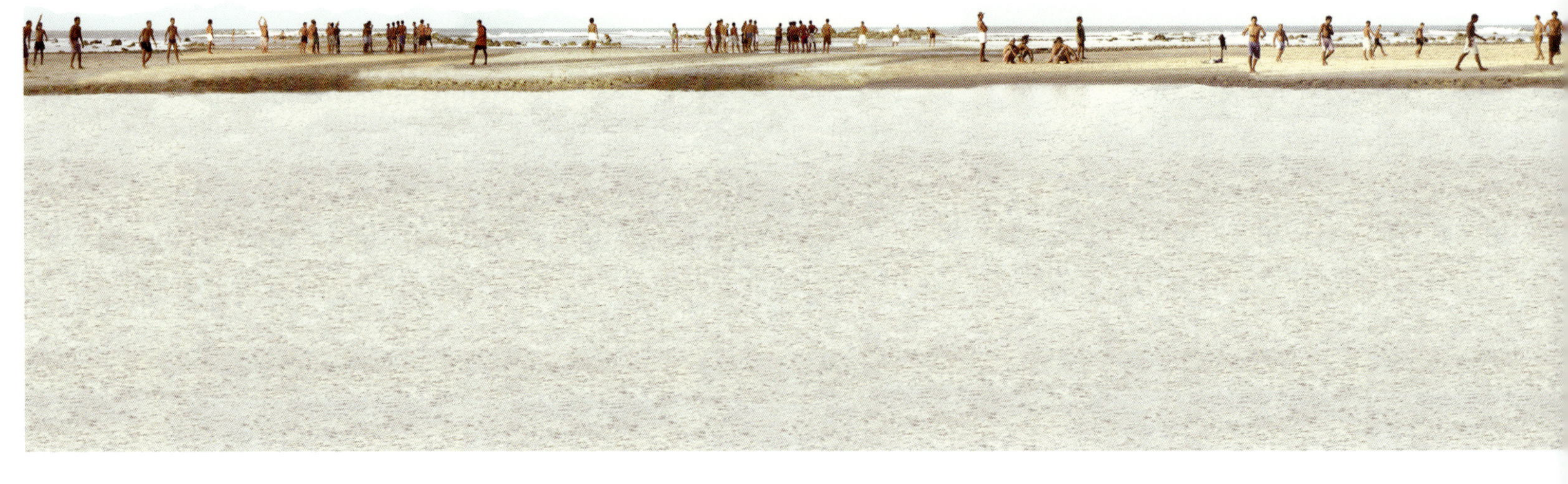

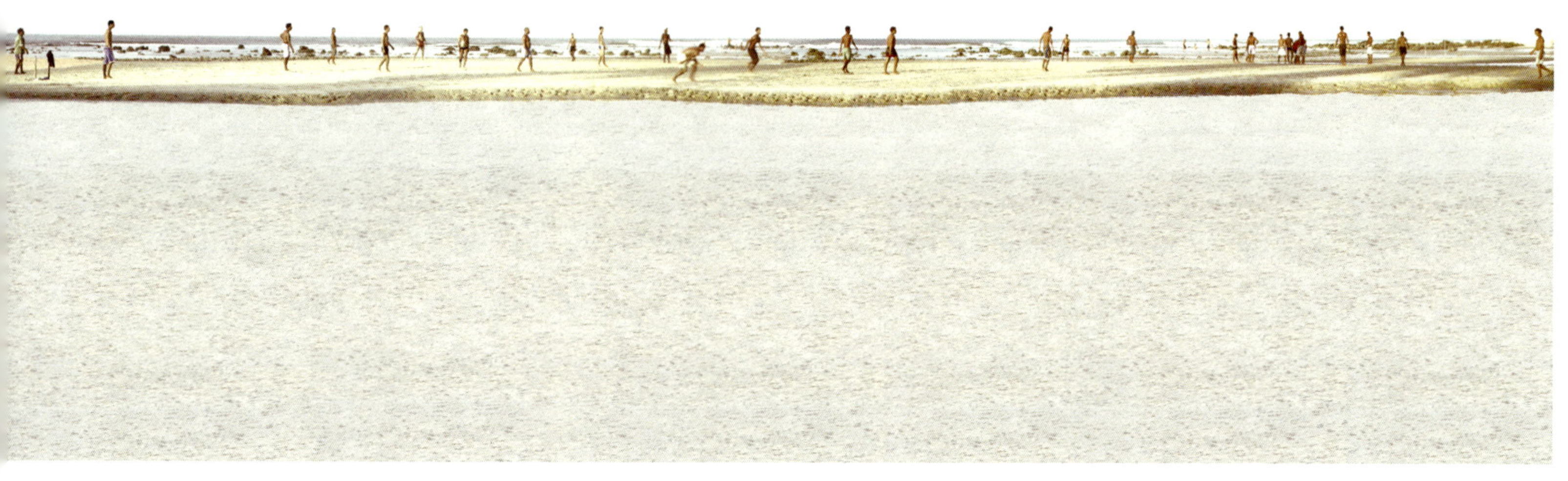

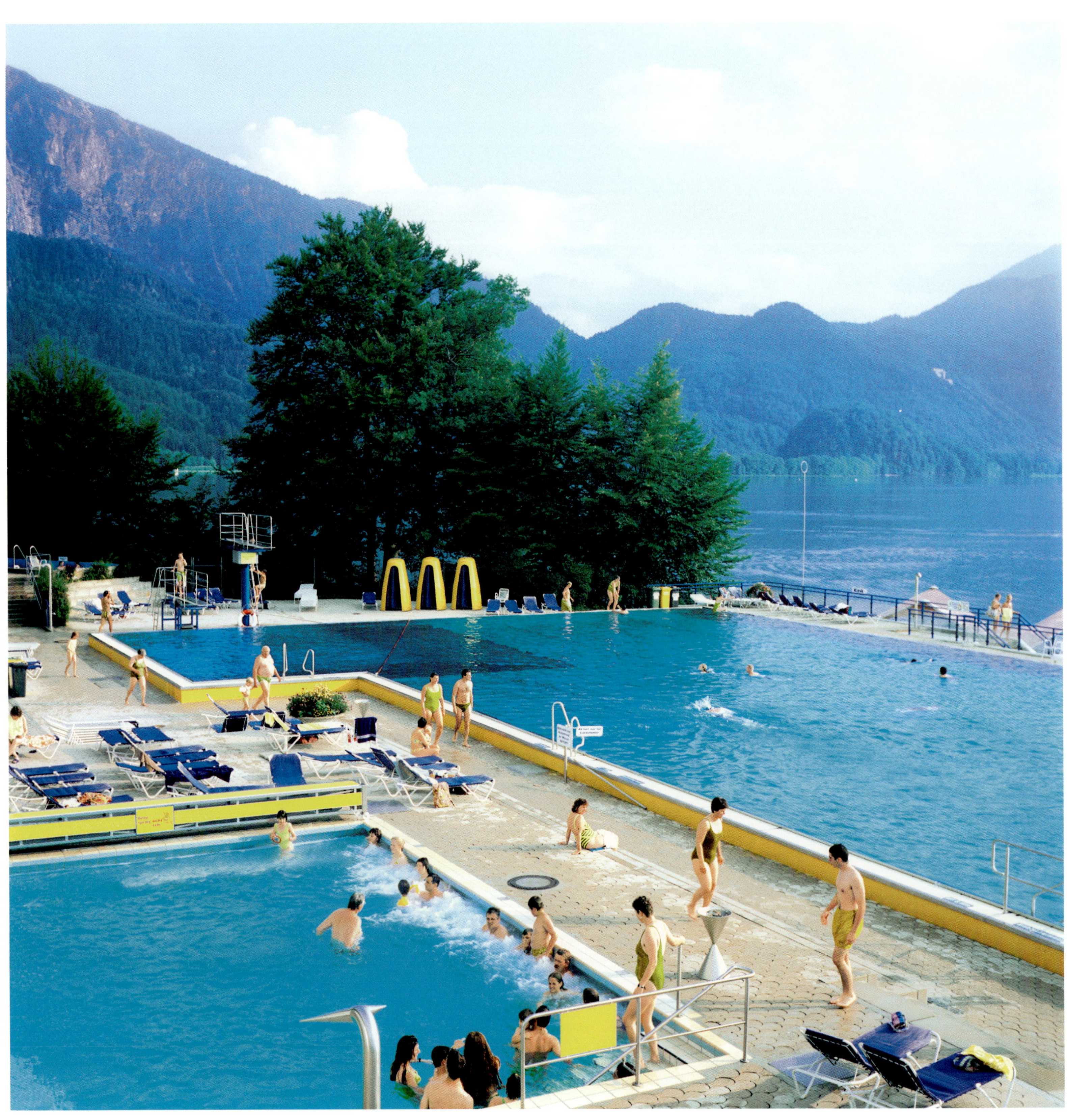

164   **SCHWIMMBAD / SWIMMING POOL** 100 × 100 cm / 39.38 × 39.38 in.

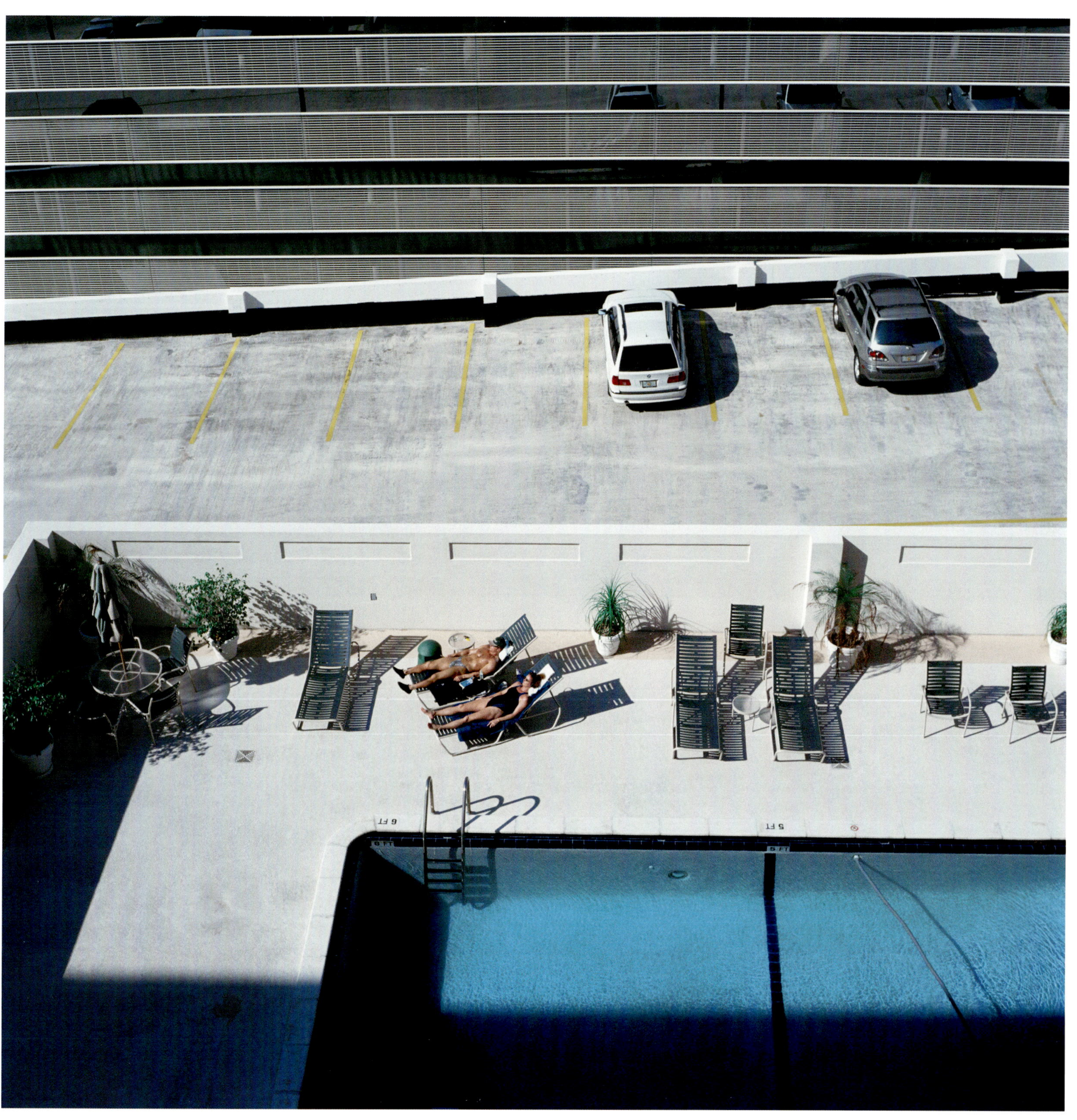

POOL 117 × 117 cm / 46 × 46 in.

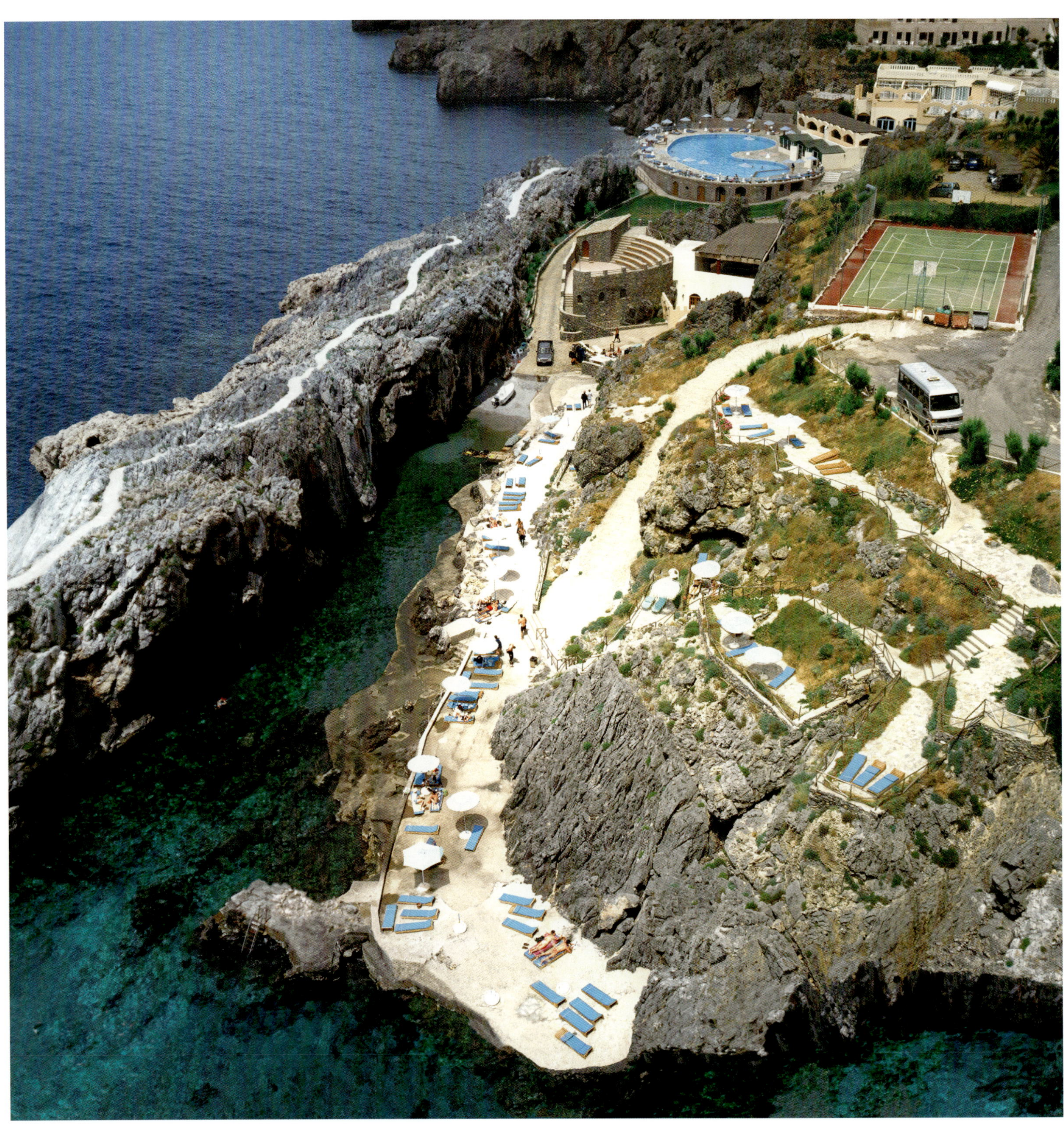

 CALYPSO 111.5 × 110.5 cm / 43.9 × 43.5 in.

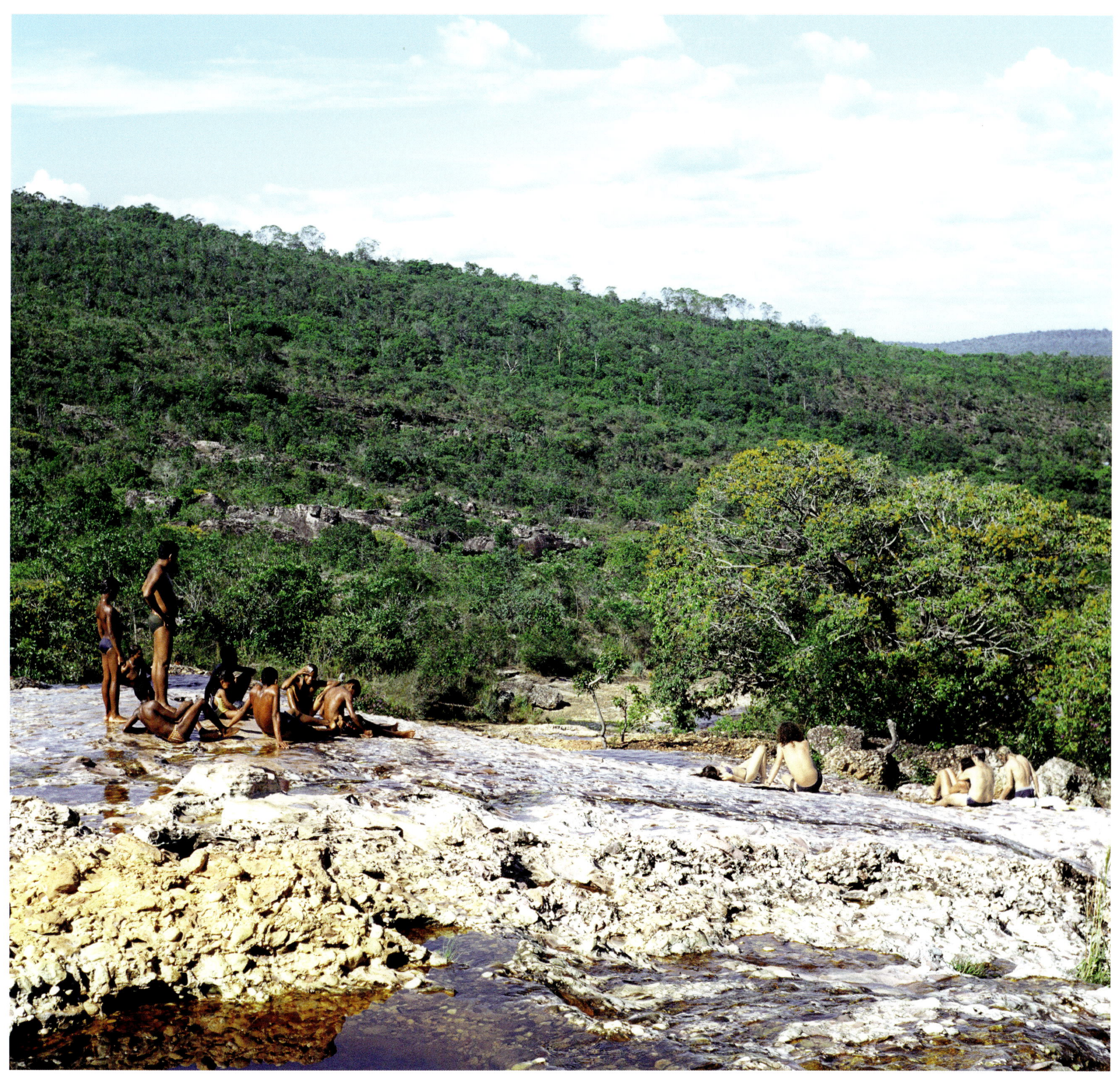

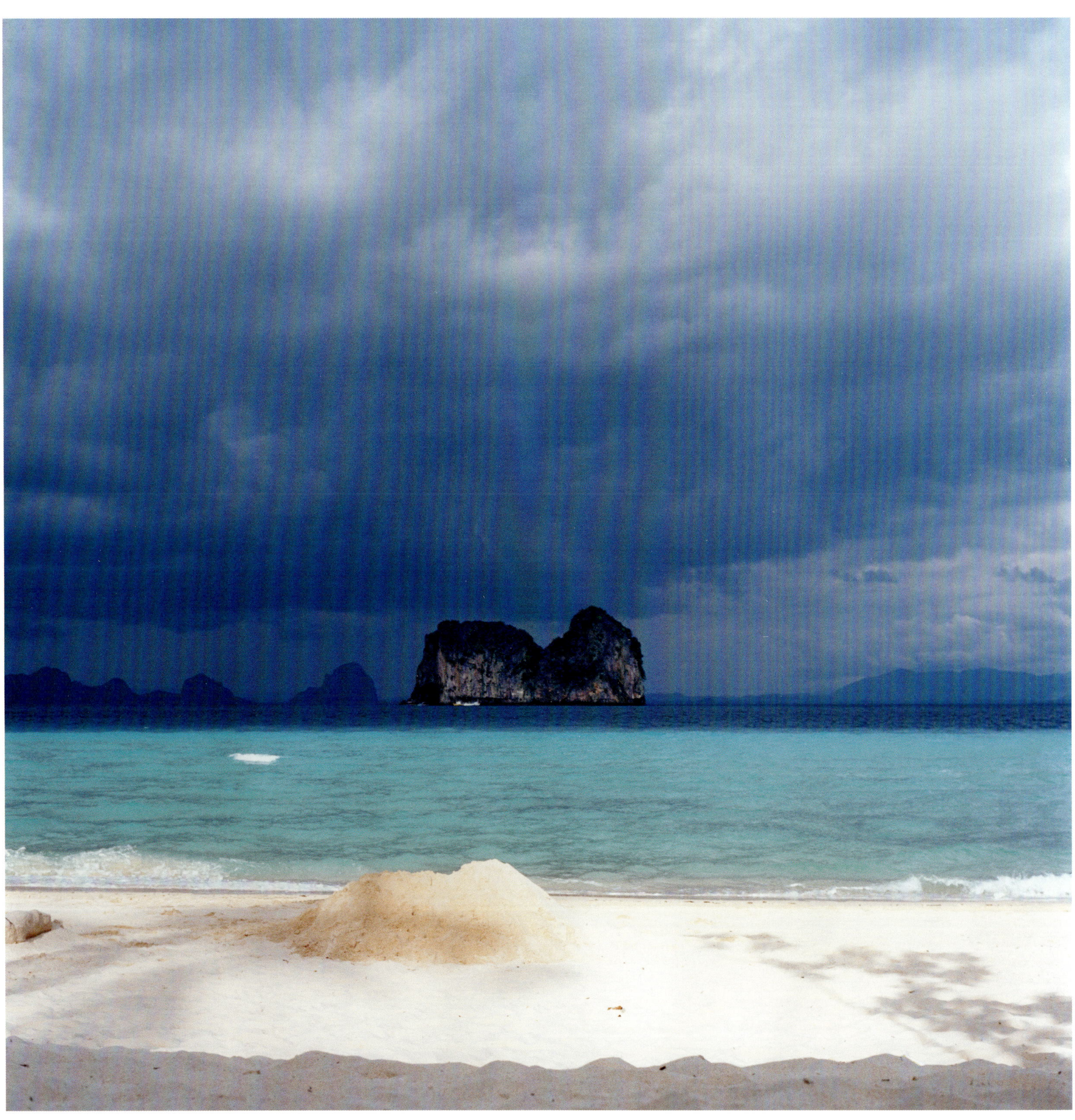

168   **TAI** 99 × 100 cm / 38.98 × 39.38 in.

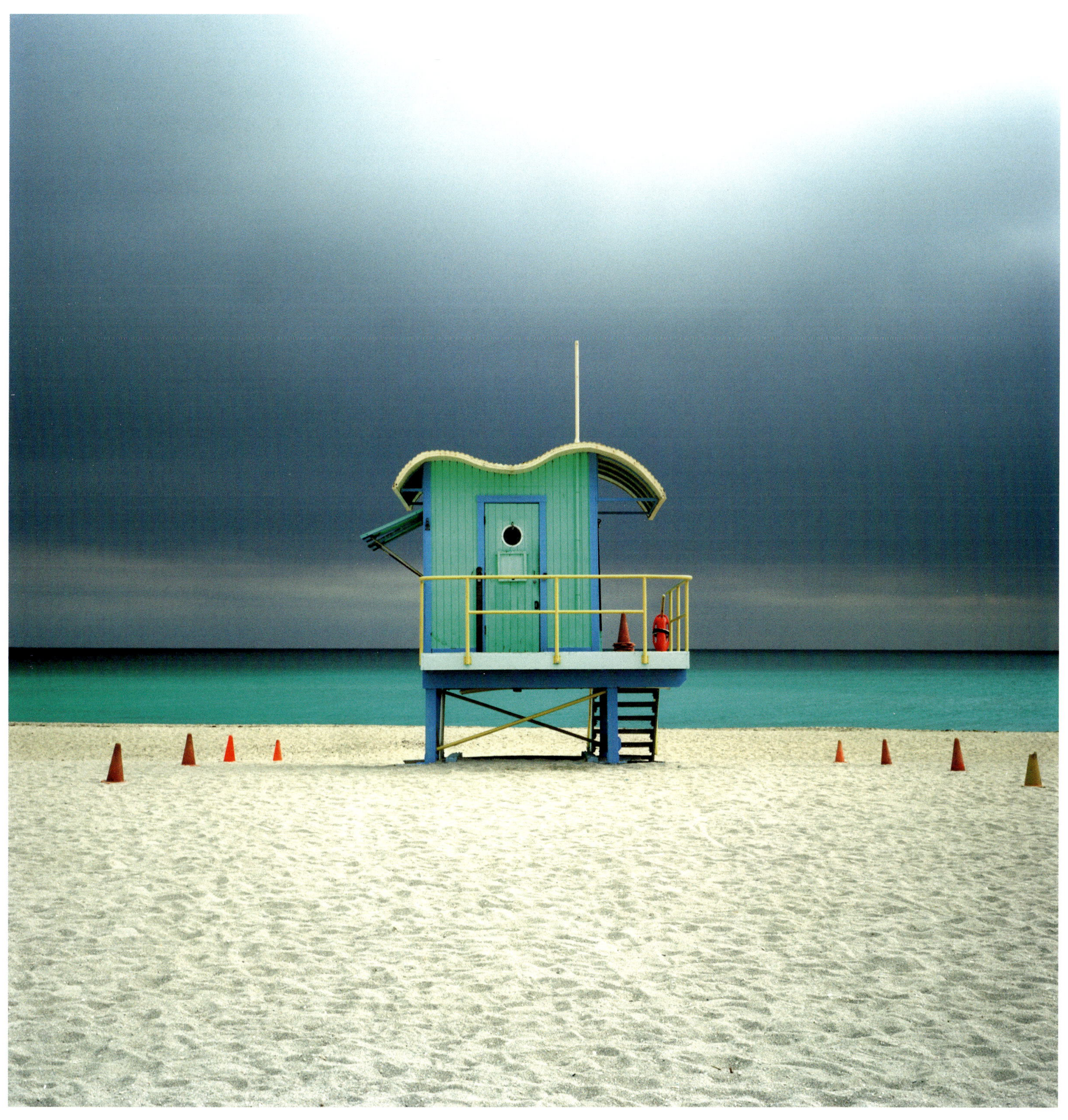

BUDE / CABIN 110 × 109 cm / 43.31 × 42.91 in.

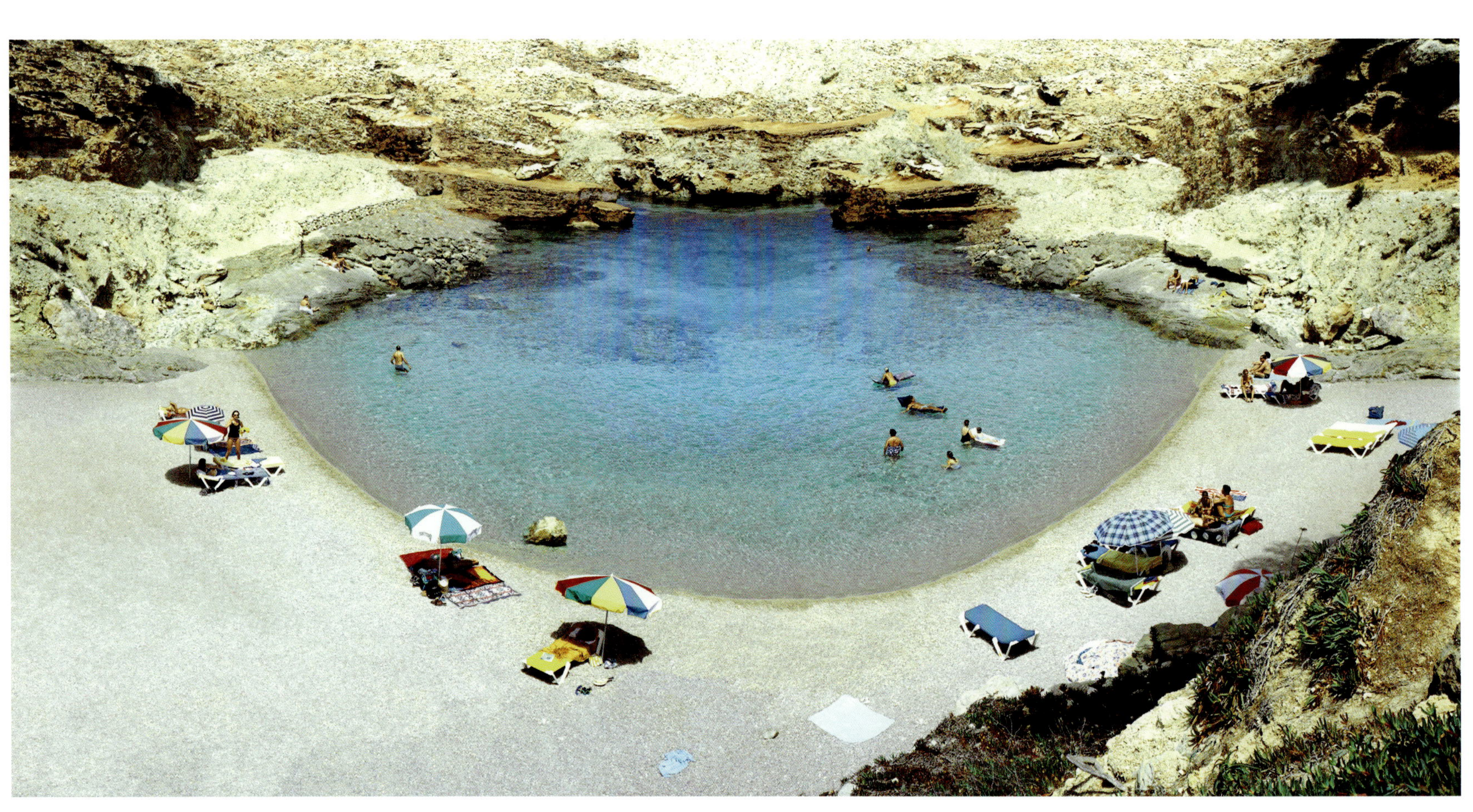

170 **BUCHT / COVE** 124 × 246 cm / 48.82 × 96.85 in.

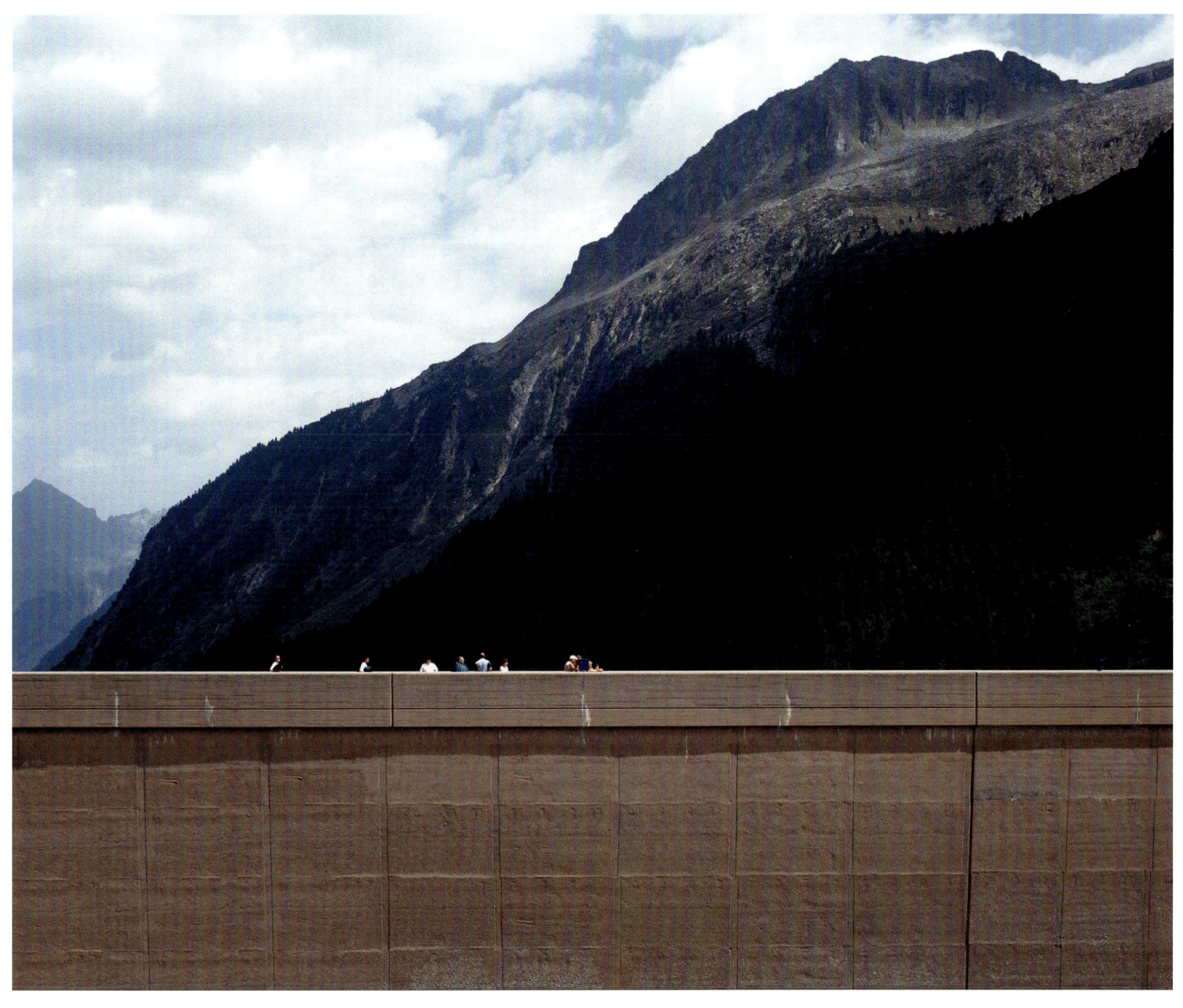

MAUER / WALL 95 × 117 cm / 37.4 × 46 in.

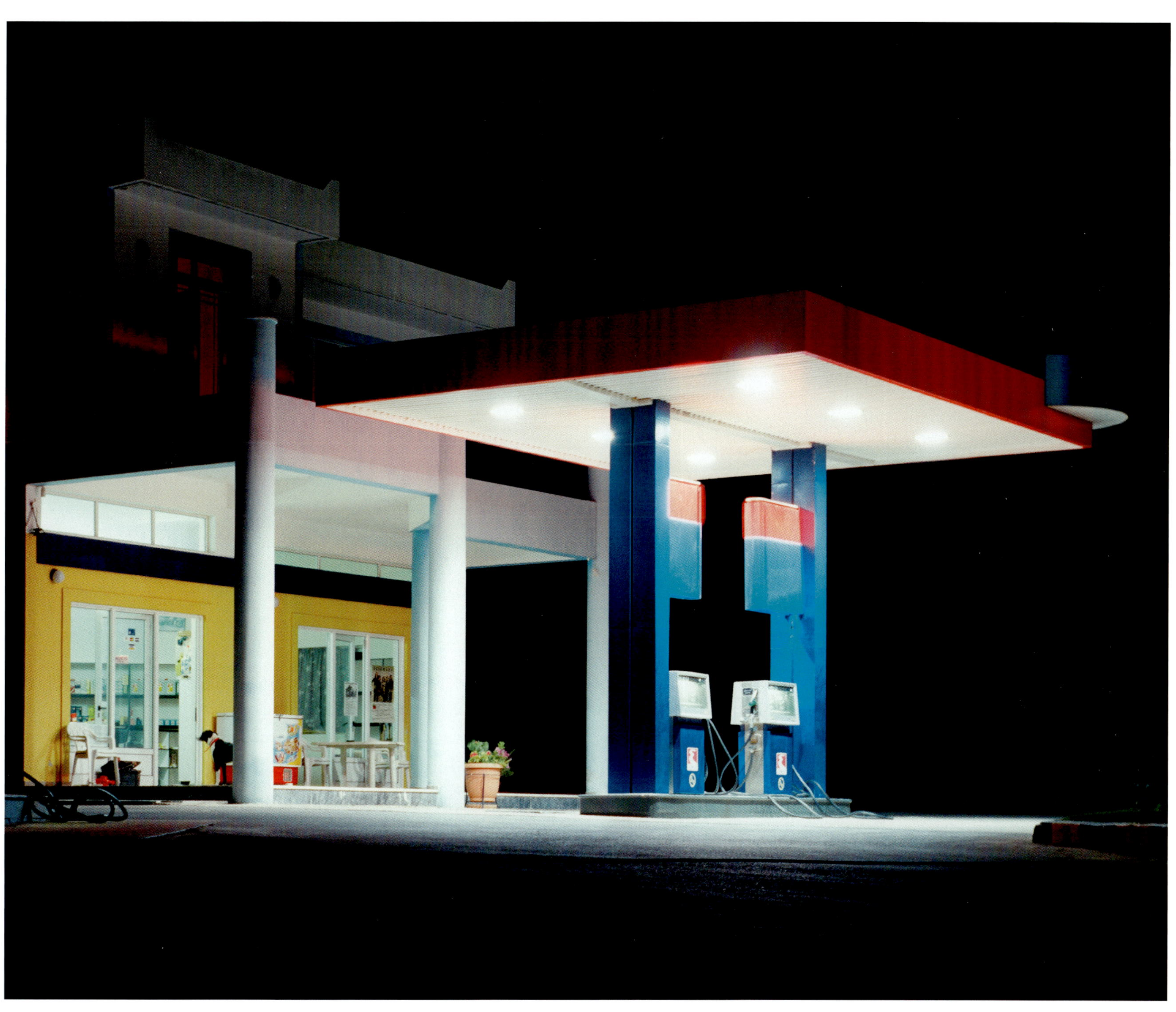

TANKSTELLE SÜD / **PETROL STATION SOUTH** 35 × 43 cm / 13.78 × 16.92 in.

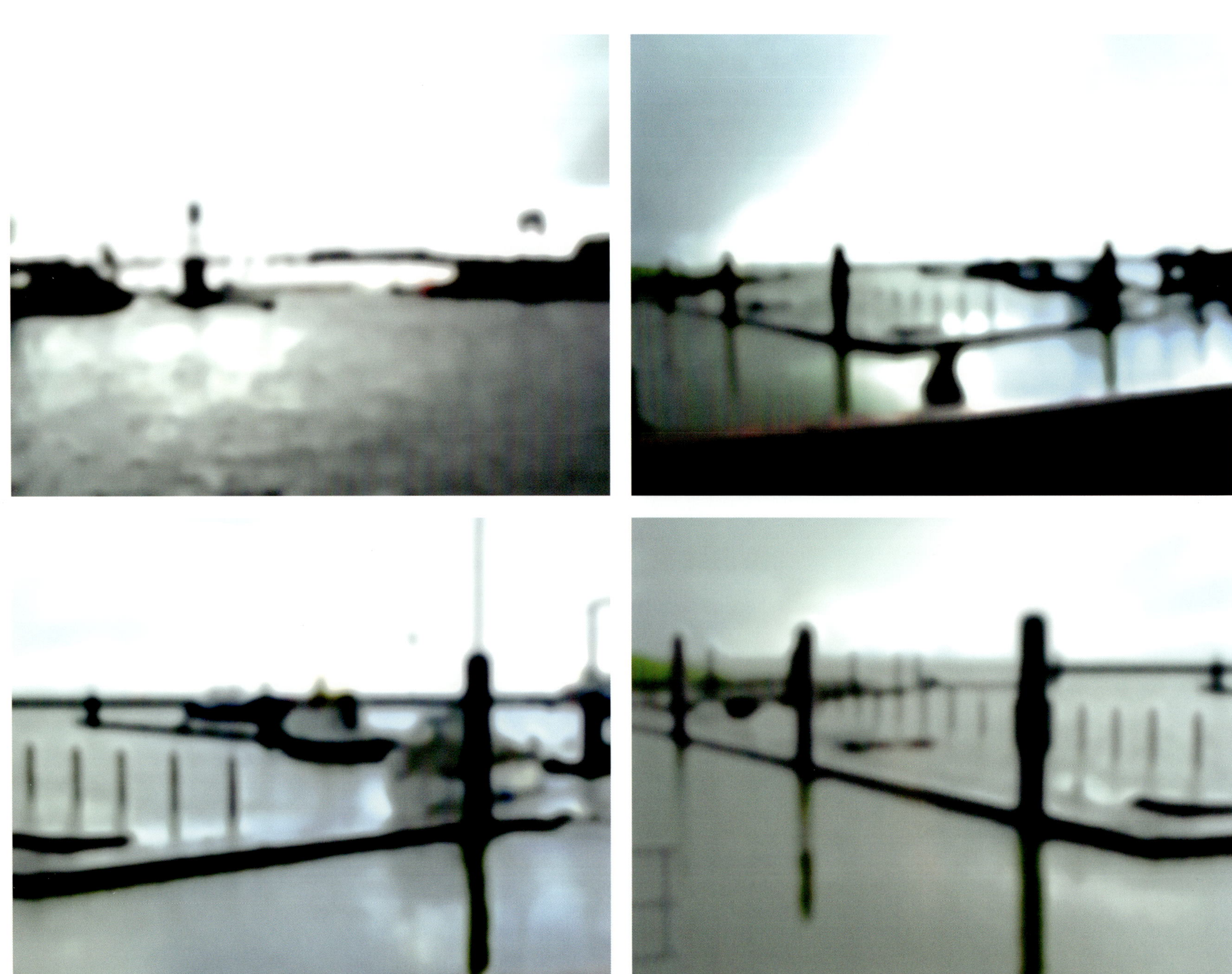

174 **HAFEN 2 / PORT 2 MOLE 3 MOLE 2 MOLE 1** 25 × 33.8 cm / 9.84 × 13.31 in.

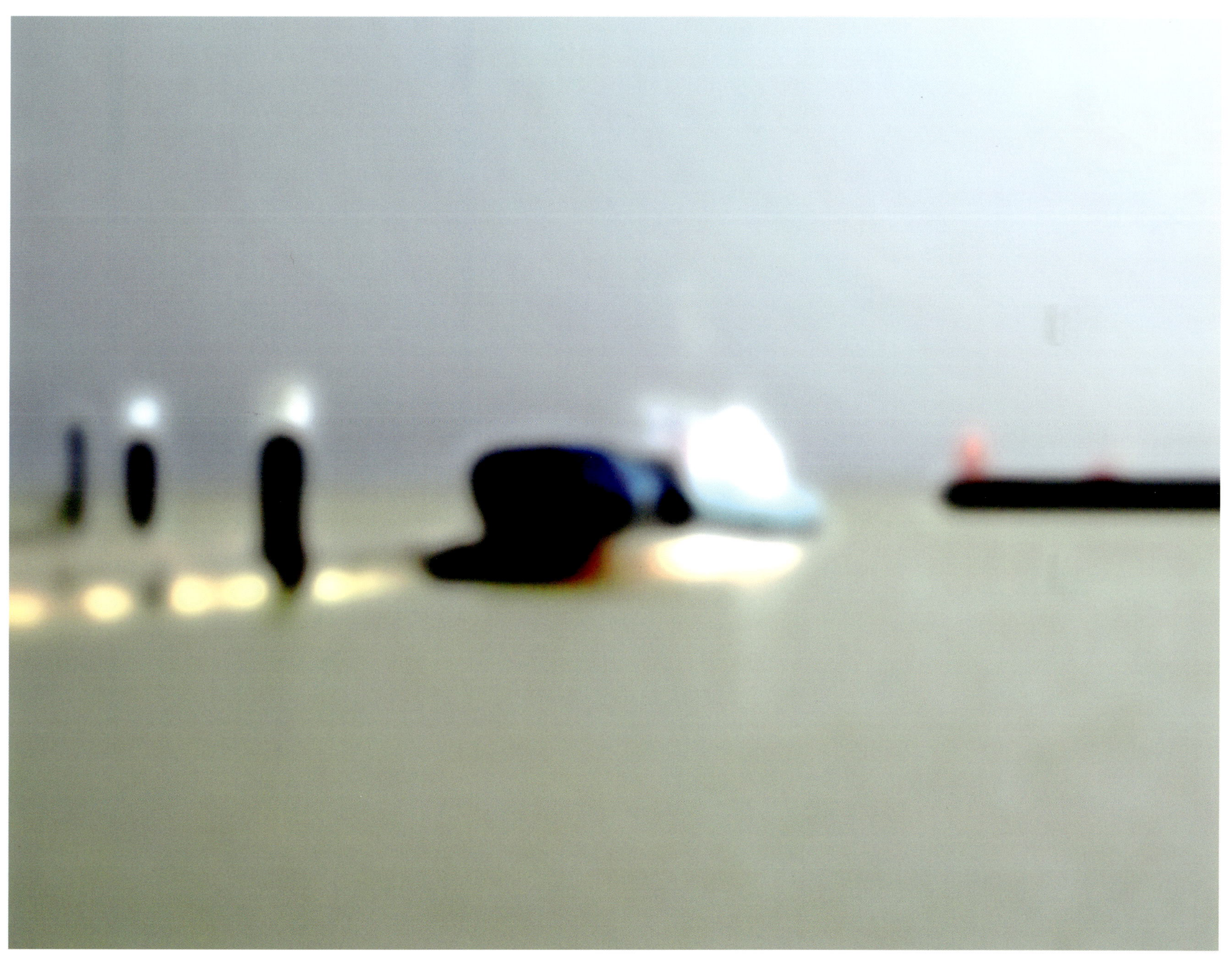

BOOT 3 / BOAT 3 25 × 33.8 cm / 9.84 × 13.31 in.

Der erste Blick entscheidet, ob mich überhaupt Signale erreichen und mein Gehirn erregen. Beim zweiten geht es dann um Verknüpfungen und um Bedeutung. Sehe ich den *Wanderer über dem Nebelmeer* und weiß, dass es sich um ein Werk von Caspar David Friedrich handelt, dann ist – vorausgesetzt, der erste Reiz ist stark genug und wird nicht von einem Bewertungsmuster abgewiesen – der zweite Schritt schon vorbereitet. Alles, was ich weiß, ist bereits eine Folie, auf der das jetzt genauer Beobachtete in mir sein Bedeutungsfeld erweitern und mein Gefühl beim Betrachten verstärken kann. Die Wirkung von Kunst und Wissen.

Aber nun steht der Wanderer als Stofftiermaus geschmackvoll gekleidet mit Stock auf dem Hügel und blickt in die Ferne (S. 184)! Gerahmt in Gold. Dieser parodistische Effekt verursacht nur auf den ersten Blick ein Schmunzeln. Die Parodie, also »das verstellt gesungene Lied«, ist eine unterschätzte Kunstform. Es ist ja das Komische, das uns oft die Tragik oder das Glück so unbegreiflich tief unter die Haut jagt. Wie stark ist das Hungergefühl durch das hochkultivierte Verspeisen einer Schuhsohle von Charles Chaplin dargestellt? Und erst mit Verzögerung bekommt unsere Ratio die Chance, zu bestätigen, was sich bereits weich in die Erkenntnisebene eingegraben hat.

Das leisten die *100 Meisterwerke* hervorragend. Jean-August-Dominique Ingres *Die Badende* ist bis in die Fußstellung hinein außerordentlich komisch (S. 188). Fast möchte man Losprusten vor Lachen. Aber dann sieh dir die Nähte am Teddykörper an. Könnten die leichten Tücher um Arm und Kopf nicht Wundverbände sein? Die leuchtende Schönheit in einem Blick vergänglich. Aber du musst jetzt nicht bedeutungsschwer dein Leben ändern. Ins Kloster gehen oder gar den körperlichen Verfall von Minute zu Minute registrieren. Denn das Komische will hier die Tragik nicht absichtsvoll hervorrufen. Die ist ja in dir. Von Anfang an. Der nächste Blick ist wieder so anrührend komisch. Du lächelst und gehst zum nächsten goldenen Rahmen, um lächelnd die nächste Einsicht subkutan zu speichern. Diese parodistische Freude kann bleiben. Ein wohltuender Erkenntnisgewinn.

The first glance tells me whether there are in fact any signals reaching and stimulating my brain. The second starts looking for meaning and associations. If I look at the *Wanderer above the Sea of Fog* in the knowledge that it is based on a work by Caspar David Friedrich, then the second step is almost inevitable—provided the picture is intriguing enough and I don't simply reject it on evaluative grounds. Once I look at it more closely, everything I know forms a background against which the picture can extend its field of meaning, heightening the feelings it evokes in me. The effect of art and knowledge.

Only this time the wanderer happens to be an elegantly dressed soft toy mouse, walking stick in hand, standing on a hill and gazing into the distance (p. 184). Framed in gold. At first sight, this parodic effect only makes you grin. Parody, the "song sung awry," is an underrated artistic form. It is often precisely through works of comedy that we come to feel tragedy or happiness most profoundly. It is hard to think of a more powerful portrayal of hunger than Charlie Chaplin eating a shoe with such perfect manners. And it is only later that our reason gets a chance to confirm what has already become softly embedded at the level of recognition.

Peters's *100 Masterpieces* manage to do this outstandingly well. Right down to the position of her feet, Jean-Auguste-Dominque Ingres's *The Bather* is quite extraordinarily funny (p. 188). It almost makes you burst out laughing. But look at the seams on the teddy bear's body. Couldn't the pieces of light material tied around its arm and head be bandages? A single glance renders this dazzling beauty ephemeral. But unlike the Greek torso of Rilke's poem, it does not demand some momentous change to your life. You need not retire to a monastery or meditate, minute by minute, upon your physical decay. For here the comic does not deliberately try to evoke the tragic. It is inside you. From the very beginning. The next glance is still so touchingly funny. You smile and go on to the next golden frame, so that, smiling, you can store the next insight under your skin. Parody can offer a lingering pleasure. An agreeable moment of recognition.

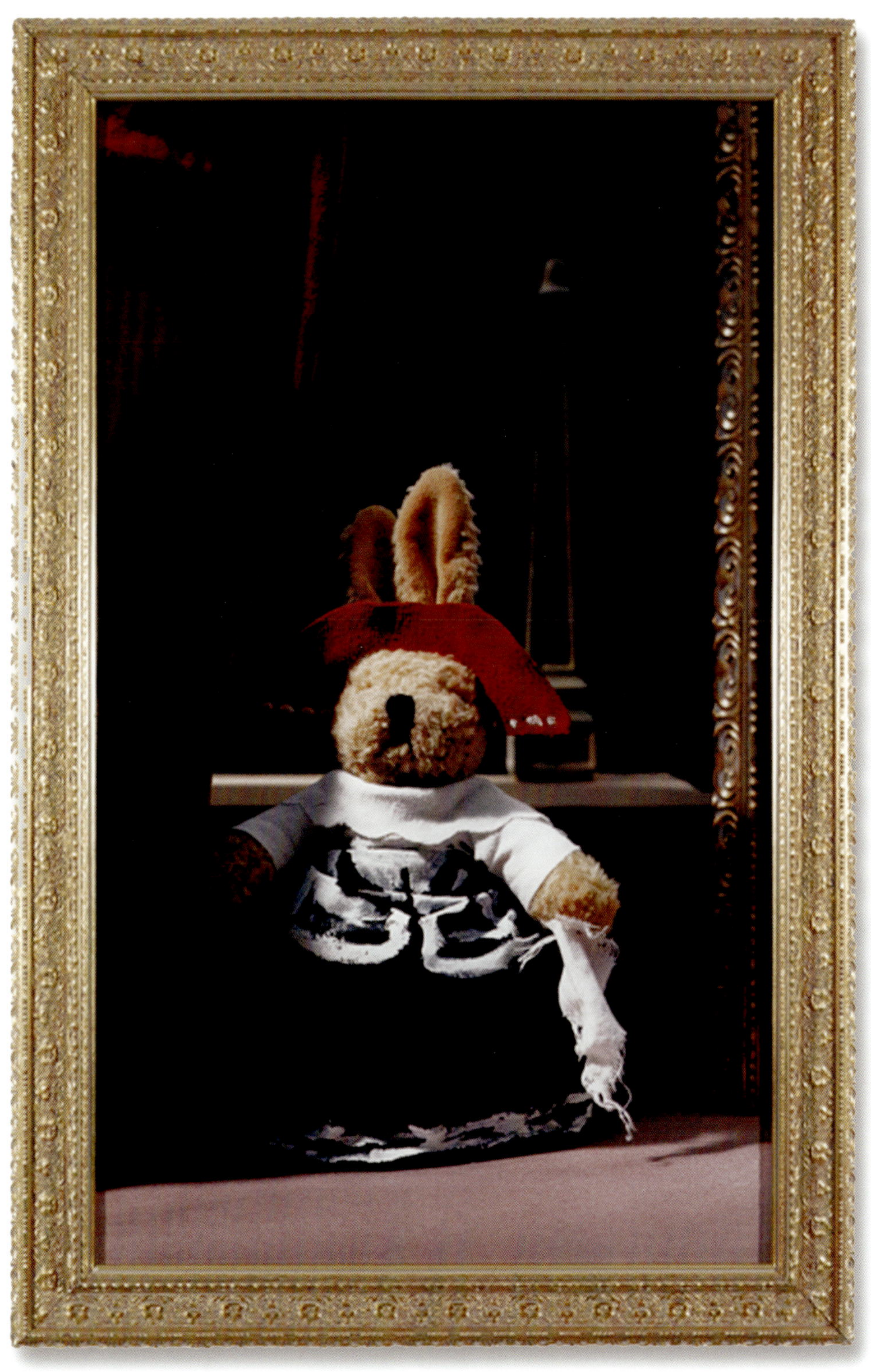

Diego Rodríguez de Silva y Velázquez **BILDNIS DER KÖNIGIN MARIANNE VON ÖSTERREICH /**
PORTRAIT OF QUEEN MARIANNE OF AUSTRIA 120 × 78 cm / 47.24 × 30.7 in.

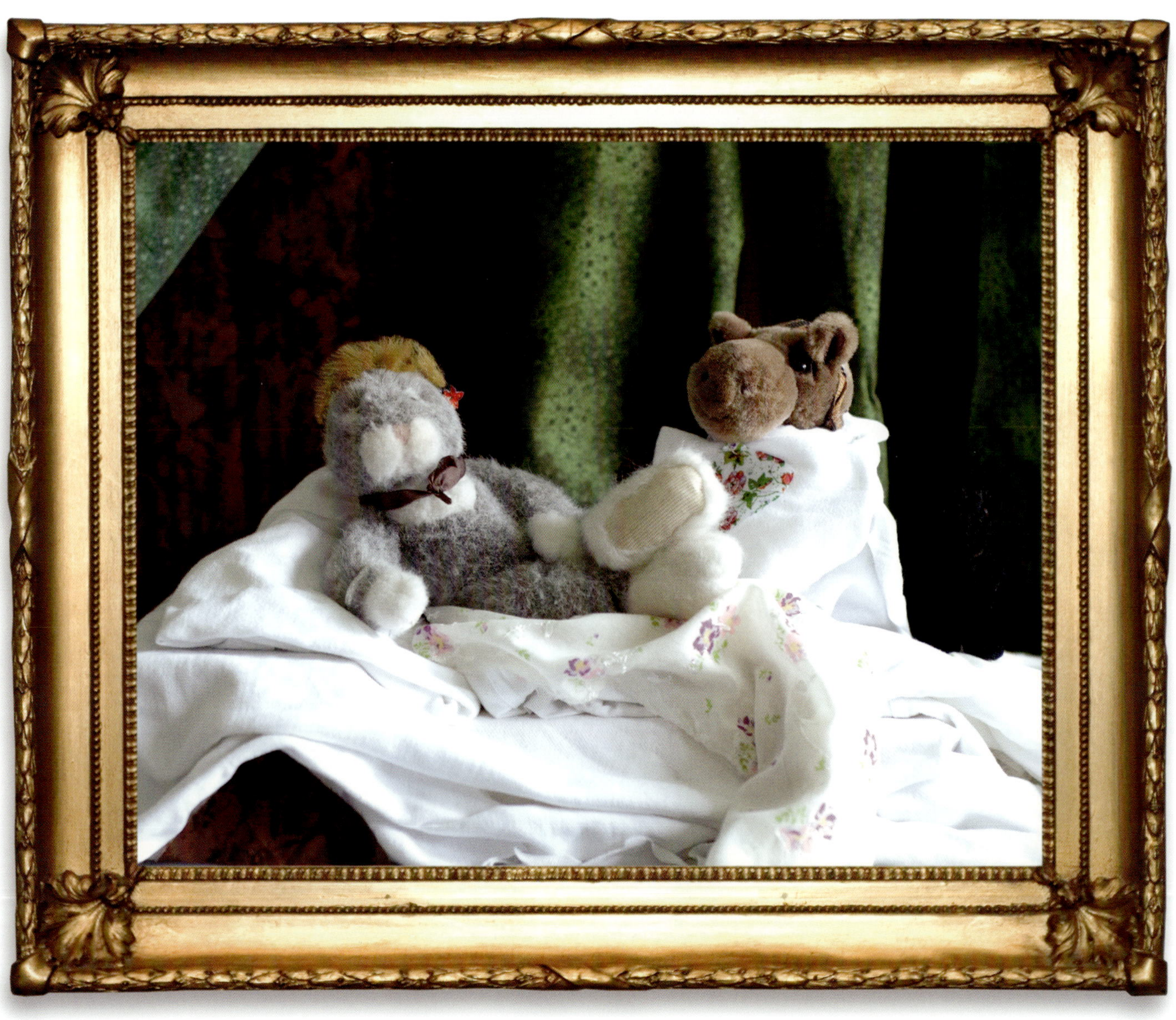

 Édouard Manet **OLYMPIA** 92 × 110 cm / 36.22 × 43.31 in.

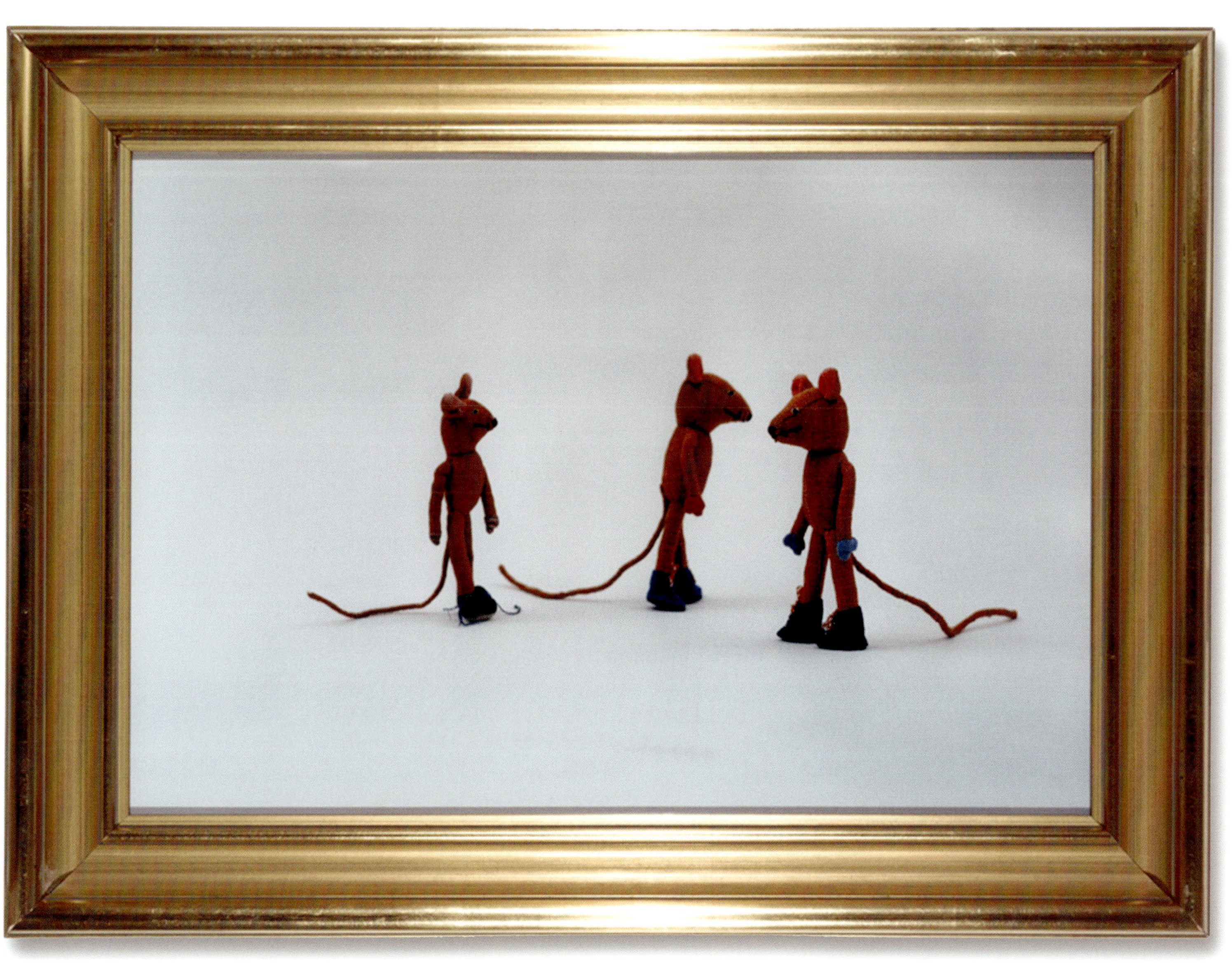

Alberto Giacometti **LA PLACE** 56 × 76 cm / 22.04 × 29.92 in.

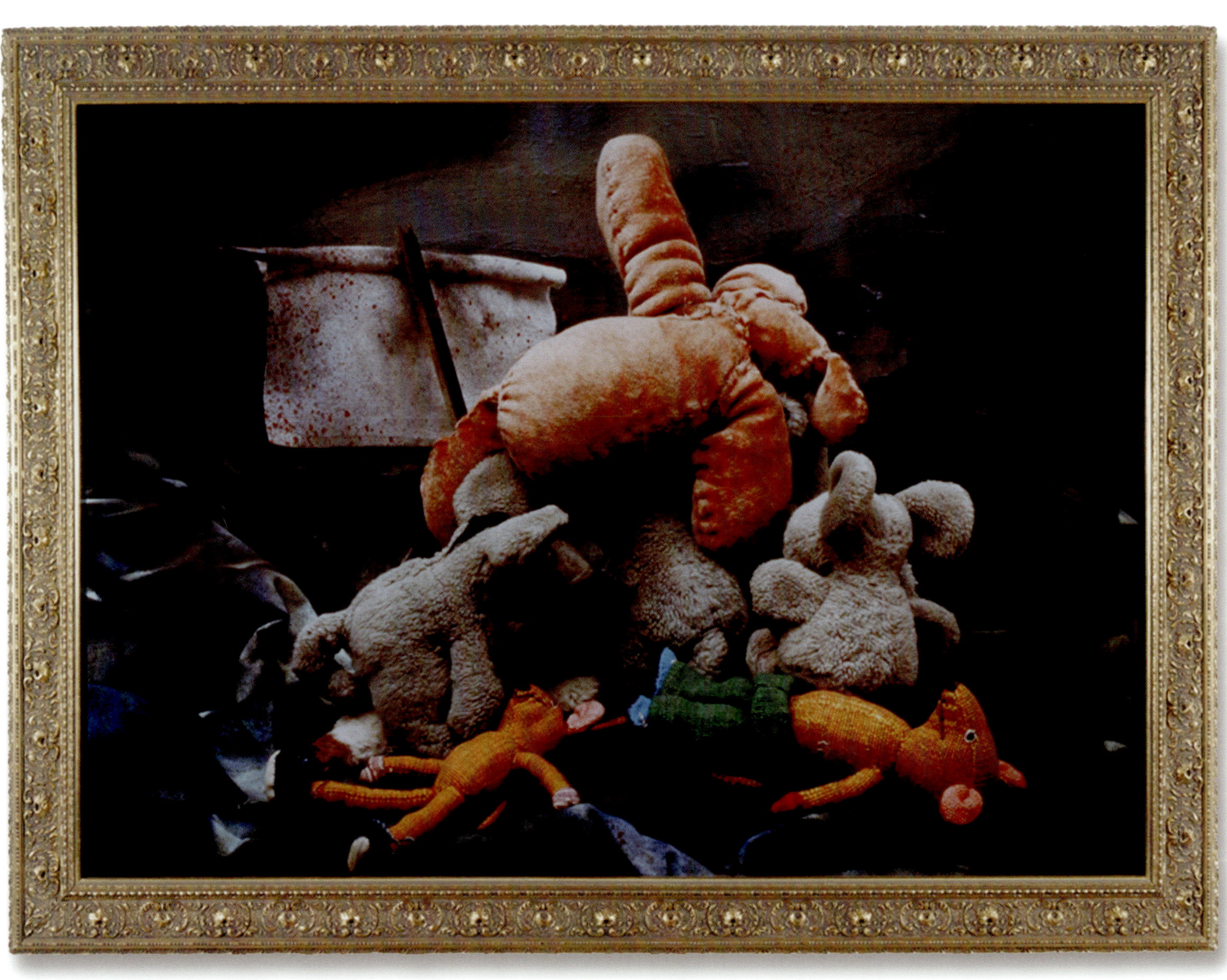

182 Théodore Géricault **DAS FLOSS DER MEDUSA / THE RAFT OF THE MEDUSA** 116 × 158 cm / 45.67 × 62.2 in.

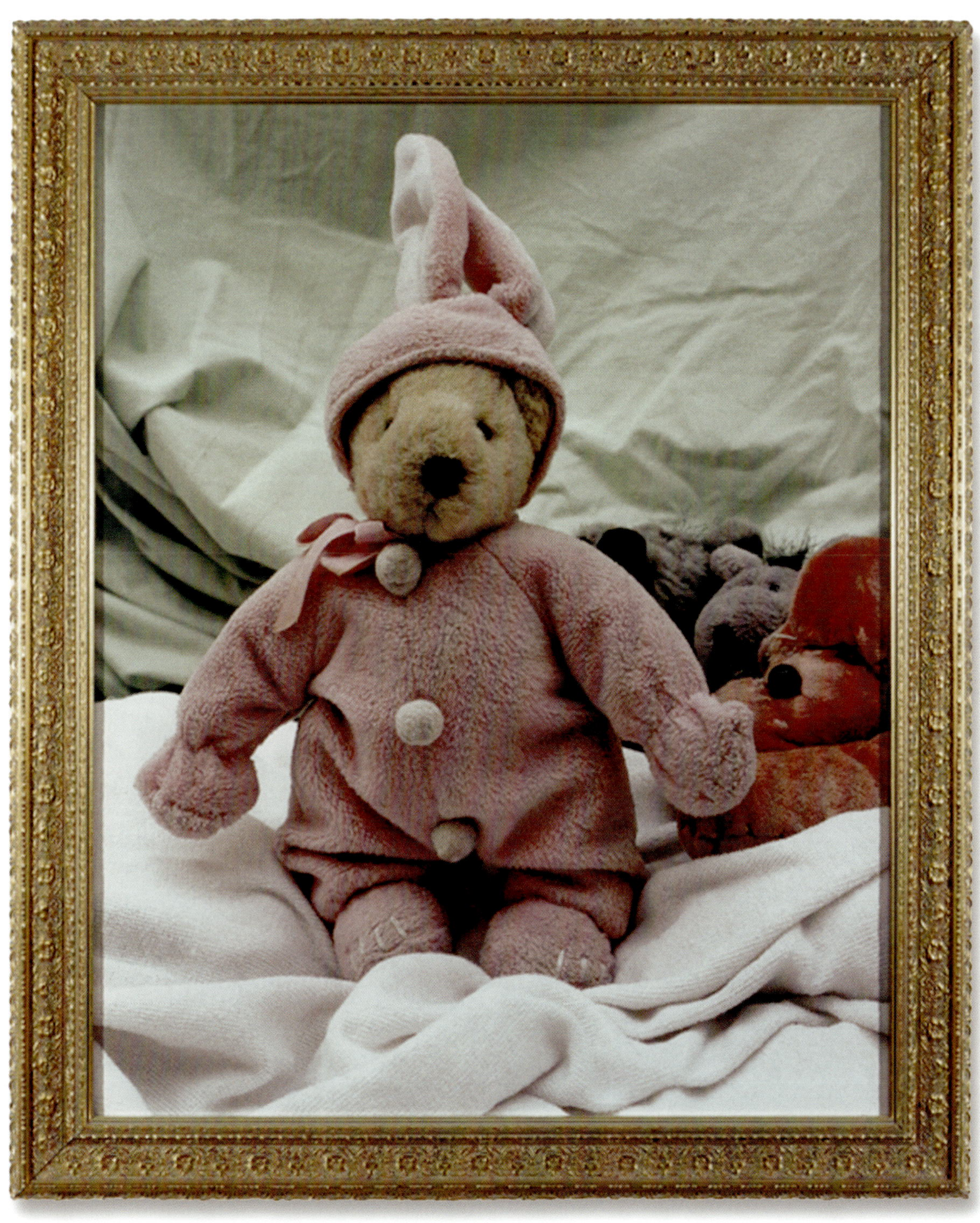

Antoine Watteau **GILLES** 106 × 89 cm / 41.73 × 35.04 in.

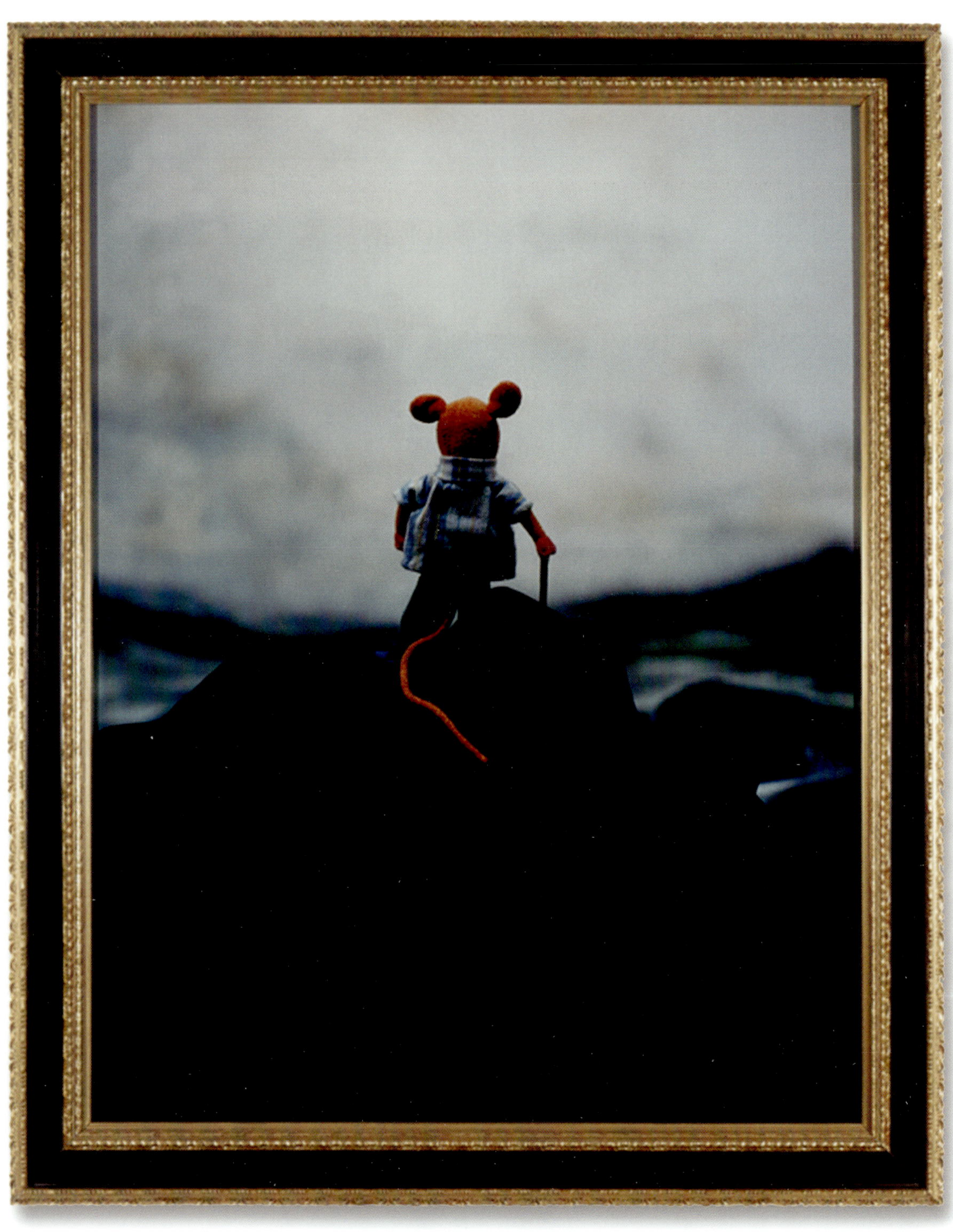

 Caspar David Friedrich **WANDERER ÜBER DEM NEBELMEER / WANDERER ABOVE THE SEA OF FOG** 108.5 × 88 cm / 42.72 × 34.64 in.

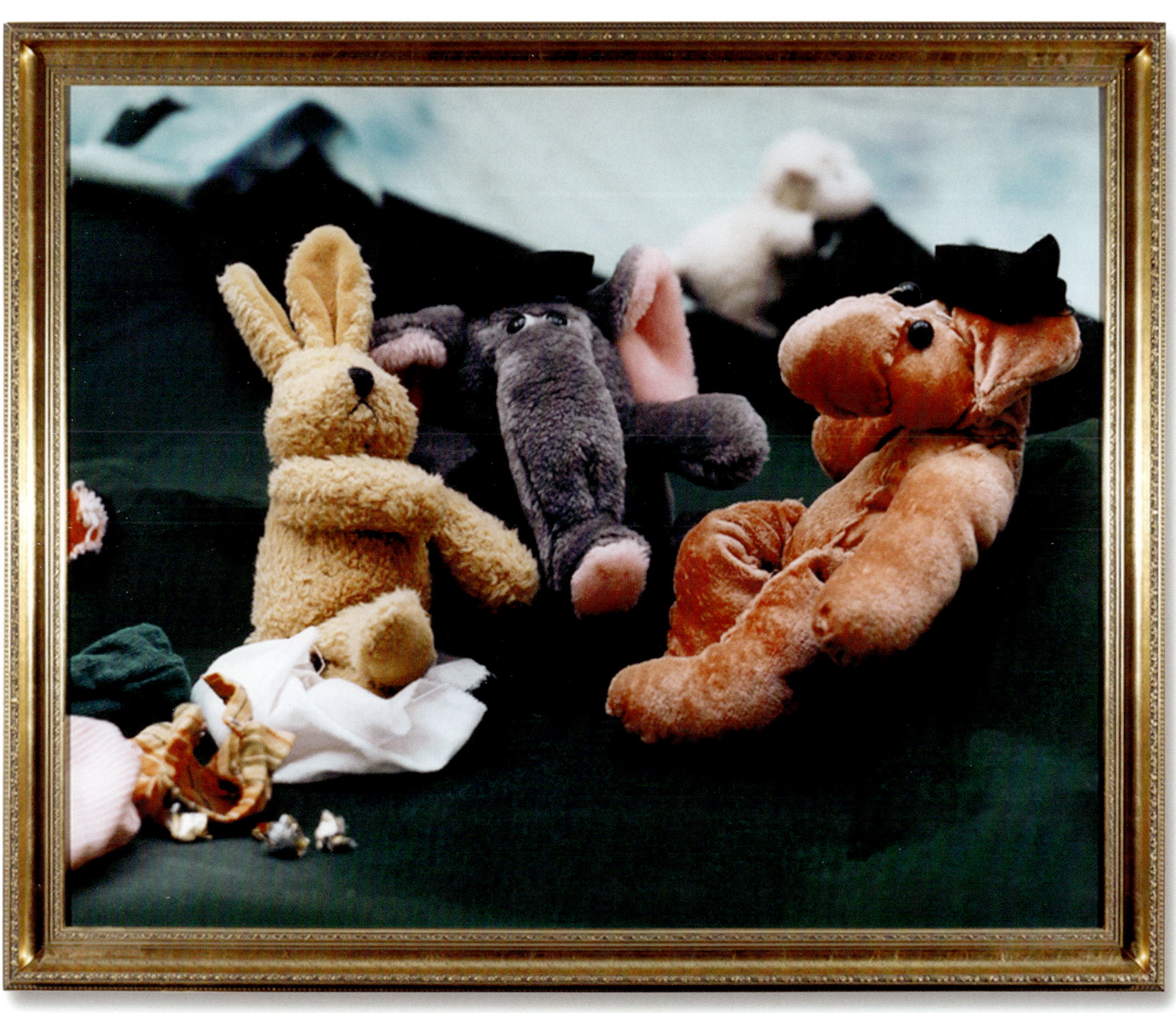

Édouard Manet **LE DÉJEUNER SUR L'HERBE** 119.5 × 146 cm / 47.05 × 57.48 in.

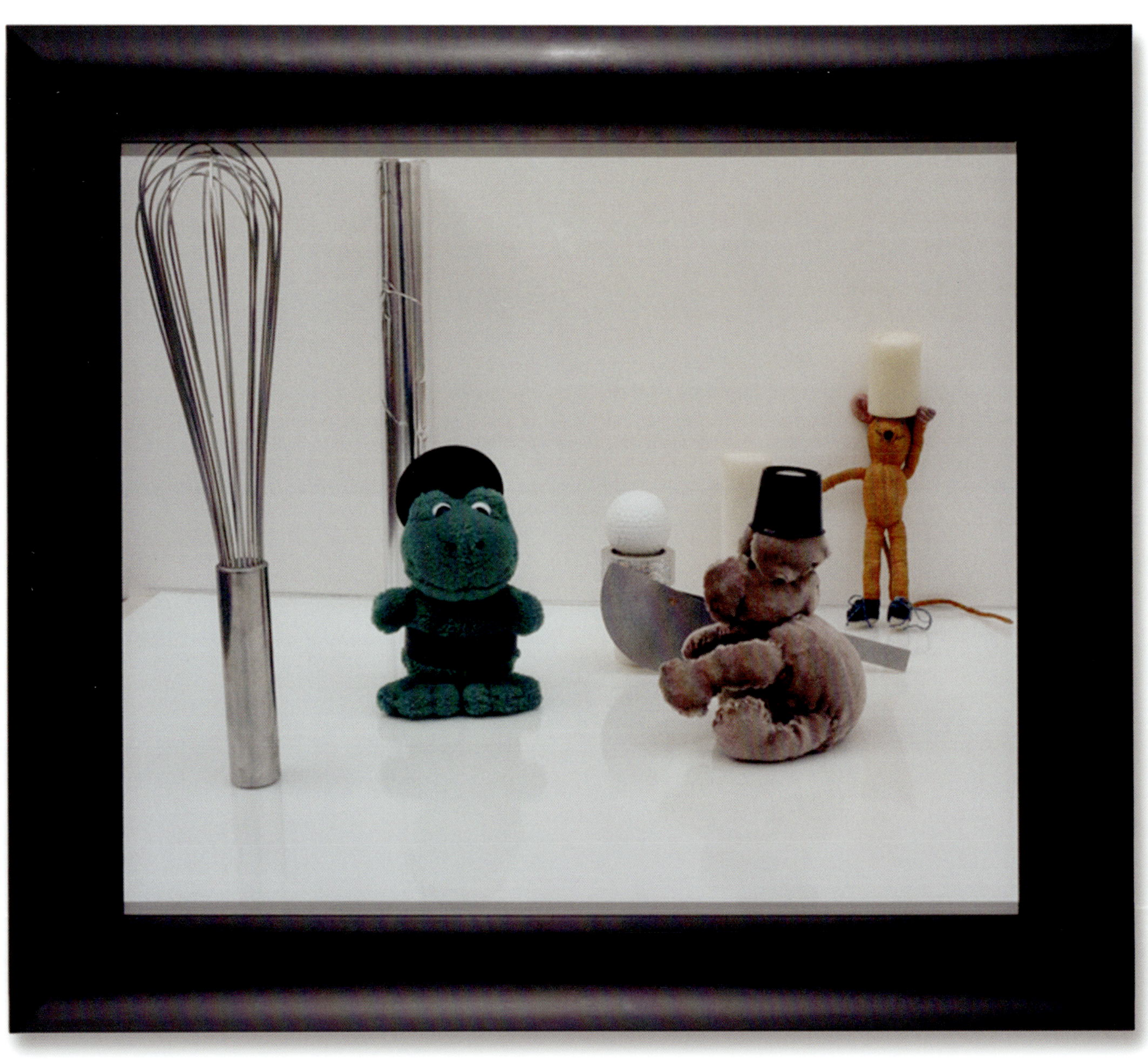

   Oskar Schlemmer **TRIADISCHES BALLETT / TRIADIC BALLET** 63 × 74 cm / 24.8 × 29.13 in.

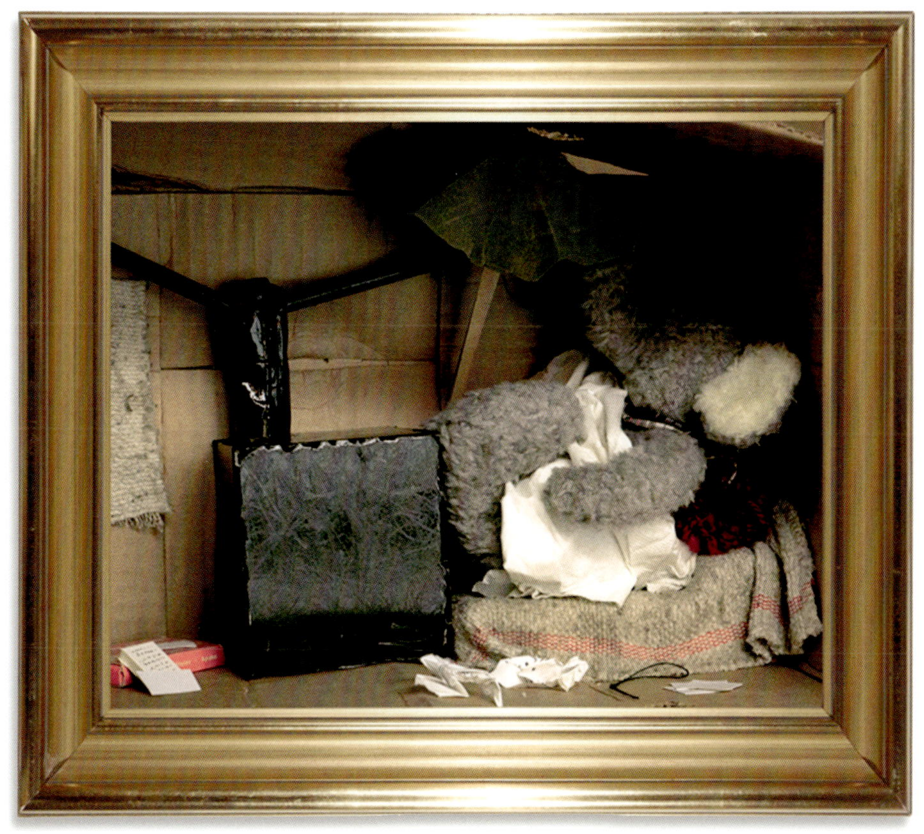

Carl Spitzweg **DER ARME POET / THE POOR POET** 45 × 54 cm / 17.72 × 21.26 in.

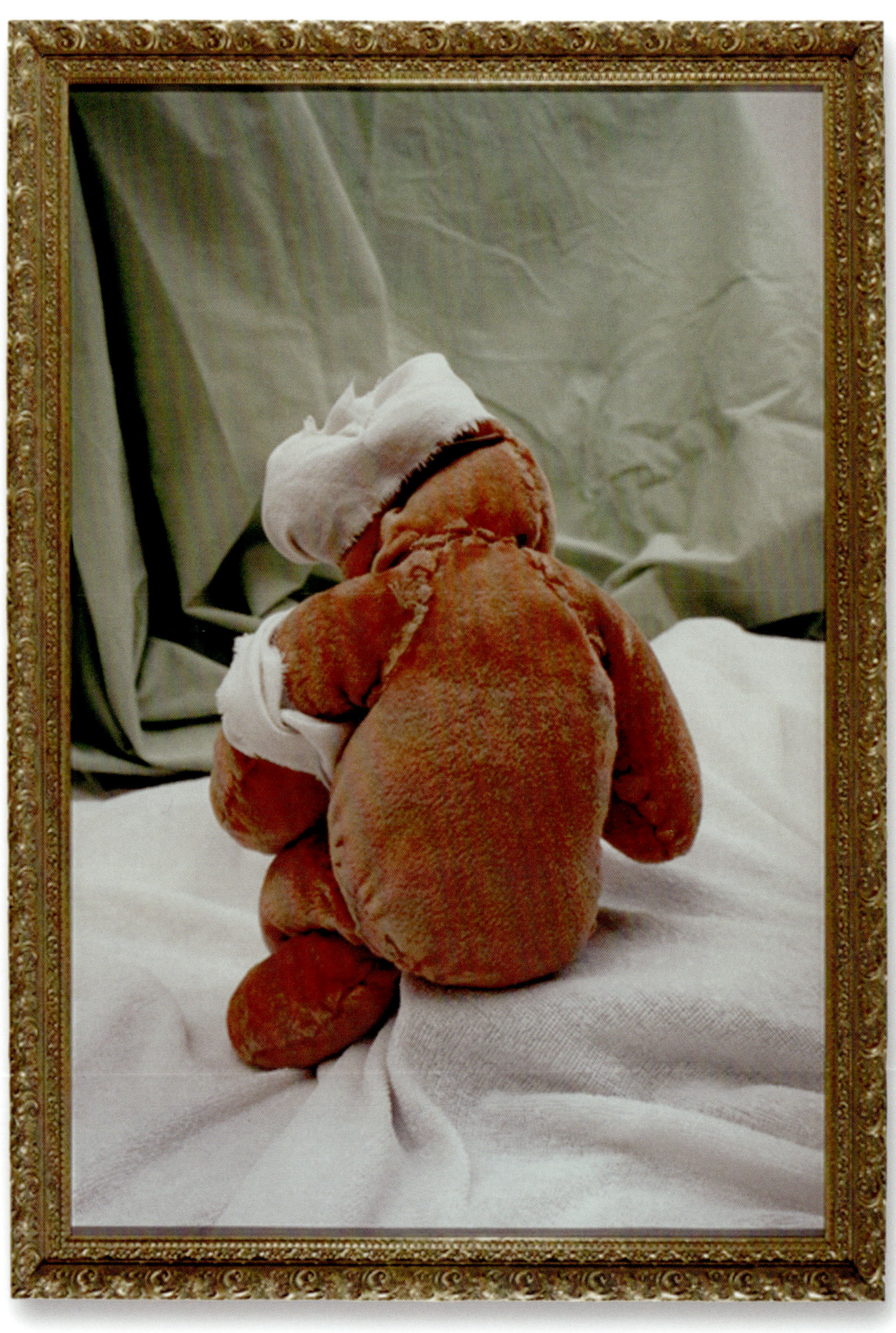

188 Jean-Auguste-Dominique Ingres **DIE BADENDE / THE BATHER** 153.5 × 107.5 cm / 60.43 × 42.32 in.

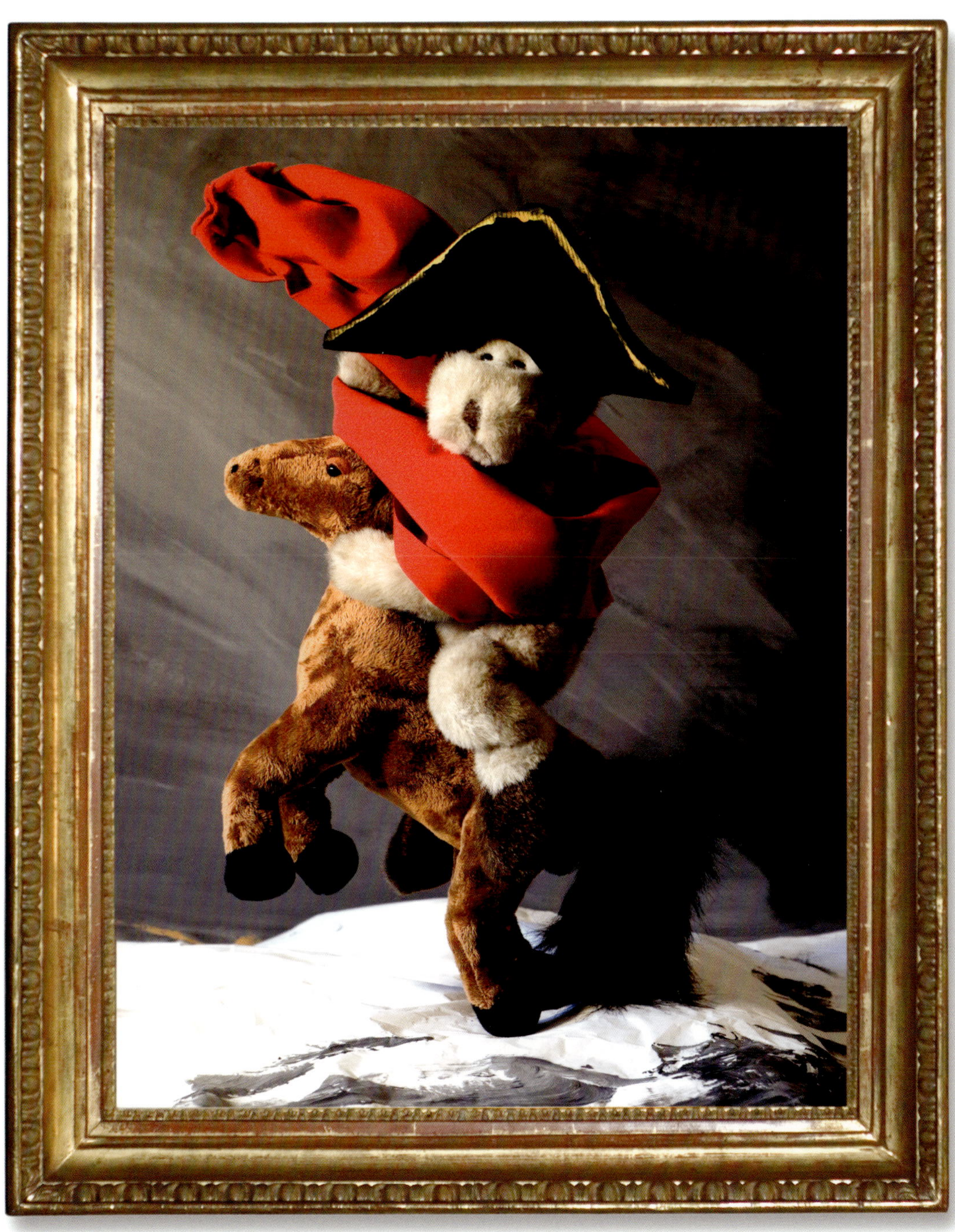

Jacques-Louis David **NAPOLEON ÜBERQUERT DIE ALPEN / NAPOLEON CROSSING THE ALPS** 95 × 77 cm / 37.4 × 30.31 in.

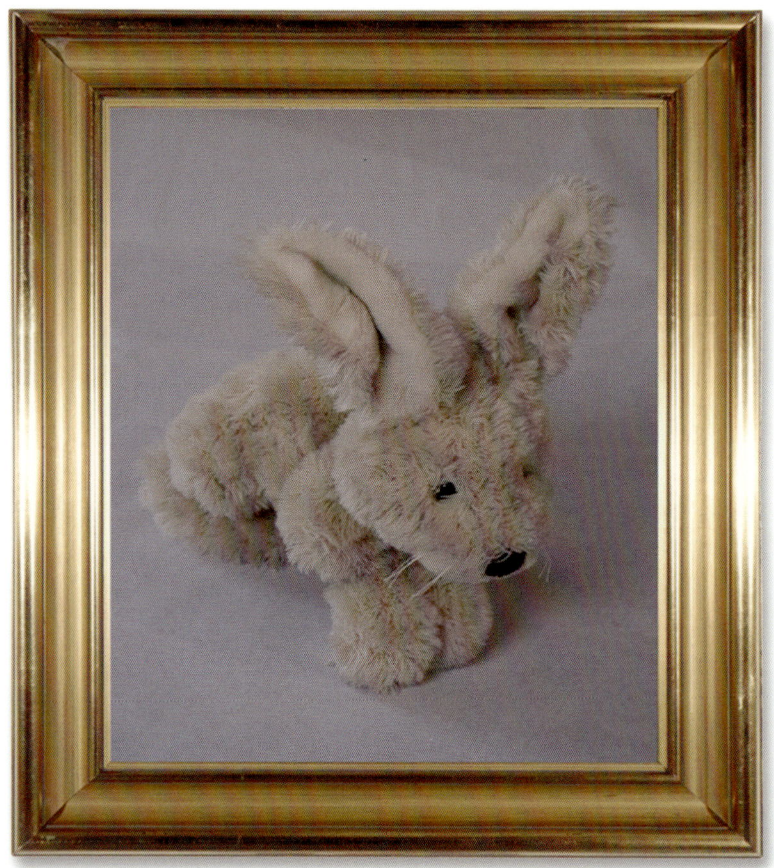

 Albrecht Dürer **DER FELDHASE / THE HARE** 50 × 47.5 cm / 19.68 × 18.5 in.

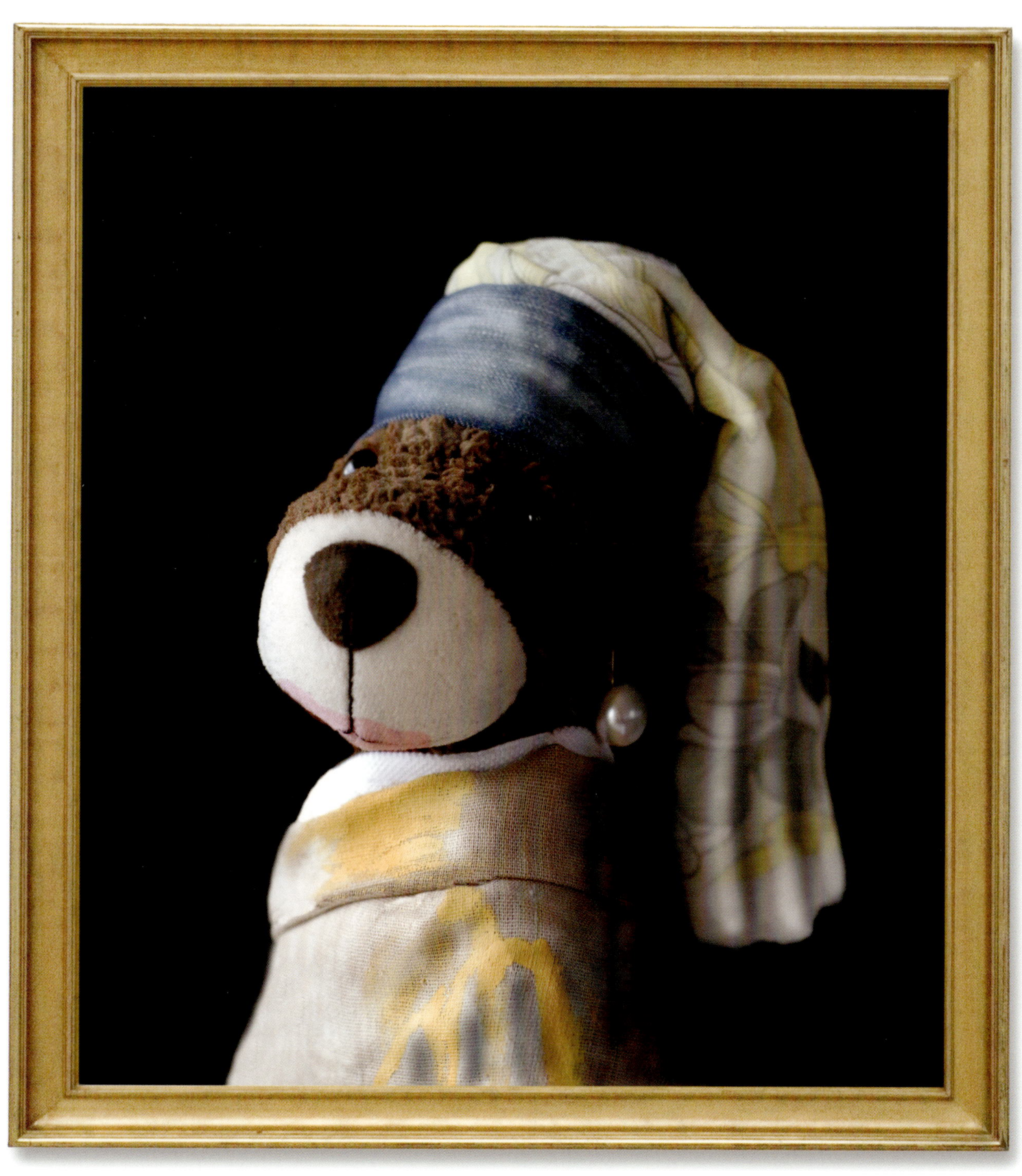

Jan Vermeer **DAS MÄDCHEN MIT DEM PERLOHRRING / GIRL WITH A PEARL EARRING** 70 × 65 cm / 27.56 × 25.59 in.

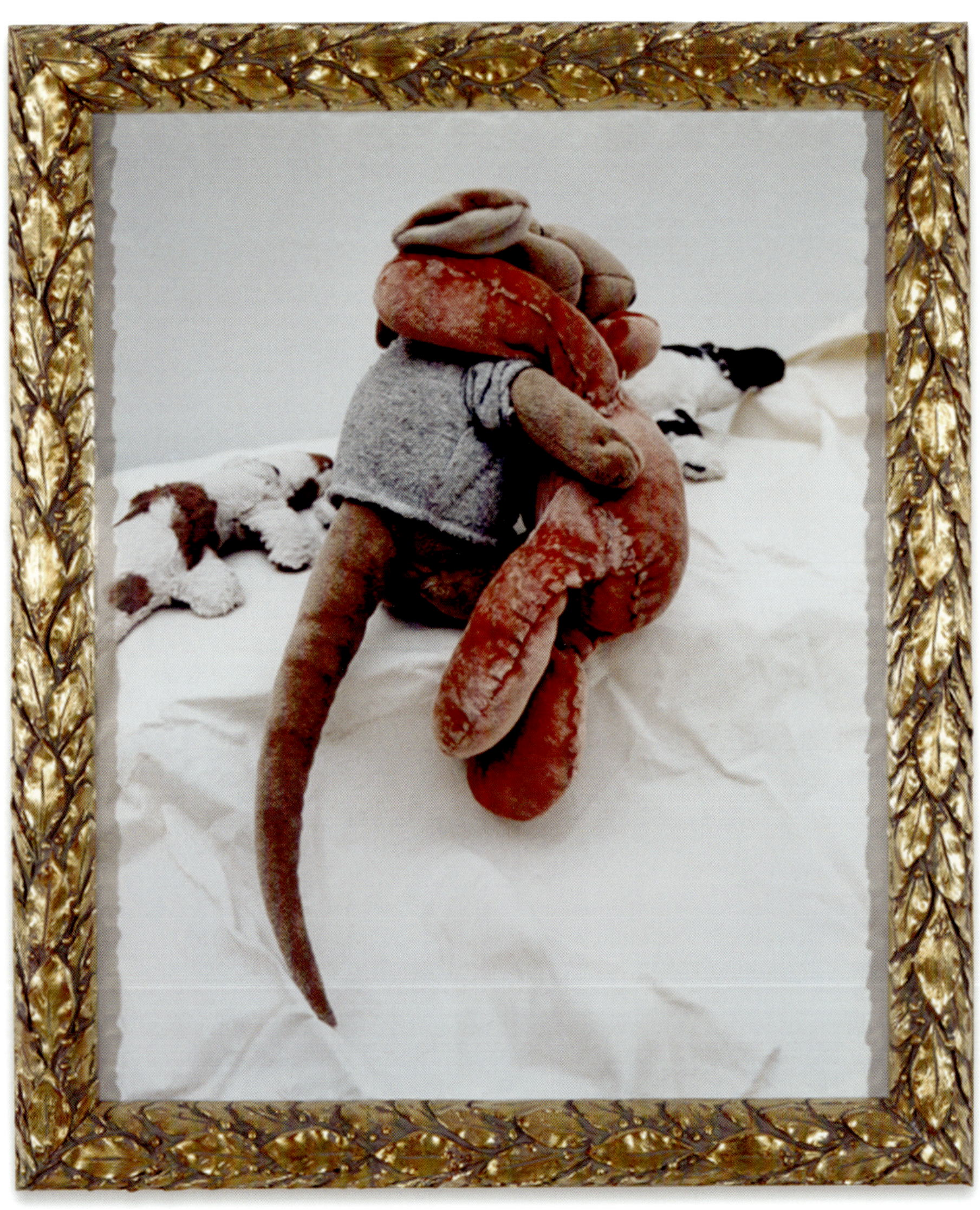

  Auguste Rodin **DIE BÜRGER VON CALAIS / THE BURGHERS OF CALAIS** 69 × 58.5 cm / 27.17 × 23.03 in.

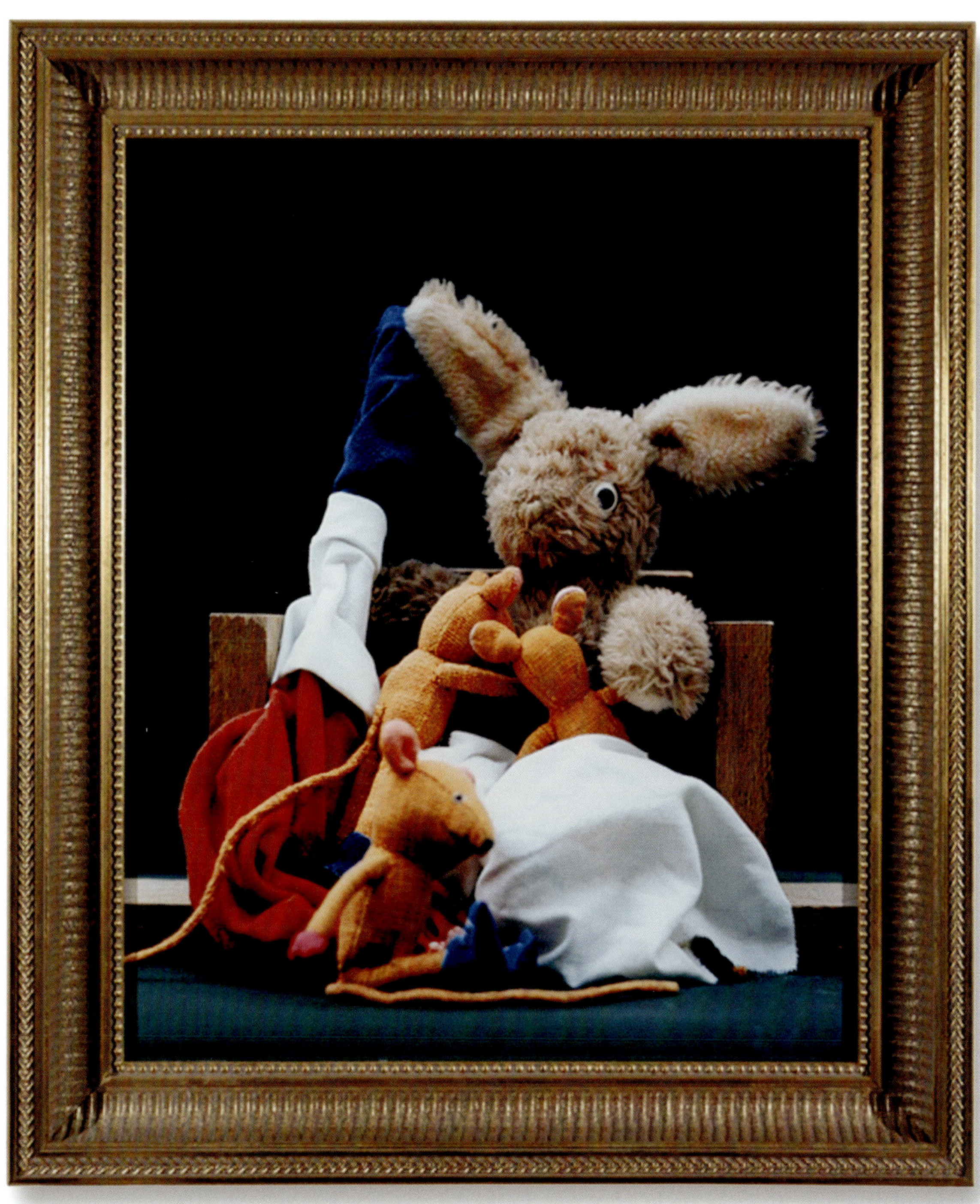

Honoré Daumier **DIE REPUBLIK / THE REPUBLIC** 89 × 75.5 cm / 35.04 × 29.72 in.

ANHANG / APPENDIX

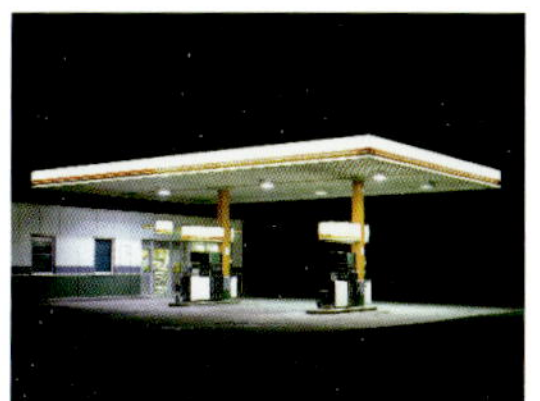

TANKSTELLEN / PETROL STATIONS **WEISS/BRAUN / WHITE/BROWN** 60 × 80 cm / 23.62 × 31.5 in. 1998 Seite / Page 13

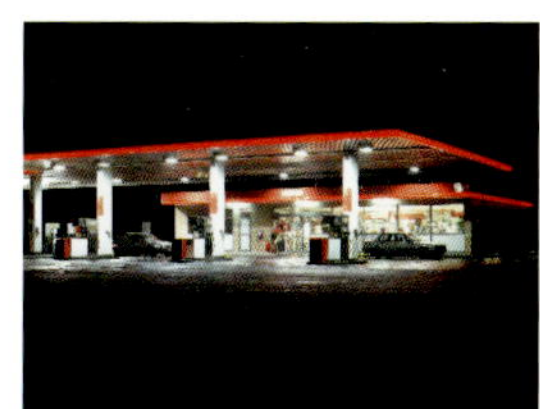

TANKSTELLEN / PETROL STATIONS **ROT/WEISS/ROT / RED/WHITE/RED** 60 × 80 cm / 23.62 × 31.5 in. 1998 Seite / Page 19

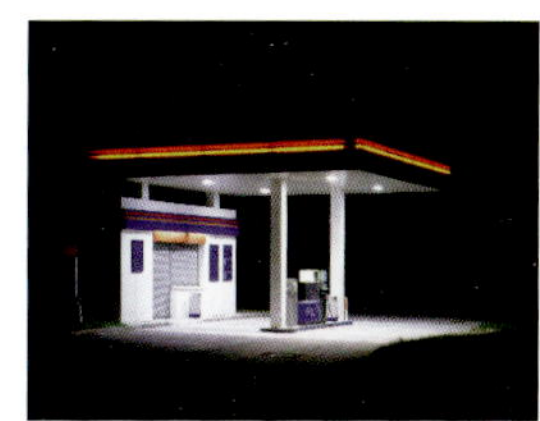

TANKSTELLEN / PETROL STATIONS **BLAU/ROT/GELB / BLUE/RED/YELLOW** 60 × 80 cm / 23.62 × 31.5 in. 1998 Seite / Page 22

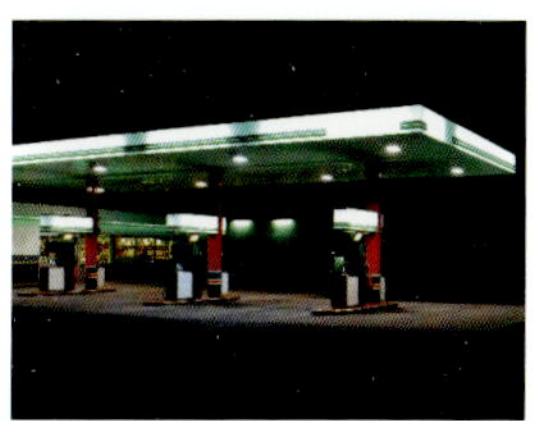

TANKSTELLEN / PETROL STATIONS **GRÜN/WEISS / GREEN/WHITE** 60 × 80 cm / 23.62 × 31.5 in. 1998 Seite / Page 14

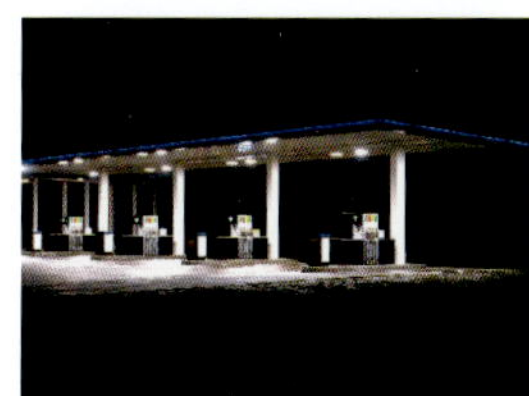

TANKSTELLEN / PETROL STATIONS **BLAU/WEISS / BLUE/WHITE** 60 × 80 cm / 23.62 × 31.5 in. 1998 Seite / Page 19

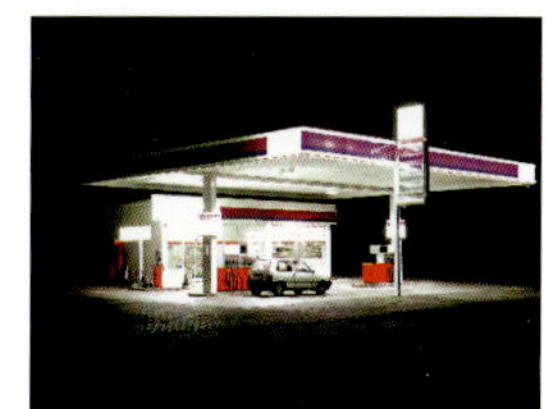

TANKSTELLEN / PETROL STATIONS **LILA / PURPLE** 60 × 80 cm / 23.62 × 31.5 in. 1998 Seite / Page 23

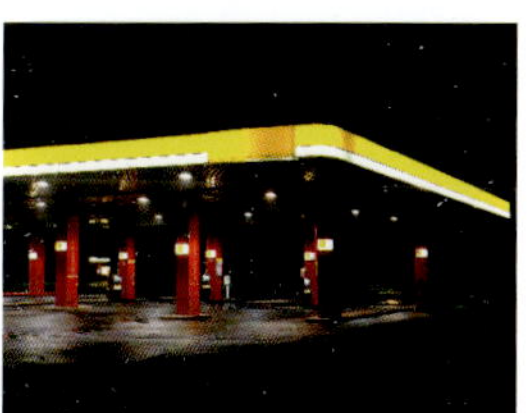

TANKSTELLEN / PETROL STATIONS **ROT/WEISS/GELB / RED/WHITE/YELLOW** 60 × 80 cm / 23.62 × 31.5 in. 1998 Seite / Page 15

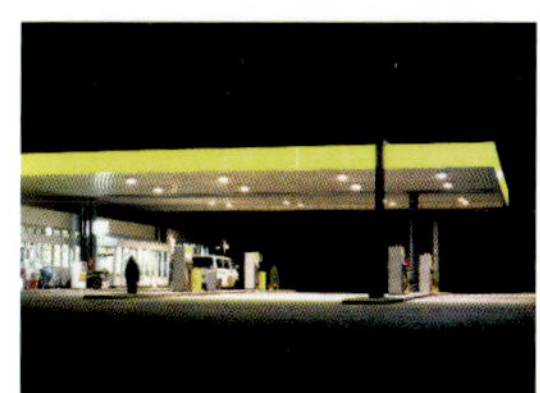

TANKSTELLEN / PETROL STATIONS **GELB/SCHWARZ / YELLOW/BLACK** 60 × 80 cm / 23.62 × 31.5 in. 1998 Seite / Page 20

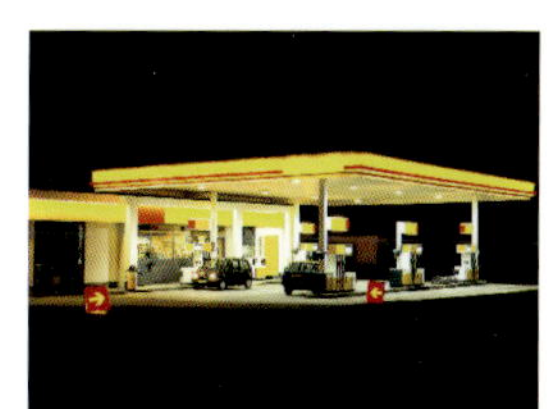

TANKSTELLEN / PETROL STATIONS **GELB NEU / YELLOW NEW** 60 × 80 cm / 23.62 × 31.5 in. 1998 Seite / Page 24

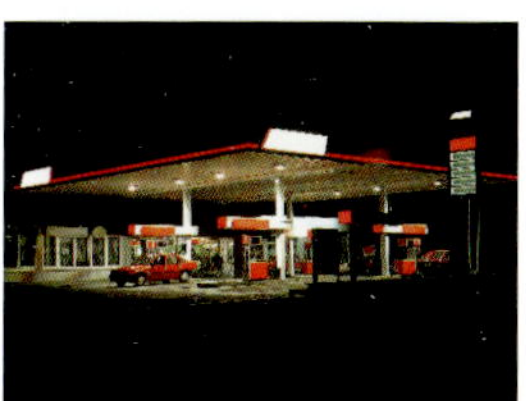

TANKSTELLEN / PETROL STATIONS **ROT/SCHWARZ / RED/BLACK** 60 × 80 cm / 23.62 × 31.5 in. 1998 Seite / Page 16

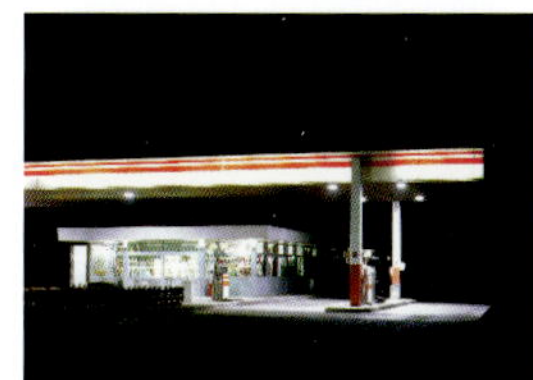

TANKSTELLEN / PETROL STATIONS **ROT/GELB / RED/YELLOW** 60 × 80 cm / 23.62 × 31.5 in. 1998 Seite / Page 20

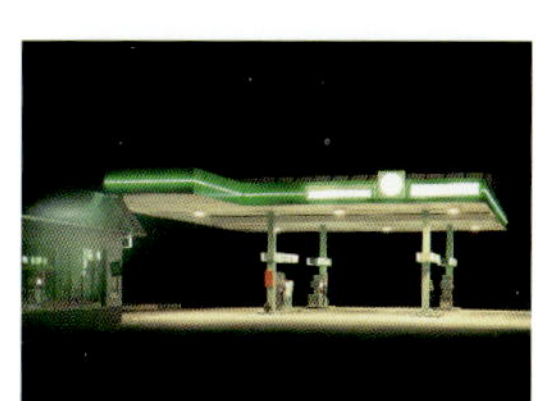

TANKSTELLEN / PETROL STATIONS **GRÜN/WEISS/GRÜN / GREEN/WHITE/GREEN** 60 × 80 cm / 23.62 × 31.5 in. 1998 Seite / Page 24

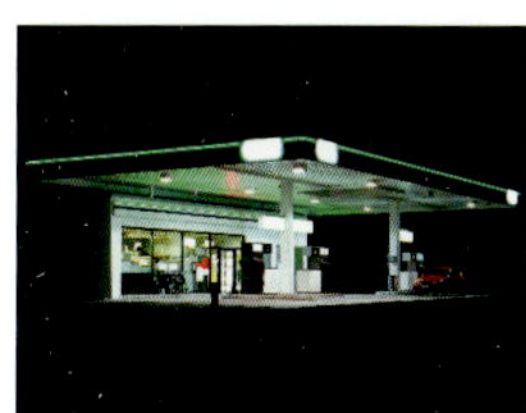

TANKSTELLEN / PETROL STATIONS **GRÜN/SCHWARZ / GREEN/BLACK** 60 × 80 cm / 23.62 × 31.5 in. 1998 Seite / Page 17

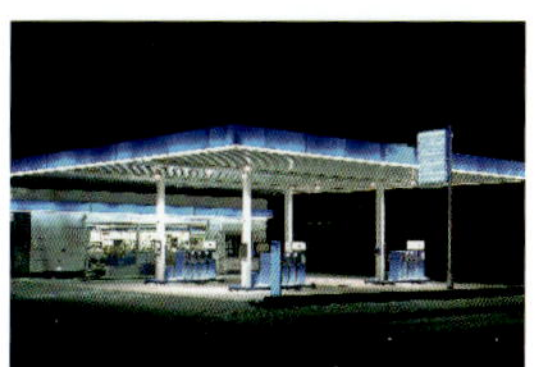

TANKSTELLEN / PETROL STATIONS **BLAU / BLUE** 60 × 80 cm / 23.62 × 31.5 in. 1998 Seite / Page 21

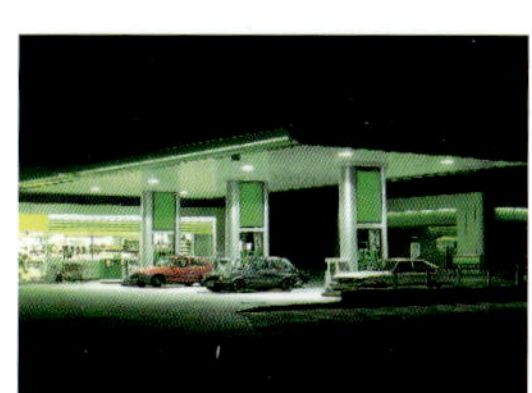

TANKSTELLEN / PETROL STATIONS **GRÜN / GREEN** 60 × 80 cm / 23.62 × 31.5 in. 1998 Seite / Page 24

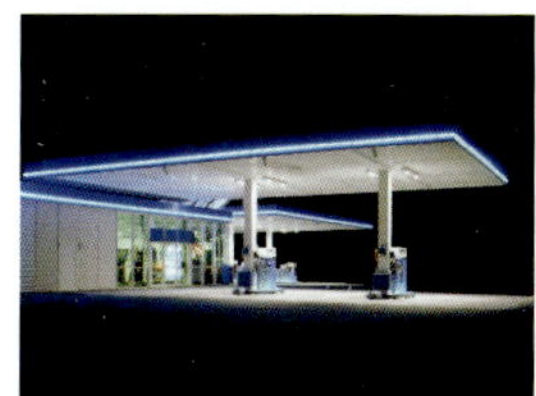

TANKSTELLEN / PETROL STATIONS **WEISS/BLAU / WHITE/BLUE** 60 × 80 cm / 23.62 × 31.5 in. 1998 Seite / Page 18

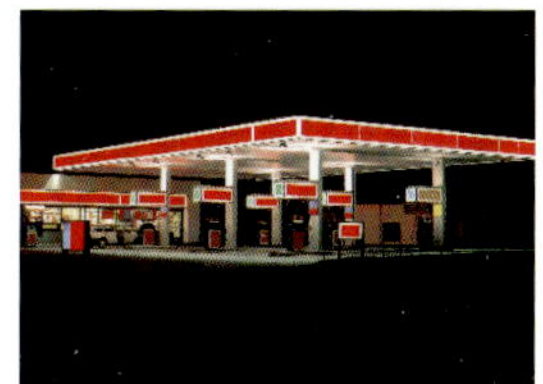

TANKSTELLEN / PETROL STATIONS **ROT / RED** 60 × 80 cm / 23.62 × 31.5 in. 1998 Seite / Page 21

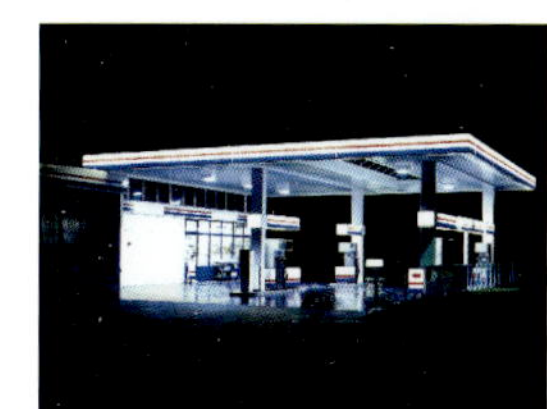

TANKSTELLEN / PETROL STATIONS **BLAU/ROT / BLUE/RED** 60 × 80 cm / 23.62 × 31.5 in. 1998 Seite / Page 24

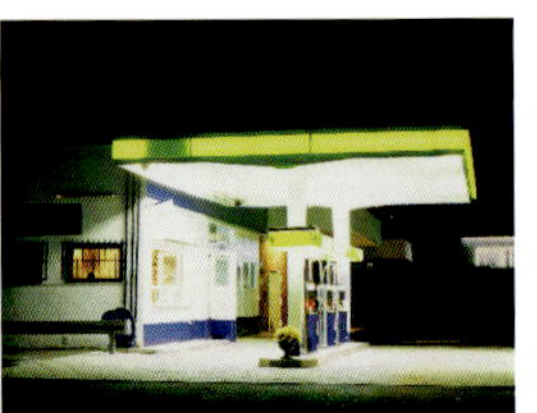

TANKSTELLEN / PETROL STATIONS **GRÜN/GELB / GREEN/YELLOW** 60 × 80 cm / 23.62 × 31.5 in. 1998 Seite / Page 25

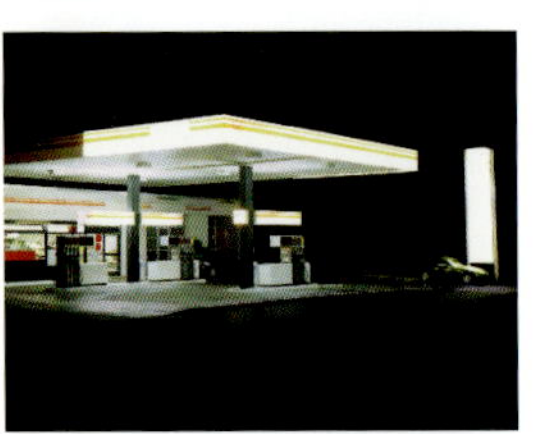

TANKSTELLEN / PETROL STATIONS **ORANGE** 60 × 80 cm / 23.62 × 31.5 in. 1998 Seite / Page 25

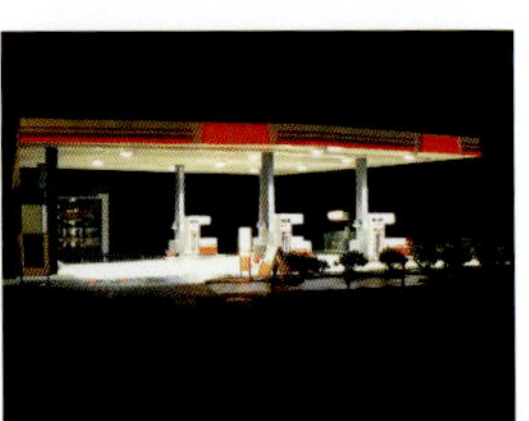

TANKSTELLEN / PETROL STATIONS **SCHWARZ/ROT / BLACK/RED** 60 × 80 cm / 23.62 × 31.5 in. 1998 Seite / Page 25

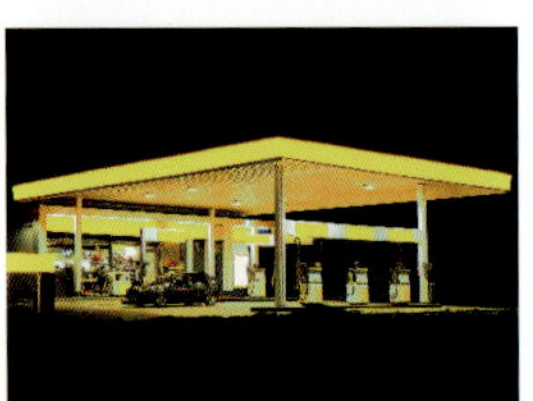

TANKSTELLEN / PETROL STATIONS **GELB / YELLOW** 60 × 80 cm / 23.62 × 31.5 in. 1998 Seite / Page 25

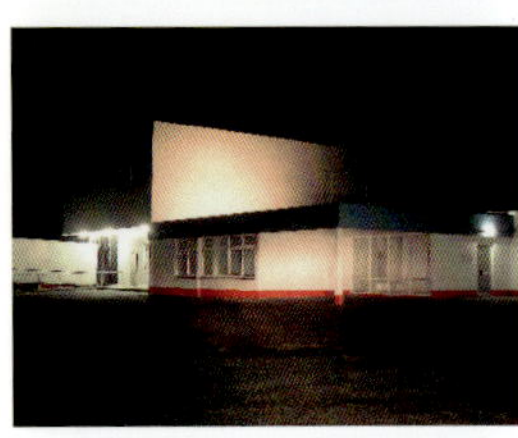

SUPERMÄRKTE / SUPERMARKETS **BLAU/ROT / BLUE/RED** 60 × 80 cm / 23.62 × 31.5 in. 1998 Seite / Page 27

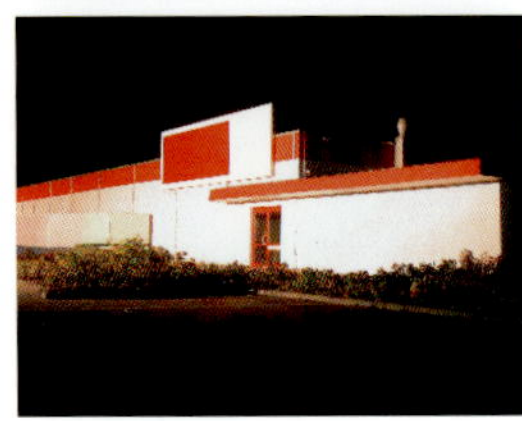

SUPERMÄRKTE / SUPERMARKETS **ROT / RED** 60 × 80 cm / 23.62 × 31.5 in. 1998 Seite / Page 27

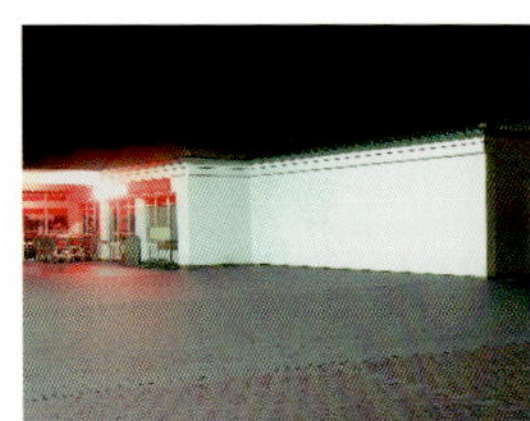

SUPERMÄRKTE / SUPERMARKETS **ROT/GRÜN / RED/GREEN** 60 × 80 cm / 23.62 × 31.5 in. 1998 Seite / Page 27

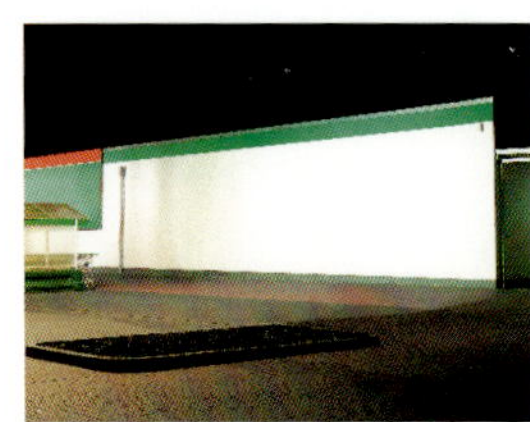

SUPERMÄRKTE / SUPERMARKETS **GRÜN / GREEN** 60 × 80 cm / 23.62 × 31.5 in. 1998 Seite / Page 27

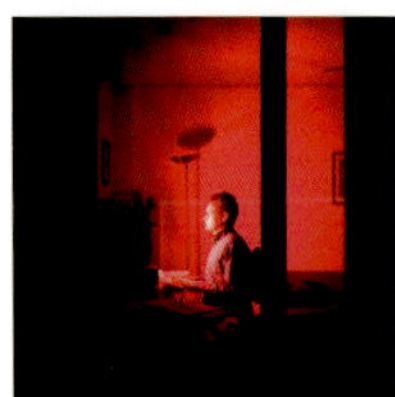

PORTRÄTS BEI NACHT / PORTRAITS BY NIGHT **ROT / RED** 110 × 110 cm / 43.31 × 43.31 in. 1998 Seite / Page 29

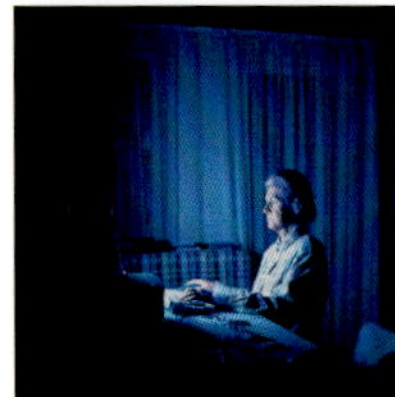

PORTRÄTS BEI NACHT / PORTRAITS BY NIGHT **BLAU / BLUE** 110 × 110 cm / 43.31 × 43.31 in. 1998 Seite / Page 30

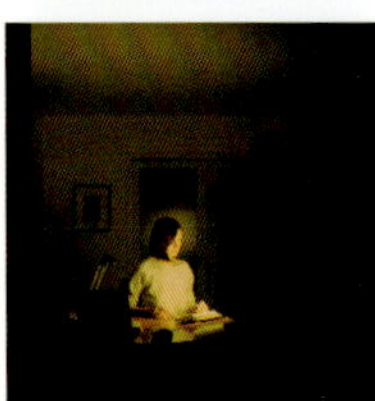

PORTRÄTS BEI NACHT / PORTRAITS BY NIGHT **GELB / YELLOW** 110 × 110 cm / 43.31 × 43.31 in. 1998 Seite / Page 31

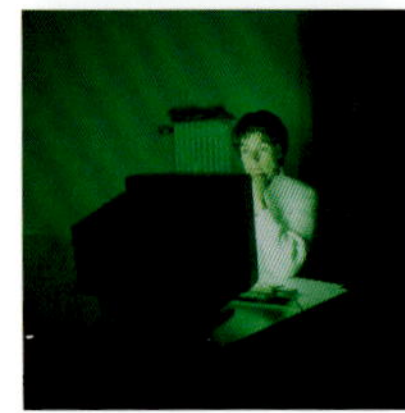

PORTRÄTS BEI NACHT / PORTRAITS BY NIGHT **GRÜN / GREEN** 110 × 110 cm / 43.31 × 43.31 in. 1998 Seite / Page 32

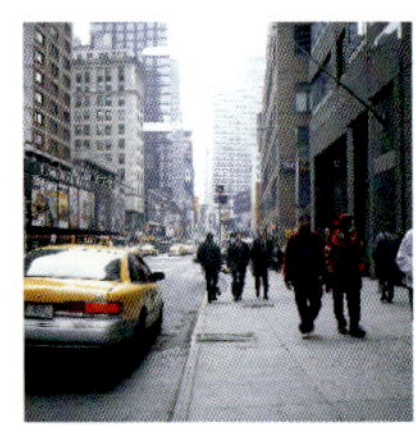

MÄNNER/FRAUEN / MEN/WOMEN **9TH AVENUE** 110 × 110 cm / 43.31 × 43.31 in. 1998/99 Seite / Page 35

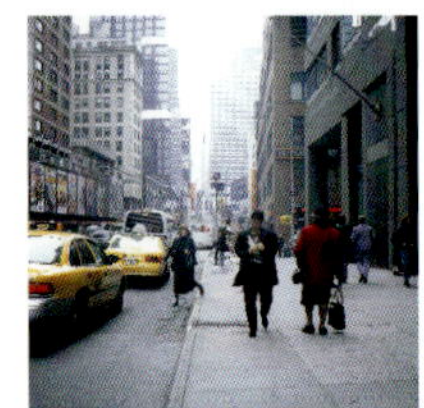

MÄNNER/FRAUEN / MEN/WOMEN **9TH AVENUE** 110 × 110 cm / 43.31 × 43.31 in. 1998/99 Seite / Page 35

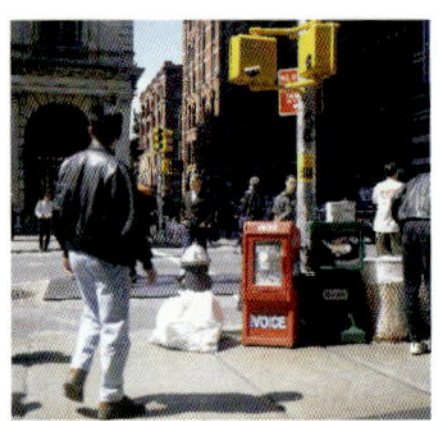

MÄNNER/FRAUEN / MEN/WOMEN **BROADWAY** 102 × 110 cm / 40.16 × 43.31 in. 1998/99 Seite / Page 35

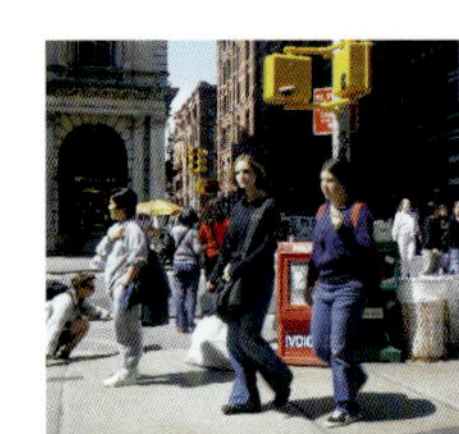

MÄNNER/FRAUEN / MEN/WOMEN **BROADWAY** 102 × 110 cm / 40.16 × 43.31 in. 1998/99 Seite / Page 35

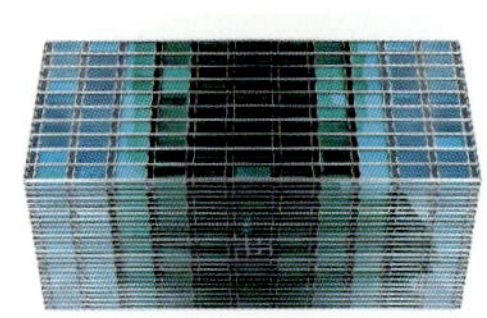

BOX **# 1** 124 × 202 cm / 48.82 × 79.67 in. 1999/2000 Seite / Page 37

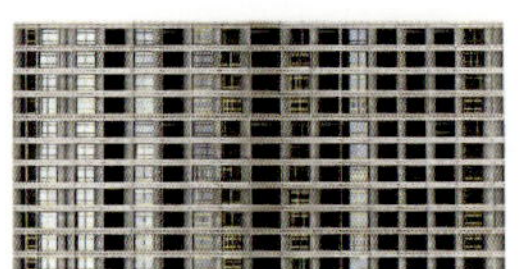

BOX **# 6** 124 × 223 cm / 48.82 × 87.84 in. 1999/2000 Seite / Page 38

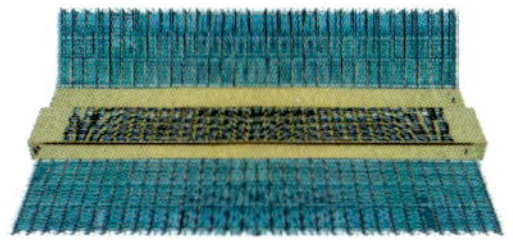

BOX **# 7** 124 × 266 cm /
48.82 × 104.83 in. 1999/2000
Seite / Page 39

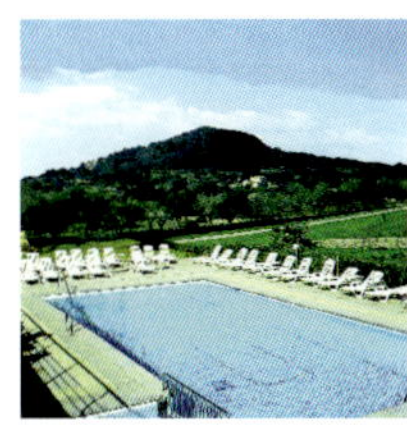

MIX **TILJO** 100 × 100 cm /
39.38 × 39.38 in. 2000/01
Seite / Page 46

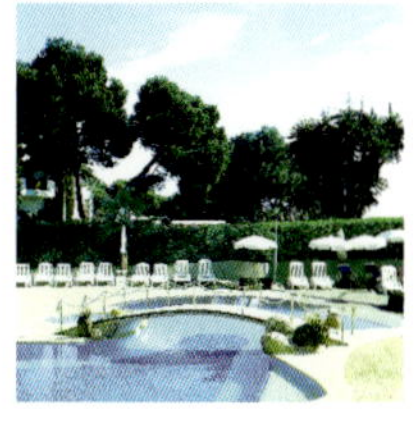

MIX **TUSAN** 100 × 100 cm /
39.38 × 39.38 in. 2000/01
Seite / Page 49

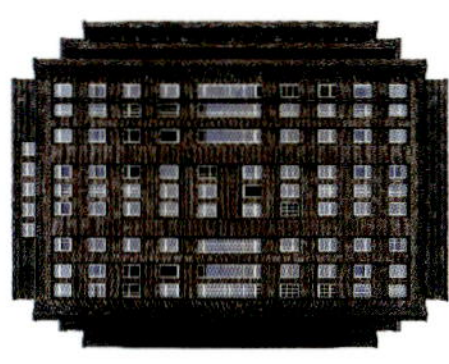

BOX **# 5** 124 × 181 cm /
48.82 × 71.3 in. 1999/2000
Seite / Page 40

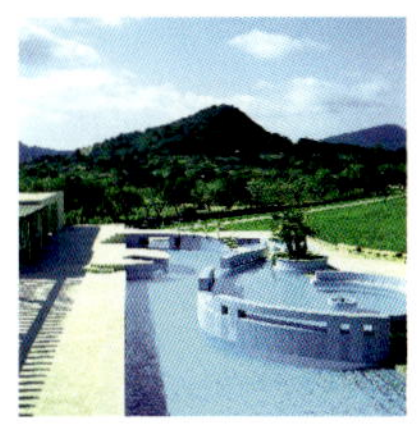

MIX **RAMANO** 100 × 100 cm /
39.38 × 39.38 in. 2000/01
Seite / Page 47

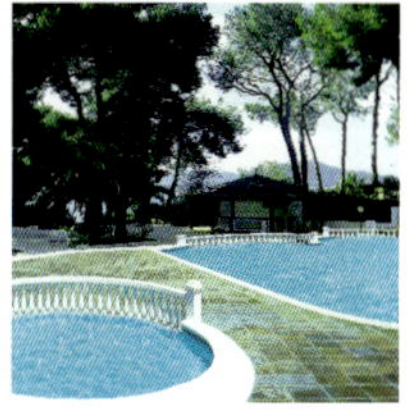

MIX **RALMARA** 100 × 100 cm /
39.38 × 39.38 in. 2000/01
Seite / Page 49

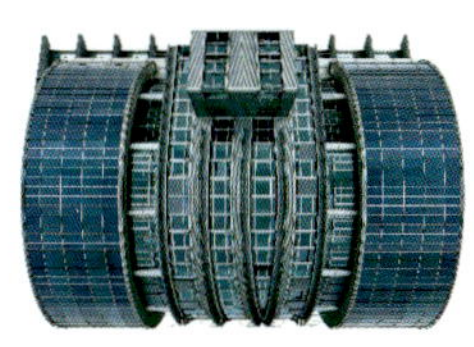

BOX **# 3** 124 × 192 cm /
48.82 × 75.83 in. 1999/2000
Seite / Page 41

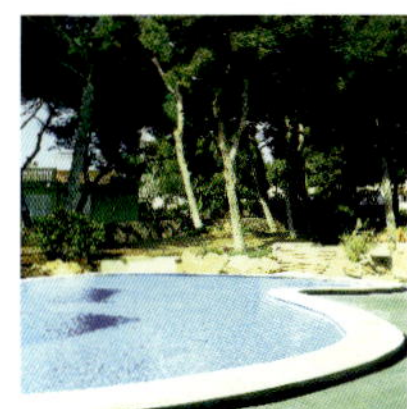

MIX **CALTARA** 100 × 100 cm /
39.38 × 39.38 in. 2000/01
Seite / Page 48

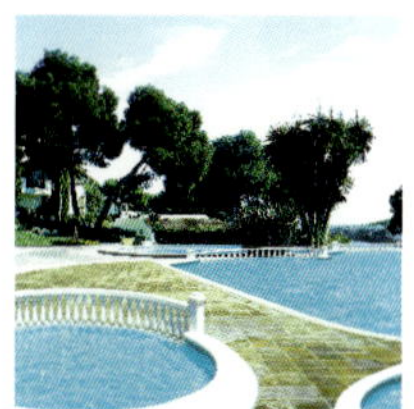

MIX **MASERA** 100 × 100 cm /
39.38 × 39.38 in. 2000/01
Seite / Page 49

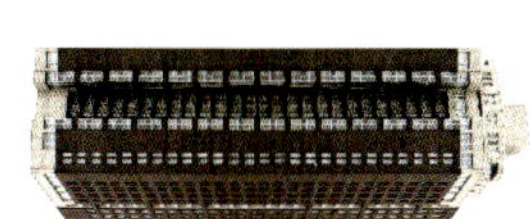

BOX **# 4** 124 × 282 cm /
48.82 × 111 in. 1999/2000
Seite / Page 42

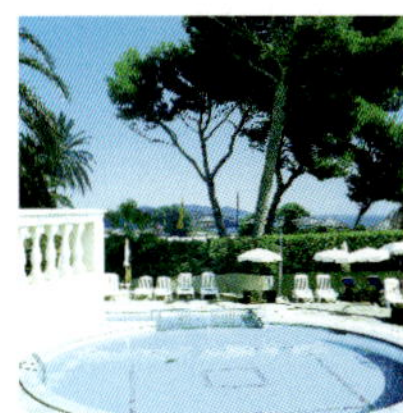

MIX **ZITUS** 100 × 100 cm /
39.38 × 39.38 in. 2000/01
Seite / Page 48

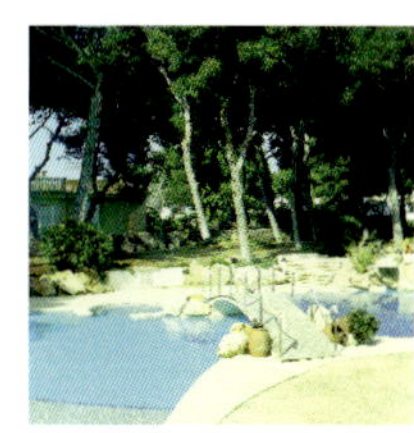

MIX **ZINOLA** 100 × 100 cm /
39.38 × 39.38 in. 2000/01
Seite / Page 49

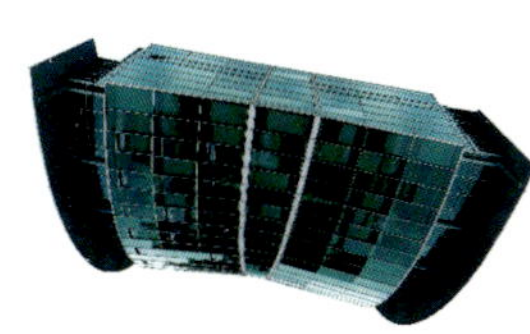

BOX **# 2** 124 × 216 cm /
48.82 × 85.12 in. 1999/2000
Seite / Page 43

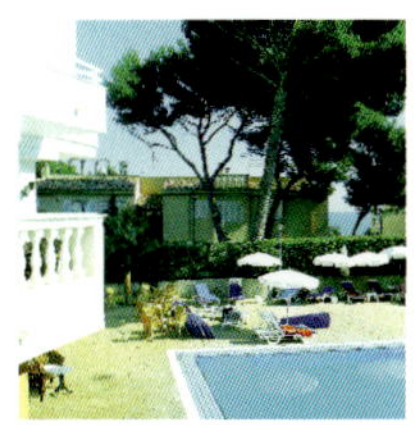

MIX **OLAN** 100 × 100 cm /
39.38 × 39.38 in. 2000/01
Seite / Page 48

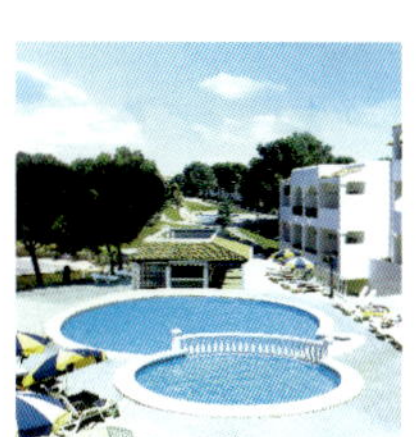

MIX **TAMMARA** 100 × 100 cm /
39.38 × 39.38 in. 2000/01
Seite / Page 50

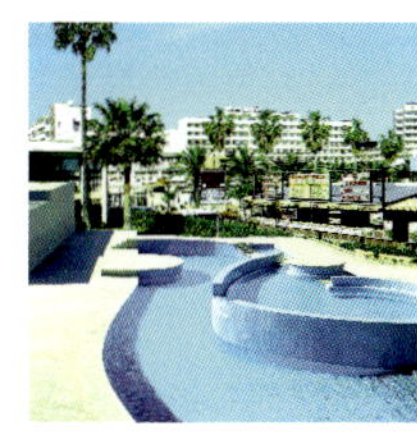

MIX **TANJO** 100 × 100 cm /
39.38 × 39.38 in. 2000/01
Seite / Page 45

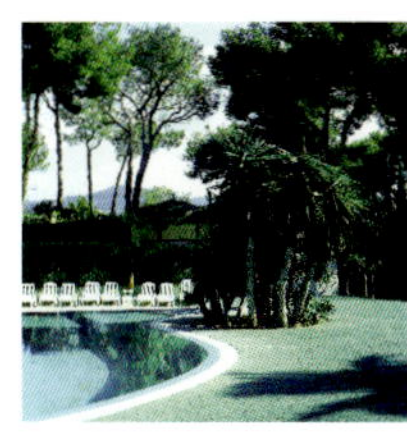

MIX **MALA** 100 × 100 cm /
39.38 × 39.38 in. 2000/01
Seite / Page 48

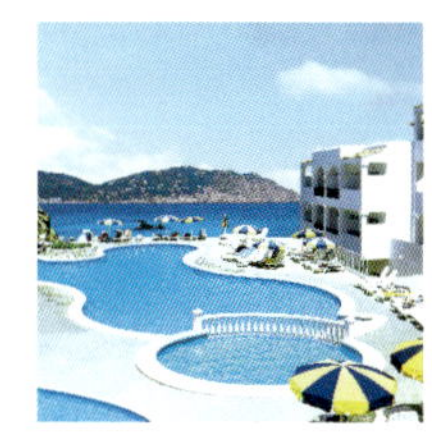

MIX **TANA** 100 × 100 cm /
39.38 × 39.38 in. 2000/01
Seite / Page 51

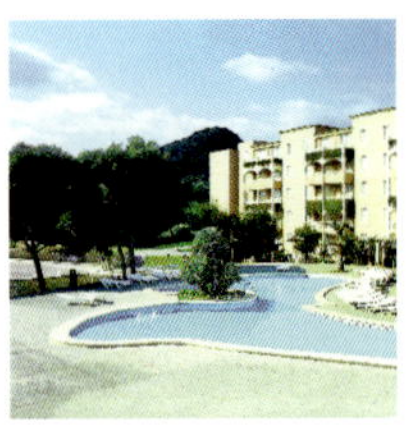

MIX **MELANIE** 100 × 100 cm /
39.38 × 39.38 in. 2000/01
Seite / Page 52

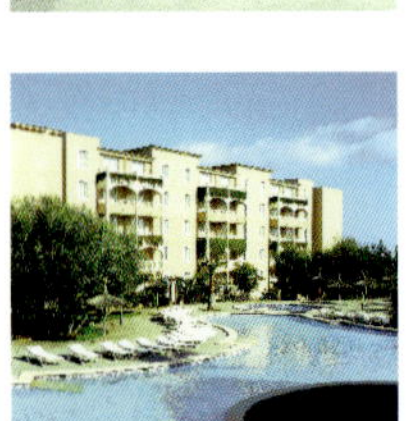

MIX **SONJA** 100 × 100 cm /
39.38 × 39.38 in. 2000/01
Seite / Page 52

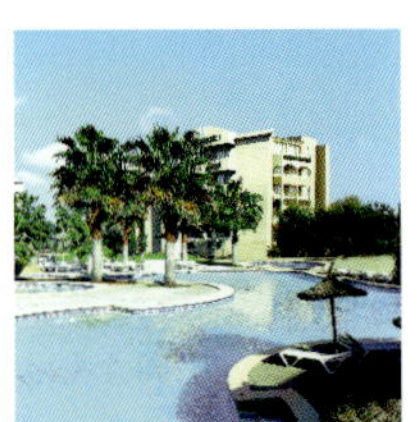

MIX **SALINA** 100 × 100 cm /
39.38 × 39.38 in. 2000/01
Seite / Page 53

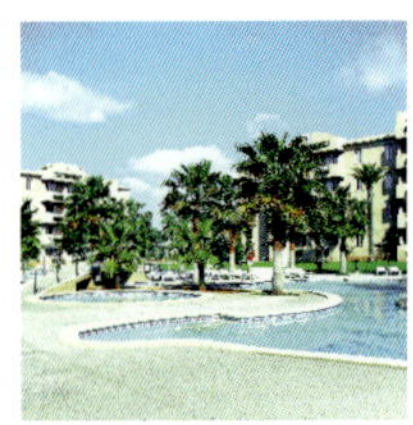

MIX **ALDIANE** 100 × 100 cm /
39.38 × 39.38 in. 2000/01
Seite / Page 53

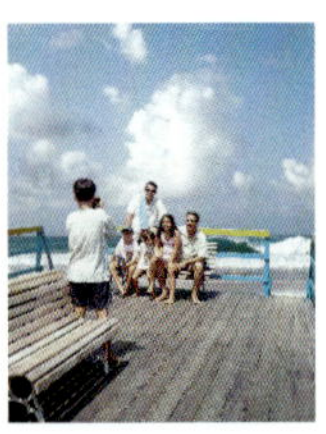

PORTRÄTS VON PORTRÄTS /
PORTRAITS OF PORTRAITS
SCHIFF / SHIP 100 × 80 cm /
39.38 × 31.5 in. 2001
Seite / Page 55

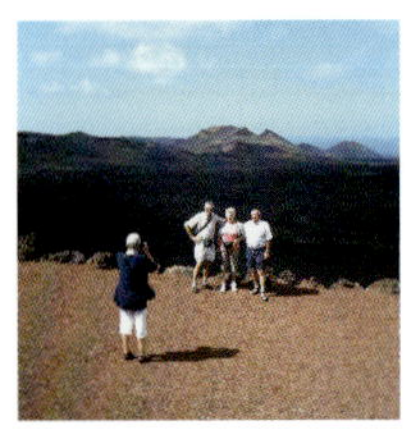

PORTRÄTS VON PORTRÄTS /
PORTRAITS OF PORTRAITS
LANZAROTE 100 × 100 cm /
39.38 × 39.38 in. 2001
Seite / Page 56

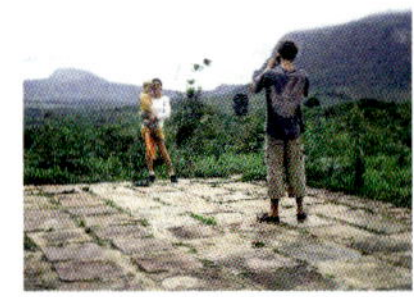

PORTRÄTS VON PORTRÄTS /
PORTRAITS OF PORTRAITS
PAAR / COUPLE 100 × 100 cm /
39.38 × 39.38 in. 2001
Seite / Page 56

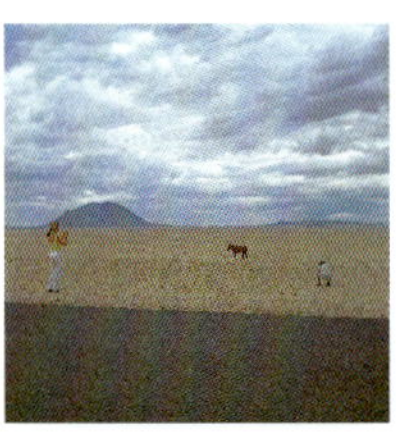

PORTRÄTS VON PORTRÄTS /
PORTRAITS OF PORTRAITS
PFERD / HORSE 100 × 100 cm /
39.38 × 39.38 in. 2001
Seite / Page 57

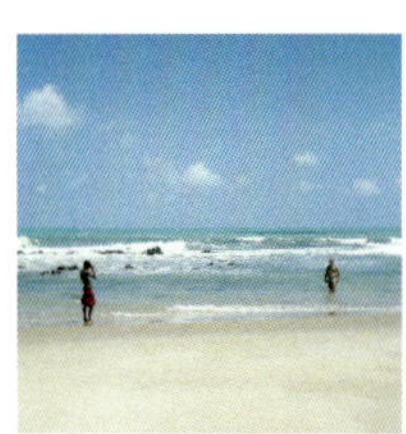

PORTRÄTS VON PORTRÄTS /
PORTRAITS OF PORTRAITS
JUNGE/MANN / BOY/MAN
100 × 100 cm / 39.38 × 39.38 in.
2001 Seite / Page 57

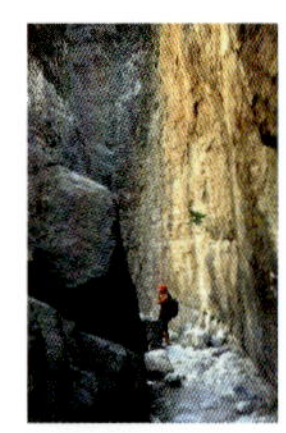

PORTRÄTS VON PORTRÄTS /
PORTRAITS OF PORTRAITS
ROTE KAPPE / RED CAP
100 × 65 cm / 39.38 × 25.59 in.
2001 Seite / Page 58

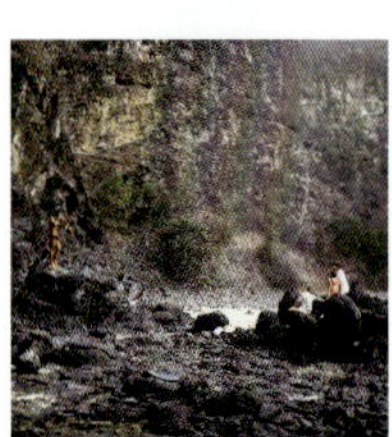

PORTRÄTS VON PORTRÄTS /
PORTRAITS OF PORTRAITS
SCHLUCHT / GULLEY
100 × 100 cm / 39.38 × 39.38 in.
2001 Seite / Page 59

SKYLINE **CONTAINER /
CONTAINERS** 190 × 108 cm /
74.83 × 42.52 in. 2002–2009
Seite / Page 69

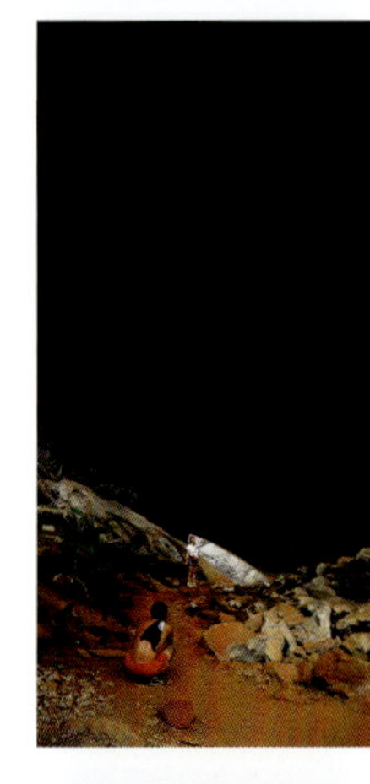

SKYLINE **GROTTE / GROTTO**
190 × 90 cm / 74.83 × 35.43 in.
2002–2009 Seite / Page 70

SKYLINE **SCHNORCHEL /
SNORKEL** 190 × 90 cm /
74.83 × 35.20 in. 2002–2009
Seite / Page 71

SKYLINE **SAL** 190 × 81 cm /
74.83 × 32 in. 2002–2009
Seite / Page 72

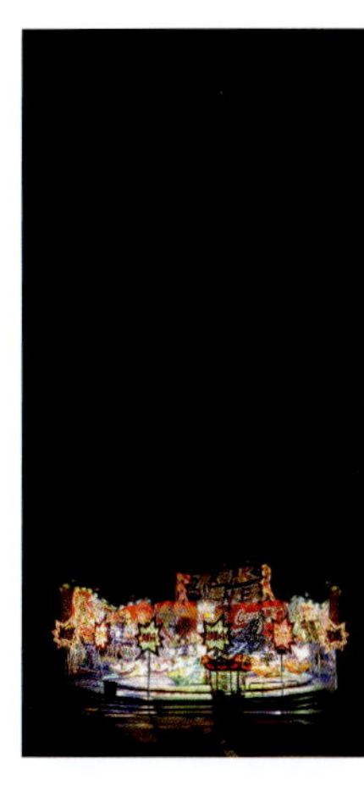

SKYLINE **KARUSSELL /
CAROUSEL** 190 × 95 cm /
74.83 × 37.4 in. 2002–2009
Seite / Page 75

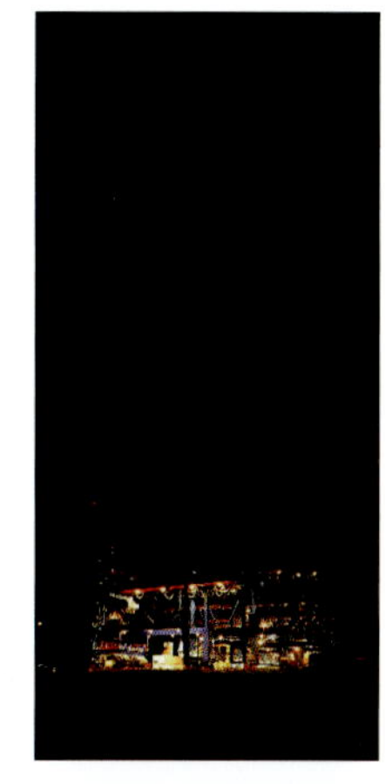

SKYLINE **TERMINAL**
190 × 90 cm / 74.83 × 35.43 in.
2002–2009 Seite / Page 78

SKYLINE **HAFEN / PORT**
190 × 70 cm / 74.83 × 27.55 in.
2002–2009 Seite / Page 73

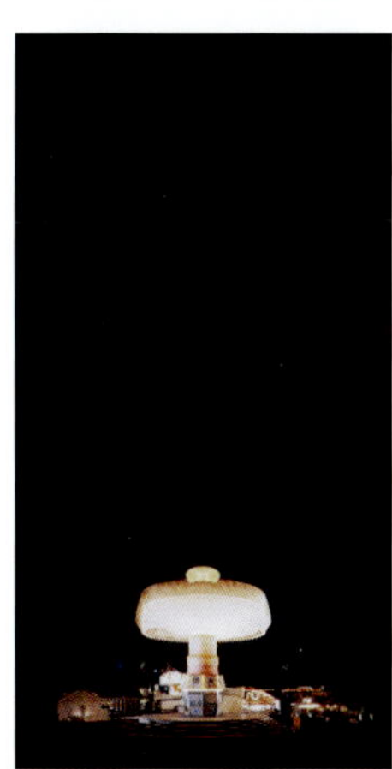

SKYLINE **TRUDEL / SPIN**
190 × 100 cm / 74.83 × 39.38 in.
2002–2009 Seite / Page 76

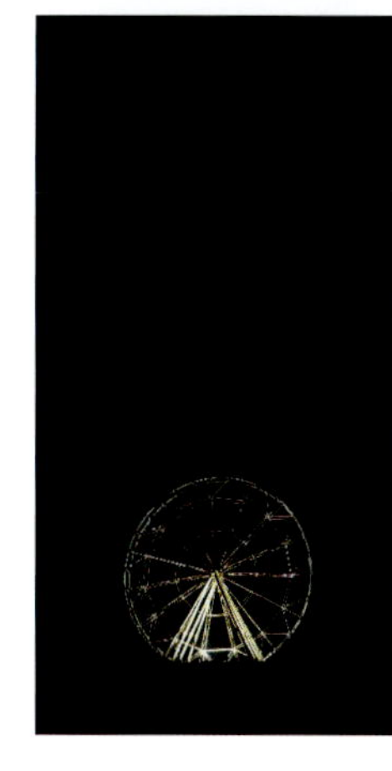
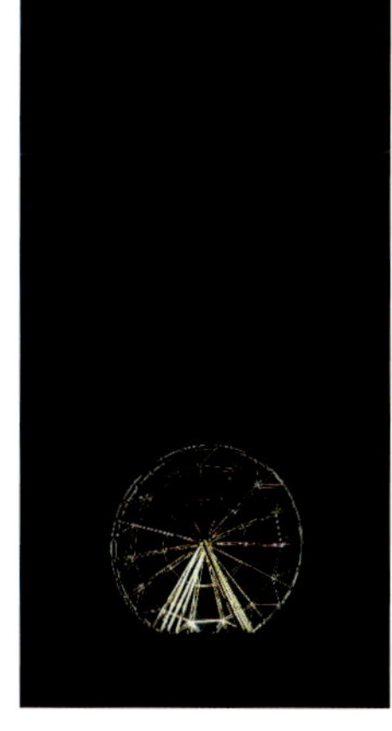

SKYLINE **RAD / WHEEL**
190 × 98 cm / 74.83 × 38.58 in.
2002–2009 Seite / Page 79

SKYLINE **STREIFEN / LINES**
190 × 90 cm / 74.83 × 35.43 in.
2002–2009 Seite / Page 74

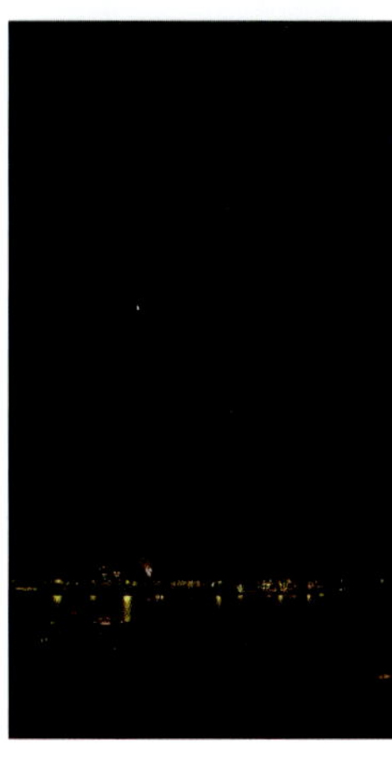

SKYLINE **FEUERWERK /
FIREWORKS** 190 × 105 cm /
74.83 × 41.33 in. 2002–2009
Seite / Page 77

SKYLINE **WELLE / WAVE**
190 × 90 cm / 74.83 × 35.43 in.
2002–2009 Seite / Page 80

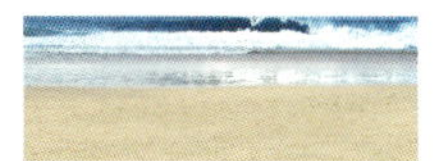

SKYLINE **FRASER** 190 × 95 cm /
74.83 × 37.4 in. 2002–2009
Seite / Page 81

SKYLINE **FLUSS/MEER /
RIVER/SEA** 190 ×100 cm /
74.83 × 39.38 in. 2002–2009
Seite / Page 84

SKYLINE **KRUSTE / CRUST**
190 × 100 cm / 74.83 × 39.38 in.
2002–2009 Seite / Page 87

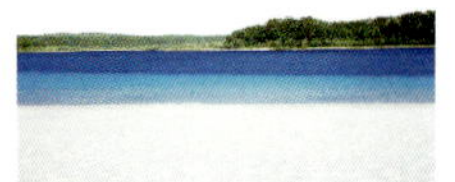

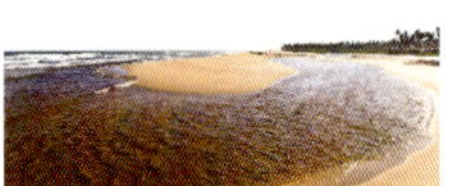

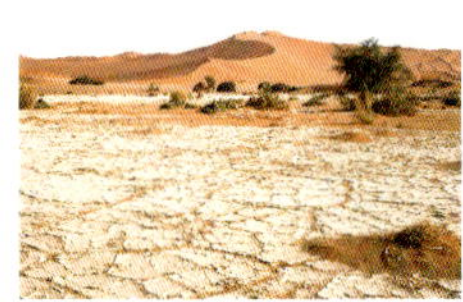

SKYLINE **HÜGEL / HILL**
190 × 100 cm / 74.83 × 39.38 in.
2002–2009 Seite / Page 82

SKYLINE **BÄUME / TREES**
190 × 105 cm / 74.83 × 41.34 in.
2002–2009 Seite / Page 85

SKYLINE **FERNANDO**
190 × 72 cm / 74.83 × 28.35 in.
2002–2009 Seite / Page 88

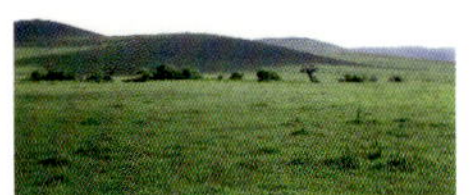

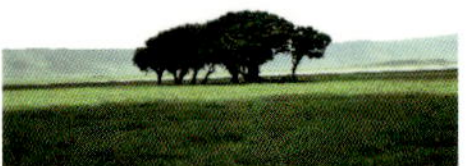

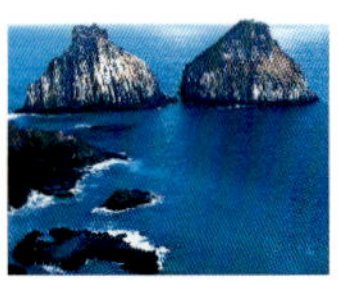

SKYLINE **MARMOLADA**
190 × 100 cm / 74.83 × 39.38 in.
2002–2009 Seite / Page 83

SKYLINE **TRAUM / DREAM**
190 × 80 cm / 74.83 × 31.5 in.
2002–2009 Seite / Page 86

SKYLINE **DÜNE / DUNE**
190 × 110 cm / 74.83 × 43.31 in.
2002–2009 Seite / Page 89

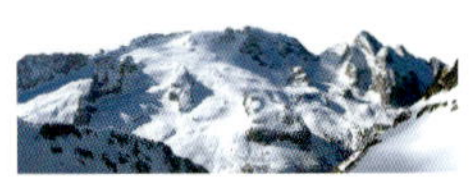

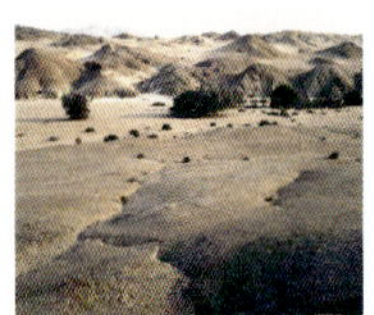

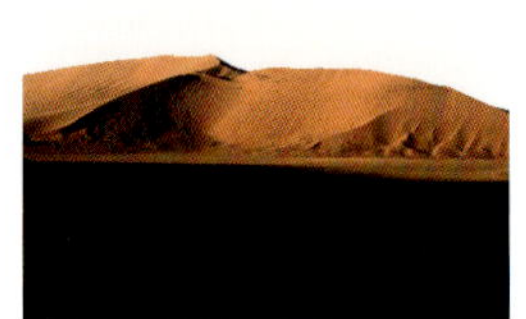

SKYLINE **NGORONGORO**
190 × 90 cm / 74.83 × 35.43 in.
2002–2009 Seite / Page 90

SKYLINE **VIC FALLS**
190 × 90 cm / 74.83 × 35.43 in.
2002–2009 Seite / Page 93

SKYLINE **KRETA / CRETE**
190 × 67 cm / 74.83 × 26.38 in.
2002–2009 Seite / Page 96

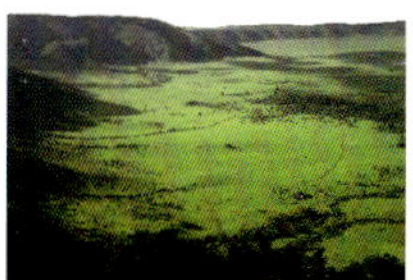

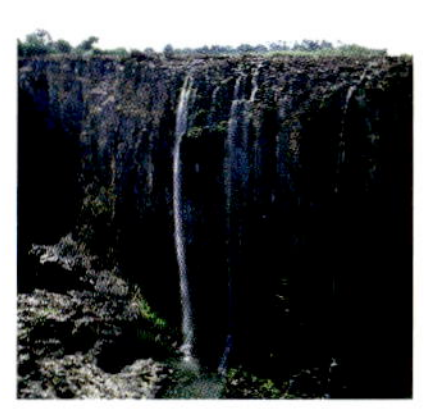

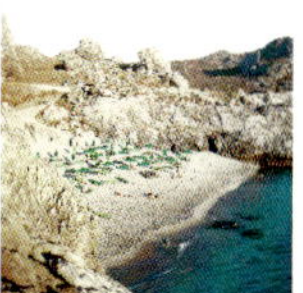

SKYLINE **SSUSS** 190 × 95 cm /
74.83 × 37.4 in. 2002–2009
Seite / Page 91

SKYLINE **TEMPEL MITTE /
TEMPLE CENTER** 190 × 83 cm /
74.83 × 32.68 in. 2002–2009
Seite / Page 94

SKYLINE **MITTE / CENTER**
190 × 95 cm / 74.83 × 37.4 in.
2002–2009 Seite / Page 97

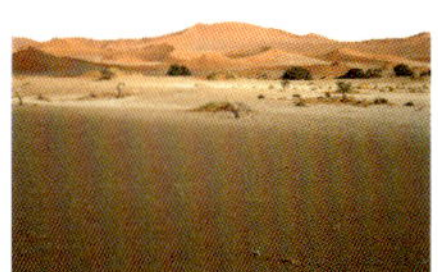

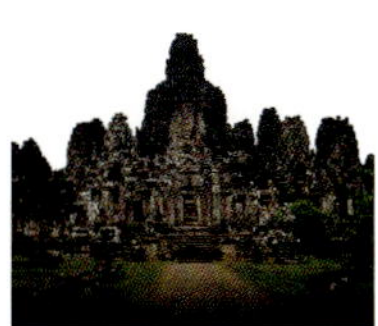

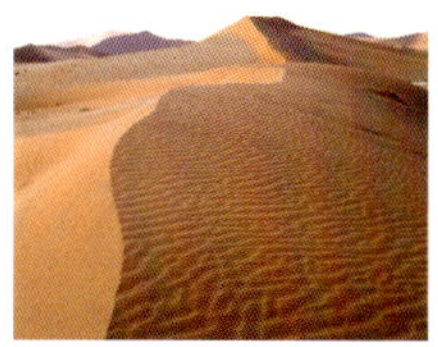

SKYLINE **TAL / VALLEY**
190 × 78 cm / 74.83 × 30.71 in.
2002–2009 Seite / Page 92

SKYLINE **SEAM MITTE /
SEAM CENTER** 190 × 94 cm /
74.83 × 37 in. 2002–2009
Seite / Page 95

SKYLINE **TEMPEL KLEIN /
TEMPLE SMALL** 190 × 100 cm /
74.83 × 39.38 in. 2002–2009
Seite / Page 98

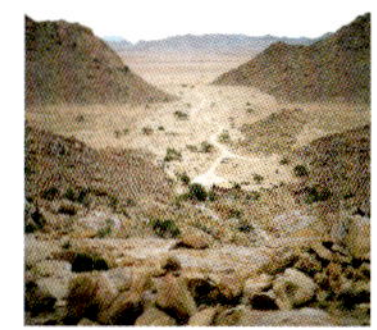

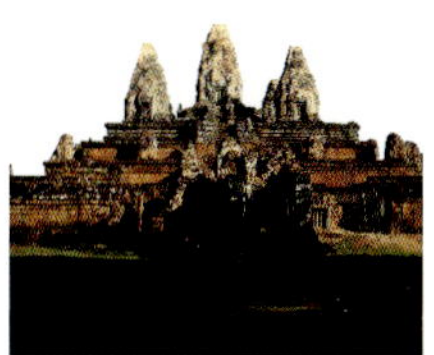

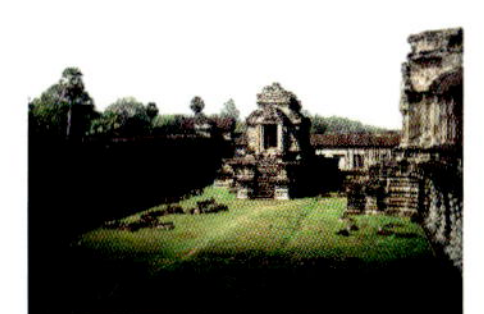

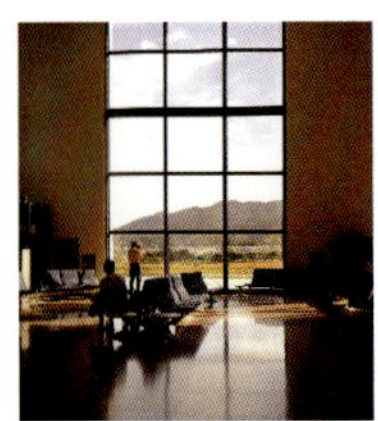 INDOOR **# 3** 120 ×110 cm /
47.24 × 43.31 in. 2001/02
Seite / Page 101

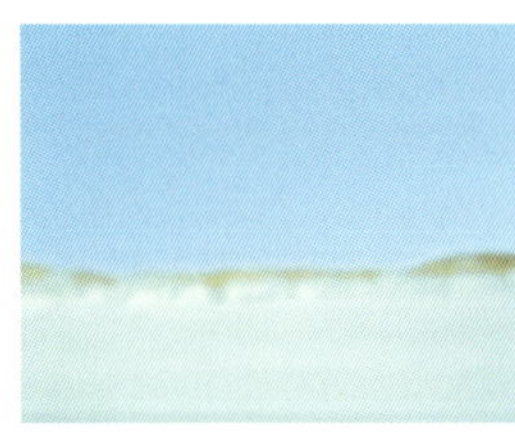 CANDIES **# 16** 70 × 100 cm /
27.56 × 39.38 in. 2002/03
Seite / Page 104

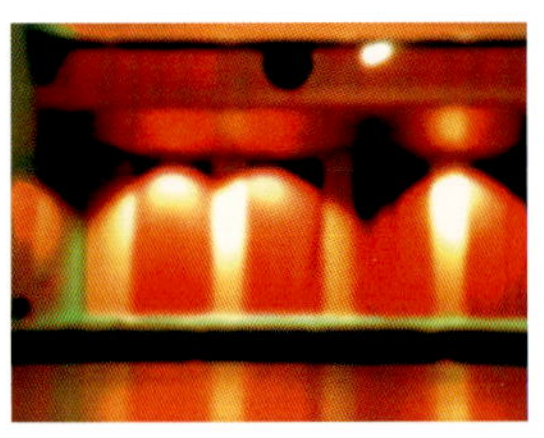 CANDIES **# 54** 70 × 100 cm /
27.56 × 39.38 in. 2002/03
Seite / Page 106

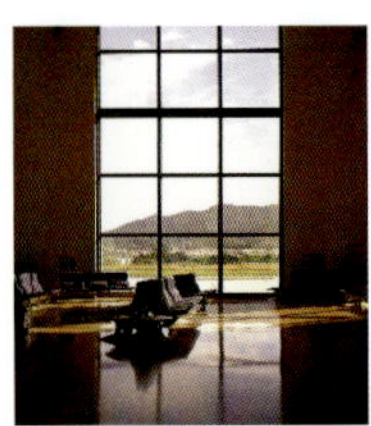 INDOOR **# 4** 120 ×110 cm /
47.24 × 43.31 in. 2001/02
Seite / Page 102

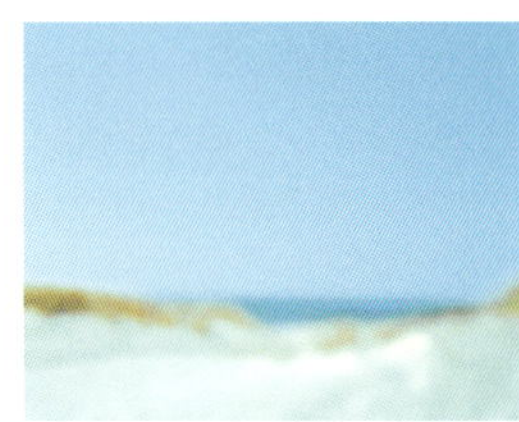 CANDIES **# 18** 70 × 100 cm /
27.56 × 39.38 in. 2002/03
Seite / Page 105

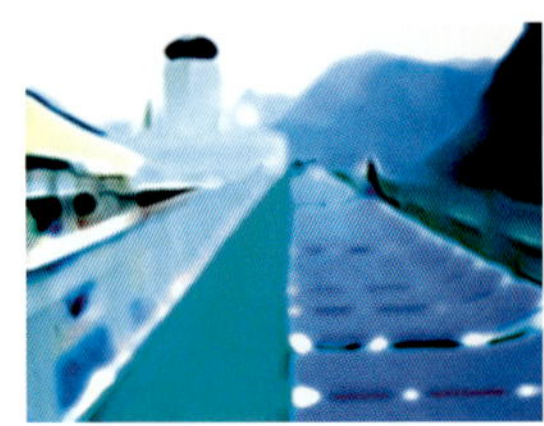 CANDIES **# 14** 70 × 100 cm /
27.56 × 39.38 in. 2002/03
Seite / Page 107

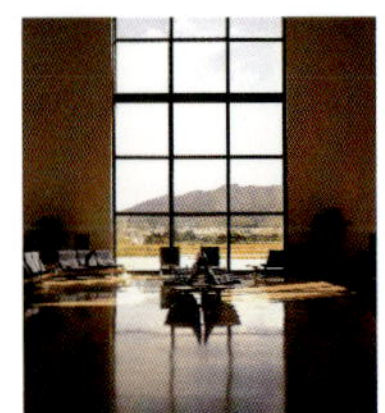 INDOOR **# 2** 120 ×110 cm /
47.24 × 43.31 in. 2001/02
Seite / Page 102

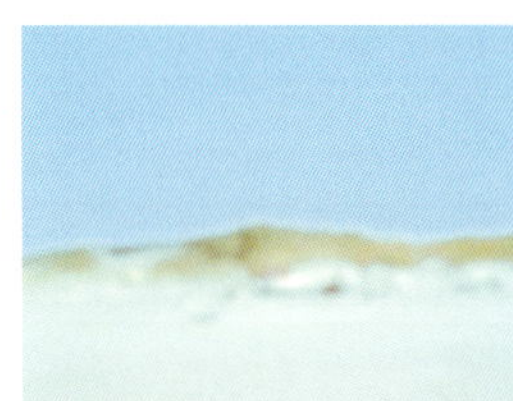 CANDIES **# 17** 70 × 100 cm /
27.56 × 39.38 in. 2002/03
Seite / Page 105

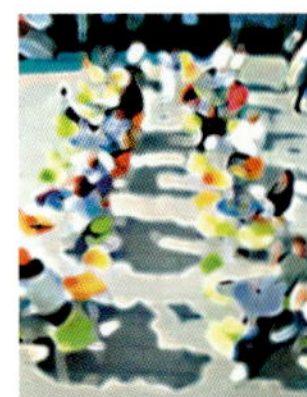 CANDIES **# 36** 100 × 70 cm /
39.38 × 27.56 in. 2002/03
Seite / Page 108

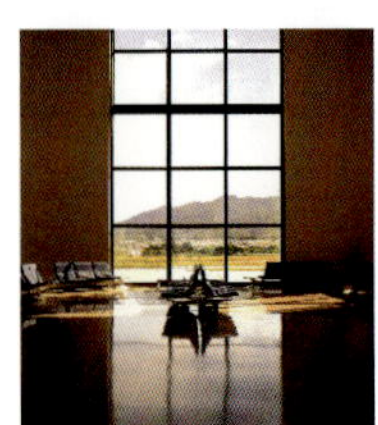 INDOOR **# 6** 120 ×110 cm /
47.24 × 43.31 in. 2001/02
Seite / Page 102

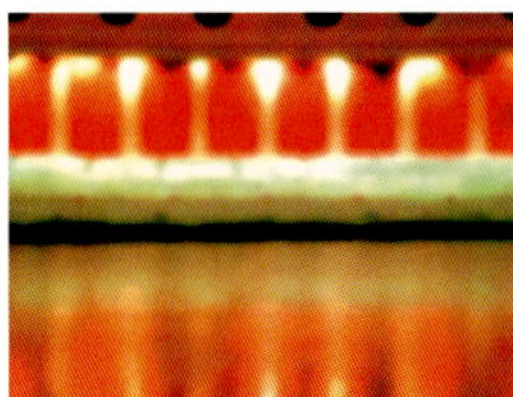 CANDIES **# 35** 70 × 100 cm /
27.56 × 39.38 in. 2002/03
Seite / Page 106

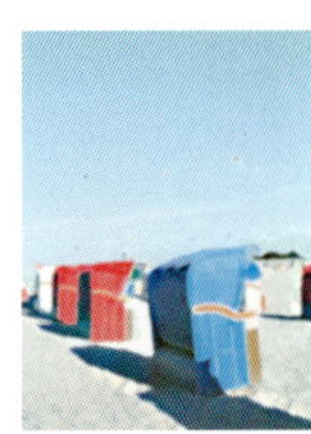 CANDIES **# 30** 100 × 70 cm /
39.38 × 27.56 in. 2002/03
Seite / Page 108

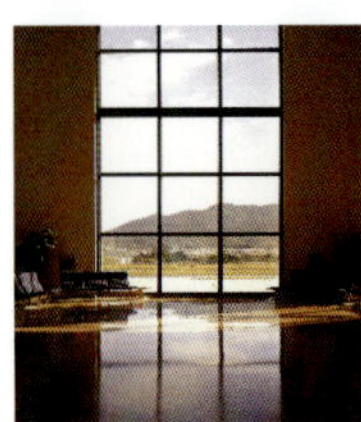 INDOOR **# 5** 120 ×110 cm /
47.24 × 43.31 in. 2001/02
Seite / Page 102

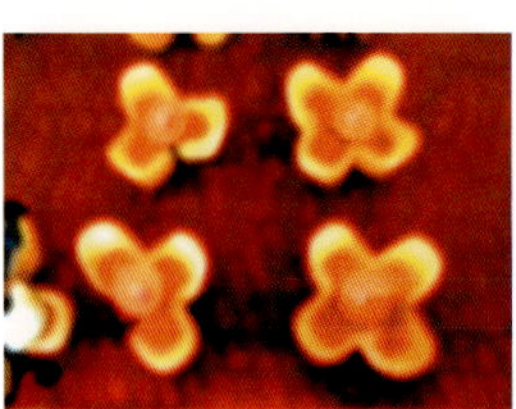 CANDIES **# 10** 70 × 100 cm /
27.56 × 39.38 in. 2002/03
Seite / Page 106

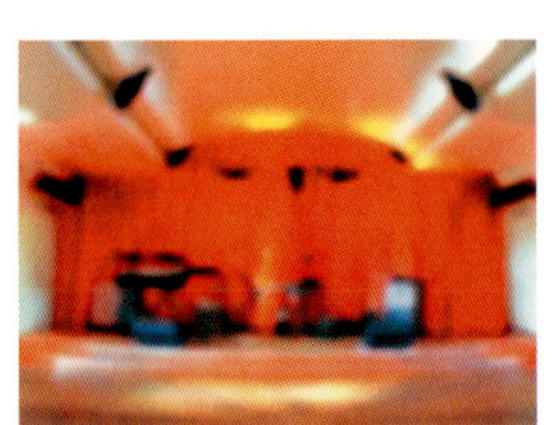 CANDIES **# 7** 70 × 100 cm /
27.56 × 39.38 in. 2002/03
Seite / Page 109

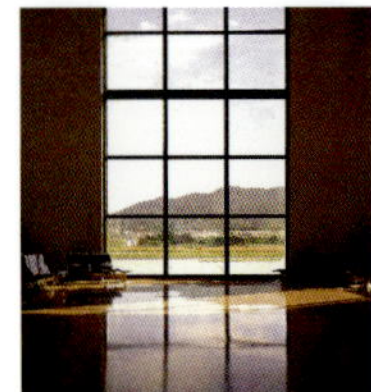 INDOOR **# 1** 120 ×110 cm /
47.24 × 43.31 in. 2001/02
Seite / Page 103

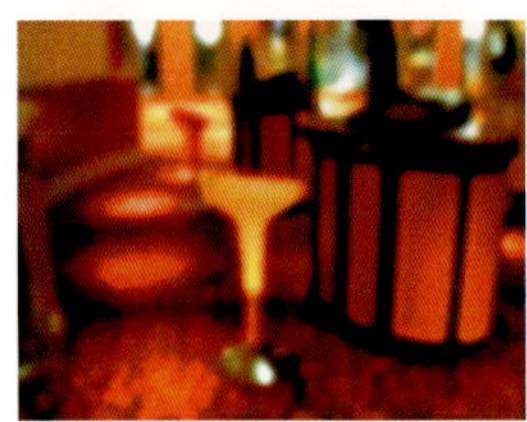 CANDIES **# 6** 70 × 100 cm /
27.56 × 39.38 in. 2002/03
Seite / Page 106

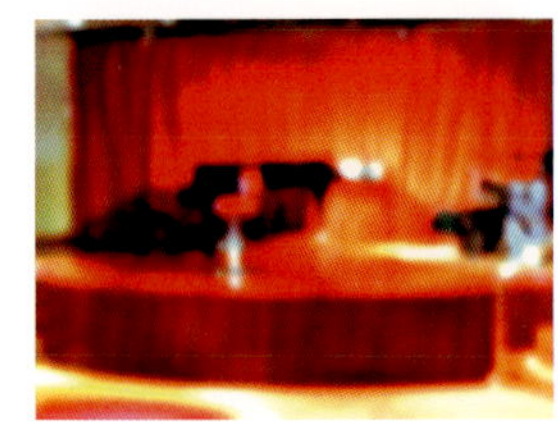 CANDIES **# 44** 70 × 100 cm /
27.56 × 39.38 in. 2002/03
Seite / Page 109

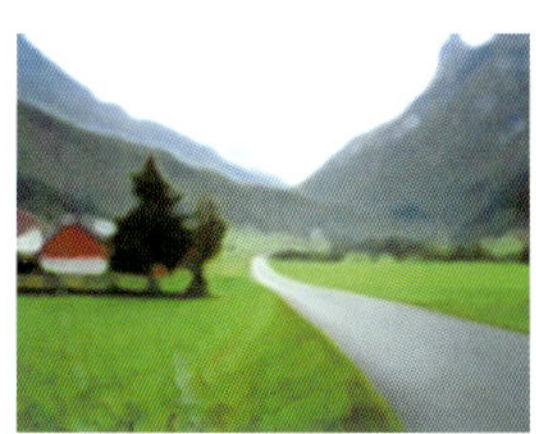

CANDIES **# 48** 70 × 100 cm /
27.56 × 39.38 in. 2002/03
Seite / Page 110

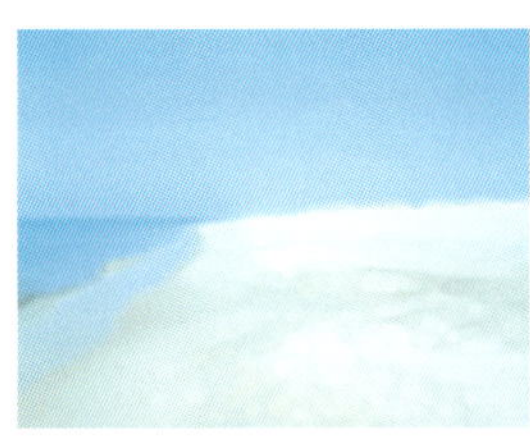

CANDIES **# 23** 70 × 100 cm /
27.56 × 39.38 in. 2002/03
Seite / Page 113

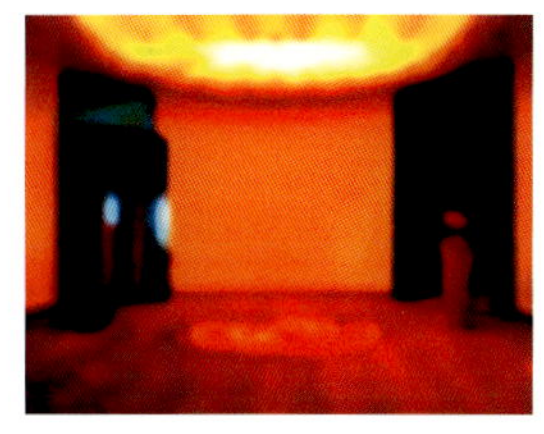

CANDIES **# 8** 70 × 100 cm /
27.56 × 39.38 in. 2002/03
Seite / Page 116

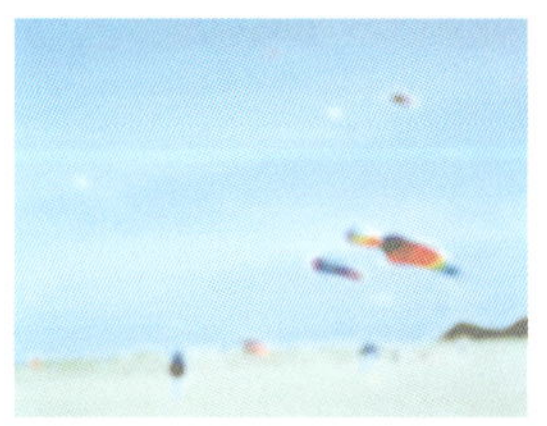

CANDIES **# 25** 70 × 100 cm /
27.56 × 39.38 in. 2002/03
Seite / Page 110

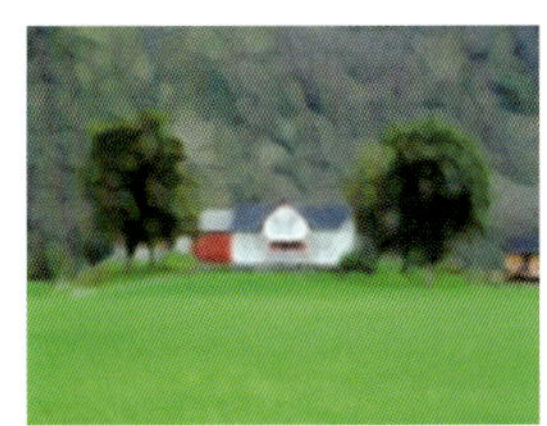

CANDIES **# 49** 70 × 100 cm /
27.56 × 39.38 in. 2002/03
Seite / Page 113

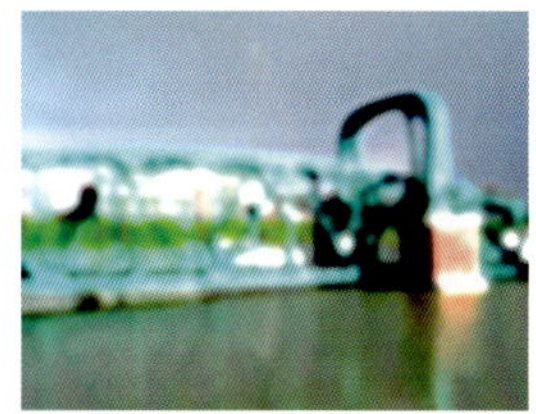

CANDIES **# 50** 70 × 100 cm /
27.56 × 39.38 in. 2002/03
Seite / Page 117

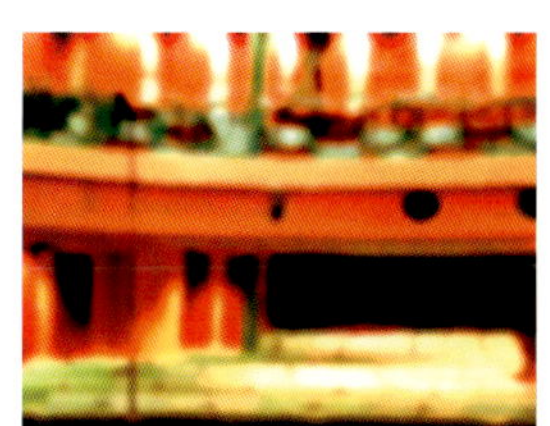

CANDIES **# 46** 70 × 100 cm /
27.56 × 39.38 in. 2002/03
Seite / Page 110

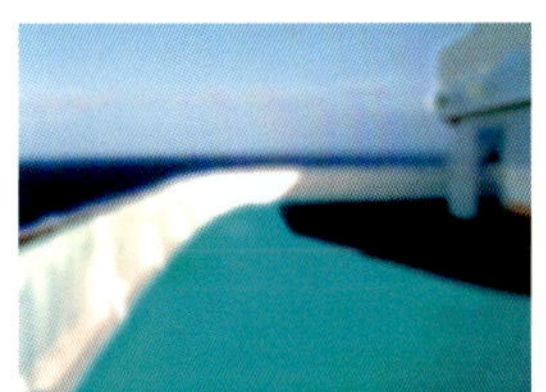

CANDIES **# 38** 70 × 100 cm /
27.56 × 39.38 in. 2002/03
Seite / Page 113

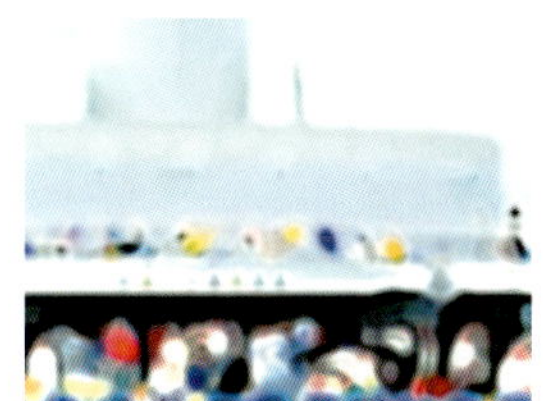

CANDIES **# 22** 70 × 100 cm /
27.56 × 39.38 in. 2002/03
Seite / Page 117

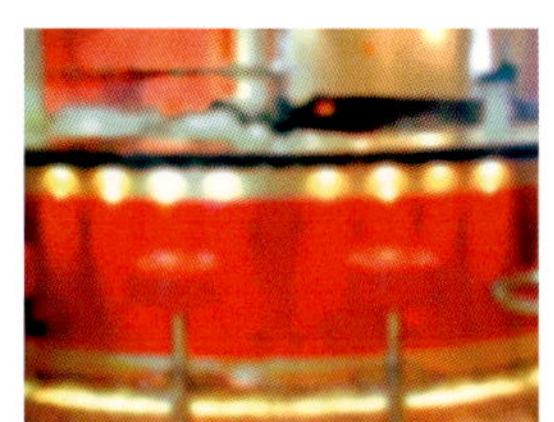

CANDIES **# 45** 70 × 100 cm /
27.56 × 39.38 in. 2002/03
Seite / Page 110

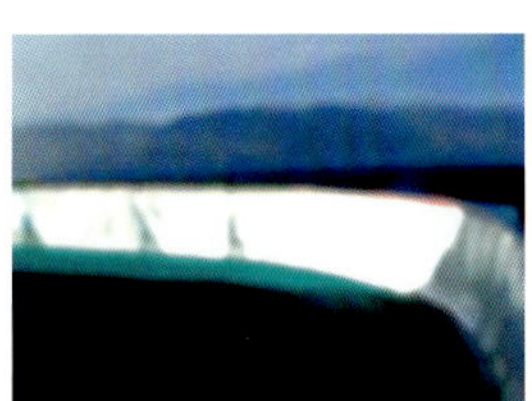

CANDIES **# 39** 70 × 100 cm /
27.56 × 39.38 in. 2002/03
Seite / Page 113

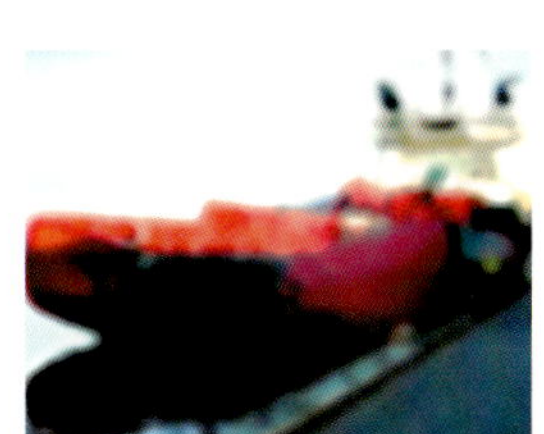

CANDIES **# 15** 70 × 100 cm /
27.56 × 39.38 in. 2002/03
Seite / Page 117

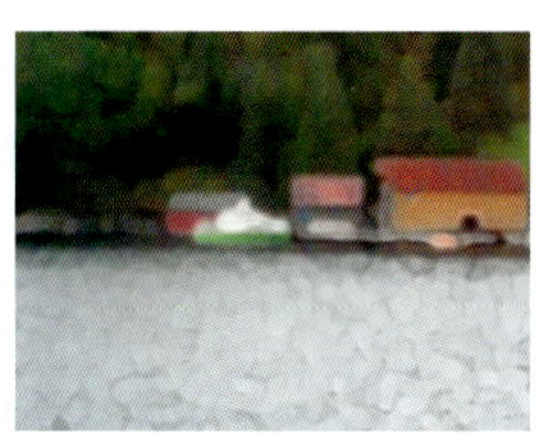

CANDIES **# 11** 70 × 100 cm /
27.56 × 39.38 in. 2002/03
Seite / Page 111

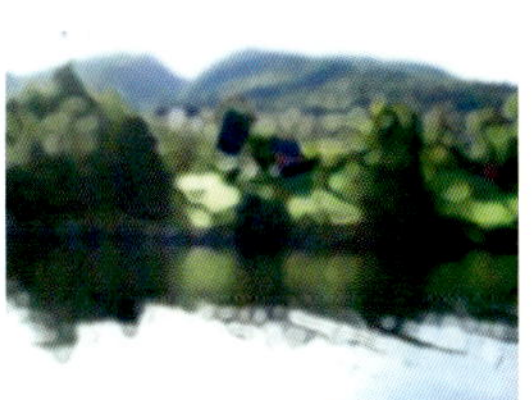

CANDIES **# 12** 70 × 100 cm /
27.56 × 39.38 in. 2002/03
Seite / Page 114

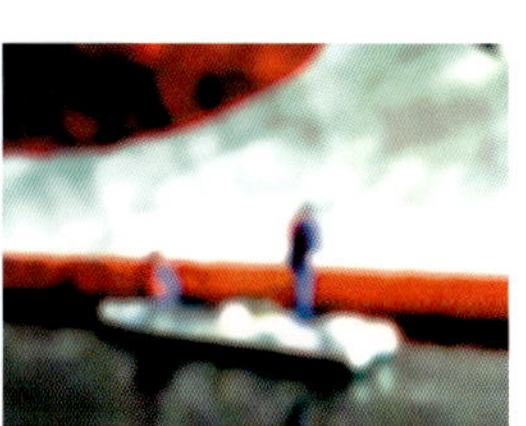

CANDIES **# 31** 70 × 100 cm /
27.56 × 39.38 in. 2002/03
Seite / Page 117

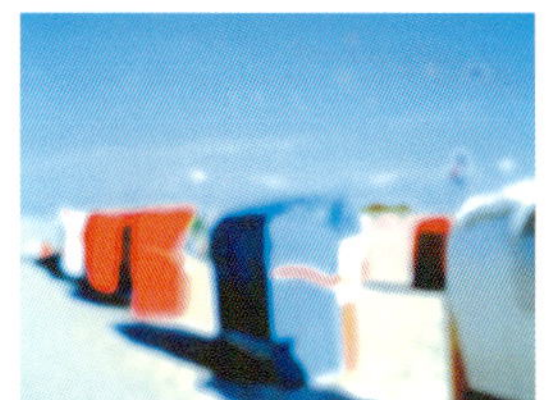

CANDIES **# 24** 70 × 100 cm /
27.56 × 39.38 in. 2002/03
Seite / Page 112

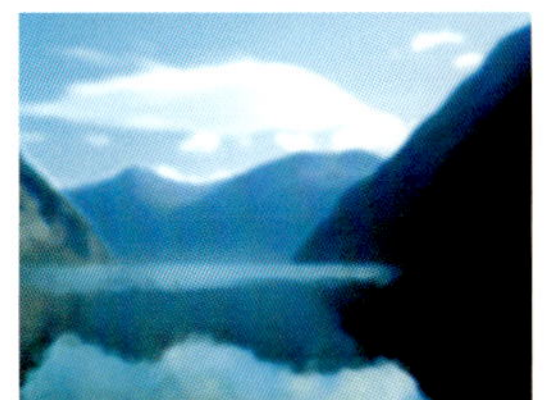

CANDIES **# 13** 70 × 100 cm /
27.56 × 39.38 in. 2002/03
Seite / Page 115

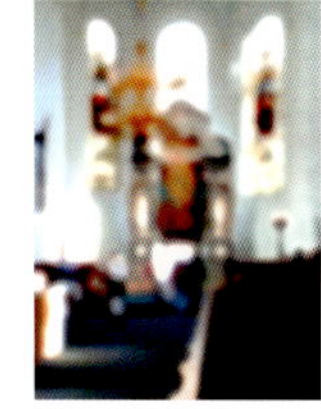

CANDIES **# 37** 100 × 70 cm /
39.38 × 27.56 in. 2002/03
Seite / Page 118

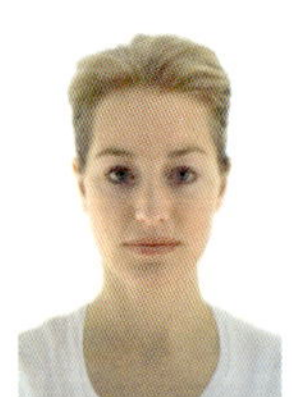

DIFFERENT PERSONS
SUSANNE 76 × 52 cm /
29.92 × 20.47 in. 2006
Seite / Page 127

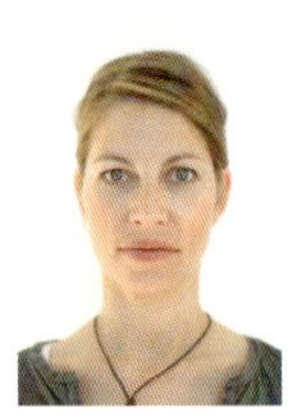

DIFFERENT PERSONS **TINA**
76 × 52 cm / 29.92 × 20.47 in.
2006 Seite / Page 128

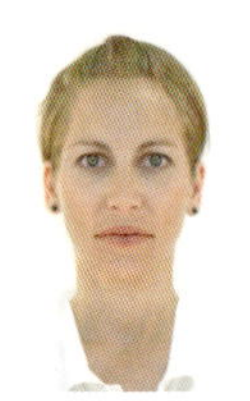

DIFFERENT PERSONS **ANETTE**
76 × 52 cm / 29.92 × 20.47 in.
2006 Seite / Page 129

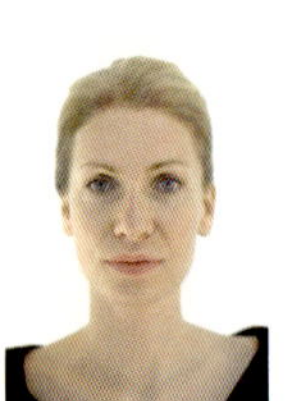

DIFFERENT PERSONS **STEFFI**
76 × 52 cm / 29.92 × 20.47 in.
2006 Seite / Page 130

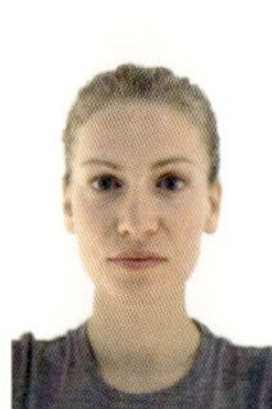

DIFFERENT PERSONS
KONSTANZE 76 × 52 cm /
29.92 × 20.47 in. 2006
Seite / Page 131

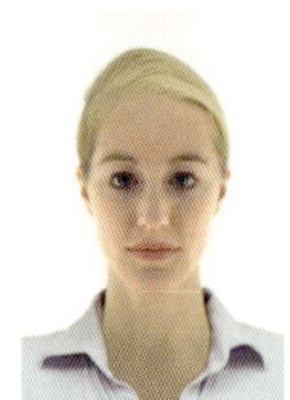

DIFFERENT PERSONS **CAROLL**
76 × 52 cm / 29.92 × 20.47 in.
2006 Seite / Page 132

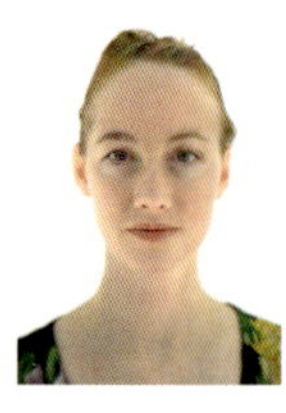

DIFFERENT PERSONS
MARION 76 × 52 cm /
29.92 × 20.47 in. 2006
Seite / Page 133

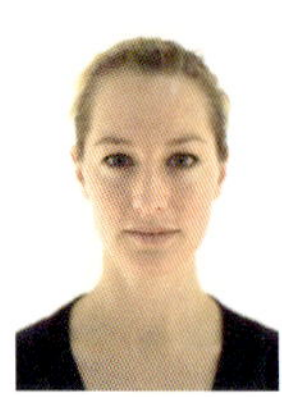

DIFFERENT PERSONS **INSA**
76 × 52 cm / 29.92 × 20.47 in.
2006 Seite / Page 134

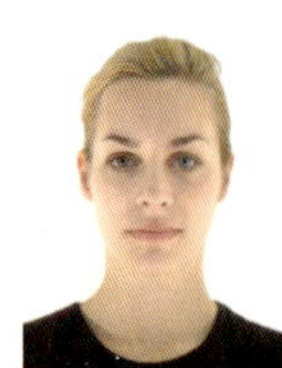

DIFFERENT PERSONS **TANJA**
76 × 52 cm / 29.92 × 20.47 in.
2006 Seite / Page 135

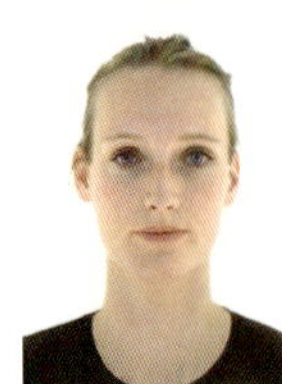

DIFFERENT PERSONS **SASKIA**
76 × 52 cm / 29.92 × 20.47 in.
2006 Seite / Page 136

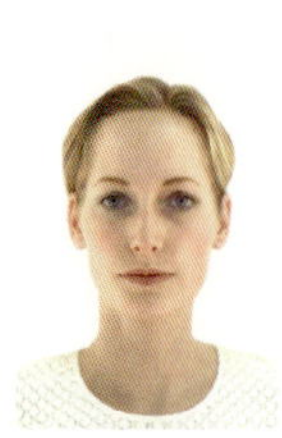

DIFFERENT PERSONS **SABINE**
76 × 52 cm / 29.92 × 20.47 in.
2006 Seite / Page 137

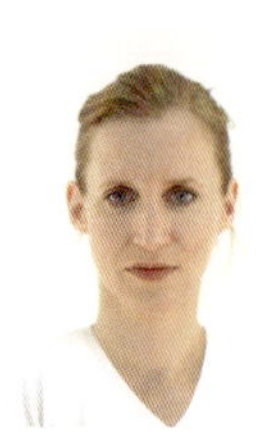

DIFFERENT PERSONS **SYBILLE**
76 × 52 cm / 29.92 × 20.47 in.
2006 Seite / Page 138

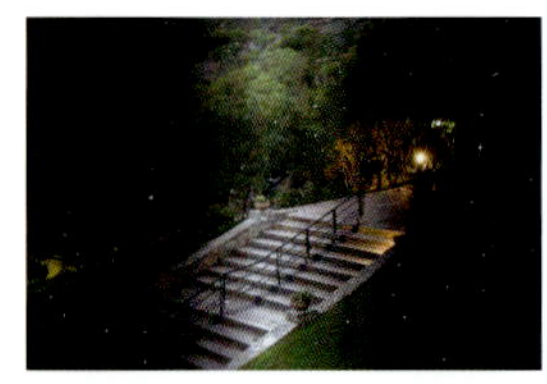

24 HOURS **TREPPE / STAIRS**
70 × 100 cm / 27.56 × 39.38 in.
2008 Seite / Page 141

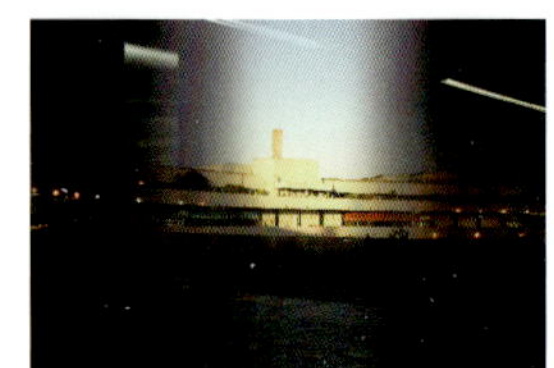

24 HOURS **FLUGHAFEN /
AIRPORT** 70 × 100 cm /
27.56 × 39.38 in. 2008
Seite / Page 142

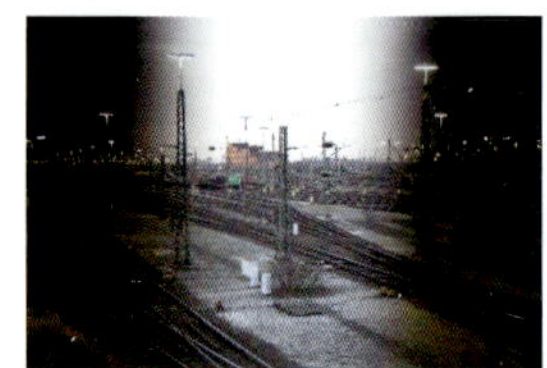

24 HOURS **RANGIERBAHNHOF /
MARSHALLING YARD**
70 × 100 cm / 27.56 × 39.38 in.
2008 Seite / Page 143

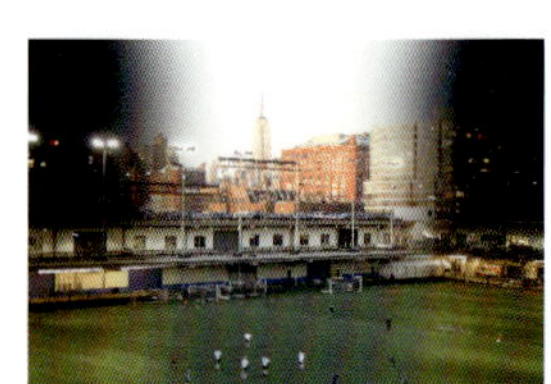

24 HOURS **EMPIRE**
70 × 100 cm / 27.56 × 39.38 in.
2008 Seite / Page 144

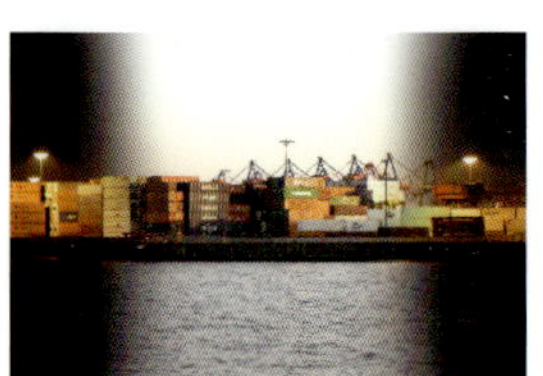

24 HOURS **CONTAINER /
CONTAINERS** 70 × 100 cm /
27.56 × 39.38 in. 2008
Seite / Page 145

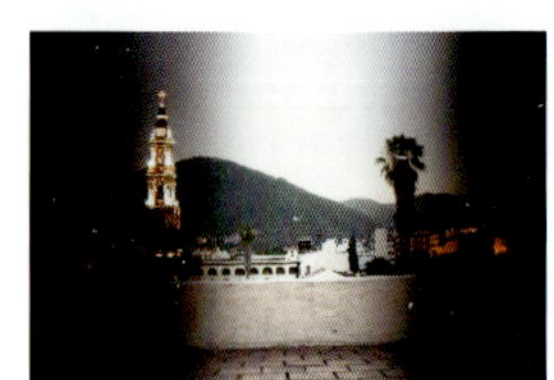

24 HOURS **KIRCHTURM /
CHURCH TOWER** 70 × 100 cm /
27.56 × 39.38 in. 2008
Seite / Page 146

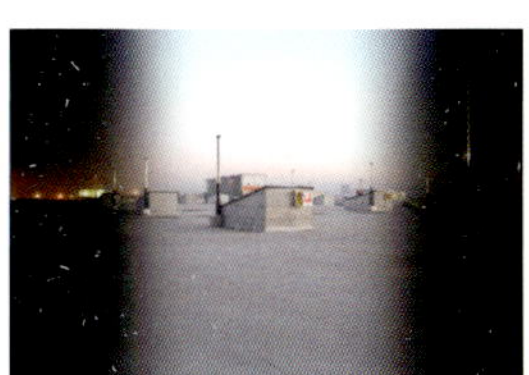

24 HOURS **DACH / ROOF**
70 × 100 cm / 27.56 × 39.38 in.
2008 Seite / Page 147

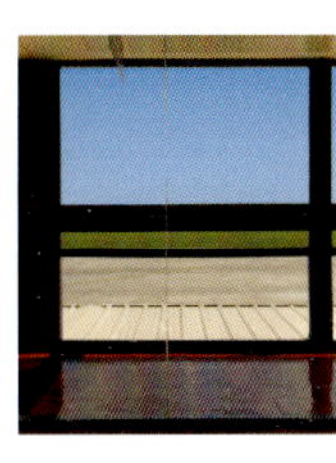

SALTA **# 1** 110 × 91 cm /
43.31 × 35.83 in. 2008
Seite / Page 154

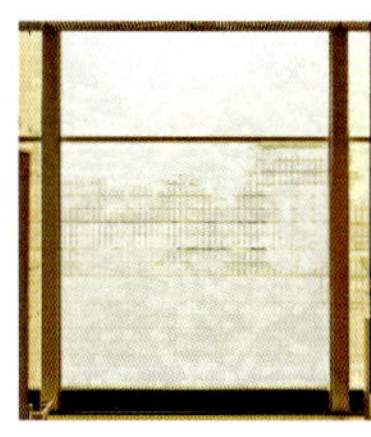

SEOUL **# 1** 90 × 82.6 cm /
35.43 × 32.52 in. 2009
Seite / Page 158

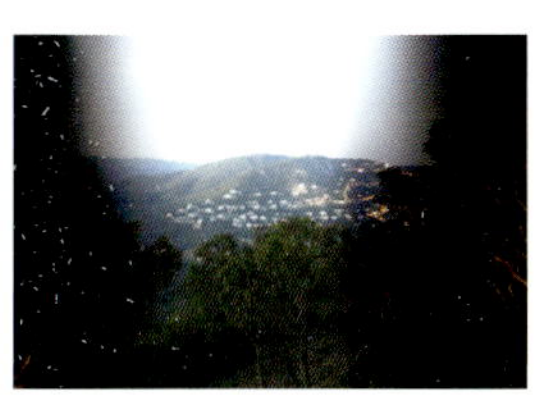

24 HOURS **BERG / MOUNTAIN**
70 × 100 cm / 27.56 × 39.38 in.
2008 Seite / Page 148

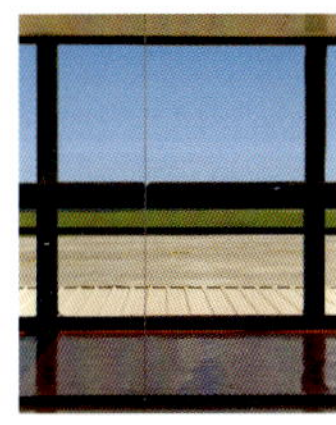

SALTA **# 2** 110 × 91 cm /
43.31 × 35.83 in. 2008
Seite / Page 154

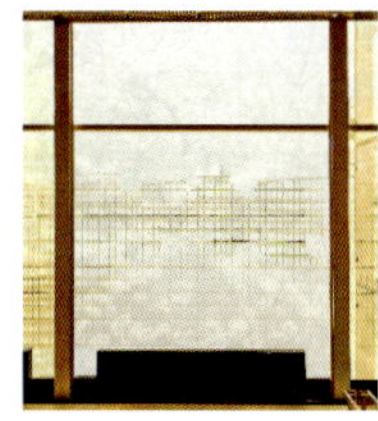

SEOUL **# 2** 90 × 82.6 cm /
35.43 × 32.52 in. 2009
Seite / Page 159

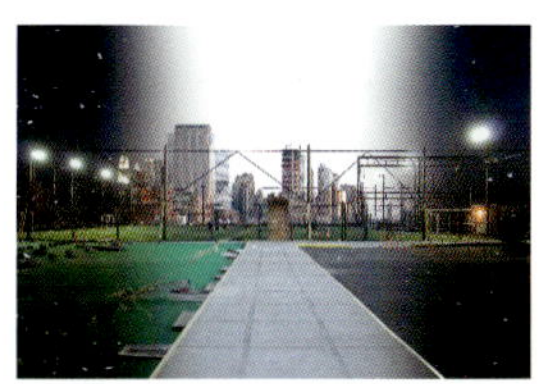

24 HOURS **WORLD TRADE**
70 × 100 cm / 27.56 × 39.38 in.
2008 Seite / Page 149

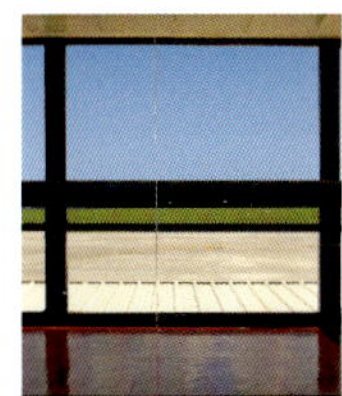

SALTA **# 3** 110 × 91 cm /
43.31 × 35.83 in. 2008
Seite / Page 155

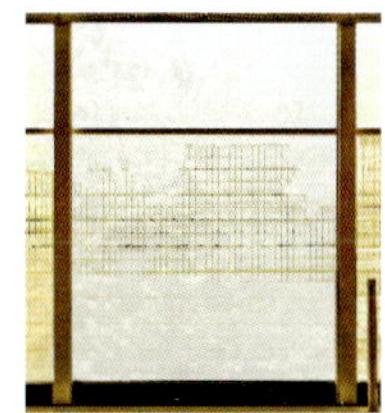

SEOUL **# 3** 90 × 82.6 cm /
35.43 × 32.52 in. 2009
Seite / Page 159

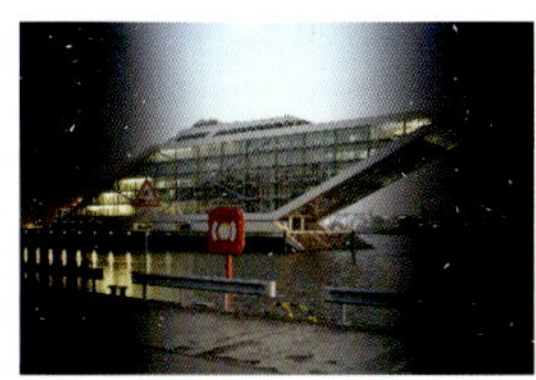

24 HOURS **HAFENHAUS /
HARBOR BUILDING**
70 × 100 cm / 27.56 × 39.38 in.
2008 Seite / Page 150

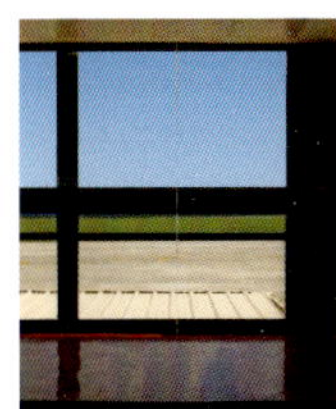

SALTA **# 4** 110 × 91 cm /
43.31 × 35.83 in. 2008
Seite / Page 155

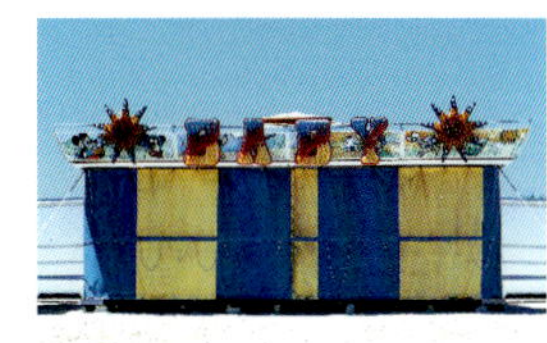

EINZELARBEITEN / INDIVIDUAL
WORKS **BABY** 65.5 × 90.5 cm /
25.79 × 35.63 in. 2000
Seite / Page 161

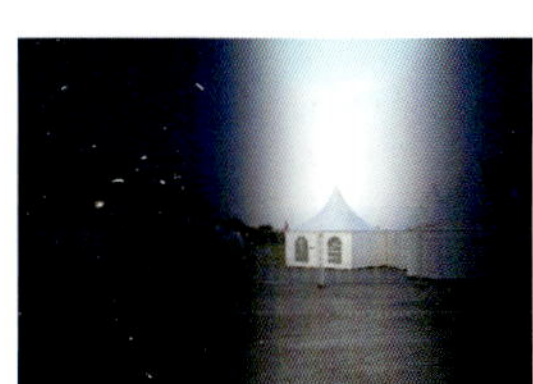

24 HOURS **ZELTE / TENTS**
70 × 100 cm / 27.56 × 39.38 in.
2008 Seite / Page 151

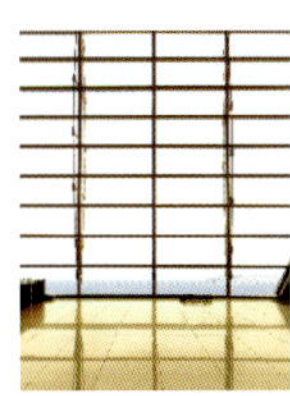

SAR **# 1** 100 × 80 cm /
39.38 × 31.5 in. 2009
Seite / Page 156

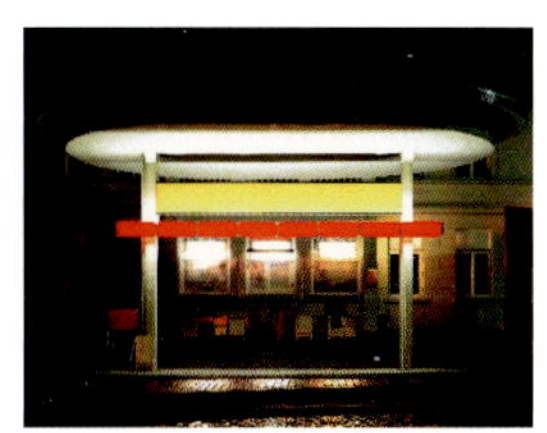

EINZELARBEITEN / INDIVIDUAL
WORKS **UELZEN** 61.5 × 83.5 cm /
24.21 × 32.87 in. 2001
Seite / Page 161

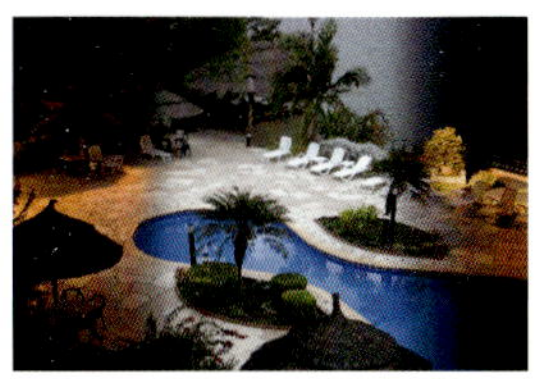

24 HOURS **HOTEL** 70 × 100 cm /
27.56 × 39.38 in. 2008
Seite / Page 152

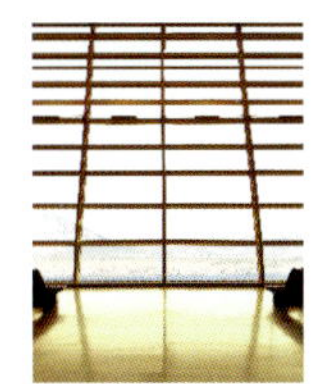

SAR **# 2** 100 × 80 cm /
39.38 × 31.5 in. 2009
Seite / Page 157

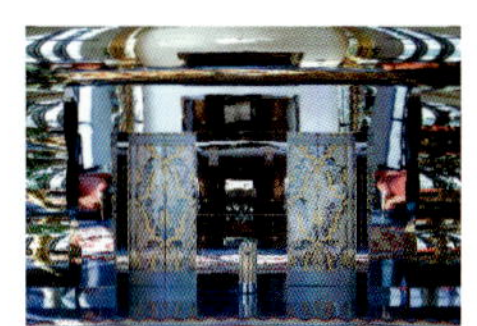

EINZELARBEITEN / INDIVIDUAL
WORKS **BUR** 50 × 70 cm /
19.69 × 27.56 in. 2007
Seite / Page 161

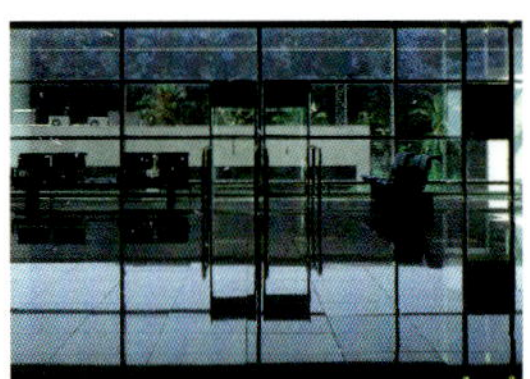

EINZELARBEITEN / INDIVIDUAL WORKS **FENSTER / WINDOW** 21 × 30 cm / 8.27 × 11.81 in. 2003 Seite / Page 161

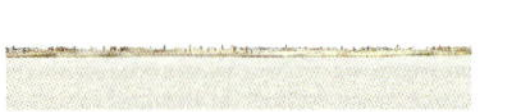

EINZELARBEITEN / INDIVIDUAL WORKS **FUSSBALL / SOCCER** 95 × 221 cm / 37.4 × 87 in. 2002 Seite / Pages 162/163

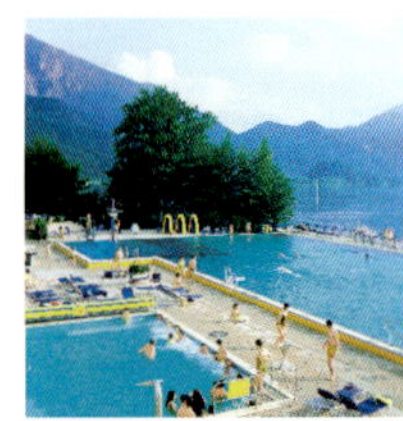

EINZELARBEITEN / INDIVIDUAL WORKS **SCHWIMMBAD / SWIMMING POOL** 100 × 100 cm / 39.38 × 39.38 in. 1999 Seite / Page 164

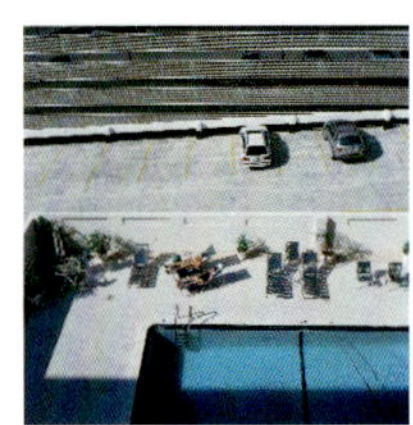

EINZELARBEITEN / INDIVIDUAL WORKS **POOL** 117 × 117 cm / 46 × 46 in. 2002 Seite / Page 165

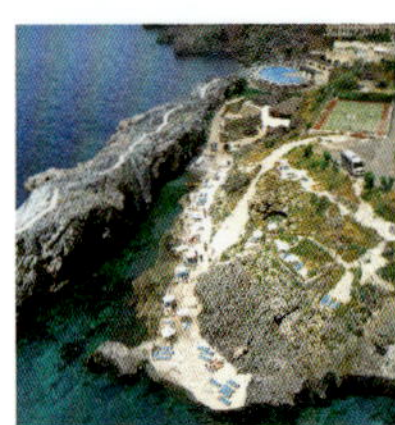

EINZELARBEITEN / INDIVIDUAL WORKS **CALYPSO** 111.5 × 110.5 cm / 43.9 × 43.5 in. 2003 Seite / Page 166

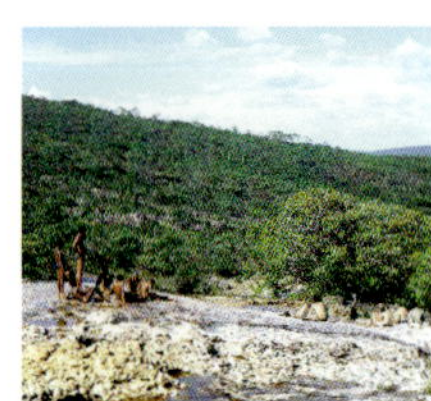

EINZELARBEITEN / INDIVIDUAL WORKS **SCHWARZ/WEISS / BLACK/WHITE** 110 × 110 cm / 43.31 × 43.31 in. 2003 Seite / Page 167

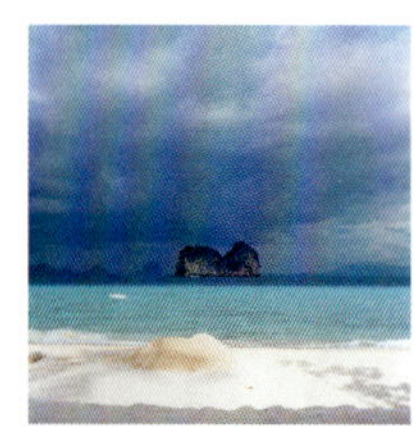

EINZELARBEITEN / INDIVIDUAL WORKS **TAI** 99 × 100 cm / 38.98 × 39.38 in. 2005 Seite / Page 168

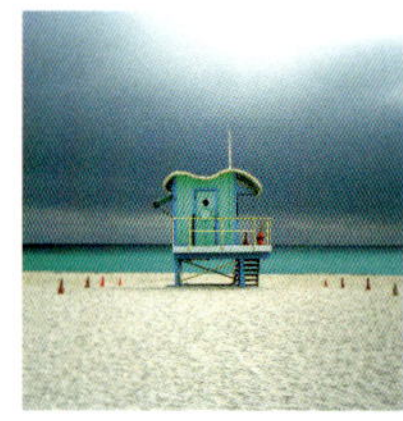

EINZELARBEITEN / INDIVIDUAL WORKS **BUDE / CABIN** 110 × 109 cm / 43.31 × 42.91 in. 2005 Seite / Page 169

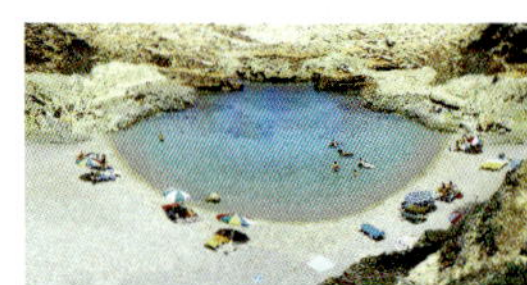

EINZELARBEITEN / INDIVIDUAL WORKS **BUCHT / COVE** 124 × 246 cm / 48.82 × 96.85 in. 1999 Seite / Page 170

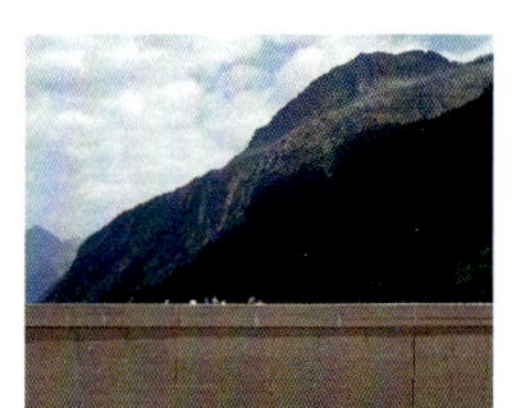

EINZELARBEITEN / INDIVIDUAL WORKS **MAUER / WALL** 95 × 117 cm / 37.4 × 46 in. 2003 Seite / Page 171

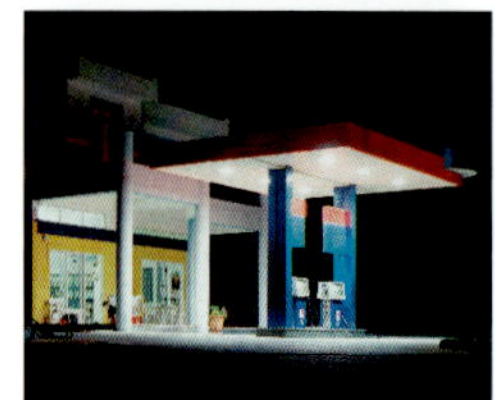

EDITIONEN / EDITIONS **TANKSTELLE SÜD / PETROL STATION SOUTH** 35 × 43 cm / 13.78 × 16.92 in. 2005 Seite / Page 173

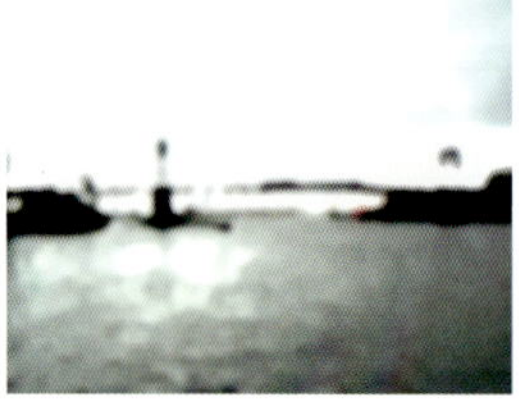

EDITIONEN / EDITIONS **HAFEN 2 / PORT 2** 25 × 33.8 cm / 9.84 × 13.31 in. 2004 Seite / Page 174

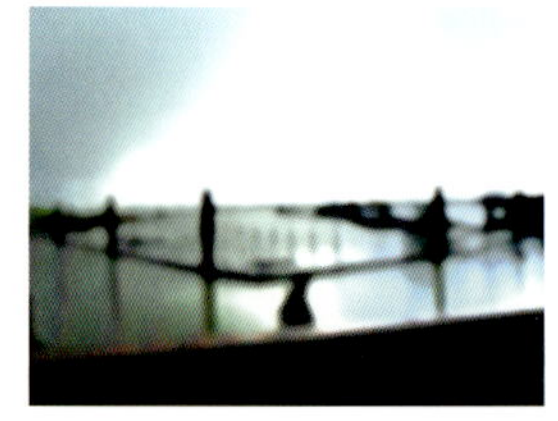

EDITIONEN / EDITIONS **MOLE 3** 25 × 33.8 cm / 9.84 × 13.31 in. 2004 Seite / Page 174

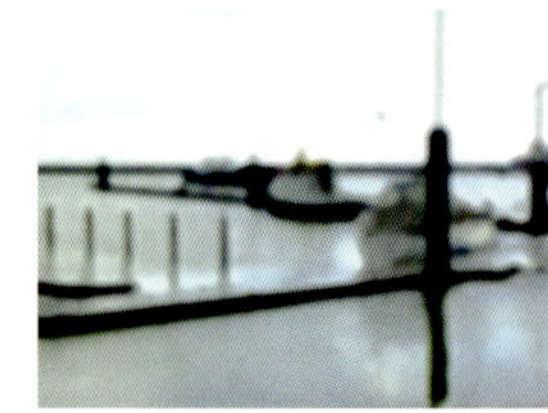

EDITIONEN / EDITIONS **MOLE 2** 25 × 33.8 cm / 9.84 × 13.31 in. 2004 Seite / Page 174

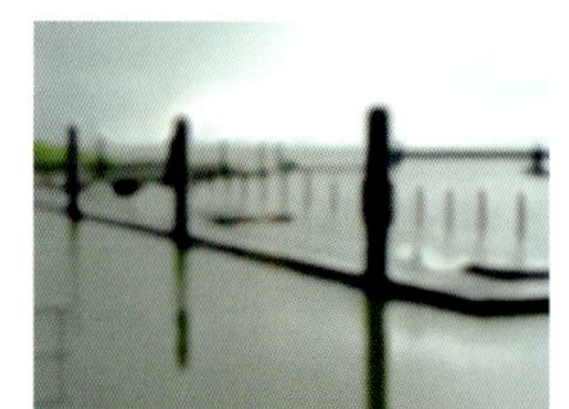

EDITIONEN / EDITIONS **MOLE 1** 25 × 33.8 cm / 9.84 × 13.31 in. 2004 Seite / Page 174

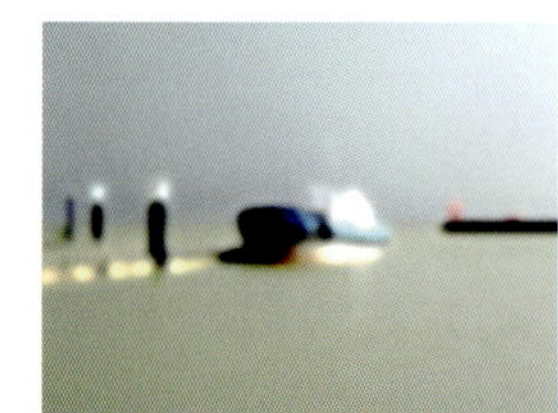

EDITIONEN / EDITIONS **BOOT 3 / BOAT 3** 25 × 33.8 cm / 9.84 × 13.31 in. 2004 Seite / Page 175

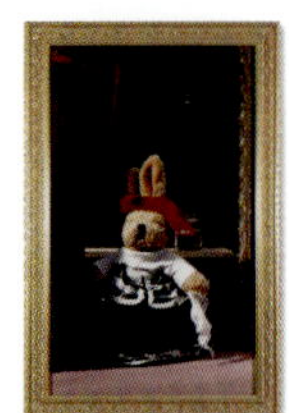

100 MEISTERWERKE / 100 MASTERPIECES **BILDNIS DER KÖNIGIN MARIANNE VON ÖSTERREICH / PORTRAIT OF QUEEN MARIANNE OF AUSTRIA** 120 × 78 cm / 47.24 × 30.7 in. 1995/2009 Seite / Page 179

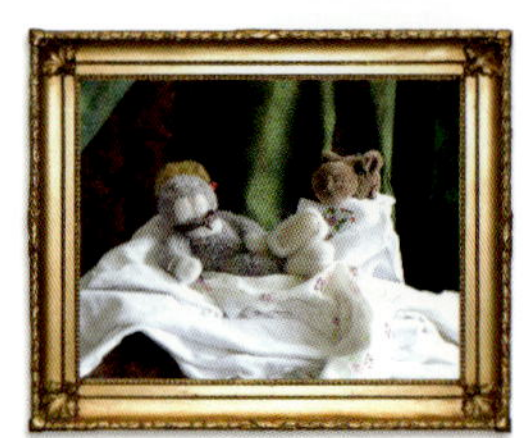

100 MEISTERWERKE / 100 MASTERPIECES **OLYMPIA** 92 × 110 cm / 36.22 × 43.31 in. 1995/2009 Seite / Page 180

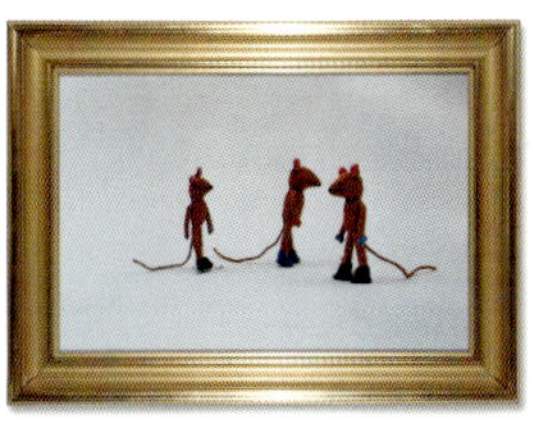

100 MEISTERWERKE /
100 MASTERPIECES
LA PLACE 56 × 76 cm /
22.04 × 29.92 in. 1995/2009
Seite / Page 181

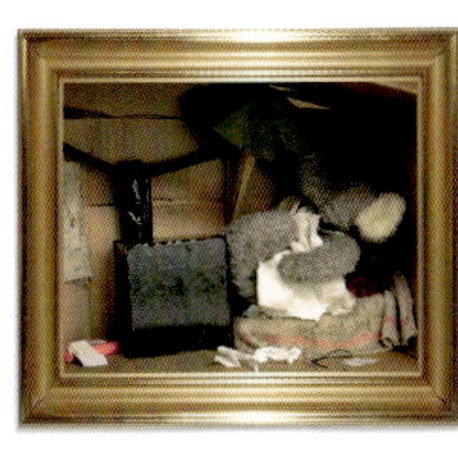

100 MEISTERWERKE /
100 MASTERPIECES **DER ARME
POET / THE POOR POET**
45 × 54 cm / 17.72 × 21.26 in.
1995/2009 Seite / Page 187

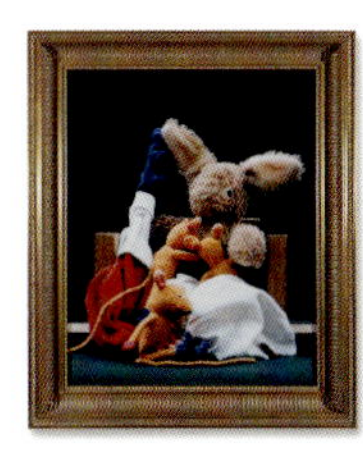

100 MEISTERWERKE /
100 MASTERPIECES
DIE REPUBLIK / THE REPUBLIC
89 × 75.5 cm / 35.04 × 29.72 in.
1995/2009 Seite / Page 193

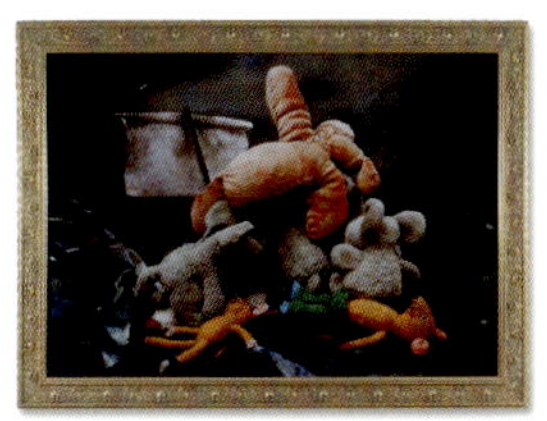

100 MEISTERWERKE /
100 MASTERPIECES **DAS FLOSS
DER MEDUSA / THE RAFT OF
THE MEDUSA** 116 × 158 cm /
45.67 × 62.2 in. 1995/2009
Seite / Page 182

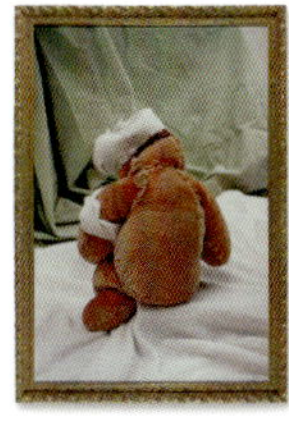

100 MEISTERWERKE /
100 MASTERPIECES
DIE BADENDE / THE BATHER
153.5 × 107.5 cm / 60.43 × 42.32 in.
1995/2009 Seite / Page 188

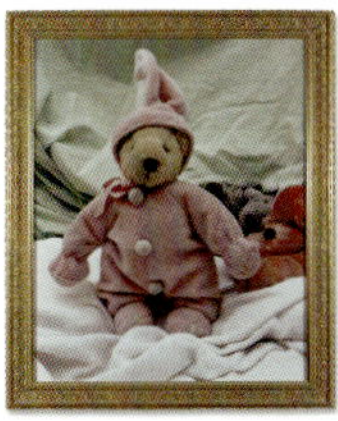

100 MEISTERWERKE /
100 MASTERPIECES **GILLES**
106 × 89 cm / 41.73 × 35.04 in.
1995/2009 Seite / Page 183

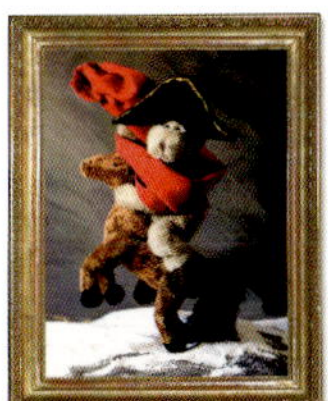

100 MEISTERWERKE /
100 MASTERPIECES
**NAPOLEON ÜBERQUERT
DIE ALPEN / NAPOLEON
CROSSING THE ALPS**
95 × 77 cm / 37.4 × 30.31 in.
1995/2009 Seite / Page 189

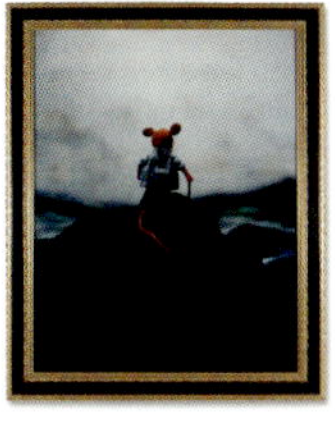

100 MEISTERWERKE /
100 MASTERPIECES
**WANDERER ÜBER DEM
NEBELMEER / WANDERER
ABOVE THE SEA OF FOG**
108.5 × 88 cm / 42.72 × 34.64 in.
1995/2009 Seite / Page 184

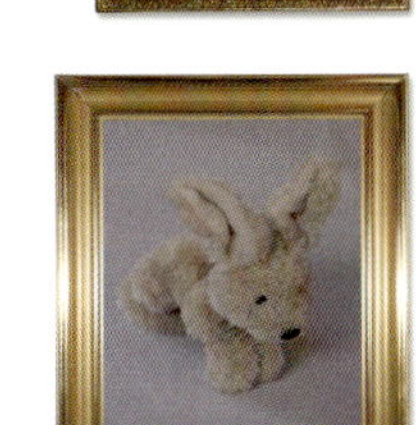

100 MEISTERWERKE /
100 MASTERPIECES
DER FELDHASE / THE HARE
50 × 47.5 cm / 19.68 × 18.5 in.
1995/2009 Seite / Page 190

100 MEISTERWERKE /
100 MASTERPIECES
LE DÉJEUNER SUR L'HERBE
119.5 × 146 cm / 47.05 × 57.48 in.
1995/2009 Seite / Page 185

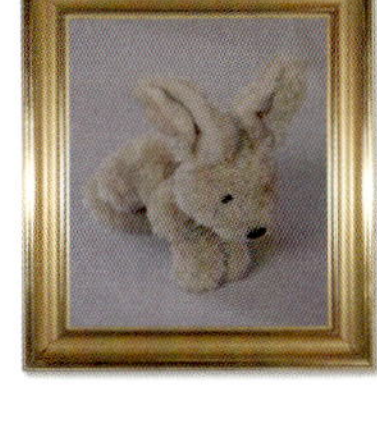

100 MEISTERWERKE /
100 MASTERPIECES **DAS MÄDCHEN MIT DEM
PERLOHRRING / GIRL WITH
A PEARL EARRING** 70 × 65 cm /
27.56 × 25.59 in. 1995/2009
Seite / Page 191

Die Arbeiten sind auf Acryl kaschiert (Diasec), *24 Hours*
sowie die *Editionen* sind Lambda-Prints. Die Maße von
24 Hours verstehen sich inklusive des weißen Rands, der
nicht abgebildet ist, die von *100 Meisterwerke* einschließlich
des goldenen Rahmens. / The photographs are laminated
with acrylic (Diasec), *24 Hours* and *Editions* are Lambda
prints. The dimensions of *24 Hours* include the white border
not shown here, those of the *100 Masterpieces* include
the gold frame.

Die Fotografien erscheinen in einer Auflage von 5 + 2 a.p.,
die *Porträts bei Nacht*, *Candies* und *24 Hours* in einer
Auflage von 3 + 1 a.p. / The photographs are available in
an edition of 5 + 2 a.p., *Portraits by Night*, *Candies*, and
24 Hours in an editon of 3 + 1 a.p.

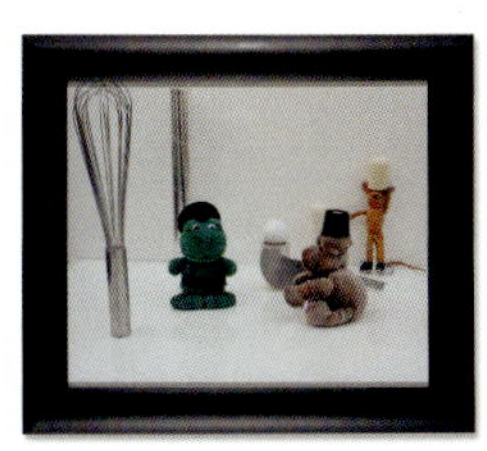

100 MEISTERWERKE /
100 MASTERPIECES
**TRIADISCHES BALLETT /
TRIADIC BALLET** 63 × 74 cm /
24.8 × 29.13 in. 1995/2009
Seite / Page 186

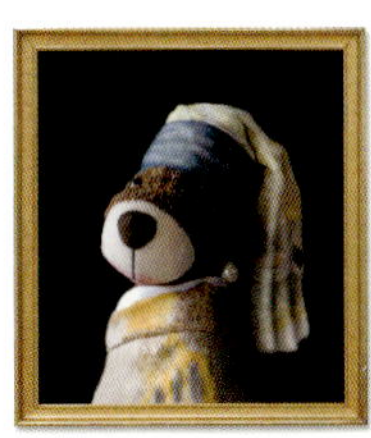

100 MEISTERWERKE /
100 MASTERPIECES
**DIE BÜRGER VON CALAIS /
THE BURGHERS OF CALAIS**
69 × 58.5 cm / 27.17 × 23.03 in.
1995/2009 Seite / Page 192

BIOGRAFIE / BIOGRAPHY

Ralf Peters

Geboren 1960 in Lüneburg, Deutschland / Born 1960 in Lüneburg, Germany

1985–1991	Akademie der Bildenden Künste, München / Munich
1984	Ecole des Beaux-Arts, Nîmes
1982/83	Hochschule für Bildende Künste, Braunschweig

Einzelausstellungen (Auswahl) / Solo Exhibitions (Selection)

2009 *Sky Lightening,* Base Gallery, Tokyo

2008 *24 Hours,* Diana Lowenstein Fine Arts, Miami; Bernhard Knaus Fine Art, Frankfurt am Main

2007 *Inter Pares,* Kunstverein Mannheim

2005 *Coloured Smarties,* Diana Lowenstein Fine Arts, Miami
Candies, Galerie Dörrie & Priess, Hamburg

2004 *Plastische Fotografie,* Kunsthalle Wilhelmshaven; Galerie Bernhard Knaus, Mannheim; Museum Schloss Agathenburg; Kunstverein Grafschaft Bentheim; Galerie der Stadt Nordhorn (Kat. / cat.)

2003 *Boxes und Indoor,* Galerie Mosel & Tschechow, München / Munich
Games 2003, Kunstverein Wolfenbüttel

2001 *Mix,* Kunstverein Springhornhof, Neuenkirchen (Kat. / cat.)
Pools, Galerie Mosel & Tschechow, München / Munich
Outdoor, Kunstverein Recklinghausen (Kat. / cat.)

2000 *Neue Arbeiten,* Kunstverein Heidenheim
Boxes, Kulturforum Lüneburg
Bäder und Boxen, Galerie Dörrie & Priess, Hamburg

1998 *Open Studies,* Galerie Mosel & Tschechow, München / Munich (Kat. / cat.)

1996 *Hundert Meisterwerke,* Galerie Raffl, Meran

1995 *Geschenke an Architekten,* Kunstforum Lenbachhaus, München / Munich (Kat. / cat.)
Temperatur der Räume, Galerie der Stadt Nordhorn (Kat. / cat.)

1994 *32 Modelle,* Kunstverein Nürnberg (mit / with Gerhard Winkler) (Kat. / cat.)
64 Modelle, Galerie Mosel & Tschechow, München / Munich (Kat. / cat.)

1993 *Ralf Peters,* Ladengalerie Lothringerstraße, München / Munich (Kat. / cat.)

1992 *Zwischendurch,* Museum für das Fürstentum Lüneburg

Gruppenausstellungen (Auswahl) / Group Exhibitions (Selection)

2010 *Es werde Dunkel!,* Stadtgalerie Kiel; Kunstmuseum Mühlheim an der Ruhr in der Alten Post

2009 *Es werde Dunkel!,* Städtische Galerie, Bietigheim-Bissingen (Kat. / cat.)
Patterns in Nature, Städtische Galerie Neunkirchen;
Bernhard Knaus Fine Art, Frankfurt am Main (Kat. / cat.)
Our Dear Friends, Galleria Torbandena, Triest / Trieste

2007 *More than meets the eye,* Collection Deutsche Bank, Museo de Artes Modernas, Lima;
Fundación Cultural Plaza Mulato Gil de Castro, Santiago de Chile;
Museu de Arte Moderna, São Paulo;
Pabellon de las Bellas Artes, Pontificia Universidad Católica, Buenos Aires
Die Liebe zum Licht, Museum Bochum
Kopf an Kopf. Serielle Portraitfotografie, Kunsthalle Tübingen (Kat. / cat.)
Statement, Bernhard Knaus Fine Art, Frankfurt am Main

2006	*Lead Award*, Deichtorhallen, Hamburg
	Vom Pferd erzählen, Kunsthalle Göppingen (Kat. / cat.)
	More than meets the eye, Collection Deutsche Bank, Marco Museum, Monterrey;
	Colegio de San Ildefonso, Mexico City;
	Museo de Arte del Banco de la República, Bogota (Kat. / cat.)
	Polemos, Fortezza di Gavi, Gavi (Kat. / cat.)
	Die Liebe zum Licht, Kunstmuseum Celle (Robert-Simon-Stiftung);
	Städtische Galerie Delmenhorst (Kat. / cat.)
2005	*Haben wir den Ozean verloren?*, Städtische Galerie im Rathauspark, Gladbeck
2004	*Landschaft + Stillleben*, Internationale Tage Ingelheim (Kat. / cat.)
	Poesie, Galerie Mosel & Tschechow, München / Munich
	Sammlung der HVB, Kunsthaus Hamburg
	Dreamscapes, Aeroplastics Contemporary, Brüssel / Brussels
2003	*Summer Holiday*, Galerie Bernhard Knaus, Mannheim
	Ornament ... oder die neue Lust am Verbrechen in der zeitgenössischen Kunst,
	Kunsthalle Wilhelmshaven
2002	*smax®*, Villa de Bank, Enschede (Kat. / cat.)
	Zeitgenössische deutsche Fotografie der Alfried Krupp v. Bohlen und Halbach-Stiftung,
	Museum Folkwang, Essen; State Art Museum, Arsenal Exhibition House, Riga;
	The State Russian Museum, Department of Contemporary Art, St. Petersburg (Kat. / cat.)
2001	*close up*, Kunstverein Hannover
	Nightscapes, Stadthaus Ulm (Kat. / cat.)
	Ein Treppenhaus für die Kunst, Niedersächsisches Ministerium für Wissenschaft und Kultur,
	Hannover (Kat. / cat.)
	Trade, Fotomuseum Winterthur; Foto Institut, Rotterdam (Kat. / cat.)
2000	*Essensbilder*, Galerie Dörrie & Priess, Hamburg
	close up, Kunstverein Freiburg; Kunstverein Baselland (Kat. / cat.)
	einlräumen, Hamburger Kunsthalle, Galerie der Gegenwart, Hamburg (Kat. / cat.)
	11 Positionen Fotografie, Hans-Thoma-Gesellschaft, Reutlingen
1998	*Der Liter fünf Mark*, Galerie Dörrie & Priess, Hamburg
	Griffelkunst, Altonaer Museum, Hamburg (Kat. / cat.)
1996	*Utopia*, Biennale der Stadt Aalst (Kat. / cat.)
1995	*Förderpreise 1995*, Lothringerstraße, München / Munich (Kat. / cat.)
1994	*Scharf im Schauen*, Haus der Kunst, München / Munich (Kat. / cat.)
1993	*Die Mysterien finden im Hauptbahnhof statt ...*, Galerie Mosel & Tschechow, München / Munich
	hier & there, Goethe-Institut, London
1992	*Fotografie*, Akademie der Bildenden Künste, München / Munich (Kat. / cat.)
	Modell, Ritterwerke, München / Munich (Kat. / cat.)

IMPRESSUM / IMPRINT

Der Herausgeber und der Künstler danken den folgenden Personen, die zu der Veröffentlichung dieses Buches nicht nur durch ihre Unterstützung in Form von wertvollen Hinweisen und kritischen Beiträgen, sondern auch durch ihr besonderes Engagement und ihre Kontakte beigetragen haben / The editor and artist would like to thank the following people without whose valuable support rendered in the form of essays, critical comment, commitment and contacts, the publication of this book would not have been possible:

Walter Albertoni, Selini Andres, Susanne Baumgart, Benedict Caesar, Anne Denecke, Charlotte Dreschke, Klaus Honnef, Barbara Huygen, Heinz Kattner, Gudrun Knaus, Eva Koba, Laura Köpke, Diana Lowenstein, Marc Naroska, Gregor Nusser, Toshikatsu Onishi, Ulrich Pohlmann, Renate Puvogel, Alessandro Rosada, Haide Rost, Dominik Saam, Raimar Stange, Elena Zonca

Ralf Peters Until Today

Herausgeber / Editor
Bernhard Knaus

Grafische Gestaltung und Satz / Graphic design and typesetting
Naroska, Berlin
www.naroska.de

Verlagslektorat / Copyediting
Simone Albiez (Deutsch / German), Melanie Newton (Englisch / English)

Übersetzungen / Translations
Nathaniel McBride

Verlagsherstellung / Production
Stefanie Langner

Reproduktionen / Reproductions
Ralf Peters

Druck / Printing
Dr. Cantz'sche Druckerei, Ostfildern

Papier / Paper
170 g/m², Galaxi Supermat

Schrift / Typeface
Avenir

Buchbinderei / Binding
Conzella Verlagsbuchbinderei, Urban Meister GmbH, Aschheim-Dornach

© 2010 Hatje Cantz Verlag, Ostfildern, und Autoren / and authors

© 2010 für die abgebildeten Werke von Ralf Peters: beim Künstler / for the reproduced works by Ralf Peters: the artist

Erschienen im / Published by
Hatje Cantz Verlag
Zeppelinstr. 32
73760 Ostfildern
Deutschland / Germany
Tel. +49 711 4405-200
Fax +49 711 4405-220
www.hatjecantz.com

Hatje Cantz books are available internationally at selected bookstores. For more information about our distribution partners, please visit our homepage at www.hatjecantz.com.

ISBN 978-3-7757-2608-5

Printed in Germany

Umschlagabbildungen / Cover illustrations
Karussell / Carousel (S. / p. 75)
Tankstellen, Weiß/Blau / Petrol Stations, White/Blue (S. / p. 18)